"Vertiginous and voluminous. Just reading the introduction to this sizeable and updated book made me dizzy! As an Edwards scholar, I like to think I am aware of recent work in the field, but the labor of the editors to prepare this material for publication is truly remarkable. Why would anyone start anywhere else in their Edwardsean research?"

—**RHYS BEZZANT**, Senior Lecturer in Church History, Ridley College, Parkville, Victoria, Australia

"Following in the footsteps of M. X. Lesser, Adriaan Neele and his associate editors have compiled an invaluable resource for Edwards studies. Every researcher, whether undergraduate, master's, or doctoral, will benefit immeasurably by consulting *Reading Jonathan Edwards: An Annotated Bibliography, 2006–2023*. The volume is exhaustive in scope. It not only promises to save scholars significant amounts of time but opens before them a breathtaking portrait of the vast array of Edwards scholarship that has emerged over the past two decades."

—**CHRIS CHUN**, Director of Jonathan Edwards Center, Gateway Seminary, Los Angeles, California

"Max Lesser's legacy lives on in this much desired update of the *Annotated Jonathan Edwards Bibliography*. Edwards scholars from various disciplines and pastors alike will all benefit from this comprehensive yet judicious review of the literature from 2006 to 2023. The editors' thematically arranged introduction is a delightful bonus."

—**PHILIP JOHN FISK**, Guest Associate Professor in Historical Theology, Evangelische Theologische Faculteit, Leuven, Belgium

"The Jonathan Edwards renaissance continues, as amply revealed in this new and useful bibliography that collects and describes secondary writings on the eighteenth-century Christian philosopher and preacher since 2006. The field is vast, encompassing many disciplines and vocations, and this collection provides a sort of scholarly GPS to guide us. Along with M. X. Lesser's *Reading Jonathan Edwards*, this volume should sit on any serious Edwards student's shelf—within easy reach."

—**Kenneth P. Minkema**, Director, The Jonathan Edwards Center, Yale University

"Jonathan Edwards continues to fascinate, challenge, teach, inspire, and contradict us. To develop a spiritually sophisticated, scientifically nuanced, and theologically precise view of Edwards's insights, we cannot avoid the community of Edwards scholars. *Reading Jonathan Edwards: An Annotated Bibliography, 2006–2023* is an indispensable guide to take us around in and introduce us to the landscape of Edwards studies. So, the quality of our understanding of Jonathan Edwards increases even more."

—**Willem van Vlastuin**, Director, Jonathan Edwards Center Benelux, Vrije Universiteit Amsterdam, The Netherlands

Reading Jonathan Edwards

Reading Jonathan Edwards

An Annotated Bibliography, 2006–2023

Editor
Adriaan C. Neele

Associate Editors
Allen M. Stanton, Brandon James Crawford, and Marco Barone

☙PICKWICK *Publications* • Eugene, Oregon

READING JONATHAN EDWARDS
An Annotated Bibliography, 2006–2023

Copyright © 2025 Wipf and Stock Publishers. All rights reserved. Except for brief quotations in critical publications or reviews, no part of this book may be reproduced in any manner without prior written permission from the publisher. Write: Permissions, Wipf and Stock Publishers, 199 W. 8th Ave., Suite 3, Eugene, OR 97401.

Pickwick Publications
An Imprint of Wipf and Stock Publishers
199 W. 8th Ave., Suite 3
Eugene, OR 97401

www.wipfandstock.com

PAPERBACK ISBN: 979-8-3852-3858-3
HARDCOVER ISBN: 979-8-3852-3859-0
EBOOK ISBN: 979-8-3852-3860-6

Cataloguing-in-Publication data:

Names: Neele, Adriaan C., editor. | Stanton, Allen M., editor. | Crawford, Brandon James, editor. | Barone, Marco, editor.

Title: Reading Jonathan Edwards : an annotated bibliography, 2006–2023 / edited by Adriaan C. Neele, Allen M. Stanton, Brandon James Crawford, and Marco Barone.

Description: Eugene, OR : Pickwick Publications, 2025 | **Includes bibliographical references and index.**

Identifiers: ISBN 979-8-3852-3858-3 (paperback) | ISBN 979-8-3852-3859-0 (hardcover) | ISBN 979-8-3852-3860-6 (ebook)

Subjects: LCSH: Edwards, Jonathan, 1703–1758—Bibliography.

Classification: Z8255.5 .R35 2025 (paperback) | Z8255.5 (ebook)

VERSION NUMBER 11/20/25

Contents

Introduction | 1

Reading Jonathan Edwards:
An Annotated Bibliography, 2006–2023

  2006 | 27
  2007 | 39
  2008 | 52
  2009 | 64
  2010 | 79
  2011 | 94
  2012 | 105
  2013 | 117
  2014 | 126
  2015 | 140
  2016 | 151
  2017 | 165
  2018 | 178
  2019 | 191
  2020 | 204
  2021 | 214
  2022 | 228
  2023 | 238

Appendix I | 247
Index | 251

Introduction

THIS BOOK IS IN memory of Marvin X. ("Max") Lesser, who died on September 22, 2017, at the age of eighty-nine. A scholar of Jonathan Edwards, he was a member of the Yale edition of Edwards's *Works*, editing a volume of sermons. He also wrote a biography of Edwards, contributed to *The Cambridge Companion to Jonathan Edwards*, and wrote many reviews, essays, and articles on the same subject.[1] However, this book commemorates his nearly comprehensive resource, *Reading Jonathan Edwards: An Annotated Bibliography in Three Parts, 1729-2005*.[2] Reviewers have said that Lesser's volume was an "exceptional" and "impressive" book[3] and that he gave us a "clear guide to the [Edwards] liter-

---

1. M. X. Lesser, ed., *Sermons and Discourses, 1734-1738*, vol. 19 of *The Works of Jonathan Edwards* (New Haven, CT: Yale University Press, 2001); M. X. Lesser, *Jonathan Edwards* (Boston: Twayne, 1988); "Edwards in American Culture," in *The Cambridge Companion to Jonathan Edwards*, ed. Stephen J. Stein (Cambridge University Press, 2007), 280-99; Alexander V. G. Allen, *Jonathan Edwards: The First Critical Biography, 1889*, foreword by M. X. Lesser (Eugene, OR: Wipf & Stock, 2008); "Edwards, Jonathan," in *The Reader's Companion to American History*, ed. Eric Foner and John A. Garraty (Boston: Houghton Mifflin, 1991), 327-28; Review of *Delightful Conviction*, by Stephen R. Yarbrough and John C. Adams, *William and Mary Quarterly* 50 (1993) 825-27; "'An Honor Too Great': Jonathan Edwards in Print Abroad," in *Jonathan Edwards at Home and Abroad: Historical Memories, Cultural Movement, Global Horizons*, ed. David W. Kling and Douglas A. Sweeney (Columbia: University of South Carolina Press, 2003), 297-319; and M. X. Lesser and Patience Ford, "A Transcendentalist Conversion Narrative," *Massachusetts Historical Review* 11 (2009) 153-67.

2. M. X. Lesser, *Reading Jonathan Edwards: An Annotated Bibliography in Three Parts, 1729-2005* (Grand Rapids: Eerdmans, 2008).

3. Randall J. Pederson, Review of *Reading Jonathan Edwards: An Annotated Bibliography in Three Parts, 1729-2005*, by M. X. Lesser. *Westminster Theological Journal* 71 (2009) 244-45.

ary maze."[4] One analysis said that "this work will be essential for any future work done on Edwards."[5] With this effort, Lesser put scholars, professors, pastors, and theologians "all in his debt."[6]

Lesser's bibliography concluded with publications from 2005. But in the meantime, the resurgence of interest in Edwards has continued. Monographs, articles, essays, and reviews have mounted up between 2006 and 2023. These interpretive works on Edwards and Edwardseanism relate to nearly every academic discipline—theology, philosophy, history, literature, and others. Furthermore, seemingly every Christian denomination has been represented in this surge of productivity—Anglicans, Congregationalists, Presbyterians, Baptists, Methodists, Pentecostals, and Charismatics. And, while engagement with Edwards continues to be strong in North America, scholars, commentators, and religious leaders from Europe, Asia, Australia, Africa, and Latin America are a growing constituency.[7]

The following bibliography takes up where Lesser left off, and brings the literature up to 2023. Not only that, but this compilation emulates Lesser's methodology by providing brief descriptions of each item—an "annotated" bibliography. We have attempted, in every way, to honor his style, demonstrating that we have not left Lesser behind but are perpetuating his efforts.

By way of introduction, we have identified several themes which may assist future scholarship. As we see it, the most important topics that are covered in this volume are historical, literary, philosophical, ecclesiastical, missional, exegetical, theological, pastoral, and global. We have divided these up accordingly and discussed the work that has been done previously in certain areas. We will explore these subjects chronologically and briefly in the pages that follow.

---

4. Randall J. Pederson, Review of *Reading Jonathan Edwards: An Annotated Bibliography in Three Parts, 1729–2005*, by M. X. Lesser. *Puritan Reformed Journal* 1 (2009) 296–98.

5. David W. Bebbington, Review of *Reading Jonathan Edwards: An Annotated Bibliography in Three Parts*, by M. X. Lesser. *Church History: Studies in Christianity and Culture* 78 (2009) 693–94.

6. Hans Madueme, Review of *Reading Jonathan Edwards: An Annotated Bibliography in Three Parts, 1729–2005*, by M. X. Lesser. *Themelios* 35 (2010) 170–71.

7. See Douglas A. Sweeney and Jan Stievermann, eds., *The Oxford Handbook of Jonathan Edwards* (Oxford: Oxford University Press, 2021), 463–582.

HISTORICAL CONTEXT

The first theme Edwards scholars have explored since 2006 is *historical context*. Readers now have several avenues of research besides the biographies of Marsden and Gura. Three titles are particularly important scholarly contributions to this area. First, the *Cambridge Companion to Jonathan Edwards*, published in 2007, is a tremendous help for learning the various contexts of Edwards's labors and ministry.[8] Second, the *Jonathan Edwards Encyclopedia*, published in 2017, contains over 400 essays from reputable scholars exploring a wide range of topics.[9] Finally, *The Oxford Handbook of Jonathan Edwards*, published in 2021, has thirty-seven essays on Edwards's background, theological, religious and social practices, and global reception.[10] Beyond these titles, other scholars have written on Edwards's historical context, including Mark Noll,[11] Michael McClymond and George McDermott,[12] and again, George Marsden.[13] Still, one would do well to begin with these volumes.

In the area of Edwards's historical context, it is pertinent to talk about the much-debated subject of race and slavery. Historical evidence reveals that Edwards personally owned slaves. Because scholars generally disagree with his views regarding slavery, the question persists of how highly we should regard Edwards's teaching in other areas. After Kenneth Minkema first brought the subject of Edwards's slaves to the fore, other writers continued his theme.[14]

---

8. Stephen J. Stein, ed., *The Cambridge Companion to Jonathan Edwards* (Cambridge: Cambridge University Press, 2007).

9. Harry S. Stout et al., eds., *The Jonathan Edwards Encyclopedia* (Grand Rapids: Eerdmans, 2017).

10. Douglas A. Sweeney and Jan Stievermann, eds., *The Oxford Handbook of Jonathan Edwards* (Oxford: Oxford University Press, 2021).

11. Mark A. Noll, *The Rise of Evangelicalism: The Age of Edwards, Whitefield and the Wesleys* (Downers Grove, IL: InterVarsity, 2010).

12. Michael McClymond and George R. McDermott, *The Theology of Jonathan Edwards* (Oxford: Oxford University Press, 2012).

13. Marsden has written two more biographical treatments: *The Short Life of Jonathan Edwards* (Grand Rapids: Eerdmans, 2008); *An Infinite Fountain of Light: Jonathan Edwards for the Twenty-First Century* (Downers Grove, IL: InterVarsity, 2023).

14. Kenneth P. Minkema, "Jonathan Edwards's Defense of Slavery," *Massachusetts Historical Review* 4 (2005) 23–59; Kenneth P. Minkema and Harry S. Stout, "The Edwardsean Tradition and the Antislavery Debate, 1740–1865," *Journal of American History* 92 (2005) 47–74; Kenneth P. Minkema, "A New Edwards Document: Receipt for a Slave," *Jonathan Edwards Studies* 9.2 (2019) 98–99.

In 2007, Ava Chamberlain wrote an essay for the *Cambridge Companion* entitled "Edwards and Social Issues," speaking on the slavery issue.[15] In 2015, Wayne Detzler took a different approach and theorized that Edwards played a key role in the emergence of Protestant missions which included the abolition of slavery and the evangelization of Africa.[16] In 2018–2019, John Ericson and Joy Craun focused on Jonathan Edwards Jr. and his role in the abolition of slavery.[17] Joseph Lee wrote his doctoral dissertation comparing Edwards, the slaveholder, and Samuel Hopkins, the abolitionist.[18] In 2021, Brown wrote his dissertation on race and slavery and chastised Edwards for acting more from contemporary practices of slavery and race rather than the Bible.[19] John T. Lowe and Daniel N. Gullotta edited *Jonathan Edwards Within the Enlightenment* wherein "topics of slavery, colonialism, racism, gender, populism, violence, pain, and witchcraft" were addressed.[20] In 2022, Lowe wrote his dissertation on the subject and made the case that it wasn't just the Edwardseans that argued for the abolition of slaves but Edwards himself contemplated and wrote of race abundantly.[21] In applying Edwards's theology to the twenty-first century, George Marsden says, "In summary, while Edwards was wrong to have owned enslaved Africans . . . that surely does not nullify the value of his insights on many other matters."[22] There is room for

---

15. Ava Chamberlain, "Edwards and Social Issues," in *The Cambridge Companion to Jonathan Edwards*, ed. Stephen J. Stein (Cambridge: Cambridge University Press, 2007), 325–44.

16. Wayne A. Detzler, "Jonathan Edwards, Slavery, and Africa Missions," *Evangelical Review of Theology* 39 (2015) 229–42.

17. John Ericson, "When God Ceased Winking: Jonathan Edwards the Younger's Evolution on the Problem of Slavery," *Connecticut History Review* 57.1 (2018) 7–32; Joy Craun, "We Are Them: The Golden Rule as a Theological Impetus in the Anti-Slavery and Abolitionist Movement," *Jonathan Edwards Studies* 9.1 (2019) 25–48.

18. Joseph W. Lee, "Jonathan Edwards, Samuel Hopkins, and Theological Ethics of Social Concern" (PhD diss., Dallas Theological Seminary, 2018).

19. Geoffrey Todd Brown, "Exegetical Soundness Regarding Race: How White American Evangelicals Were Influenced by Contemporary Racial Opinions of Their Day Rather Than Consistent with Application of Biblical Hermeneutics" (PhD diss., Southeastern Baptist Theological Seminary, 2021).

20. John T. Lowe and Daniel N. Gullotta, eds., *Jonathan Edwards Within the Enlightenment: Controversy, Experience, and Thought*. New Directions in Jonathan Edwards Studies (Göttingen: Vandenhoeck & Ruprecht, 2019).

21. John Thomas Lowe, "'The Practice That Prevails': Jonathan Edwards, Slavery, and Race" (PhD diss., Vrije Universiteit Amsterdam, 2022).

22. George Marsden, *An Infinite Fountain of Light: Jonathan Edwards for the Twenty-First Century* (Downers Grove, IL: InterVarsity, 2023), 13–17, cited from 14–15.

further inquiry regarding the implications of Edwards's views on race and slavery, specifically the effects they have on his reputation as a credible theologian.

LITERARY CONTEXT

Considering that M. X. Lesser was a literary scholar, it would be ironic if we didn't explore Edwards's literary context. The *Cambridge Companion to Jonathan Edwards* contains two essays that involve Edwards's literary appropriation. Philip F. Gura wrote about Edwards's influence on American literature and Lesser wrote on "Edwards in American Culture."[23] In 2009, Wilson A. Kimnach contributed an essay "The Literary Life of Jonathan Edwards," where he viewed Edwards as an "author of scientific, philosophic, and theological writing."[24] Since 2009, others have likened Edwards to authors such as John Bunyan, Herman Melville, Nathaniel Hawthorne, Emily Dickinson, William Faulkner, William James, and W. E. B. Dubois.[25] However, not many have spoken of his resemblances to the Reformed scholastics, with few exceptions such as Adriaan Neele and Ken Minkema.[26]

---

23. Philip F. Gura, "Edwards and American Literature," in *The Cambridge Companion to Jonathan Edwards*, ed. Stephen J. Stein (Cambridge: Cambridge University Press, 2007), 262–79; M. X. Lesser, "Edwards in 'American Culture,'" in *The Cambridge Companion to Jonathan Edwards*, ed. Stephen J. Stein (Cambridge: Cambridge University Press, 2007), 300–324.

24. Wilson H. Kimnach, "The Literary Life of Jonathan Edwards," in *Understanding Jonathan Edwards*, ed. Gerald McDermott (Oxford: Oxford University Press, 2009), 133–45.

25. Harold Simonson, *Jonathan Edwards: Theologian of the Heart* (Eugene, OR: Wipf & Stock, 2009); Andrea Knutson, "'Something That Is Seen, That Is Wonderful': Jonathan Edwards and the Feeling of Conviction," in *American Spaces of Conversion: The Conductive Imaginaries of Edwards, Emerson, and James* (New York: Oxford University Press, 2010), 54–82; Carole Lynn Stewart, *Strange Jeremiahs: Civil Religion and the Literary Imaginations of Jonathan Edwards, Herman Melville, and W. E. B. Du Bois* (Albuquerque: University of New Mexico Press, 2010); Jennifer L. Leader, *Knowing, Seeing, Being: Jonathan Edwards, Emily Dickinson, Marianne Moore and American Typological Interpretation* (Amherst: University of Massachusetts Press, 2016); Kenneth P. Minkema, "The Pilgrim's Progress and Jonathan Edwards," *Bunyan Studies* 23 (2019) 62–75; Michael Boyden, *Predicting the Past: The Paradoxes of American Literary History* (Leuven: Leuven University Press, 2021); and Sandra M. Gustafson, "Edwards's Place and Importance in Anglo-American Literature," in *The Oxford Handbook of Jonathan Edwards*, ed. Douglas A. Sweeney and Jan Stievermann (Oxford: Oxford University Press, 2021), 495–513.

26. Adriaan C. Neele, "Jonathan Edwards (1703–1758) and the Nature of Theology," *Studia Historiae Ecclesiasticae* 38.2 (2012) 273–86; *Before Jonathan Edwards: Sources of*

PHILOSOPHICAL CONTEXT

Edwards's philosophical perspective is analyzed in numerous works throughout this era (2006–2023). For example, *The Princeton Companion to Jonathan Edwards*, published in 2005 and edited by Sang Hyun Lee, has received mixed reviews.[27] In the past decade and a half and more, several academics, including Oliver Crisp, Richard Muller, Paul Helm, Marco Barone, and Sebastian Rehnman, have written on Edwards's philosophy.[28] Some have supported the views taken by the *Princeton Companion*, while others have deviated. Many writings could have been cited for enlightening the philosophical Edwards; however, Lee's edition is an appropriate place to start.

New England Theology (Oxford: Oxford University Press, 2019); Kenneth P. Minkema, "Jonathan Edwards Reads John Owen," *Studies in Puritanism & Piety* 1.1 (2019) 97–108; "A 'Dordtian Philosophe': Jonathan Edwards, Calvin, and Reformed Orthodoxy," *Church History and Religious Culture* 91.1–2 (2011) 241–53.

27. See M. X. Lesser, *Reading Jonathan Edwards: An Annotated Bibliography in Three Parts, 1729–2005* (Grand Rapids: Eerdmans, 2008), 601–4 [2005.23].

28. Examples of this are Oliver Crisp and Paul Helm, eds., *Jonathan Edwards: Philosophical Theologian* (Farnham, UK: Ashgate, 2003); Oliver Crisp, "Jonathan Edwards's Ontology: A Critique of Sang Hyun Lee's Dispositional Account of Edwardsian Metaphysics," *Religious Studies* 46.1 (2010) 1–20; "Jonathan Edwards' Panentheism," in *Jonathan Edwards as Contemporary: Essays in Honor of Sang Hyun Lee*, ed. Don Schweitzer (New York: Peter Lang, 2010), 107–26; *Jonathan Edwards on God and Creation* (New York: Oxford University Press, 2012). Paul Helm and Richard Muller went back and forth in an explanation of the *Freedom of the Will* and produced opposite conclusions. For Paul Helm, see "Jonathan Edwards and the Parting of the Ways?" *Jonathan Edwards Studies* 4.1 (2014) 42–60; "Turretin and Edwards Once More," *Jonathan Edwards Studies* 4.3 (2014) 286–96; "Francis Turretin and Jonathan Edwards on Compatibilism," *Journal of Reformed Theology* 12.4 (2018) 335–55. For Richard Muller, see "Jonathan Edwards and Francis Turretin on Necessity, Contingency, and Freedom of Will. In Response to Paul Helm," *Jonathan Edwards Studies* 4.3 (2014) 266–85; *Providence, Freedom, and the Will in Early Modern Reformed Theology* (Grand Rapids: Reformation Heritage, 2022). See also Marco Barone, "The Relationship Between God's Nature, God's Image in Man, and Freedom in the Philosophy of Jonathan Edwards," *Jonathan Edwards Studies* 8.1 (2018) 37–51; "Jonathan Edwards on Necessity and Contingency: A Reconsideration," *Jonathan Edwards Studies* 10.1 (2020) 2–19. For Sebastian Rehnman, see "Is the Distinction Between Natural and Moral Attributes Good? Jonathan Edwards on Divine Attributes," *History of Philosophy Quarterly* 27.1 (2010) 57–78; *Edwards on God* (London: Routledge, 2021). Each has written further contributions on Edwards's philosophy.

ECCLESIASTICAL CONTEXT

Edwards's ecclesiastical context received less attention. Yet, there are exceptions. In 2010, Amy Plantinga Pauw authored the "Practical Ecclesiology in John Calvin and Jonathan Edwards" and "Jonathan Edwards' Ecclesiology."[29] This theme continued in 2011 when Rhys Bezzant completed his doctoral dissertation on the subject, which was then published in 2014 as *Jonathan Edwards and the Church*.[30] Pauw commended Bezzant for producing the first "synthetic analysis of Edwards' ecclesiology."[31] McClymond and McDermott included a chapter on "The Church" in *The Theology of Jonathan Edwards*,[32] and again, Bezzant wrote an essay on "Ecclesiology" in the *Jonathan Edwards Encyclopedia* followed by an article in the *Oxford Handbook*.[33] However, given the stature of Edwards and the importance the church played in his life, more needs to be done on his ecclesiology.

MISSIONARY CONTEXT

To present a full picture of Jonathan Edwards, we must explore the topic of Edwards in his role of missionary at Stockbridge, Massachusetts, from 1751–1757. Douglas Sweeney has said of his missionary activity, this "is still the least understood aspect of his life."[34] Stephen Nichols drew attention to Edwards's mission work in a presentation in 2003 and published in a post-conference book. He cleverly entitled this essay "Last of the

---

29. Amy Plantinga Pauw, "Practical Ecclesiology in John Calvin and Jonathan Edwards," in *John Calvin's American Legacy*, ed. Thomas J. Davis (Oxford: Oxford University Press, 2010), 91–110; "Jonathan Edwards' Ecclesiology," in *Jonathan Edwards as Contemporary: Essays in Honor of Sang Hyun Lee*, ed. Don Schweitzer (New York: Peter Lang, 2010), 175–86.

30. Rhys Stewart Bezzant, "Orderly but Not Ordinary: Jonathan Edwards's Evangelical Ecclesiology" (ThD diss., Australian College of Theology, 2011); *Jonathan Edwards and the Church* (Oxford: Oxford University Press, 2014).

31. Ava Chamberlain, Review of *Jonathan Edwards and the Church*, by Rhys Bezzant. *The Journal of Religion* 95.4 (2015) 540–42.

32. Michael J. McClymond and Gerald R. McDermott, "The Church," in *The Theology of Jonathan Edwards* (New York: Oxford University Press, 2014), 451–64.

33. Rhys Bezzant, "Ecclesiology and Sacraments," in *The Oxford Handbook of Jonathan Edwards*, ed. Douglas A. Sweeney and Jan Stievermann (Oxford: Oxford University Press, 2021), 267–80.

34. Endorsement of Roy M. Paul, *Jonathan Edwards and the Stockbridge Mohican Indians: His Mission and Sermons* (Ontario, Canada: B&H, 2020).

Mohican Missionaries: Jonathan Edwards at Stockbridge."[35] His work drew attention to the scholarly neglect of the subject.[36] Roland Baines and Ian McFarland opined that Edwards's missionary status was rarely explored.[37] However, Rachel Wheeler made a breakthrough in scholarship when she wrote her doctoral dissertation and Oxford University Press published it as *To Live Upon Hope: Mohicans and Missionaries in the Eighteenth-Century Northeast*.[38] Wheeler's work opened the doors for further exploration from writers such as Jonathan Gibson,[39] McClymond and McDermott,[40] Brian Russel Franklin,[41] Jon Payne,[42] Roy Paul,[43] and Brandon Crawford.[44] Although this has been a real advancement in Jonathan Edwards Studies, scholars should continue to write in this area and illuminate Edwards in his missionary context.

---

35. See M. X. Lesser, *Reading Jonathan Edwards: An Annotated Bibliography in Three Parts, 1729–2005* (Grand Rapids: Eerdmans, 2008), 564–66 [2003.36].

36. Stephen J. Nichols, "Last of the Mohican Missionaries: Jonathan Edwards at Stockbridge," in *The Legacy of Jonathan Edwards: American Religion and the Evangelical Tradition,* ed. D. G. Hart et al. (Grand Rapids: Baker Academic, 2003), 47–63.

37. Roland S. Baines, "Thy Kingdom Come: The Missionary Theology and Practice of Jonathan Edwards" (MA thesis, Reformed Theological Seminary, 2006); Ian D. McFadden, "Amidst the Great Darkness: The Practical Missiology of Jonathan Edwards at Stockbridge, 1751–1758" (STM thesis, Yale Divinity School, 2008).

38. Rachel Wheeler, "Edwards as a Missionary," in *The Cambridge Companion to Jonathan Edwards*, ed. Stephen J. Stein (Cambridge: Cambridge University Press, 2006), 196–216; *To Live Upon Hope: Mohican and Missionaries in the Eighteenth-Century Northeast* (Ithaca, NY: Cornell University Press, 2008).

39. Jonathan Gibson, "Jonathan Edwards: A Missionary?" *Themelios* 36.4 (2011) 380–402.

40. Michael J. McClymond and Gerald R. McDermott, "Edwards on (and in) Mission," in *The Theology of Jonathan Edwards* (New York: Oxford University Press, 2014), 549–65.

41. Brian Russel Franklin, "Mission and Missiology," in *The Jonathan Edwards Encyclopedia*, ed. Harry S. Stout et al. (Grand Rapids: Eerdmans, 2017), 384–85.

42. Jon D. Payne, "Jonathan Edwards: Missionary to the Indians," *The Evangelical Times* 50.2 (2016) 23, 29.

43. Roy M. Paul, *Jonathan Edwards and the Stockbridge Mohican Indians: His Mission and Sermons* (Ontario, Canada: B&H, 2020).

44. Brandon J. Crawford, "Making Their Hopes Prevail: The Stockbridge Indians and Jonathan Edwards" (PhD diss., Puritan Reformed Theological Seminary, 2023).

BIBLICAL EXEGETICAL CONTEXT

Stephen J. Stein's monumental labors in editing Edwards's "Blank Bible," "Notes on Scripture," and "Notes on the Apocalypse"[45] have led scholars to take notice of Edwards's devotion to biblical interpretation. Although it had always been assumed that biblical exegesis contributed to the work of Edwards's preaching, it had seldom been explored in secondary literature. As Stein commented, "Only in recent decades has this oversight begun to be corrected as more of Edwards' commentaries have been published."[46]

This "oversight" began to be "corrected" when, in 2007, Brandon Withrow wrote his dissertation on Edwards's exegetical method.[47] In 2011, Stephen R. C. Nichols completed his study and published it as *The Harmony of Biblical Exegesis in the Work of Jonathan Edwards*,[48] and Jeongmo Yoo wrote "Jonathan Edwards' Interpretation of the Major Prophets."[49] David Barshinger also published in 2014 *Jonathan Edwards on the Psalms*, and he has written articles on Isaiah and the imprecatory Psalms.[50] Douglas A. Sweeney advanced this theme as he published *Edwards the Exegete* in 2016.[51] Sweeney and Barshinger furthered the discussion in their work

---

45. Stephen J. Stein, ed., *The "Blank Bible,"* vol. 24 of *The Works of Jonathan Edwards* (New Haven, CT: Yale University Press, 2006); *Notes on Scripture*, vol. 15 of *The Works of Jonathan Edwards* (New Haven, CT: Yale University Press, 1998); *Apocalyptic Writings*, vol. 5 of *The Works of Jonathan Edwards* (New Haven, CT: Yale University Press, 1977).

46. Stephen J. Stein, "Edwards as Biblical Exegete," in *The Cambridge Companion to Jonathan Edwards*, ed. Stephen J. Stein (Cambridge: Cambridge University Press, 2006), 181–95, cited on 182.

47. Brandon G. Withrow, "'Full of Wondrous and Glorious Things': The Exegetical Mind of Jonathan Edwards in His Anglo-American Cultural Context" (PhD diss., Westminster Theological Seminary, 2007).

48. Stephen R. C. Nichols, *Jonathan Edwards's Bible: The Relationship of the Old and New Testaments* (Eugene, OR: Pickwick, 2013).

49. Jeongmo Yoo, "Jonathan Edwards's Interpretation of the Major Prophets: The Book of Isaiah, Jeremiah, and Ezekiel," *Puritan Reformed Journal* 3.2 (2011) 160–92.

50. David Barshinger, *Jonathan Edwards and the Psalms: A Redemptive-Historical Vision of Scripture* (Oxford: Oxford University Press, 2014). He also has written of Edwards's exegesis in "The Only Rule of Our Faith and Practice: Jonathan Edwards' Interpretation of the Book of Isaiah as a Case Study of His Exegetical Boundaries," *Journal of the Evangelical Theological Society* 52.4 (2009) 811–29; "'So Much of the Gospel . . . Shining in It': Jonathan Edwards' Redemptive-Historical Vision of the Psalms," *Trinity Journal* 33.2 (2012) 285; "Spite or Spirit? Jonathan Edwards on the Imprecatory Language in the Psalms," *Westminster Theological Journal* 77 (2015) 53–69.

51. Douglas A. Sweeney, *Edwards the Exegete: Biblical Interpretations and the Anglo-Protestant Culture on the Edge of the Enlightenment* (Oxford: Oxford University Press, 2016).

Edwards as an Interpreter of Scripture published in 2018.[52] Interpreters have also narrowed their researches to illuminate Edwards's views on a particular book of the Bible. For instance, Donny Landrum, Brian Borgman, and Brian Steven each conducted studies of Edwards's exegesis of Genesis.[53]

The emphasis on biblical interpretation has led to the further exploration of Edwards's typology, whether in nature or Scripture. Robert Brown, Sarah and Robert Boss, and Cameron Schweitzer have led the way.[54]

THEOLOGICAL CONTEXT

Edwards's exegesis led to theological development. Two instrumental questions concerning his doctrinal statements are: How did he continue to teach from his Reformed Puritan forebears? And, in what way did the Enlightenment affect him and his developments? Scholars often deal with these questions and interpret them differently. One needs to read these works with these questions in mind.

The first topic to be mentioned in this regard is Edwards's doctrine of the Trinity. In previous secondary sources, trinitarian research was at a standstill. In the period 2006–2023, many scholars have filled that void by writing on Edwards and the Trinity, including Stephen Studebaker,[55]

---

52. David Barshinger and Douglas Sweeney, eds., *Jonathan Edwards and Scripture: Biblical Exegesis in British North America* (New York: Oxford University Press, 2018).

53. See Douglas Blake Landrum, "Jonathan Edwards's Exegetical Reflections of Genesis: A Puritan Literal Hermeneutic?" (PhD diss., Mid-America Baptist Theological Seminary, 2014), later published as *Jonathan Edwards' Exegesis of Genesis: A Puritan Hermeneutic?* (Mustang, OK: Tate, 2015); Brian Borgman, *Jonathan Edwards on Genesis: Hermeneutics, Homiletics, and Theology* (ThM thesis, Puritan Reformed Theological Seminary, 2020), subsequently published under the same title, *Jonathan Edwards on Genesis: Hermeneutics, Homiletics, and Theology* (Eugene, OR: Wipf & Stock, 2021); and Brian Steven, "Jonathan Edwards (1703–1758) on the Book of Genesis" (ThM thesis, Puritan Reformed Theological Seminary, 2020).

54. Robert E. Brown, "Jonathan Edwards and the Discourses of Nature," in *Nature and Scripture in the Abrahamic Religions: 1700–Present*, ed. Jitse M. van der Meer and Scott Mandelbrote (Leiden: Brill, 2008), 83–114; Sarah Boss, "Edwards and Thoreau: Typologies of Lakes," *Augustine Collective*, April 1, 2016. http://augustinecollective.org/augustine/edwards-and-thoreau-typologies; Robert Boss, *Thunder God, Wonder God: Exploring the Emblematic Visions of Jonathan Edwards* (Fort Worth, TX: JESociety, 2023); Cameron Schweitzer, "Towards a Clearer Understanding of Jonathan Edwards's Biblical Typology: A Case Study in The 'Blank Bible'" (PhD diss., Gateway Seminary, 2022).

55. Stephen M. Studebaker, *Jonathan Edwards' Social Augustinian Trinitarianism in Historical and Contemporary Perspectives* (Piscataway, NJ: Gorgias, 2008).

Robert Caldwell III,[56] McClymond and McDermott,[57] Oliver Crisp,[58] Kyle Strobel,[59] Ralph Cunnington,[60] Amy Plantinga Pauw,[61] and Seng-Kong Tan.[62] Scholars have begun to see that Edwards's theology was, first and foremost, a trinitarian theology, which led the way for William Danaher to speak about Edwards's "trinitarian ethics."[63] Further, Robert Caldwell and Michael A. G. Haykin have contributed to the issue by writing about Edwards's doctrine of the Holy Spirit.[64]

Academic treatises are advancing the notion of Edwards's concept of theosis or divination. McClymond and McDermott have a chapter on divination in *The Theology of Jonathan Edwards*.[65] Kyle Strobel has argued that Edwards did not have a concept of theosis, but did utilize the grammar of the doctrine.[66] W. Ross Hastings in his book *Jonathan Edwards and the Life of God* expounded on Edwards's doctrine in its three relations: the

---

56. Steven M. Studebaker and Robert W. Caldwell III, *The Trinitarian Theology of Jonathan Edwards: Text, Context, and Application* (Farnham, UK: Ashgate, 2012).

57. Michael J. McClymond and Gerald R. McDermott, "God as Trinity: Father, Son, and Holy Spirit," in *The Theology of Jonathan Edwards* (New York: Oxford University Press, 2014), 193–206.

58. Oliver D. Crisp, "Jonathan Edwards on the Trinity," *Jonathan Edwards Studies* 4.1 (2014) 21–41.

59. Oliver D. Crisp and Kyle C. Strobel, *Jonathan Edwards: An Introduction to His Thought* (Grand Rapids: Eerdmans, 2018). Kyle Strobel also contributed an article on the Trinity, "The Nature of God and the Trinity," in *The Oxford Handbook of Jonathan Edwards*, ed. Douglas A. Sweeney and Jan Stievermann (Oxford: Oxford University Press, 2021), 118–34.

60. Ralph Cunnington, "A Critical Examination of Jonathan Edwards's Doctrine of the Trinity," *Themelios* 39.2 (2014) 224–40.

61. Amy Plantinga Pauw, "Trinity," in *The Jonathan Edwards Encyclopedia*, ed. Harry S. Stout et al. (Grand Rapids: Eerdmans, 2017), 570–73.

62. Seng-Kong Tan, *Fullness Received and Returned: Trinity and Participation in Jonathan Edwards* (Minneapolis: Fortress, 2014).

63. William J. Danaher, *The Trinitarian Ethics of Jonathan Edwards* (Louisville, KY: Westminster John Knox, 2004).

64. Robert W. Caldwell III, *Communion in the Spirit: The Holy Spirit as the Bond of Union in the Theology of Jonathan Edwards*. Studies in Evangelical History and Thought (Waynesboro, GA: Paternoster, 2006). Republished under the same title, *Communion in the Spirit: The Holy Spirit as the Bond of Union in the Theology of Jonathan Edwards* (Eugene, OR: Wipf & Stock, 2006).

65. Michael J. McClymond and Gerald R. McDermott, "The Theme of Divination," in *The Theology of Jonathan Edwards* (New York: Oxford University Press, 2014), 410–23.

66. Kyle Strobel, "Jonathan Edwards and the Polemics of Theosis," *Harvard Theological Review* 105 (2012) 259–79.

Trinity, the hypostatic union, and believers, and brings Edwards into dialogue with patristic and Reformed authors.[67] Divination was addressed again in the controversial work of James R. Salladin.[68] Reviewers of this volume were mixed, but largely positive.[69] Nevertheless, more work could and ought to be done on theosis.

Perry Miller famously said that Edwards departed from the Reformed tradition in respect of the covenants.[70] Carl Bogue, Gilsun Ryu, and Paul Hoehner have demurred. They have written high-quality volumes on the nature of the covenants that have received favorable reviews.[71] Several articles that appeared since 2006 have maintained Edwards's views on the covenant, including those by Cornelis van der Knijff and Willem van Vlastuin,[72] and Christopher Woznicki on the covenant of redemption.[73] Moreover, van Vlastuin has written an essay in the *Oxford Handbook of Jonathan Edwards*, "Federalism and Reformed Scholasticism."[74] However, this is a small portion of research that deserves much more attention.

Edwards on worship has attracted the attention of a new cadre of scholars. Principal among them is Ted Rivera, in his PhD dissertation

---

67. W. Ross Hastings, *Jonathan Edwards and the Life of God: Toward an Evangelical Theology of Participation* (Minneapolis: Fortress, 2015).

68. James R. Salladin, *Jonathan Edwards and Deification: Reconciling Theosis and the Reformed Tradition* (Downers Grove, IL: InterVarsity, 2022). He also contributed an essay on "Theosis," in *The Jonathan Edwards Encyclopedia*, ed. Harry S. Stout et al. (Grand Rapids: Eerdmans, 2017), 563–64.

69. Jonathan M. Carter, Review of *Jonathan Edwards and Deification: Reconciling Theosis and the Reformed Tradition*, by James Salladin. *International Journal of Systematic Theology* 25.4 (2023) 648–50. Carter's review criticized the work of Salladin for being too "verbose" and "significant difference of opinion amongst Reformed orthodox puritans." Carter is not "convinced that Edwards was breaking ground as much as suggested."

70. Perry Miller, *Errand in the Wilderness* (San Francisco: Harper and Row, 1964), 98.

71. Carl Bogue, *Jonathan Edwards and the Covenant of Grace* (Eugene, OR: Wipf & Stock, 2009); Gilsun Ryu, *The Federal Theology of Jonathan Edwards: An Exegetical Perspective* (Bellingham, WA: Lexham, 2021); and Paul J. Hoehner, *The Covenant Theology of Jonathan Edwards: Law, Gospel, and Evangelical Obedience* (Eugene, OR: Pickwick, 2021).

72. Cornelis van der Knijff and Willem van Vlastuin, "Why Edwards Did Not Understand Thomas Boston: A Comparison of Their Views on the Covenants," *Jonathan Edwards Studies* 5.1 (2015) 44–57.

73. Christopher Woznicki, "The Son in the Hands of a Violent God? Assessing Violence in Jonathan Edwards's Covenant of Redemption," *Journal of the Evangelical Theological Society* 58.3 (2015) 583–97.

74. Willem van Vlastuin, "Federalism and Reformed Scholasticism," in *The Oxford Handbook of Jonathan Edwards*, ed. Douglas A. Sweeney and Jan Stievermann (Oxford: Oxford University Press, 2021), 183–98.

and 2008 publication, *Jonathan Edwards and Worship*.[75] Studies were published on the subject by Peter Beck,[76] Graham Beynon,[77] and Matthew Raley.[78] Zachary Jones and Hyun Jin wrote on this topic in their doctoral dissertations.[79] Kirkland brought psalm-singing to the fore, reiterating that Edwards retained psalm-singing in corporate worship, but introduced Isaac Watts's hymns weekly at "religious conferences."[80] Yet, David W. Music, based on his reading of a thanksgiving sermon, has contended that this conclusion was incorrect.[81]

A lot of ink has been spilled in the debate of whether Edwards's doctrine of justification is consistent with the Reformed tradition, or leaned toward a Catholic view, or if it was somewhere in between. Scholars, pastors, and theologians are all interested in this issue because, as Martin Luther said, it is the doctrine on which the church stands or falls.[82] In Edwards Studies this has produced more controversy than anything else in Edwards's theology. It was debated before this period,[83]

---

75. Ted Rivera, "Jonathan Edwards on Worship: Public and Private Devotion to God" (PhD diss., Southeastern Baptist Theological Seminary, 2007). Rivera later published his dissertation as *Jonathan Edwards on Worship: Public and Private Devotion to God* (Eugene, OR: Pickwick, 2010).

76. Peter Beck, "Worship God with Our Minds: Theology as Doxology Among the Puritans," *Puritan Reformed Journal* 5.2 (2013) 193–203.

77. Graham Beynon, "Tuning the Heart: A Historical Survey of the Affections in Corporate Worship, with Special Reference to Jonathan Edwards," *Foundations* 76 (2019) 84–109.

78. Matthew Raley, "A Rational and Spiritual Worship: Comparing J. S. Bach and Jonathan Edwards," *Journal of the Evangelical Theological Society* 62.3 (2019) 583–97.

79. Zachary Jones, "Recognizing Revelation: Illuminating the Epistemology Context of Biblical Worship" (PhD diss., Southeastern Baptist Theological Seminary, 2021); Hyun H. Jin, "Jonathan Edwards, Trinity, and Worship Theology: The Practical Value of Edwards' Trinitarian Covenant Theology for Christian Worship" (PhD diss., Southeastern Baptist Theology Seminary, 2023).

80. E. Trevor Kirkland, "Jonathan Edwards and Psalmody," *Free Church Witness* 10 (2016) 16–18.

81. David W. Music, "Jonathan Edwards and the Theology and Practice of Congregational Song in Puritan New England: Jonathan Edwards's Singing Lecture Sermon," *Hymn* 57.1 (2006) 43–44.

82. Martin Luther, *Lectures on Galatians (1535)*, vol. 26 of *Luther's Works*, ed. Jaroslav Pelikan (St. Louis, MO: Concordia, 1963), 3.

83. For example, Samuel T. Logan Jr., "The Doctrine of Justification in the Theology of Jonathan Edwards," *Westminster Theological Journal* 46 (1984) 26–52; John J. Bombaro, "Jonathan Edwards's Vision of Salvation," *Westminster Theological Journal* 65 (2003) 45–67; George Hunsinger, "Dispositional Soteriology: Jonathan Edwards on Justification by Faith Alone," *Westminster Theological Journal* 66 (2004) 107–20; and Jeffrey C. Waddington, "Jonathan Edwards's 'Ambiguous Somewhat Precarious'

but it has been discussed with some intensity since 2006. Edwards's doctrine of justification has been widely considered beginning in 2008 with Gerald McDermott, who recruited a panoply of scholars who have held forth on the subject: Michael McClymond,[84] Douglas Sweeney,[85] Michael McClenahan,[86] Lawrence Rast,[87] Michael Horton,[88] Hyun-Jin Cho,[89] S. Mark Hamilton,[90] Jonathan Huggins,[91] Josh Moody,[92] Christopher Atwood,[93] Brent Rempel,[94] and Shawn Welch.[95] Scholars must take this

---

Doctrine of Justification," *Westminster Theological Journal* 66 (2004) 357–72.

84. Gerald R. McDermott, "Jonathan Edwards on Justification by Faith—More Protestant or Catholic?" *Pro Ecclesia* 17.1 (2008) 92–111; Michael J. McClymond and Gerald R. McDermott, "Justification and Sanctification," in *The Theology of Jonathan Edwards* (New York: Oxford University Press, 2014), 389–409.

85. Douglas A. Sweeney, "Jonathan Edwards and Justification: The Rest of the Story," in *Jonathan Edwards as Contemporary: Essays in Honor of Sang Hyun Lee*, ed. Don Schweitzer (New York: Peter Lang, 2010), 151–74.

86. Michael McClenahan, "Jonathan Edwards' Doctrine of Justification in the Period up to the Great Awakening" (DPhil thesis, University of Oxford, 2007). He later published his dissertation as *Jonathan Edwards and Justification by Faith* (Farnham, UK: Ashgate, 2012).

87. Lawrence R. Rast Jr., "Jonathan Edwards on Justification by Faith," *Concordia Theological Quarterly* 72.4 (2008) 347–62.

88. Michael Horton, *Covenant and Salvation: "Union" with Christ* (Louisville, KY: Westminster John Knox, 2007).

89. Hyun-Jin Cho, "Jonathan Edwards on Justification: Reformed Development of the Doctrine in Eighteenth-Century New England" (PhD diss., Trinity International University, 2010). He later published his dissertation under the same title, *Jonathan Edwards on Justification: Reformed Development of the Doctrine in Eighteenth-Century New England* (Lanham, MD: University Press of America, 2012).

90. S. Mark Hamilton, "Jonathan Edwards on Justification: A Reassessment" (MA thesis, Southwestern Baptist Theological Seminary, 2010).

91. See Jonathan R. Huggins, "Jonathan Edwards on Justification by Faith Alone: An Analysis of His Thought and Defense of His Orthodoxy" (PhD diss., University of Stellenbosch, 2012); *Living Justification: A Historical-Theological Study of the Reformed Doctrine in the Writings of John Calvin, Jonathan Edwards, and N. T. Wright* (Eugene, OR: Wipf & Stock, 2013).

92. Josh Moody, ed., *Jonathan Edwards and Justification* (Wheaton, IL: Crossway, 2012).

93. Christopher S. Atwood, "Jonathan Edwards's Doctrine of Justification: A New Reading of Edwards's Treatises, Sermons, and Miscellanies" (PhD diss., Wheaton College, 2014).

94. Brent Anders Rempel, "The Invisible Redemption of God: Justification and Union with Christ in Jonathan Edwards and Seventeenth-Century Puritanism" (MA thesis, Providence Theological Seminary, 2016).

95. Shawn Welch, "Justified: The Pragmaticization of American Evangelicalism from Jonathan Edwards to the Social Gospel" (PhD diss., University of Michigan, 2020).

literature seriously, and the various viewpoints presented, in order to deal with the doctrine of justification responsibly.

On the other hand, Edwards's doctrine of sanctification has been comparatively neglected in the past decade and a half. However, there are a few exceptions. In 2010, D. N. Luke's dissertation and Dane Ortlund's article both centered on Edwards's engagement with sanctification.[96] In 2017, Kevin Hall completed his doctorate on this subject and Heejoon Jeon followed suit in 2019.[97] Even so, the doctrine of sanctification remains to be further explored.

Since the preaching on hell in the (in)famous sermon in 1741, *Sinners in the Hands of an Angry God*, few scholars and pastors have debated what Edwards meant by hell. However, Bruce Davidson expounded what Edwards wrote about hell in a series of articles in the *Journal of the Evangelical Society*. He maintained that Edwards preached on hell in the traditional view according to biblical exegesis.[98] Glenn R. Kreider examined this exposition and creatively called it "Sinners in the Hands of a *Gracious God*." He conducted an analysis on the sermon and said, "one must not ignore the other major categories of the divine attributes," that there is more "grace, mercy, compassion, patience and love" than anger.[99] Although Edwards's sermon *Sinners* is the most-well known, Marsden made the case that the *Divine and Supernatural Light* was the most representative of Edwards's sermons.[100]

Scholars frequently have forgotten what Edwards said about heaven. However, academics such as Stephen Nichols, Katherine

---

96. D. N. Luke, "The Doctrine of Sanctification in the Theology of Jonathan Edwards" (PhD diss., Queen's University, Belfast, 2010); Dane Ortlund, "Sanctification by Justification: The Forgotten Insight of Bavinck and Berkouwer on Progressive Sanctification," *Scottish Bulletin of Evangelical Theology* 28.1 (2010) 43–61.

97. Kevin David Hall, "Jonathan Edwards and Sanctification: The Pursuit of Happiness Found in Union and Obedience" (PhD diss., Southern Baptist Theological Seminary, 2017); Heejoon Jeon, "The Role of Sanctification in the Ethics of Jonathan Edwards" (PhD diss., Trinity International University, 2019).

98. Bruce W. Davidson, "Glorious Damnation: Hell as an Essential Element in the Theology of Jonathan Edwards," *Journal of the Evangelical Theological Society* 54.4 (2011) 809–22; "Narcissism: The Root of All Hypocrisy in the Theological Psychology of Jonathan Edwards," *Journal of the Evangelical Theological Society* 57.1 (2014) 135–45; "Unholy Hate: The Essence of Human Evil in the Theology of Jonathan Edwards," *Journal of the Evangelical Theological Society* 64.4 (2021) 643–55.

99. Glenn R. Kreider, "Sinners in the Hands of a Gracious God," *Bibliotheca Sacra* 163 (2006) 259–75.

100. George Marsden, *An Infinite Fountain of Light: Jonathan Edwards for the Twenty-First Century* (Downers Grove, IL: InterVarsity, 2023), 66–67.

Paisley, Adrian Chastain Weimer, Robert Caldwell III, and Gerald McDermott highlighted what Edwards said about heaven in his corpus.[101] Meanwhile specialists, such as Owen Strachan and Douglas Sweeney,[102] Dustin Benge,[103] and Matthew Everhard, have highlighted how Edwards was heavenly minded.[104]

Scholars have always been concerned with the definition of "affections" in Edwards's *Treatise on Religious Affections*. Rather than "emotions" or "passions," Marsden contends that by "affections" Edwards meant "religious *loves*."[105] Craig Biehl and Sam Storms have given a reader's guide to these *Religious Affections*,[106] and other scholars have written on this treatise including Melanie Ross,[107] Larry Hubbard,[108]

---

101. Stephen J. Nichols, *Heaven on Earth: Capturing Jonathan Edwards' Vision of Living in Between* (Wheaton, IL: Crossway, 2006); Katherine T. Paisley, "Windows into Heaven: The Homiletic Scenes of Jonathan Edwards and the Preaching of Redemption" (PhD diss., Vanderbilt University, 2006); Adrian Chastain Weimer, "Heaven and Heavenly Piety in Colonial American Elegies," in *The Church, the Afterlife, and the Fate of the Soul: Papers Read at the 2007 Summer Meeting and the 2008 Winter Meeting of the Ecclesiastical History Society*, ed. Peter Clarke and Tony Claydon (Woodbridge, Suffolk, UK: Boydell, 2009), 258–67; Robert Caldwell III, "A Brief History of Heaven in the Writings of Jonathan Edwards," *Calvin Theological Journal* 46.1 (2011) 48–71; Gerald R. McDermott, "The Saints in Heaven as Spectators of Providence: Edwards and the Tradition," *Jonathan Edwards Studies* 10.2 (2020) 193–201.

102. Owen Strachan and Douglas Sweeney, *Jonathan Edwards on Heaven and Hell* (Chicago: Moody, 2010).

103. Dustin W. Benge, ed., *A Journey Toward Heaven: Daily Devotions from the Sermons of Jonathan Edwards* (Grand Rapids: Reformation Heritage, 2012).

104. Matthew Everhard, *A Theology of Joy: Jonathan Edwards and Eternal Happiness in the Holy Trinity* (Fort Worth, TX: JESociety, 2018). He also wrote an article, "Jonathan Edwards: The Theologian of Joy," *Modern Reformation* 27.5 (2018) 34–43.

105. George Marsden, *An Infinite Fountain of Light: Jonathan Edwards for the Twenty-First Century* (Downers Grove, IL: InterVarsity, 2023), 105.

106. Craig Biehl, *Reading "Religious Affections": A Study Guide to Jonathan Edwards' Classic on the Nature of True Christianity* (Birmingham, AL: Solid Ground Christian, 2012); Sam C. Storms, *Signs of the Spirit: An Interpretation of Jonathan Edwards' "Religious Affections"* (Wheaton, IL: Crossway, 2007).

107. Melanie Ross, "Jonathan Edwards: Advice to Weary Theologians," *Scottish Journal of Theology* 59.1 (2006) 14–26.

108. Larry A. Hubbard, "Using Jonathan Edwards's Treatise Concerning Religious Affections to Equip Selected Members of Riverside Baptist Church, Denham" (DMin thesis, New Orleans Baptist Theological Seminary, 2009).

Elizabeth Agnew Cochran,[109] and Paul Helm.[110] Perhaps the most important contribution during the period under consideration was by Ryan Martin, with his book entitled *Understanding Affections in the Theology of Jonathan Edwards: "The High Exercises of Divine Love."* It garnered many mostly positive academic reviews.[111]

The controversy over Edwards's *Freedom of the Will* of 1754 during this period primarily concerned the debate of Richard Muller and Paul Helm. It began as a disagreement in the *Jonathan Edwards Studies* journal in which Muller said that Edwards had departed from the Reformed tradition in his notions of contingency and necessity.[112] Helm demurred and called upon Francis Turretin to assist him in his deliberation with Muller.[113] This has produced at least one publication from Muller[114] and another from Helm.[115] Philip Fisk and Marco Barone, among others, have added to the debate.[116] Given the two sides, more research must be contributed to reach a satisfactory conclusion.

Many researchers have embraced themes of aesthetics and beauty in life, thought, preaching, and works in the mind of Jonathan Edwards;

---

109. Elizabeth Agnew Cochran, "The Moral Significance of Religious Affections: A Reformed Perspective on Emotions and Moral Formation," *Studies in Christian Ethics* 28.2 (2015) 150–62.

110. Paul Helm, "Jonathan Edwards, John Locke, and The Religious Affections," *Jonathan Edwards Studies* 6.1 (2016) 3–15.

111. Ryan J. Martin, *Understanding Affections in the Theology of Jonathan Edwards: "The High Exercises of Divine Love"* (London: T&T Clark, 2018).

112. Richard A. Muller, "Jonathan Edwards and the Absence of Free Choice: A Parting of Ways in the Reformed Tradition," *Jonathan Edwards Studies* 1.1 (2011) 3–23; "Jonathan Edwards and Francis Turretin on Necessity, Contingency, and Freedom of Will. In Response to Paul Helm," *Jonathan Edwards Studies* 4.3 (2014) 266–85.

113. Paul Helm, "Jonathan Edwards and the Parting of the Ways?" *Jonathan Edwards Studies* 4.1 (2014) 42–60; "Turretin and Edwards Once More," *Jonathan Edwards Studies* 4.3 (2014) 286–96.

114. Richard A. Muller, *Providence, Freedom, and the Will in Early Modern Reformed Theology* (Grand Rapids: Reformation Heritage, 2022).

115. Paul Helm, *Human Nature from Calvin to Edwards* (Grand Rapids: Reformation Heritage, 2018).

116. Robert J. Fisk, *Jonathan Edwards's Turn from Classic-Reformed Tradition of the Freedom of the Will* (Gröningen: Vandenhoeck & Ruprecht, 2016); Marco Barone, "Jonathan Edwards on Necessity and Contingency: A Reconsideration," *Jonathan Edwards Studies* 10.1 (2020) 2–19.

among these are Choi,[117] Helseth,[118] Louie,[119] Mitchell,[120] Geschiere,[121] Gibson,[122] Sholl,[123] Scalise,[124] Venter,[125] McClymond and McDermott,[126] Kim,[127] Martin,[128] Higgins,[129] Kerley,[130] Zhu,[131] Shin,[132] Dyrness and

---

117. Ki Joo Choi, "The Role of Beauty in Moral Discernment: An Appraisal from Rahnerian and Edwardsean Perspectives" (PhD diss., Boston College, 2006). He also wrote an article on this topic, "The Deliberative Practices of Aesthetic Experience: Reconsidering the Moral Functionality of Art," *Journal of the Society of Christian Ethics* 29.1 (2009) 193–218.

118. Paul Kjoss Helseth, "Christ-Centered, Bible-Based, and Second-Rate? 'Right Reason' as the Aesthetic Foundation of Christian Education," *The Westminster Theological Journal* 69.2 (2007) 383–401.

119. K. Y. Louie, "The Theological Aesthetics of Jonathan Edwards" (PhD diss., University of Edinburgh, 2007).

120. Louis J. Mitchell, "The Theological Aesthetics of Jonathan Edwards," *Theology Today* 64.1 (2007) 36–46.

121. Charles L. Geschiere, "Taste and See That the Lord Is Good: The Aesthetic-Affectional Preaching of Jonathan Edwards" (ThM thesis, Calvin Theological Seminary, 2008).

122. Michael D. Gibson, "The Beauty of the Redemption of the World: The Theological Aesthetics of Maximus the Confessor and Jonathan Edwards," *Harvard Theological Review* 101.1 (2008) 45–76.

123. Brian Keith Sholl, "The Excellency of Minds: Jonathan Edwards's Theological Style" (PhD diss., University of Virginia, 2008).

124. Brian T. Scalise, "Wilderness Beauty: A Means to Resolve Volitional Doubt," *Eleutheria* 1.1 (2010) 2–22.

125. Rian Venter, "Trinity and Beauty: The Theological Contribution of Jonathan Edwards," *Dutch Reformed Theological Journal* 51.3-4 (2010) 185–92.

126. Michael J. McClymond and Gerald R. McDermott, "Beauty and Aesthetics," in *The Theology of Jonathan Edwards* (New York: Oxford University Press, 2012), 93–101.

127. Hyunkwan Kim, "Jonathan Edwards's Reshaping of Lockean Terminology into a Calvinistic Aesthetic Epistemology in His Religious Affections," *Puritan Reformed Journal* 6.2 (2014) 103–22.

128. James Alfred Martin, *Beauty and Holiness: The Dialogue Between Aesthetics and Religion* (Princeton, NJ: Princeton University Press, 2014).

129. August J. Higgins, "The Aesthetic Foundations of Religious Experience in the Writings of Jonathan Edwards and Ralph Waldo Emerson," *American Journal of Theology & Philosophy* 38 (2017) 152–66.

130. Tyler Kerley, "The Beauty of the Cross: Retrieving Penal Substitutionary Atonement on Jonathan Edwards' Aesthetic Basis," *Jonathan Edwards Studies* 7.2 (2017) 79–102.

131. Xinying Zhu, "A Beautiful Vision of Glory: Jonathan Edwards's Use of Scripture in His Aesthetic Approach to God's End of Creation" (MA thesis, Trinity Evangelical Divinity School, 2018).

132. Joyce Sue-Mee Shin, "Faith in an Age of Cultural Pluralism: An Aesthetic Approach to Transformation" (PhD diss., University of Chicago, 2020).

Wells,[133] Kim,[134] and Lucas.[135] The most creative articles were from Kornu and Cochran. In 2014, Kornu took Edwards's theological beauty and suggested that it promotes the practice of medicine.[136] In 2018, Cochran applied Edwards's aesthetic to our duty to prevent intellectual disability from hindering civic participation.[137]

PASTORAL AND SPIRITUAL CONTEXT

Edwards's primary calling was as a pastor, and many Edwards scholars have written upon certain aspects of his vocation such as his preaching, revivalism, prayer, the sacraments, and his spirituality. Researchers such as Dooley,[138] Paisley,[139] Rivera,[140] Kimnach,[141] Carrick,[142] Geschiere,[143]

---

133. William Dyrness and Christi Wells, "Aesthetics," in *The Oxford Handbook of Jonathan Edwards*, ed. Douglas A. Sweeney and Jan Stievermann (Oxford: Oxford University Press, 2021), 296–308.

134. Youngrae Kim, "The Aesthetics of Jonathan Edwards as Seen in His Biblical Theology" (PhD diss., Trinity Evangelical Divinity School, 2023).

135. Sean Luke, "Beatific Satisfaction," *Perichoresis (Oradea)* 21.3 (2023) 143–58.

136. Kimbell Kornu, "The Beauty of Healing: Covenant, Eschatology, and Jonathan Edwards' Theological Aesthetics: Toward a Theology of Medicine," *Christian Bioethics* 20.1 (2014) 43–58.

137. Elizabeth Agnew Cochran, "Relational Consent: Reflections on Disability and Jonathan Edwards's Aesthetics," *Journal of Disability & Religion* 22.2 (2018) 177–86.

138. Adam B. Dooley, "Utilizing Biblical Persuasion Techniques in Preaching Without Being Manipulative" (PhD diss., Southern Baptist Theological Seminary, 2006). He appealed to Edwards's *Religious Affection* to indicate that Edwards was not manipulative.

139. Katherine T. Paisley, "Windows into Heaven: The Homiletic Scenes of Jonathan Edwards and the Preaching of Redemption" (PhD diss., Vanderbilt University, 2006).

140. Ted Rivera, "Jonathan Edwards on Worship: Public and Private Devotion to God" (PhD diss., Southeastern Baptist Theological Seminary, 2007).

141. Wilson Kimnach, "Edwards as a Preacher," in *The Cambridge Companion to Jonathan Edwards*, ed. Stephen J. Stein (Cambridge: Cambridge University Press, 2006), 103–24.

142. John Carrick, *The Preaching of Jonathan Edwards* (Edinburgh: Banner of Truth, 2008).

143. Charles L. Geschiere, "Taste and See That the Lord Is Good: The Aesthetic-Affectional Preaching of Jonathan Edwards" (ThM thesis, Calvin Theological Seminary, 2008).

Holloway,[144] Lucas,[145] Hall,[146] and Sweeney focused extensively on Edwards's preaching.[147] Other scholars such as Stout,[148] Wood,[149] Cooper,[150] Noll,[151] Choiński,[152] Hall,[153] Peterson,[154] Thomas,[155] Caldwell,[156] Friend,[157]

---

144. Charles S. Holloway, "The Homiletical Theology of Jonathan Edwards, Gilbert Tennent, and Samuel Davies" (PhD diss., Southwestern Baptist Theological Seminary, 2008).

145. Sean M. Lucas, "'Divine Light, Holy Heat': Jonathan Edwards, the Ministry of the Word, and Spiritual Formation," *Presbyterion* 34.1 (2008) 1–11. Lucas also wrote a book that took on this theme; see "Means of Grace: The Ministry of the Word," in *God's Grand Design* (Wheaton, IL: Crossway, 2011), 133–46.

146. Brent E. Hall, "The Methodology of Persuasion in the Preaching of Jonathan Edwards" (ThM thesis, Dallas Theological Seminary, 2009).

147. Douglas A. Sweeney, *Jonathan Edwards and the Ministry of the Word: A Model of Faith and Thought* (Downers Grove, IL: IVP Academic, 2009).

148. Harry S. Stout, "Edwards as a Revivalist," in *The Cambridge Companion to Jonathan Edwards*, ed. Stephen J. Stein (Cambridge: Cambridge University Press, 2006), 125–43.

149. Dustin A. Wood, "Rhetoric of Revival: An Analysis of Exemplary Sermons from America's Great Awakenings" (MA thesis, University of Cincinnati, 2009).

150. William Henry Cooper, *Great Revivalists in American Religion, 1740–1944: The Careers and Theology of Jonathan Edwards, Charles Finney, Dwight Moody, Billy Sunday and Aimee Semple McPherson* (Jefferson, NC: McFarland, 2010).

151. Mark A. Noll, *The Rise of Evangelicalism: The Age of Edwards, Whitefield and the Wesleys* (Downers Grove, IL: InterVarsity, 2010).

152. Michał Choiński, "Rhetoric of the Revival: A Pragma-Rhetorical Analysis of the Language of the Great Awakening Preachers" (PhD diss., University of Kraków, Poland, 2011). He subsequently published his dissertation under the same title, *The Rhetoric of the Revival: The Language of the Great Awakening Preachers* (Göttingen: Vandenhoeck & Ruprecht, 2016).

153. Kenley Hall, "The Great Awakening: Calvinism, Arminianism and Revivalistic Preaching: Homiletical Lesson for Today," *The Journal of Evangelical Homiletics Society* 12.2 (2012) 31–40.

154. Cheryl M. Peterson, "The Great Awakening as an 'Outpouring of the Spirit' in the Work of Redemption According to Jonathan Edwards: A New Interpretive Framework," *Jonathan Edwards Studies* 4.1 (2014) 61–80.

155. David R. Thomas, "'They Cannot Forbear Crying Out'—A Critical Study of Travailing Prayer as a Pattern of Preparedness for Revival, Examining It Historically in the Theology and Practice of Jonathan Edwards and Charles Finney" (PhD diss., Asbury Theological Seminary, 2015).

156. Robert W. Caldwell III, *Theologies of the American Revivalists: From Whitefield to Finney* (Downers Grove, IL: IVP Academic, 2017).

157. Nathan Friend, "Inventing Revivalist Millennialism: Edwards and the Scottish Connection," *Journal of Religious History* 41.1 (2017) 1–20.

Halambiec,[158] Moga,[159] Todd,[160] Strobel and Chun,[161] Story,[162] and Ramini pointed out that his preaching stirred the Great Awakening and concentrated on Edwards's revivalism.[163]

Pastors may be interested to learn that Joel Beeke, Brian Najapfour, Peter Beck, John Hannah, and David Kling make the case that Edwards was, above all, a theologian of prayer.[164] Another topic during this time (2006–2023) focused on "Edwards and the Sacraments." This theme is traced by several scholars such as Oliver Crisp,[165] Ted Rivera,[166] Michael McClymond and Gerald McDermott,[167] David McDowell,[168] Mark

---

158. Kamil M. Halambiec, "Jonathan Edwards and Charles Finney on the Theology and Methodology of Religious Revivals" (STM thesis, Yale Divinity School, 2017).

159. Dinu Moga wrote three articles for *Perichoresis*; see "Jonathan Edwards and His Understanding of Revival," *Perichoresis* 17.1 (2019) 37–54; "Jonathan Edwards and His Theology of Revival," *Perichoresis* 17.1 (2019) 55–70; and "Jonathan Edwards and His Methodology Promoting Concern for Revival," *Perichoresis* 17.1 (2019) 71–89.

160. Obbie Tyler Todd, "The Grammar of Revival: The Legacy of Jonathan Edwards' Teleological Language in Religion Affections (1746)," *Calvin Theological Journal* 54.1 (2019) 35–56.

161. Chris Chun and Kyle C. Strobel, eds., *Regeneration, Revival, and Creation: Religious Experience and the Purposes of God in the Thought of Jonathan Edwards* (Eugene, OR: Pickwick, 2020).

162. Allan F. Story, *Utmost Endeavor: An Introduction to Jonathan Edwards on Revival* (Six Mile, SC: F. Allan Story Jr., 2021).

163. Ashwin Ramini, "Revive Us Again: Evaluating a Sermon Series on Revival" (PhD diss., Asbury Theological Seminary, 2023).

164. Joel R. Beeke and Brian G. Najapfour, *Taking Hold of God: Reformed and Puritan Perspectives on Prayer* (Grand Rapids: Reformation Heritage, 2011); Brian G. Najapfour, *Jonathan Edwards: His Doctrine of and Devotion to Prayer* (Caledonia, MI: Biblical Spirituality, 2013); Peter Beck, *The Voice of Faith: Jonathan Edwards' Theology of Prayer* (Ontario, Canada: Joshua, 2010); John D. Hannah, "Jonathan Edwards' Thoughts on Prayer," *Bibliotheca Sacra* 173.689 (2016) 80–96; and David W. Kling, "Jonathan Edwards, Petitionary Prayer, and the Cognitive Science of Religion," *Theology and Science* 18.1 (2020) 113–36.

165. Oliver D. Crisp, "Jonathan Edwards and the Closing of the Table: Must the Eucharist Be Open to All?" *Ecclesiology* 5.1 (2009) 48–68.

166. Ted Rivera, "Jonathan Edwards on Worship: Public and Private Devotion to God" (PhD diss., Southeastern Baptist Theological Seminary, 2007). He subsequently published his dissertation under the same title, *Jonathan Edwards on Worship: Public and Private Devotion to God* (Eugene, OR: Pickwick, 2010).

167. Michael J. McClymond and Gerald R. McDermott, "The Sacrament: Baptism and the Lord's Supper," in *The Theology of Jonathan Edwards* (New York: Oxford University Press, 2012), 465–81.

168. David Paul McDowell, *Beyond the Half-Way Covenant: Solomon Stoddard's Understanding of the Lord's Supper as a Converting Ordinance* (Eugene, OR: Wipf & Stock, 2012).

Dever,[169] Rhys Bezzant,[170] and lastly, David Luke.[171] These topics have been frequently treated, but more could be done and especially on sacrament of baptism.

The spirituality of Edwards has been explored by many scholars. For example, Philip A. Gura's work *Jonathan Edwards: America's Evangelical*[172] answers the question, "What can be learned from Edwards spirituality and how we can make the world a better place?"[173] In 2007 Darryl Frayne compared Edwards to a contemplative.[174] Arthur Holder and Timothy Hessel-Robinson wrote on Edwards in a collection of the spiritual classics.[175] Belden Lane[176] contributed to the Reformed concept, and Brandon Withrow focuses on Edwards's incarnation spirituality.[177] In 2016, Willem van Vlastuin's article centered on the reappraisal of Edwards's piety, and in 2018, Bruce Hindmarsh concentrated on the spirituality of early evangelicals, including Edwards.[178]

---

169. Mark E. Dever, "Believers Only: Jonathan Edwards on Communion," *Bibliotheca Sacra* 172 (2015) 259–67.

170. Rhys Bezzant, "Ecclesiology and Sacrament," in *The Oxford Handbook of Jonathan Edwards*, ed. Douglas A. Sweeney and Jan Stievermann (Oxford: Oxford University Press, 2021), 267–80.

171. David Luke, *Meeting Christ at His Table: Jonathan Edwards and the Lord's Supper* (Fort Worth, TX: JESociety, 2023).

172. See M. X. Lesser, *Reading Jonathan Edwards: An Annotated Bibliography in Three Parts, 1729-2005* (Grand Rapids: Eerdmans, 2008), 601 [2005.11].

173. Gerald R. McDermott, Review of *Jonathan Edwards: America's Evangelical*, by Philip F. Gura. *History: Reviews of New Books* 34.2 (2006) 46.

174. Darryl R. Frayne, "The Contemplative Foundations of Genuine Religious Experience in the Life and Pastoral Ministry of Jonathan Edwards" (MACS thesis, Regent College, 2007).

175. Timothy Hessel-Robinson, "Jonathan Edwards (1703–1758): *A Treatise Concerning Religious Affections*," in *Christian Spirituality: The Classics*, ed. Arthur G. Holder (London: Routledge, 2009), 269–80.

176. Belden C. Lane, *Ravished by Beauty: The Surprising Legacy of Reformed Spirituality* (New York: Oxford University Press, 2011); "A Reformed Vision of the World: Trinitarian Beauty and Environmental Ethics," in *Spirit and Nature: The Study of Christian Spirituality in a Time of Ecological Urgency*, ed. Timothy Hessel-Robinson and Ray Maria McNamara (Eugene, OR: Pickwick, 2011), 70–97.

177. Brandon G. Withrow, *Becoming Divine: Jonathan Edwards's Incarnational Spirituality Within the Christian Tradition* (Eugene, OR: Wipf & Stock, 2011).

178. Willem van Vlastuin, "Jonathan Edwards' Spiritualis: Towards a Reconstruction of His Theology of Spirituality," *Journal for the History of Reformed Pietism* 2.1 (2016) 23–46; Bruce D. Hindmarsh, *The Spirit of Early Evangelicalism: True Religion in a Modern World* (Oxford: Oxford University Press, 2018).

In 2019, Obbie Tyler Todd studied the spirituality of David Brainerd in which Edwards was the primary editor of his life.[179] That same year, a most significant contribution edited by Kyle Strobel, Kenneth Minkema, and Adriaan Neele collected essays on Edwards's spirituality with glowing reviews.[180] Nathan Finn acclaims it as a "signal contribution."[181] In 2020, Justin Deeter wrote his dissertation on the subject,[182] and Rhys Bezzant's *Edwards the Mentor* centers on the impressions that he made on his disciples such as Samuel Hopkins, Jonathan Edwards Jr., and Joseph Bellamy, to name a few.[183] In 2021, Song Kim compared Edwards to Bernard of Clairvaux,[184] and Jonathan Liem Yoe Gie likened him to Teresa of Avila.[185] Lisanne D'Andrea Winslow characterized Edwards's concept of the beauty of nature that has bearing to the current climate crisis.[186] The last area involving Edwards's spirituality is Steven Studebaker and Amos Yong, who edited *Pentecostal Theology and Jonathan Edwards*, where scholars made the case that Edwards left a considerable stamp on Pentecostal and Charismatic denominations.[187] Willem van Vlastuin said, "It is striking that Pentecostals are inspired by Jonathan Edwards' theology and spirituality."[188]

---

179. Obbie Tyler Todd, "The Grammar of Revival: The Legacy of Jonathan Edwards's Teleological Language in Religious Affections (1746)," *Calvin Theological Journal* 54.1 (2019) 35–56.

180. Kyle Strobel et al., eds., *Jonathan Edwards: Spiritual Writings* (New York: Paulist, 2019).

181. Nathan Finn, Review of *Jonathan Edwards: Spiritual Writings*, ed. Kyle Strobel et al. *Themelios* 45.2 (2020) 438–39.

182. Justin Baine Deeter, "Communion with God and the Means of Grace in the Spirituality of Jonathan Edwards" (PhD diss., Southeastern Baptist Theological Seminary, 2020).

183. Rhys S. Bezzant, *Edwards the Mentor* (Oxford: Oxford University Press, 2019).

184. Song Kim, "Mysticism in Jonathan Edwards's Theology of Spirituality: A Comparison Between Edwards's and Bernard of Clairvaux's Understanding of Union and Communion with Christ," *Jonathan Edwards Studies* 11.1 (2021) 1–28.

185. Jonathan Liem Yoe Gie, "Teresa of Avila and Jonathan Edwards on Prayer and Spirituality," *Veritas* 20.2 (2021) 219–35.

186. Lisanne D'Andrea-Winslow, "An Ecospirituality of Nature's Beauty: A Hopeful Conversation in the Current Climate Crisis," *HTS Theological Studies* 79.2 (2023) 1–6.

187. Steven M. Studebaker and Amos Yong, *Pentecostal Theology and Jonathan Edwards* (London: T&T Clark, 2019).

188. Willem van Vlastuin, Review of *Pentecostal Theology and Jonathan Edwards*, ed. Steven M. Studebaker and Amos Yong. *Journal of Reformed Theology* 17.3–4 (2023) 374–75.

It would be an interesting study to examine how Edwards's spirituality affected other denominations such as Presbyterians, Baptists, and Methodists. Although many analyses have been published on Edwards's influence on these denominations, his spirituality is not explored in depth.

GLOBAL CONTEXT

Michael McClymond and Gerald McDermott have produced a source inspiring a study of the effect Edwards had on global Christianity. They write, "A new agenda needs to be scripturally based, open to vibrant, Spirit-led experience, engaged with non-Christian religions, and ecumenically fruitful." For them, Edwards provides a "bridge" between "Catholics and Protestants, the Christian East and West, Charismatics and non-Charismatics, and liberals and conservatives."[189]

Following in their path, Kyle Strobel edited a book called *The Ecumenical Edwards*, which brought together prominent Catholics, Orthodox, and Protestant theologians to evaluate Edwards's thought.[190] Furthermore, in 2017, Rhys Bezzant edited a volume on *The Global Edwards: Papers from the Jonathan Edwards Congress Held in Melbourne*.[191] Bezzant's study collected essays exploring Edwards's worldwide impact and includes chapters on Edwards's legacy in Britain, Australia, China, and Poland.

In 2020, the editors of the *Jonathan Edwards Studies* collected papers to show how Edwards had influenced the world. Dolf Britz offered "Jonathan Edwards on the Cape of Good Hope" and Franklin Ferreira contributed "Jonathan Edwards's Works in Brazil." Joel Burnell and Wojciech Szczerba wrote "Jonathan Edwards Center at Poland," and Willem van Vlastuin wrote a paper on the reception of Edwards in Amsterdam. Lastly, Mark Noll composed "Jonathan Edwards in Scotland: An Alternate History."[192]

---

189. Gerald R. McDermott and Michael J. McClymond, "Jonathan Edwards and the Future of Global Christianity," *Theology Today* 69 (2013) 478–85.

190. Kyle Strobel, ed., *The Ecumenical Edwards: Jonathan Edwards and the Theologians* (Farnham, UK: Ashgate, 2015).

191. Rhys S. Bezzant, ed., *The Global Edwards: Papers from the Jonathan Edwards Congress Held in Melbourne* (Eugene, OR: Wipf & Stock, 2017).

192. Dolf Britz, "Jonathan Edwards on the Cape of Good Hope," *Jonathan Edwards Studies* 20.2 (2020) 137–49; Franklin Ferreira, "'They Are Precious Gifts of Heaven': Jonathan Edwards's Works in Brazil," *Jonathan Edwards Studies* 20.2 (2020) 157–66; Joe Burnell and Wojciech Szczerba, "After Ten Years: The Jonathan Edwards Center

This theme continued with the editors of the *Oxford Handbook of Jonathan Edwards*.¹⁹³ Jonathan Yeager contributed an essay on Edwards's influence of "Britain and Europe." He states that "Edwards' current popularity is firmly situated in America, but it is spilling over into Britain and Europe."¹⁹⁴ Dongsoo Han recalled that publications in Asia, "where the second-largest group of Edwardseans in the world is actively working," have been "largely unacknowledged."¹⁹⁵ Stuart Piggin contributed to this theme about Australia, stating, "There is a wide gap between Edwards' influence on Australia . . . for which there is no abundant evidence."¹⁹⁶ He asserts that Edwards's reception stemmed from nineteenth-century missionaries but is greater now than ever before.

Adriaan Neele wrote on Edwards's reception in "Africa" as he contends that "Even less attention, however, has been given to the reception of Edwards's works in Africa. This absence in Edwards research is *remarkable*, as many of his works have been reprinted, translated, and published from the eighteenth century onwards, particularly by those who had a vested interest in missionary movements and societies labouring through Africa."¹⁹⁷ Finally, Heber Carlos De Campos Jr. contributed to Edwards's influence on "Latin America." He speaks of Edwards's reception especially on Pentecostals and the popularity of Reformation theology that has been pertinent toward Edwards's work of spirituality and revivalism.¹⁹⁸

Poland—Past, Present, and Future," *Jonathan Edwards Studies* 20.2 (2020) 208–15; Willem van Vlastuin, "Jonathan Edwards in Amsterdam," *Jonathan Edwards Studies* 10.2 (2020) 216–26; Mark A. Noll, "Jonathan in Scotland: An Alternate History," *Jonathan Edwards Studies* 10.2 (2020) 227–50.

193. Douglas A. Sweeney and Jan Stievermann, eds., *The Oxford Handbook of Jonathan Edwards* (Oxford: Oxford University Press, 2021), 463–567.

194. Jonathan Yeager, "Britain and Europe," in *The Oxford Handbook of Jonathan Edwards*, ed. Douglas A. Sweeney and Jan Stievermann (Oxford: Oxford University Press, 2021), 492.

195. Dongsoo Han, "Asia," in *The Oxford Handbook of Jonathan Edwards*, ed. Douglas A. Sweeney and Jan Stievermann (Oxford: Oxford University Press, 2021), 514.

196. Stuart Piggin, "Australia," in *The Oxford Handbook of Jonathan Edwards*, ed. Douglas A. Sweeney and Jan Stievermann (Oxford: Oxford University Press, 2021), 528.

197. Adriaan C. Neele, "Africa," in *The Oxford Handbook of Jonathan Edwards*, ed. Douglas A. Sweeney and Jan Stievermann (Oxford: Oxford University Press, 2021), 542.

198. Heber Carlos de Campos Jr., "Latin America," in *The Oxford Handbook of Jonathan Edwards*, ed. Douglas A. Sweeney and Jan Stievermann (Oxford: Oxford University Press, 2021), 555–67.

Edwards's global impact continues to be displayed, particularly in South America and Korea. However, more scholarship needs to be devoted to other countries and territories that have been unexplored, for example Canada, Hawaii, Russia, and Turkey.

CONCLUSION

To ensure the most usefulness in continuing Jonathan Edwards scholarship, one needs to ask, "What has been said on the issue before?" We have presented themes of scholarly contributions in Edwards's historical, literary, philosophical, missionary, theological, pastoral-spiritual, and global context during the years 2006–2023. With the information provided, the landscape of thinking can be changed and, through responsible reading of Edwardsean scholarship, we can confidently move the discussion forward.

The Editors

Reading Jonathan Edwards
An Annotated Bibliography, 2006–2023

2006

1. Adams, Kimberly V. "Family Influences on 'The Minister's Wooing' and 'Oldtown Folks': Henry Ward Beecher and Calvin Stowe." *Religion & Literature* 38.4 (2006) 27–61.

    Argues that Harriet Beecher Stowe's *The Minister's Wooing* (1859) and *Oldtown* (1869) were set in New England which was marked by theological debate. Her father, Calvin Stowe, objected to the Edwardsean Calvinism that came from Andover Seminary. Calvin was a professor of Sacred Literature at Andover (1852–1864).

2. Andrews, Edward E. Review of *The Creation of the British Atlantic World*, edited by Elizabeth Mancke and Carole Shammas. *Journal of World History* 17.3 (2006) 339–42.

    Studies of the exchange of ideas, people, culture, and capital between Europe, Africa, and the Americas. Makes the case that "merchants, African slaves, Indians, missionaries, migrants, botanists, painters, Quakers, and lawyers were all crucial actors in the production of this British Atlantic."

3. Bademan, R. Bryan. "The Edwards of History and the Edwards of Faith." *Reviews in American History* 34.2 (2006) 131–49.

    Reviews several books about the works of theology of Edwards, including *Jonathan Edwards and the Bible*, by Robert E. Brown; *Jonathan Edwards: America's Evangelical*, by Philip F. Gura; and *Jonathan Edwards: A Life*, by George M. Marsden.

4. Baines, Ronald S. "Thy Kingdom Come: The Missionary Theology and Practice of Jonathan Edwards." MA thesis, Reformed Theological Seminary, 2006.

    States that the missionary activity of Edwards is rarely explored.

5. Baxter, Tony. Review of *The Salvation of Souls*, by Jonathan Edwards, edited by Richard A. Bailey and Gregory A. Wills. *Evangel* 24.3 (2006) 92.

    Commends these nine sermons of Edwards to Christians as "a sobering and needful book!"

6. Beck, Peter. "Edwards and Indians: Inclusivism or Evangelism?" *Fides et Historia* 38.2 (2006) 23–33.

    Contends that Edwards was committed to evangelizing the Native Americans because he loved them despite modern opinions that he did not.

7. Bennett, M. Jay. "A Synthesis of Jonathan Edwards's Thoughts on Theodicy and Its Pastoral Implications." MA thesis, Dallas Theological Seminary, 2006.

    Implications of Edwards's synthesis that "God is absolutely loving and absolutely sovereign" is that *"the all-loving God has purposed the existence of evil to enlighten the understanding and incline the affections of his intelligent creatures to his glory, thereby increasing their happiness forever."*

8. Bush, Alfred L. "Otterskins, Eagle Feathers, and Native American Alumni at Princeton." *Princeton University Library Chronicle* 67.2 (2006) 420–34.

    Examines the short tenure that Edwards served as the president of the College of New Jersey. He inherited a few articles of Indian influence, such as Johannis Buxtorf's *Lexicon Hebraicum et Chaldaicum* and David Brainerd's Bible, which were both wrapped in otter skin.

9. Caldwell, Robert W. *Communion in the Spirit: The Holy Spirit as the Bond of Union in the Theology of Jonathan Edwards*. Studies in Evangelical History and Thought. Milton Keynes; Waynesboro, GA: Paternoster, 2006.

    Reprints his dissertation under a new title. See M. X. Lesser, *Reading Jonathan Edwards: An Annotated Bibliography in Three Parts, 1729–2005* (Grand Rapids: Eerdmans, 2008), 560 [2003.17].

10. ———. *Communion in the Spirit: The Holy Spirit as the Bond of Union in the Theology of Jonathan Edwards*. Studies in Evangelical History and Thought. Eugene, OR: Wipf & Stock, 2006.
    Reprint (2006.9).

11. Cayton, Mary K. "The Expanding World of Jacob Norton: Reading, Revivalism, and the Construction of a 'Second Great Awakening' in New England, 1787–1804." *Journal of the Early Republic* 26.2 (2006) 221–48.
    Disputes that Norton expanded the world through the printing of Jonathan Edwards to set in motion the Second Great Awakening.

12. Choi, Ki Joo. "The Role of Beauty in Moral Discernment: An Appraisal from Rahnerian and Edwardsean Perspectives." PhD diss., Boston College, 2006.
    Appraises the beautiful and moral realism of Edwards. He argues that the perception of transcendental beauty can be a powerful means to promote moral discernment. "This theory of beauty offers an aesthetic perspective to current debates in Christian ethics on the nature of moral knowledge, especially on the viability of moral realism."

13. Chun, Chris. "A Mainspring of Missionary Thought: Andrew Fuller on 'Natural and Moral Inability.'" *American Baptists Quarterly* 25.4 (2006) 335–55.
    Explores Edwards's *Freedom of the Will* as it influenced Andrew Fuller.

14. Crain, Chris T. Review of *America's God: From Jonathan Edwards to Abraham Lincoln*, by Mark Noll. *Presbyterion* 32.1 (2006) 55–57.
    Praises Noll's book as a scholarly "ten-course meal" and an "intellectual" and "theological feast for the mind."

15. Crampton, W. Gary. *A Conversation with Jonathan Edwards*. Grand Rapids: Reformation Heritage, 2006.
    Offers a readable conversational manner to introduce laymen to Jonathan Edwards.

16. Danaher, William J., Jr. Review of *The Princeton Companion to Jonathan Edwards*, edited by Sang Hyun Lee. *Theological Studies* 67.3 (2006) 706–7.
    Remarks that the individual scholars have provided historical studies that are exceptional; however, this does not reflect "the

variety of perspectives on Edwards or the ambiguity that additional voices would have added."

17. Davies, Ron E. "Missionary Benefactor and Strange Bedfellow: Isaac Hollis, Jonathan Edwards' English Correspondent." *Baptist Quarterly* 41.5 (2006) 263–80.

    Summarizes the account of Isaac Hollis through his wills, diaries, and correspondence as he was the primary benefactor of Edwards's time as a missionary.

18. Ditmore, Michael G. Review of *Jonathan Edwards: America's Evangelical*, by Philip F. Gura. *Christianity and Literature* 55.4 (2006) 595–98.

    Suggests that this biography by Gura should not be overshadowed by Marsden. It should stand on its own merit because it is a "penetrating treatment" of Edwards's thought and career.

19. Dooley, Adam B. "Utilizing Biblical Persuasion Techniques in Preaching Without Being Manipulative." PhD diss., Southern Baptist Theological Seminary, 2006.

    Appeals to Edwards's *Religious Affections* to persuade the reader that he maintained pure biblical persuasion that keeps him from resorting to manipulation.

20. Edwards, Jonathan. *The Blank Bible*. Vol. 24 of *The Works of Jonathan Edwards*. Edited by Stephen J. Stein. New Haven, CT: Yale University Press, 2006.

21. ———. *The Jonathan Edwards Center at Yale University*. New Haven, CT: Yale Divinity School, 2006.

22. ———. *Sermons and Discourses, 1743–1758*. Vol. 25 of *The Works of Jonathan Edwards*. Edited by Wilson H. Kimnach. New Haven, CT: Yale University Press, 2006.

23. Gerstner, John. *The Theology of Jonathan Edwards*. Grand Rapids: Institute of Theological Studies, 2006.

    Analysis of Jonathan Edwards's theology on its.edu.

24. Graham, Kenneth W. Review of *Imagining the Sciences: Expressions of New Knowledge in the "Long" Eighteenth Century*, edited by Robert C. Leitz III and Kevin L. Cope. *The Modern Language Review* 101.3 (2006) 827–28.

Expresses that Edwards's motivation to Calvinism comes through in his famous sermon, "Sinners in the Hands of an Angry God."

25. Harrison, Douglas. "The Will in Contemporary Evangelicalism: Or, How (Not) to Domesticate Jonathan Edwards." *The Journal of the Midwest Modern Language Association* 39.1 (2006) 1–13.

    Conducts a brief narrative about Edwards's intellectual and spiritual development that attempts to mediate between theological absolutes and human experience.

26. Haykin, Michael A. G. *Jonathan Edwards, The Holy Spirit in Revival: The Lasting Influence of the Holy Spirit in the Heart of Man.* Webster, NY: Evangelical, 2005.

    Traces the life and ministry of Edwards and the works that particularly concern revival, such as the "Faithful Narrative," "Religious Affection," and the "Humble Attempt."

27. Henard, William D. "An Analysis of the Doctrine of Seeking in Jonathan Edwards's Conversion Theology as Revealed Through Representative Northampton Sermons and Treatises." PhD diss., Southern Baptist Theological Seminary, 2006.

    Maintains that the sermons from Northampton are insightful for Edwards's theology of conversion as they reveal the doctrine of "seeking." Henard offers "an in-depth study of the specific sermons that address the issues of conversion theology, seeking, God's sovereignty, and humanity's responsibility."

28. Holifield, Brooks E. Review of *The Princeton Companion to Jonathan Edwards*, edited by Sang Hyun Lee. *Theology Today* 63.2 (2006) 274–76.

    Guides "eighteen experts in the thought of Jonathan Edwards" and the authors have written "twenty exceptionally useful essays on Edwards' views."

29. Holmes, Stephen R. "Everlasting Punishment and the Goodness of God: Some Contribution to the Current Debate from Jonathan Edwards." *Philosophia Christi* 8.2 (2006) 327–42.

    Claims that Edwards's account of "God's act of self-glorification in reprobation and damnation of sinner is theologically incoherent."

30. Huggins, Jonathan R. "Jonathan Edwards on Justification by Faith Alone: An Analysis of His Thought and Defense of His Orthodoxy." MA thesis, Reformed Theological Seminary, 2006.

    Argues that Edwards was "a strong defender of this historic doctrine," and "it will be shown" in his thesis that "is in full harmony with the historic reformed doctrine of justification by faith alone."

31. Hunter, George G. "The 'Emotionally Relevant' Congregations." *Journal of the American Society for Church Growth* 17.3 (2006) 3–17.

    Presents a case study of Presbyterian pastors to see whether their congregations are "Emotionally Relevant." Edwards's is given the title "Church growth scholar" as the "reflective leader" of the Great Awakening he "employed field observation, interviews, and historical analysis" to make "sense of a Christian movement," offering Edwards as an example of what ought to be done in the Presbyterian ministers who claim to be "emotionally relevant."

32. Jull, David. "Jonathan Edwards and the Christian Education of Today's Young People." *Journal of Christian Education* 49 (2006) 15–21.

    Investigates what Edwards has to tell us about Christian education of children.

33. ———. "Towards an Understanding of the Effect of Revival Evidenced in the Writings of George Whitefield and Jonathan Edwards." PhD diss., University of Otago, 2006.

    Appeals to the works of Jonathan Edwards and George Whitefield from 1736 to 1743 and relays their understanding of revival, propagation, techniques, defense, and passing it on to other revivalists.

34. Knutson, Andrea. "American Spaces of Conversion: The Conductive Imaginaries of Jonathan Edwards, Ralph Waldo Emerson, and William James." PhD diss., City University of New York, 2006.

    Explores the concept of conversion as evidenced through Thomas Shepard, Jonathan Edwards, Ralph Waldo Emerson, and William James. The author analyzes the varying continuity and discontinuities of the said parties.

35. Kosits, Russell D. Review of *Jonathan Edwards: A Life*, by George M. Marsden. *Journal of the History of the Behavioral Sciences* 42.2 (2006) 183–84.

    Reviews *Jonathan Edwards: A Life*, by George M. Marsden.

36. Kreider, Glenn R. Review of *The Glory and Honor of God: Volume Two of the Previously Unpublished Sermons of Jonathan Edwards*, edited by Michael D. McMullen. *Bibliotheca Sacra* 163.651 (2006) 380–81.

   Consists of twenty of Edwards's sermons that are contained in this book and are "highly recommended for all Christians."

37. ———. "Sinners in the Hands of a Gracious God." *Bibliotheca Sacra* 163 (2006) 259–75.

   Studies Edwards's sermon "Sinners in the Hands of an Angry God" and concludes that God's anger is directed toward sinners; however, "one must not ignore the other major categories of the divine attributes," that there is more "grace, mercy, compassions, patience and love" than anger.

38. Leader, Jennifer L. "'In Love with the Image': Transitive Being and Typological Desire in Jonathan Edwards." *Early American Literature* 41.2 (2006) 153–81.

   Shows how close attention to the textual level operation of Edwards's types yields a more intricate diagram of the subjectivity in Edwards's thinking than does attention to conceptual theology alone.

39. Longaker, Mark G. "Puritan Sermon Method and Church Government: Solomon Stoddard's Rhetorical Legacy." *The New England Quarterly* 79.3 (2006) 439–60.

   Examines the sermons of early eighteenth-century Congregationalist minister and grandfather of Edwards Solomon Stoddard. Stoddard provides insight into church government of the time.

40. Maffly-Kipp, Laurie F., et al., eds. *Practicing Protestants: Histories of Christian Life in America, 1630–1965*. Lived Religions. Baltimore: Johns Hopkins University Press, 2006.

   Essays that have bearing on Edwards are in "Part I: Puritan and Evangelical Practice in New England, 1630–1800," by Catherine A. Brekus. She examines Edwards's devotional diary, and this was representative of New England. Valeri's article made much of Edwards's preaching on forgiveness. He argued that he preached forgiveness in the Puritan style but never made it to the evangelical style.

41. McClenahan, Michael. Review of *Jonathan Edwards and the Enlightenment: Knowing the Presence of God*, by Josh Moody. *Journal of Religion* 86.4 (2006) 685–86.

   Asserts that Moody's book states in essence that Edwards is "archetypal Puritan foe" of Deism.

42. ———. Review of *The Protestant Interest: New England After Puritanism*, by Thomas S. Kidd. *Journal of Religion* 86.1 (2006) 126–27.

   Laments that Kidd never mentioned Edwards by his name. That was to his great oversight.

43. McClymond, Michael J. Review of *The Legacy of Jonathan Edwards: American Religion and the Evangelical Tradition*, edited by D. G. Hart, Sean Michael Lucas, and Stephen J. Nichols. *Church History* 75.3 (2006) 699–701.

   Opines this work as by "evangelical scholars" who "generally regard Edwards as a model, mentor, and motivator" in contrast to Edwards scholars situating Edwards's place in his world for other scholars.

44. McDermott, Gerald R. Review of *Jonathan Edwards: America's Evangelical*, by Philip F. Gura. *History: Reviews of New Books* 34.2 (2006) 46.

   Summarizes the book's central thesis as what we can learn from Edwards's spirituality and do better in the world. According to McDermott, this is its greatest weakness.

45. ———. Review of *The Trinitarian Ethics of Jonathan Edwards*, by William Danaher. *Journal of Religion* 86.3 (2006) 483–84.

   As McDermott says, this volume is the "finest attempt to date related to Edwards's ethics."

46. McKinley, David W. Review of *Jonathan Edwards: A Life*, by George Marsden. *Evangelical Review of Theology* 30.3 (2006) 274–75.

   Lauds Marsden's biography of Edwards as "a masterful work." He criticizes the work by saying that Marsden often says that Edwards was a Calvinist but never offers a definition of what that meant.

47. McPherson, Jeffrey A. "Jonathan Edwards and Alfred North Whitehead: The Possibility of a Constructive Dialogue in Metaphysics." PhD diss., McMaster University, Canada, 2006.

Constructs a comparative study of Jonathan Edwards and Alfred North Whitehead (1861–1947), asking: (1) What is the commonality of their thought? (2) What distinguishes their thoughts? and (3) Can their thoughts be enriched by each other? He argues that this is beneficial to scholarship because it eliminates stagnation.

48. Mensch, Elizabeth. "Democracy and Virtue: Optimism or Faith?" *Journal of Law and Religion* 21.2 (2005) 401–5.

    Alludes to Edwards when she divides up "theology in this pre-Civil war period" and "the rationalists (centered at Harvard)" and "the strict Calvinist of Jonathan Edwards variety."

49. Miller, Mark J. "Voicing Abjection: Evangelic Discourse, Suffering and Speech in Early American Literature." PhD diss., University of Pennsylvania, 2006.

    Examines the view of masochism in Edwards, William Apess, Harriet Beecher Stowe, and Herman Melville.

50. Miller, Samuel. *Life of Jonathan Edwards*. Edinburgh: Puritan Reprints, 2006.

    Reprint. See M. X. Lesser, *Reading Jonathan Edwards: An Annotated Bibliography in Three Parts, 1729–2005* (Grand Rapids: Eerdmans, 2008), 78 [1837.1].

51. Mills, D. E. Review of *Jonathan Edwards: Philosophical Theologian*, edited by Paul Helm and Oliver Crisp. *Scottish Journal of Theology* 59.4 (2006) 483–85.

    Criticizes the book as only looking to Locke in paying attention to "Edwards's philosophy"; however, "other giant contemporaries like Berkeley and Leibniz [and Newton]" were "largely ignored."

52. Mitchell, Louis J. Review of *The Princeton Companion to Jonathan Edwards*, edited by Sang Hyun Lee. *Journal of Church & State* 48.4 (2006) 874–75.

    Says it is a "good and useful book."

53. Moody, Josh. *The God-Centered Life: Insights from Jonathan Edwards for Today*. Downers Grove, IL: InterVarsity, 2006.

    Calls readers to listen to Edwards as an example of how to "start living the God-centered life."

54. Music, David W. "Jonathan Edwards and the Theology and Practice of Congregational Song in Puritan New England: Jonathan Edwards's Singing Lecture Sermon." *Hymn* 57.1 (2006) 43–44.

   Examines two sermons of Edwards: one on "Thanksgiving" (1734) and the other "For a Singing Meeting" (1736). Edwards said about disregarding the command to congregational singing that this is our "due calling" on earth and as a "duty, public, containing of the word of God, and done with grace in our hearts." To disregard that duty is a sin.

55. New, Elisa. "Variety as Religious Experience: The Poetics of the Plain Style." *Religion & Literature* 38.1 (2006) 9–25.

   Shows how Christianity remains an article of aesthetic and faith for a "distinctive American poetics." She then takes us "two virtuosos," Jonathan Edwards and Edwards Taylor, to examine this.

56. Nichols, Stephen J. *Heaven on Earth: Capturing Jonathan Edwards' Vision of Living in Between*. Wheaton, IL: Crossway, 2006.

   Argues that Edwards understood that heaven isn't only about the future. Nichols explores sermons and demonstrates how this can change the life of the Christian.

57. Paisley, Katherine T. "Windows into Heaven: The Homiletic Scenes of Jonathan Edwards and the Preaching of Redemption." PhD diss., Vanderbilt University, 2006.

   Expounds Edwards's homiletic strategy in preaching on the doctrine of heaven, as he believed that God's purpose of the work of redemption is only fulfilled in heaven. His sermonic imagery reveals the beauty, love, and challenge of heaven for his own time and for ours. Edwards encourages a model of preaching designed to increase our longing for the Divine, with transformational possibilities for our lives in the present.

58. Phillips, Charles W. "The Last Edwardsean: Edwards Amasa Park and the Rhetoric of Improved Calvinism." PhD diss., University of Stirling, 2005.

   Contends that Park has been incorrectly identified as a Taylorite, as Park re-casts Hopkinsian theology in a way that extended the revivalist inheritance of Edwards and Hopkins through the rhetoric of New Divinity to a nineteenth-century audience.

59. Pryor, John M. "The Trinitarian Missiology of Jonathan Edwards." MA thesis, Gordon Conwell Theological Seminary, 2006.

   Concerns the "Trinitarian foundations for the missiology of Jonathan Edwards" as the glory of God "visibly indwelled in the life of the church."

60. Rhoda, Alan R., Gregory A. Boyd, and Thomas G. Belt. "Open Theism, Omniscience, and the Nature of the Future." *Faith and Philosophy* 23.4 (2006) 432–59.

   Develops two arguments that are the "key issues" in open theism—an "open future" and the "denial of foreknowledge"—which Edwards dispels in *The Freedom of the Will*.

61. Rivera, Ted. "Jonathan Edwards's 'Hermeneutics': A Case Study of the Sermon 'Christian Knowledge.'" *Journal of the Evangelical Theological Society* 49.2 (2006) 273–86.

   Argues that the sermon "Christian Knowledge" dictates Edwards's method of biblical interpretation.

62. Roland, James W. "'A Diamond in the Sun': The Idea of 'Glory' in the Teleology of Jonathan Edwards." MA thesis, Trinity Evangelical Divinity School, 2006.

   Examines Edwards's *Dissertation Concerning the End for Which God Created the World* (1755) as identified with God's glory. Roland believes he substantiates the hypothesis that "Edwards arrives at this most mature conclusion about the purpose of the world" through biblical exegesis.

63. Ross, Melanie. "Jonathan Edwards: Advice to Weary Theologians." *Scottish Journal of Theology* 59.1 (2006) 14–26.

   Insists that reading Edwards gives a cure for spiritual lethargy. The essay consists of two parts. Part I examines his *Treatise Concerning Religious Affections*. Part II focuses on Edwards's biography, examining his diary, resolutions, and the Personal Narrative. Using insights from the public and private writings of Edwards can actually cure spiritual fatigue.

64. Schultz, Walter. "Jonathan Edwards's End of Creation: An Exposition and Defense." *Journal of the Evangelical Theological Society* 49.2 (2006) 247–71.

Summarizes, makes annotations, and introduces modern applications of Edwards's *Dissertation Concerning the End for Which God Created the World*.

65. Seay, Scott D. Review of *The Trinitarian Ethics of Jonathan Edwards*, by William Danaher. *Journal of the Society of Christian Ethics* 26.1 (2006) 188–90.

    Insists that scholars have underestimated how deeply Edwards's Trinitarianism informed his understanding of morality and Christian duty. Edwards has much to contribute to contemporary theological discussions of virtue, human free will, love, and evil.

66. Stenschke, Christoph. Review of *History of New Testament Research, Volume Two: From Jonathan Edwards to Rudolf Bultmann*, by William Baird. *European Journal of Theology* 15.1 (2006) 77–80.

    Surveys William Baird's volume on NT scholarship from Edwards to Rudolph Bultmann. See M. X. Lesser, *Reading Jonathan Edwards: An Annotated Bibliography in Three Parts, 1729–2005* (Grand Rapids: Eerdmans, 2008), 558 [2003.3].

67. Stikkers, Kenneth W. "Logics of Similitude and Logics of Difference in American and Contemporary Continental Philosophy." *The Journal of Speculative Philosophy* 20.2 (2006) 117–23.

    Refers to Edwards as having a Ramist logic and explores examples.

68. Sweeney, Douglas A., and Allen C. Guelzo, eds. *The New England Theology: From Jonathan Edwards to Edwards Amasa Park*. Grand Rapids: Baker Academic, 2006.

    Offers the Edwardseans, hence making them accessible to a broader audience.

69. Valeri, Mark. "Forgiveness: From the Puritans to Jonathan Edwards." In *Practicing Protestants: Histories of Christian Life in America, 1630–1965*, edited by Laurie F. Maffly-Kipp, Leigh E. Schmidt, and Mark Valeri, 35–50. Baltimore: Johns Hopkins University Press, 2006.

    Presents essays sponsored by the Lilly Endowment exploring the significance of practice in understanding American Protestants. Valeri wrote on forgiveness in the life and theology of Edwards.

70. Zakai, Avihu. Review of *Jonathan Edwards at Home and Abroad: Historical Memories, Cultural Movements, Global Horizon*, edited by

David W. Kling and Douglas A. Sweeney. *Journal of Presbyterian History* 84.2 (2006) 185–86.

Represents exposés from an international conference held in Miami in 2000 written by Edwards scholars engaging "historical legacy around the world."

2007

1. Adams, John C. "Jonathan Edwards, the Great Awakening, and 'Sinners in the Hands of an Angry God." In *Rhetoric, Religion, and the Roots of Identity in British Colonial America*, edited by James R. Andrews, 275–96. East Lansing: Michigan State University Press, 2007.

    Examines how the rhetoric in Edwards's "Sinners" sermon impacted the Great Awaking.

2. Allen, Alexander. *Jonathan Edwards.* Jonathan Edwards Classic Studies Series. Eugene, OR: Wipf & Stock, 2007.

    Reprint (M. X. Lesser, *Reading Jonathan Edwards: An Annotated Bibliography in Three Parts, 1729–2005* (Grand Rapids: Eerdmans), 114 [1889.1]). Stands out as the first biographer to approach him comprehensively and critically. "Allen's book deserves a place among the landmark studies on Edwards."

3. Atherstone, Andrew. Review of *The God-Centered Life: Insights from Jonathan Edwards for Today*, by Josh Moody. *Churchman* 121.3 (2007) 271–72.

    Says that Moody chastises pastors, as Edwards would, for thinking about building projects and discussions of "becoming an effective leader." A "comparison with Edwards 'reveals the poverty, brevity and superficiality of much that passes from preaching today.'"

4. Beck, Peter. "The Fall of Man and the Failure of Jonathan Edwards." *The Evangelical Quarterly* 79.3 (2007) 209–25.

    Considers it a failure on the part of Edwards that in the *Freedom of the Will* he did not take into consideration his definition of the good considering unfallen man's will. That the human will, before the Fall of Adam, had the ability to choose "the greatest apparent good" and "Adam, devoid of sin," "appeared to have no logical reason to choose it." Beck continues, how "could a good creature of God do an evil thing?" Beck describes this as a failure of Edwards.

5. Bezzant, Rhys S. "The Life of Brainerd and the State of the Church." *The Reformed Theological Review* 66.2 (2007) 97–112.

    Contends that the *Life of David Brainerd*, edited heavily by Edwards, "gives important insights into the doctrine of the church" of New England.

6. Blore, Erick J. "The Educational Philosophy of Jonathan Edwards: An Analysis and Application of His Calvinistic Psychology." MA thesis, Reformed Theological Seminary, 2007.

    Analyzes the epistemology of Jonathan Edwards "as it is related to the education of youth in America." Primary evidence of this is in "his letters from Stockbridge, sermons in which he addressed questions of youth, the mind, and education."

7. Chamberlain, Ava. "Domestic Piety in New England." In *Modern Christianity to 1900*, edited by Amanda Porterfield, 233–57, 338–40. Minneapolis, MN: Fortress, 2007.

    Focuses on the domestic life of Edwards as he was representative of the Puritans and the piety of the Puritans. He was raised with the expectation that he would become the "head of the household" along with Sarah Pierpont serving as his "helpmeet."

8. ———. Review of *The Trinitarian Ethics of Jonathan Edwards*, by William J. Danaher. *Theological Studies* 68.4 (2007) 929–30.

    Retrieves Edwards's theological ethics only by reclaiming his trinitarian position. This brings in a comparison of Edwards to contemporary ethicists as the author "aims to add a unique perspective to the modern debate on the nature of the moral life, that human morality is inseparable from the inner trinitarian life of God."

9. Charry, Ellen T. "Experience." In *The Oxford Handbook of Systematic Theology*, edited by Kathryn Tanner, John Webster, and Iain Torrance, 413–31. New York; Oxford: Oxford University Press, 2007.

    Recognizes that Christian theological experience (CTE) is the "most awkward and ambiguous." However, she uses "four classic examples" of CTE in "St. Teresa of Avila, Robert Barclay, Jonathan Edwards, and Karl Rahner."

10. Cochran, Elizabeth Agnew. "Creaturely Virtues in Jonathan Edwards: The Significance of Christology on the Moral Life." *The Journal of the Society of Christian Ethics* 27.2 (2007) 73–95.

    Presents Edwards's view of the incarnate Christ as "the moral archetype for humility" and has two implications for "contemporary ethics." First, that we need a revelation of Christ to understand and to purse virtue. Second, that there is a "relation between love and humility."

11. Crampton, W. Gary. "Edwards' Freedom of the Will: A Review and Analysis." *The Confessional Presbyterian* 3 (2007) 86–103.

    Reviews the *Freedom of the Will* favorably that nothing comes to pass without God sovereignly working it out.

12. Creegan, Nicola Hoggard. "Jonathan Edwards' Ecological and Ethical Vision of Nature." *Stimulus* 15.4 (2007) 49–51.

    Compels that Edwards's view of nature demonstrates the love of God. Shows "there are many reasons why we no longer look to nature for evidence of God's love, but Edwards at least show us what we have lost."

13. Crisp, Oliver D. "Non-Penal Substitution." *International Journal of Systematic Theology* 9.4 (2007) 415–33.

    Argues that McLeod Campbell was inspired by the work of Edwards to develop the doctrine of "vicarious penitence," as "Christ atones for human sin by repenting on behalf of human beings."

14. Danaher, James P. "Beauty, Benevolence, and Virtue in Jonathan Edwards's *The Nature of True Virtue*." *The Journal of Religion* 87.3 (2007) 386–410.

    Gives an interpretation of *True Virtue* that "destabilizes contemporary appraisals" and also responds to criticisms.

15. ———. "Human and Divine Love." *Modern Believing* 48.2 (2007) 33–43.

    Refers to John Piper as writing "extensively on Jonathan Edwards," especially *The End for Which God Created the World*.

16. ———. "Phenomenal Theology." *New Blackfriars* 88.1018 (2007) 709–21.

    Considers the *Religious Affections* in order to give "several aspects of religious experience from such a phenomenal perspective."

17. Davies, Ronald E. Review of *The Cambridge Companion to Jonathan Edwards*, edited by Stephen J. Stein. *The Baptist Quarterly* 42.2 (2007) 314–20.

    Reviews the *Cambridge Companion to Jonathan Edwards*.

18. ———. Review of *The God-Centered Life: Insights from Jonathan Edwards for Today*, by Josh Moody. *Scottish Bulletin of Evangelical Theology* 25.2 (2007) 232–33.

    Reviews Moody's book glowingly as having done a "service" to us "by illuminating the relevance of Edwards' thought and insights" that face the church today.

19. Dyrness, William A. "The Arts." In *The Oxford Handbook of Systematic Theology*, edited by Kathryn Tanner, John Webster, and Iain Torrance, 561–79. New York; Oxford: Oxford University Press, 2007.

    Investigates how in the "last two centuries" theologians "have revived a conversation of the role of art and aesthetics" in systematic theology that had been "eclipsed during the Reformation." Dyrness provides an example of art and aesthetics in the language of Jonathan Edwards. Edwards gave the "language of beauty" in the nature of God which "was at the center" of his work.

20. Fea, John. Review of *The Cambridge Companion to Jonathan Edwards*, edited by Stephen J. Stein. *History Teacher* 41.1 (2007) 134–35.

    Says this is a significant overview of Edwards's life and thought.

21. Fisk, Philip J. "Jonathan Edwards's Freedom of the Will and His Defense of the Impeccability of Jesus Christ." *Scottish Journal of Theology* 60.3 (2007) 309–25.

    Reconciles Edwards's *Freedom of the Will* (1754) with impeccability and of the will in the human soul of Jesus Christ.

22. Frayne, Darryl R. "The Contemplative Foundations of Genuine Religious Experience in the Life and Pastoral Ministry of Jonathan Edwards." MACS thesis, Regent College, 2007.

    Concerns the "significance of a contemplative spirituality for the discernment of religious experience." A test case of this is Edwards's *Personal Narrative* to demonstrate Edwards's "devotional practice."

23. Ganski, Christopher. Review of *Jonathan Edwards and the Metaphysics of Sin*, by Oliver D. Crisp. *The Journal of Ecclesiastical History* 58.2 (2007) 360.

    Offers a philosophical analysis of the controversial and neglected topic of sin in the thought of Edwards. Crisp considers the doctrine of occasionalism to be the "fatal flaw" of Edwards's metaphysics.

24. Garcia, Yvette D. "Revival Types: A Look at the Leaders of the Great Awakening Through the Lens of Psychological Type and Temperament." DMin diss., Gordon Conwell Theological Seminary, 2007.

    Involves the "lives of influential individuals during the Great Awakening," such as "Sarah Pierrepont Edwards, Gilbert Tennent, George Whitefield, and Jonathan Edwards." Gives an "analysis of these persons through the lens of psychological type."

25. Hambrick-Stowe, Charles E. Review of *The New England Theology: from Jonathan Edwards to Edwards Amasa Park*, edited by Douglas A. Sweeney and Allen C. Guelzo. *Fides et Historia* 39.2 (2007) 146–47.

    Applauds that this "superb anthology is edited by two leading historians of American religion." The reviewer's "only disappointment" is the absence of an article that explores Lemuel Haynes.

26. Heath, David Cochran. *The Best of Jonathan Edwards' Sermons*. Narrated by David Cochran Heath. Audiobook. Escondido, CA: Christianaudio, 2007.

27. Helseth, Paul Kjoss. "Christ-Centered, Bible-Based, and Second-Rate? 'Right Reason' as the Aesthetic Foundation of Christian Education." *The Westminster Theological Journal* 69.2 (2007) 383–401.

    Argues that Northwestern, Minnesota's philosophy of education, is in line with the way the Reformers speak of "right reason." To confirm this, he speaks of many Protestant theologians and focuses on Edwards as well.

28. Jackson, Brian. "Jonathan Edwards Goes to Hell (House): Fear Appeals in American Evangelism." *Rhetoric Review* 26.1 (2007) 42–59.

    Appeals to Edwards's description of hell and contemporary fundamental practice of hosting dramas called "Hell houses" used to scare people out of hell. The author considers the New Testament message of love versus the conception of hell and evaluates the advantage of each.

29. Kidd, Thomas S. *The Great Awakening: The Roots of Evangelical Christianity in Colonial America*. New Haven, CT: Yale University Press, 2007.

    Claims that the birth of the evangelical awakenings was inspired by figures like Edwards and that Whitefield changed the landscape of colonial American.

30. Kinghorn, Kevin. "Spiritual Blindness, Self-Deception and Morally Culpable Nonbelief." *Heythrop Journal* 48.4 (2007) 527–45.

    Argues that a person who does not believe the Christian gospel can be culpable of spiritual blindness. Perhaps "the two best-known articulators" within this line of thinking are "John Calvin and Jonathan Edwards," who take their "cues from Romans 1:18–20."

31. Klosko, George. Review of *Democratic Faith: Accepting Limits*, by Patrick J. Deneen. *The Review of Politics* 68.4 (2006) 675–77.

    Concludes "with a section about Jonathan Edwards and Ralph Waldo Emerson," who anticipated democratic faith.

32. Lange, Frederick de. "Becoming One Self: A Critical Retrieval of 'Choice Biography.'" *Journal of Reformed Theology* 1.3 (2007) 272–93.

    Offers the Protestant tradition as sharing the central characteristics with choice biography. This is shown by Calvin, Edwards, and Bunyan.

33. Lawrence, Anna M. "Jonathan Edwards: Puritan or Pluralist?" [Reviews of Gura, *America's Evangelical*; Lee, *Princeton Companion*; Pauw, *Supreme Harmony*]. *Eighteenth-Century Studies* 41.1 (2007) 113–16.

    Reviews Gura's and Marsden's biographies, finding Marsden's more expansive but Gura's with a "fresh and light touch." Lawrence also reviews Sang Hyun Lee's *Princeton Companion* and Amy Plantinga Pauw's *Supreme Harmony*.

34. Lesser, M. X. *Reading Jonathan Edwards: An Annotated Bibliography in Three Parts, 1729–2005*. Grand Rapids: Eerdmans, 2007.

    Examines all the references to Edwards and gathers notations in a bibliographic format.

35. Logan, Samuel T. "Puritans, Presbyterians, and Jonathan Edwards." In *Colonial Presbyterianism: Old Faith in a New Land*, edited by S. Donald Fortson III, 1–25. Eugene, OR: Pickwick, 2007.

    Focuses on Edwards as a representative of Congregational Puritanism, as he went to a congregational college and he was the pastor of Northampton Congregational Church. Yet, he was at one time an interim pastor in New York City and the president of a Presbyterian College—the College of New Jersey (later Princeton University). This symbolized how loosely Edwards was tied to the denominations of Congregationalism and Presbyterianism.

36. Louie, K. Y. "The Theological Aesthetics of Jonathan Edwards." PhD diss., Edinburgh, 2007.

    Challenges that Edwards's aesthetic usually bypasses theology, but his aesthetics are fundamental to his Trinitarian framework.

37. Marty, Martin E. "Getaway Sermon." *Christian Century* 124.4 (2007) 71.

    Outlines the last sermon that Edwards preached to the Indians in Stockbridge, Massachusetts.

38. McClenahan, Michael. "Jonathan Edwards' Doctrine of Justification in the Period up to the Great Awakening." DPhil thesis, University of Oxford, 2007.

    Rebuts recent Edwards scholarship for not formulating doctrine of justification in Edwards's understanding. Argues that regeneration, inherent holiness, and continual sanctification are simply standard Reformed theology. The Reformed denied inherent righteousness, insisting this was not in justification but sanctification, as Edwards articulates.

39. McClymond, Michael J. Review of *Jonathan Edwards: A Life*, by George Marsden. *Church History* 76.1 (2007) 207–10.

    McClymond writes, "George Marsden has filled a large lacuna in the literature with an eminently readable, exhaustively researched, and expertly reasoned tome."

40. Menzies, William W. "The Reformed Roots of Pentecostalism." *PentecoStudies* 6.2 (2007) 78–99.

    Argues that Pentecostalism has Reformed roots. By way of evidence, the teachings of John Calvin and Edwards are provided.

41. Mickle, Allen R., Jr. Review of *Jonathan Edwards: The Holy Spirit in Revival—The Last Influence of the Holy Spirit in the Heart of Man*, by Michael A. G. Haykin. *Criswell Theology Review* 5.1 (2007) 122–25.

    Recounts that "any new work from him should be seen as important." The reviewer says that "overall, this book makes a real contribution to Edwards studies and to the theology of revival and of the Holy Spirit."

42. Milder, Robert. "From Emerson to Edwards." *New England Quarterly* 80.1 (2007) 96–133.

    Recasts Perry Miller's classic, "From Edwards to Emerson," and relocates Emerson in the New England spiritual tradition, from the Puritans to William James, even as he dismissed the theological doctrines of Calvinism. Emerson increasingly came to understand himself as replicating many of the psychospiritual truths at its core.

43. Miller, Nicholas P. Review of *America's God: From Jonathan Edwards to Abraham Lincoln*, by Mark A. Noll. *Andrews University Seminary Studies* 45.1 (2007) 156–57.

    Reviews Noll's argument as "combining three historical ideas" to American Protestantism. First, the "theology of the Protestant Reformation"; second, a "philosophy of republicanism"; and third, the philosophy of "Scottish common-sense Enlightenment." Reviewer said that he "largely succeeded" in this work.

44. Mitchell, Louis J. "The Theological Aesthetics of Jonathan Edwards." *Theology Today* 64.1 (2007) 36–46.

    Contends that Edwards was a preacher and philosopher of beauty stemming from the doctrine of the Trinity, Christology, pneumatology, and soteriology.

45. Moody, Josh. *The God-Centered Life: Insights from Jonathan Edwards for Today*. Vancouver, BC: Regent College Publishing, 2007.

    Reprint. Believes that we can learn from Edwards to stop living for ourselves and live a God-centered life.

46. Nelson, David R. "A Call to Gospel Integrity: The Nature of True Christianity in Jonathan Edwards and Thomas Boston." MA thesis, Gordon-Conwell Theological Seminary, 2007.

    Encourages gospel integrity by examining the nature of true Christianity set forth in Edwards, Boston, J. Gresham Machen, Dallas Willard, John Wesley, and A. W. Tozer.

47. Puente, Eric. "A Critique of the Taxonomy of Educational Objectives by Jonathan Edwards." MA thesis, Dallas Theological Seminary, 2007.

　　Models Edwards's "effective teaching helps ministers today because its aim is to impact the will through the affection."

48. Rivera, Ted. "Jonathan Edwards on Worship: Public and Private Devotion to God." PhD diss., Southeastern Baptist Theological Seminary, 2007.

　　Describes how contemporary worship differs from Edwards as representative of Puritan worship. He analyzes reading and preaching of the word, public prayer, the sacraments, church discipline and collections for the poor among the fasting day, days of prayer and thanksgiving. Edwards spoke in key components of private worship as self-examination, private devotion, spiritual journals, family worship, the private reading of Scripture, and "conference" with another Christian and a summary consideration of how the Sabbath was to be observed. He contends that this is far removed from normal Christian worship today.

49. Ross, John S. "Claudius Buchanan: Scotland's First Missionary to the Jews." *Scottish Bulletin of Evangelical Theology* 25.1 (2009) 80–90.

　　Makes the case that Claudius Buchanan was influenced by Edwards's theology of revival, his post-millennial eschatology, and the mission to the Jews as a first sign of the millennium. Therefore, Buchanan was sent from Scotland as the first missionary to the Jews.

50. Sanders, E. Randall. "Determining Duty: The Fate of Anglo-Protestant Indian Missions After the Great Awakening." MA thesis, Wheaton College Graduate School, 2007.

　　Explains how "Christian missions" to the Native Americans, moving forward from the eighteenth century, "built on the foundation laid by men" like Brainerd, John Sergeant, Edwards, and Gideon Hawley.

51. Schweitzer, Don. "Aspects of God's Relationship to the World in the Theologies of Moltmann, Bonaventure and Jonathan Edwards." *Religious Studies* 26.1 (2007) 5–24.

　　Studies how Moltmann, Bonaventure, and Edwards understood God's goodness in light of the Trinity and compares them to each other.

52. ———. "Aspects of God's Relationship to the World in the Theologies of Jürgen Moltmann, Bonaventure and Jonathan Edwards." *Bangalore Theological Forum* 39.1 (2007) 49–66.

Same as 2007.51 but in a different journal.

53. Schweitzer, William M. "Rage Against the Machine: Jonathan Edwards Versus the God of Deism." *Scottish Bulletin of Evangelical Theology* 25.1 (2007) 61–79.

Gives us a paradigm of what it means "to apply God's eternal truths to one's own situation in a relevant and compelling way."

54. Sherry, Patrick. "The Beauty of God the Holy Spirit." *Theology Today* 64.1 (2007) 5–13.

Asserts Edwards's treatment of beauty whether in nature or in art is infused with the Holy Spirit as is described in the early church. Sherry questions why beauty is so rarely discussed by theologians.

55. Shin, Moon-Ju. "Emily Dickinson's Ecocentric Pastoralism." PhD diss., Marquette University, 2007.

Compares Emily Dickinson's love of nature demonstrated in her poetry from an "ecocritical" perspective with Edwards and Ralph Waldo Emerson's transcendental pastoralism. Dickinson shares Henry David Thoreau's acknowledgment of the physicality of nature and his humility before nature. However, she distinguishes herself from him in her acceptance of the human body as well as the Trinitarianism of her Puritan (i.e., Edwardsean) heritage.

56. Shoemaker, Stephen P. Review of *The New England Theology: From Jonathan Edwards to Edwards Amasa Park*, edited by Douglas A. Sweeney and Allen C. Guelzo. *The Journal of the Evangelical Theology Society* 50.4 (2007) 868–71.

Claims that, overall, the book does a "fine job" of introducing readers to the main ideas, but "several points" would benefit from further examination.

57. Smith, Marcus, and Glenn R. Kreider. Review of *The Trinitarian Ethics of Jonathan Edwards*, by William J. Danaher. *Bibliotheca Sacra* 164.654 (2007) 255–56.

One need not be an academic to read this book with "great profit," but it is "not an introductory or" a "simple text" as the "dialogue partners" are historians, Christian theologians, philosophers, and non-Christians as well. This volume would be "an excellent addition" to any pastor's library.

58. Stein, Stephen J., ed. *The Cambridge Companion to Jonathan Edwards.* Cambridge: Cambridge University Press, 2007.

Amasses leading scholars to give a comprehensive guide to the contexts of Edwards's life and works from various standpoints. The book is composed of seventeen essays, including an introduction by Stephen J. Stein, who divides the book into three parts.

Part I, "Edwards's Life and Context," comprises four essays. A biographical treatment from George Marsden, who has perhaps composed the most major critical biography of Edwards in existence today. The second article is from Kenneth Minkema, entitled "Personal Writings." He focuses on Edwards's "Resolution," diary, "Sarah Pierrepont," the "Personal Narrative," the "Account Book," and the "Last Will and Testament" along with the "Children's Account." David D. Hall concentrates on the Puritan background of New England. Lastly, Avihu Zakai gives the philosophical background in the "Age of the Enlightenment."

Part II contains six articles that maintain "Edwards's roles and achievements." The first essay, by Wilson Kimnach, concerns Edwards's role as a preacher, and we gain access of this by the popularity of sermon print culture in the early eighteenth century. The second, from the pen of Harry Stout, contributes to Edwards as a revivalist, concentrating on the *Faithful Narrative*; *History of the Work of Redemption*; and several "Miscellanies." In conclusion, Stout says Edwards was a preacher and chronicler of revivals. E. Brooks Holifield is assigned the task of describing Edwards as a theologian wherein he stood in continuity with the Reformed tradition, but he also immerses himself within the philosophical works of the time and thus inaugurates a "discrete Edwardseans theological tradition in America." Stephen Daniel depicts Edwards as a philosopher who contributed to a version of the Lockean idealism, and an occasionalist. Edwards spoke of foreknowledge in a way that moral creatures were judged and were of necessity to comply, yet free to conform with the ultimate or highest good that one conceives in the mind. Edwards also philosophized beauty and morality.

Another role that Edwards filled was that of biblical interpretation or, as Stephen Stein entitled this article, "Edwards as a

Biblical Exegete." Edwards's biblical interpretations were contained in the various notebooks that he composed, including the "Notes on Scripture," the various "Miscellanies," the "Blank Bible," "Note on the Apocalypse," and "Images of Divine Things." The last essay in this section, "Edwards as Missionary," written by Rachel M. Wheeler, records Edwards's Native American work in Stockbridge, Massachusetts.

The last section, Part III, consists of "Edwards's legacy and reputation." This includes six articles, and these were just starting points as his legacy continues to this day. The following authors wrote on these various platforms: Douglas Sweeney, "Evangelical Tradition in America"; D. W. Bebbington, "The Reputation of Edwards Abroad"; Philip Gura, "Edwards and American Literature"; M. X. Lesser, "Edwards in 'American Culture'"; Stephen Crocco, "Edwards's Intellectual Legacy"; and lastly, Ava Chamberlain, "Edwards and Social Issues," concentrating on the detriments of Edwards's legacy in social issues, such as gender and race—as he supported African slavery. In total, the *Cambridge Companion to Jonathan Edwards* is useful and nearly comprehensive.

59. Storms, Sam. *Signs of the Spirit: An Interpretation of Jonathan Edwards' "Religious Affections."* Wheaton, IL: Crossway, 2007.

    Believes that Edwards's treatise *Religious Affections* is an important and accurate analysis of religious experience but is misunderstood. Storms makes it more accessible to a wider audience.

60. Strange, Alan D. Review of *The New England Theology: From Jonathan Edwards to Edwards Amasa Park*, edited by Douglas A. Sweeney and Allen C. Guelzo. *Mid-America Journal of Theology* 18 (2007) 262–64.

    Praises the volume which "remains of immense value."

61. Sweeney, Douglas A. "Edwards, Jonathan." In *Dictionary of Major Biblical Interpreters*, edited by Donald K. McKim, 397–400. Downers Grove, IL: InterVarsity, 2007.

    Records Edwards's contribution as a major biblical interpreter.

62. Vaughan, David. *A Divine Light: The Spiritual Leadership of Jonathan Edwards*. Nashville: Cumberland, 2007.

    Summarizes Edwards as a pastor, revivalist, Calvinist theologian, ethicist, and philosopher.

63. Wills, Garry. *Head and Heart: American Christianities.* New York: Penguin, 2007.

   Speaks of American Christianity as a problem of being exclusively of the duality between head and the heart. Edwards is mentioned as an exception to the rule.

64. Withrow, Brandon G. "'Full of Wondrous and Glorious Things': The Exegetical Mind of Jonathan Edwards in His Anglo-American Cultural Context." PhD diss., Westminster Theological Seminary, 2007.

   Studies Edwards's approach to Scripture in his Anglo-American context. By examining his biblical exegesis and ongoing biblical interpretation, Withrow sees this as evidence of Edwards's conversion experience, and this contributes to his development of a doctrine of conversion. He sees Edwards's mature biblical reflection as coming into its own in the 1730s and 1740s when he exposits his doctrine of justification that sparks revival.

65. Wooddell, Joseph D. "Jonathan Edwards, Beauty, and Apologetics." *Criswell Theological Review* 5 (2007) 81–95.

   Focuses on Edwards's apologetic of beauty taken from *The Nature of True Virtue.*

66. Vető, Miklós. *La Pensée de Jonathan Edwards: Avec une concordance des différentes éditions de ses oeuvres.* Nouvelle édition remaniée. Paris: Harmattan, 2007.

   Reflections on Edwards's thought with a concordance of his individual works. See M. X. Lesser, *Reading Jonathan Edwards: An Annotated Bibliography in Three Parts, 1729–2005* (Grand Rapids: Eerdmans, 2008), 403 [1987.32].

67. Vlastuin, Willem van. "Does Pentecostalism Have Reformed Roots? An Analysis of the Argument of W. W. Menzies." *PentecoStudies* 6.2 (2007) 100–107.

   Argues that Menzies does not prove his point that the "reformed tradition is the source of Pentecostalism"; however, Reformed theology "is *one of* the roots" of Pentecostalism. Vlastuin calls attention to Edwards to defend his thesis.

2008

1. Allen, Alexander V. G. *Jonathan Edwards: The First Critical Biography, 1889*. Foreword by M. X. Lesser. Eugene, OR: Wipf & Stock, 2008.

    Republishes 1889.1; 2007.2. The reader benefits from a new introduction by Lesser.

2. Allen, Deborah W. "Accommodating Conscience and Culture: Mary Lyon's Appropriation of Jonathan Edwards in Personal Devotion and Public Evangelism." MA thesis, California State University, Dominguez Hills, 2008.

    Argues that Mary Lyon had religious convictions largely based on the Calvinistic theology and works of Edwards. Edwards served as a "guiding force" for her founding of Mount Holyoke Female Seminary.

3. Biehl, Craig. "The Merit of Christ's Obedience to God's Rule of Righteousness in the Theology of Jonathan Edwards." PhD diss., Westminster Theological Seminary, 2008.

    Contends that scholars tend to divorce Edwards from the Reformed tradition by paying little attention to his Trinitarian theology and work on the nature of Christology. The person and work of Christ gives glory to God in his rule, his perfect obedience, and God's unchanging righteousness.

4. Brown, Robert E. "Jonathan Edwards and the Discourses of Nature." In *Nature and Scripture in the Abrahamic Religions: 1700–Present*, edited by Jitse M. van der Meer and Scott Mandelbrote, 83–114. Leiden and Boston: Brill, 2008.

    Suggests that biblical interpretation is a key to understanding Edwards's thinking before higher criticism crossed the Atlantic. Edwards has been ignored in his interest on biblical interpretation, even though it constitutes a substantial portion of his literary output. Biblical output can be traced to every area of his life, including epistemology, historiography, and typology, whether in nature or in the biblical world, etc. His biblical understanding gave way to new scientific discoveries and anticipated the development of American religion.

5. Byrd, James P. *Jonathan Edwards for Armchair Theologians*. Louisville: Westminster John Knox, 2008.

Illuminates Edwards accessibly to a popular audience.

6. Calfano, Brian R. "Christianity and the Common Good: Generating Benevolence and Pursuing the Decent Equilibrium in International Fieldwork." *Journal of Church & State* 50.1 (2008) 101–17.

    Traces benevolence in a Christian theory in the works of Edwards, Hutchinson, and Niebuhr.

7. Carrick, John. *The Preaching of Jonathan Edwards*. Carlisle, PA: Banner of Truth Trust, 2008.

    Examines Edwards's preaching ministry both positively and critically. He primarily puts this in the homiletical context of Edwards's own time.

8. Choi, K. J. "The Deliberative Practices of Aesthetic Experience: Reconsidering the Moral Functionality of Art." *Journal of the Society of Christian Ethics* 29.1 (2009) 193–218.

    Turns to Edwards's aesthetical treatments in themes of his works.

9. Chun, Chris. "The Greatest Instruction Received from Human Writings: The Legacy of Jonathan Edwards in the Theology of Andrew Fuller." PhD diss., University of St. Andrews, 2008.

    Theorizes that Edwards had influence over the theology of Andrew Fuller. The scope of research traces the *Freedom of the Will*; *Religious Affection*; *Humble Attempt*; and *Justification by Faith Alone* as well as whether Fuller understood its primary arguments.

10. ———. "'Sense of the Heart': Jonathan Edwards' Legacy in the Writings of Andrew Fuller." *Eusebeia* 9 (2008) 117–34.

    Summarizes Chun's dissertation (2008.9).

11. Clark, John C. Review of *The New England Theology: From Jonathan Edwards to Edwards Amasa Park*, edited by Douglas A. Sweeney and Allen C. Guelzo. *Trinity Journal* 29.1 (2008) 173–75.

    Defends those underappreciated Edwardsean theologians.

12. Coleman, Mary. Review of *The Cambridge Companion to Jonathan Edwards*, edited by Stephen J. Stein. *Reviews in Religion & Theology* 15.2 (2008) 250–51.

    Applauds the essays as "all solid, reliable, and helpful essays—just what a literary companion should be."

13. Crisp, Oliver D. "Divine Beauty and Excellency: Some Lessons from Jonathan Edwards." *Crux* 44.3 (2008) 2–11.

    Discusses the problems theologians have had with divine beauty and suggests how Edwards clears matters.

14. ———. "Penal Non-Substitution." *Journal of Theological Studies* 59.1 (2008) 140–68.

    Recalls two historic approaches to Christ's atonement: governmental and penal non-substitution views. Crisp links Jonathan Edwards Jr. to the penal non-substitutional view. He points out difficulties with the penal non-substitution theory, but this idea should be taken more seriously in modern times.

15. ———. Review of *The Cambridge Companion to Jonathan Edwards*, edited by Stephen J. Stein. *Journal of Reformed Theology* 2.1 (2008) 94–95.

    Compares *The Princeton Companion to Jonathan Edwards* with *The Cambridge Companion*, where Edwards scholars concentrate on "the historical and cultural context in which Edwards wrote."

16. ———. Review of *The New England Theology: From Jonathan Edwards to Edwards Amasa Park*, edited by Douglas A. Sweeney and Allen C. Guelzo. *Themelios* 33.1 (2008) 93–94.

    Applauds the work as "sure to be very valuable" for anyone interested "in the development of theology in the nineteenth century."

17. Davidson, Bruce W. "The Four Faces of Self-Love in the Theology of Jonathan Edwards." *Journal of the Evangelical Theological Society* 51 (2008) 87–100.

    Examines Edwards's doctrine of self-love in his own context, both human and divine, and then applies it to our age.

18. Davidson, Edward H. *Jonathan Edwards: The Narrative of a Puritan Mind*. Cambridge, MA: Harvard University Press, 2008.

    Reprint. See M. X. Lesser, *Reading Jonathan Edwards: An Annotated Bibliography in Three Parts, 1729–2005* (Grand Rapids: Eerdmans, 2008), 241–42 [1966.10].

19. Edwards, Jonathan. *Catalogues of Books*. Vol. 26 of *The Works of Jonathan Edwards*. Edited by Peter J. Thuesen. New Haven, CT: Yale University Press, 2008.

20. ———. *Freedom of the Will*. Reprint, Lafayette: Sovereign Grace, 2008.

21. ———. *Heaven, a World of Love*. Edinburgh: Banner of Truth, 2008.

22. ———. *An Inquiry into the Prevailing Notions of the Freedom of the Will*. Charleston: BiblioBazaar, 2008.

23. Fisk, Philip J. "The Integral Relation of Impeccability and Freedom to the Projects of Four Theologians: Cyril of Alexandria, John Calvin, Petrus van Mastricht, and Jonathan Edwards." MA thesis, Westminster Theological Seminary, 2008.

    Aims to examine the impeccability of Jesus in the sense of *non posse pecare* through the lens of the four theologians mentioned in the title.

24. George, Christian. *Jonathan Edwards: An American Genius*. United Kingdom: Christian Focus, 2008.

    Follows Edwards through boyhood to his development as a "brilliant" theologian.

25. Geschiere, Charles L. "Taste and See That the Lord Is Good: The Aesthetic-Affectional Preaching of Jonathan Edwards." ThM thesis, Calvin Theological Seminary, 2008.

    Presents Edwards as a model, whose "topic, the text, the hearer, the goal, and, thus, the style and structure" and "aesthetic theology" are exemplified to modern preachers.

26. Gibson, David, and Daniel Strange, eds. *Engaging with Barth: Contemporary Evangelical Critiques*. Nottingham: Apollos, 2008.

    Focuses on Karl Barth and contemporary theology. However, Oliver Crisp's article compares Barth to Edwards in his view on the doctrine of reprobation.

27. Gibson, Michael D. "The Beauty of the Redemption of the World: The Theological Aesthetics of Maximus the Confessor and Jonathan Edwards." *Harvard Theological Review* 101.1 (2008) 45–76.

    Compares Edwards and Maximus from an aesthetic perspective by concentrating on their theological vision of God and the world.

28. Gilpin, W. Clark. Review of *Jonathan Edwards and the Metaphysics of Sin*, by Oliver D. Crisp. *Religious Studies* 44.1 (2008) 111–15.

    Examines Crisp's analysis of Edwards's metaphysics of sin (M. X. Lesser, *Reading Jonathan Edwards: An Annotated Bibliography in Three Parts, 1729–2005* (Grand Rapids: Eerdmans), 600 [2005.6]), concluding that his treatment of Edwards is seldom viewed as an individualistic, personal view of sin.

29. Gubbins, James P. "Positive Psychology: Friend or Foes of Religious Virtue Ethics?" *Journal of the Society of Christian Ethics* 28.2 (2008) 181–203.

    Compares very briefly the "positive psychology's vesture of humanity" in understanding of love from Aquinas, Kierkegaard, and Edwards.

30. Hall, Richard A. S., ed. *The Contribution of Jonathan Edwards to American Culture and Society: Essays on America's Spiritual Founding Father.* Northampton Tercentenary Celebration, 1703–2003. Lewiston, NY: Edwin Mellen, 2008.

    Explores select papers given at the tercentenary of Edwards's birth in 2003 at Northampton Church.

31. Harriss, M. Cooper. Review of *From Nature to Experience: The American Search for Cultural Authority*, by Roger Lundin. *Journal of Religion* 88.2 (2008) 253–55.

    Reviews Lundin's book *From Nature to Experience*, charting the development and weighing the consequences of American pragmatism in Edwards's theology.

32. Harrod, Joseph C. "'A Heart Uncommonly Devoted to God': Theology and Piety in Jonathan Edwards' Funeral Sermon for His Daughter Jerusha." *Eusebeia* 10 (2008) 7–64.

    Researches interest in Edwards's "sermonic corpus" of the death of Jerusha, Edwards's daughter.

33. Hart, Richard E. Review of *A Natural History of Pragmatism: The Fact of Feeling from Jonathan Edwards to Gertrude Stein*, by John Richardson. *Transactions of the Charles S. Peirce Society* 44.1 (2008) 159–64.

    Emphasizes Edwards's two chief phenomena: spider and light. This became a unifying experience for Edwards, as it reflects the "nature" and "religious feelings" that shape the mind.

34. Hastings, W. Ross. Review of *The Cambridge Companion to Jonathan Edwards*, edited by Stephen J. Stein. *International Journal of Systematic Theology* 10.4 (2008) 473–76.

Judges the book a must-read "for any graduate students embarking on a dissertation."

35. Herdt, Jennifer A. Review of *Virtue Reformed: Rereading Jonathan Edwards's Ethics*, by Stephen A. Wilson. *Political Theology: The Journal of Christian Socialism* 9.1 (2008) 127.

    Appreciates Wilson's *Virtue Reformed* as "the latest significant contribution to this literature." It contains virtue ethics that will be of note to philosophers and theologians.

36. Hodges, Igou. *Theology of Jonathan Edwards*. [Materials produced for distance learning course "Theology of Jonathan Edwards," by John Gerstner]. CD-ROM. Columbia, SC: Columbia International University, 2008.

    Reproduces 2006.23.

37. Holloway, Charles S. "The Homiletical Theology of Jonathan Edwards, Gilbert Tennent, and Samuel Davies." PhD diss., Southwestern Baptist Theological Seminary, 2008.

    Identifies the homiletical theology of Edwards, Tennent, and Davies during the First Great Awakening and interacts with "their views on the role of the preacher, the role of Scripture, the role of the listener, and the role of the Holy Spirit."

38. Hostetter, Xon. "The Trinitarian Philosophy of Jonathan Edwards an Ontological and Typological Exposition." PhD diss., University of Georgia, 2008.

    Studies "two of the more historically peculiar features of Jonathan Edwards' thought." He "advocates a non-Aristotelian ontology" and "extends a typological interpretation of Scripture," making the "entire cosmos" a starting point. This "suggests that the doctrine of the Trinity is the primary underlying philosophical motivation for both of these intriguing moves."

39. Hurh, John P. "Epistemology and Terror in American Literature: Edwards, Poe, Melville." PhD diss., University of California, Berkeley, 2008.

    Hypothesizes that the production of terror as advanced by Edwards, Poe, and Melville "articulates a unique view of the epistemological crisis embedded in the Enlightenment distinction between subject and object." He charts how the author adopted this methodology and "its tone of objective certainty, into literary terror."

40. Hutchins, Zachary. "Edwards and Eve: Finding Feminist Strains in the Great Awakening's Patriarch." *Early American Literature* 43.3 (2008) 671–86.

   Compares and contrasts Edwards's views about Eve with John Calvin's. He finds discontinuity in Edwards's content from Calvin.

41. Knepper, Grant. Review of *The Cambridge Companions to Jonathan Edwards*, edited by Stephen J. Stein. *Concordia Theological Quarterly* 72.4 (2008) 369–70.

   Lauds the contributors as a "veritable 'who's who'" of Edwards scholars.

42. Kreider, Glenn R. Review of *Jonathan Edwards: The Holy Spirit in Revival*, by Michael A. G. Haykin. *Bibliotheca Sacra* 165.657 (2008) 119–20.

   Applauds the book as "readable" and "accessible to a nonacademic audience."

43. ———. Review of *The New England Theology: From Jonathan Edwards to Edwards Amasa Park*, edited by Douglas A. Sweeney and Allen Guelzo. *Bibliotheca Sacra* 165.659 (2008) 382–83.

   Celebrates the authors for making an "excellent sourcebook" of New England theology.

44. ———. Review of *Heaven on Earth: Capturing Jonathan Edwards' Vision of Living in Between*, by Stephen J. Nichols. *Bibliotheca Sacra* 165.658 (2008) 250–51.

   Excels as a resource of "devotional reading, a chapter a day."

45. Lawson, Steven. *The Unwavering Resolve of Jonathan Edwards*. Long Line of Godly Men Profile. Lake Mary, FL: Reformation Trust, 2008.

   Charts the seventy "resolutions" and shows how Edwards sought to live them out.

46. Leiburg, Fred van. "Interpreting the Dutch Great Awakening (1749–1755)." *Church History* 77.2 (2008) 318–36.

   Explores the Dutch Great Awakening and Edwards's involvement in that revival campaign. Edwards's *A Faithful Narrative* was published in Dutch in 1738. He gave a prominent position to the precursor of the revivals, the Dutch minister Theodore Frelinghuysen, and was encouraged by "Dutch colleagues" for their "awakening, searching, strict, and experimental preaching." However, by 1751 or 1752, Edwards had a "criteria for the work of the Holy

Spirit" and stopped supporting the episode in Nijerk as many irregularities happened.

47. Leithart, Peter J. "Beauty Seize Us." *Touchstone: A Journal of Mere Christianity* 21.5 (2008) 6.

    Examines the aphorism "beauty is in the eye of the beholder" and states, "Jonathan Edwards knew better." He "proposed beauty as the reality that overcomes subjectivism."

48. Lesser, M. X. *Reading Jonathan Edwards: An Annotated Bibliography in Three Parts, 1729–2005*. Grand Rapids: Eerdmans, 2008.

    Reprint. Compiles all Edwards's bibliographic material in alphabetical order within the year they were published, starting from 1729 and ending with 2005.

49. Lucas, Sean M. "'Divine Light, Holy Heat': Jonathan Edwards, the Ministry of the Word, and Spiritual Formation." *Presbyterion* 34.1 (2008) 1–11.

    Reflects upon Edwards's "life's work" in the theology of preaching the Word and how this leads to spiritual maturity.

50. Madueme, Hans. Review of *A Short Life of Jonathan Edwards*, by George M. Marsden. *Themelios* 33.3 (2008) 119.

    Appraises the book as "theologically sensitive, historically insightful, and engagingly written."

51. Marsden, George M. *A Short Life of Jonathan Edwards*. Grand Rapids: Eerdmans, 2008.

    Surveys the life of Edwards as a pastor, preacher, missionary, biographer, college president, philosopher, husband, and father. This is not abridged from *Jonathan Edwards: A Life*, published in 2003, but "a concise, fresh retelling of the Edwards story."

52. McClymond, Michael J. "Jonathan Edwards." In *Oxford Handbook of Religion and Emotion*, edited by John Corrigan, 404–17. Oxford: Oxford University Press, 2008.

    Regards Edwards as a man of "deep piety" who was fascinated with religious experiences and emotions of other people. Shows how understanding, inclination, affection, passion, and love flow through religious emotions and concludes with Edwards's "legacy" of emotion.

53. McDermott, Gerald R. "Jonathan Edwards on Justification by Faith—More Protestant or Catholic?" *Pro Ecclesia* 17.1 (2008) 92–111.

   Reduces Edwards's doctrine of justification either to Protestant or Catholic, or as compared more to Luther or Aquinas, and asks, "To whom was he closer?"

54. McFadden, Ian D. "Amidst the Great Darkness: The Practical Missiology of Jonathan Edwards at Stockbridge, 1751–1758." STM thesis, Yale Divinity School, 2008.

   Explores Edwards's motivations to move to Stockbridge; contra popular scholarly opinions, he concludes "it seems most likely that Edwards chose Stockbridge because he wanted to be a missionary to the Indians there."

55. Misak, Cheryl, ed. "Jonathan Edwards." In *The Oxford Handbook of American Philosophy*, 1–18. Oxford: Oxford University Press, 2008.

   Contends that reading Edwards "as a philosopher is daunting," namely, because he names few or no references.

56. Moorhead, James H. Review of *The New England Theology: From Jonathan Edwards to Edwards Amasa Park*, edited by Douglas A. Sweeney and Allen Guelzo. *Journal of Presbyterian History* 86.2 (2008) 87–88.

   Encounters the New Divinity's "moral strenuosity and ethical absolutism, which led to vigorous advocacy of foreign missions and to attacks on slavery." The main contribution that Edwards made on the New England theologians was his determination between "natural and moral necessity."

57. Morgan, Christopher W. Review of *Communion in the Spirit: The Holy Spirit as the Bond of Union in the Theology of Jonathan Edwards*, by Robert W. Caldwell. *Fides et Historia* 40.1 (2008) 92–93.

   Shows how the Spirit is the bond of the Christ's (hypostatic) union within the Trinity and how this plays out in Edwards's theology such as the Spirit's work in creation, redemption, Christology, soteriology, regeneration, justification, sanctification, ecclesiology, and glorification.

58. Nettles, Thomas J. "The Influence of Jonathan Edwards on Andrew Fuller." *Eusebeia* 9 (2008) 97–116.

Considers how Edwards influenced the English dissenters, such as Robert Hall, John Ryland Jr., John Sutcliff, and William Carey. He spends the most time exploring how Edwards influenced Andrew Fuller.

59. Nixon, C. Robert. Review of *A Short Life of Jonathan Edwards*, by George Marsden. *Library Journal* 133.18 (2008) 72.

Commends this book as a "readable and illuminating introduction to this important figure in American religious history" and is "recommended from public and academic libraries."

60. Novak, Barbara. "Copley and Edwards: Self, Consciousness, and Thing." In *Voyages of the Self: Pairs, Parallels and Patterns in American Art and Literature*, 3–16. New York: Oxford University Press, 2009.

Demonstrates through readings, paintings, and text how "the meaning of self has influenced and changed through American identity and culture from the late eighteenth to the twentieth century." She uses Edwards as an example.

61. Olson, Ray. Review of *A Short Life of Jonathan Edwards*, by George A. Marsden. *Booklist* 105.3 (2008) 18.

Evaluates the book by what Marsden calls him: "A towering figure . . . of the first American revolution, the spiritual revolution of the awakening." The value of this book comes by "believing that assessment."

62. ———. Review of *Jonathan Edwards for Armchair Theologians*, by James Byrd. *Booklist* 105.3 (2008) 15.

Reviews the "eldritch" or uncanny fame or "imagery of Edwards" to a popular audience.

63. Rast, Lawrence R., Jr. "Jonathan Edwards on Justification by Faith." *Concordia Theological Quarterly* 72.4 (2008) 347–62.

Establishes Edwards's doctrine of justification is "based on God's grace" and is "infused into the human soul" but "requires the real consent of the human act of faith." At the same time, he "departed from a strict Reformed understanding of the justification" and "allowed the camel's nose of Arminianism into Calvinism's tent."

64. Samuel, Josh P. S. "The Doctrine of Scripture in the Theology of Jonathan Edwards." MA thesis, Tyndale Seminary, 2008.

Examines Edwards's understanding of general revelation and what could be discerned through "nature, human history, reason, and conscience" and then investigates "the authoritative role of Scripture," including what Edwards believed about "inspiration, the human writers, the canonical collection, and infallibility."

65. Schweitzer, William M. "Interpreting the Harmony of Reality: Jonathan Edwards' Theology of Revelation." PhD diss., University of Edinburgh, 2008.

    Theorizes his dissertation is "the first full-scale study of Jonathan Edwards' theology of revelation." Asks "what was Edwards' understanding of divine revelation," and "how did this understanding function in his larger theological project?" A view of Edwards's revelation "was thus distinctively tri-dimensional in that Trinitarian communication contained noetic, affectional and beatific elements."

66. Shaw, Ian J. "Theology and Transformation in Society: The Scottish Evangelical Theological Society Finlayson lecture, 2008." *Scottish Bulletin of Evangelical Theology* 26.2 (2008) 132–50.

    Gives a basic summary of the life of Edwards and his sermons on *Christian Charity* as he charts social concerns of evangelical theology.

67. Sholl, Brian Keith. "The Excellency of Minds: Jonathan Edwards's Theological Style." PhD diss., University of Virginia, 2008.

    Contrasts scholarship that separates Edwards's philosophical from his theological writing. He supports the argument that Edwards "conceives theology as an aesthetic enterprise and an aesthetic performance" for his vision of theology is the human's "engagement with God's glory and being."

68. Smart, Robert Davis. "Jonathan Edwards's Apologetic for the Great Awakening with Particular Attention to Charles Chauncy's Criticisms." PhD diss., University of Wales-Lampeter, 2008.

    Scopes out Charles Chauncy's "Old Light" criticisms of the Awakenings in the 1740s. Edwards represented the "New Lights," and responded to Chauncy's criticism.

69. Sparkes, Adam. "Salvation History, Chronology, and Crisis: A Problem with Inclusivist Theology of Religions, Part 1 of 2." *Themelios* 33.2 (2008) 7–18.

    Quotes from Edwards's *A History of the Work of Redemption*.

70. Steele, Richard B. "Transfiguring Light: The Moral Beauty of the Christian Life According to Gregory Palamas and Jonathan Edwards." *St. Vladimir's Theological Quarterly* 52.3–4 (2008) 403–39.

    Remarks that there are "surprising affinities" between the theologies of Gregory Palamas and Edwards.

71. Stout, Harry S. Review of "Bipolar Disorder: Head and Heart American Christianities," by Garry Wills. *America* 198.15 (2008) 31–33.

    Insists Wills is wrong in his assessment that Edwards was *not* influenced by Enlightenment thinkers. "If this is accurate, a large number of scholars have wasted a lot of time studying Edwards and the Great Awakening." Stout says that "happily" Wills "is far from accurate." Edwards really understood the thinking of Newton and Locke.

72. Studebaker, Steven M. *Jonathan Edwards' Social Augustinian Trinitarianism in Historical and Contemporary Perspectives.* Piscataway, NJ: Gorgias, 2008.

    Contrasts Amy Plantinga Pauw's writings as wrong-sighted in her conclusion that Edwards drew on the "psychological and social models of the Trinity." Studebaker says that Edwards did not describe a twofold model of the Trinity but rather the Augustinian model.

73. ———. "The Spirit in Creation: A Unified Theology of Grace and Creation Care." *Zygon* 43.4 (2008) 943–60.

    Identifies the neglect of Christian environmentalism in evangelical and Pentecostal theology and then develops "creation care" as a "dimension of Christian formation and sanctification."

74. Turley, Stephen R. "Awakened to the Holy: 'Sinners in the Hands of an Angry God' in Ritualized Context." *Christianity & Literature* 57.4 (2008) 507–30.

    Attempts to address the "Sinners in the Hands of an Angry God" by applying a ritual-theoretical approach to this sermon text.

75. Valeri, Mark. Review of *The Cambridge Companion to Jonathan Edwards*, edited by Stephen J. Stein. *Theological Studies* 69.2 (2008) 444–46.

    Confirms "these are all solid, reliable, and helpful essays—just what a literary companion should be."

76. ———. Review of *The Princeton Companion to Jonathan Edwards*, edited by Sang Hyun Lee. *The Journal of Ecclesiastical History* 59.1 (2008) 162–63.

   Criticizes the volume for being "somewhat more abstract and technical than he might have found to his purposes." Yet it serves as an important introduction.

77. Warner, Charles Dudley. *A Library of the World's Best Literature: Ancient and Modern*. New York: Cosimo, 2008.

   Contains the biography of Samuel Hopkins, selected sermons with introductions and notes, and the biography of Alexander V. G. Allen, etc.

78. Wheeler, Rachel. *To Live Upon Hope: Mohicans and Missionaries in the Eighteenth-Century Northeast*. Ithaca, NY: Cornell University Press, 2008.

   Explores the question of what "missionary Christianity" became for the people of the Mohicans in Stockbridge or the Shekomek in the American colonies. These had two different experiences under colonialism—"accommodations or resistance."

2009

1. Allen, Michael. "Jonathan Edwards and the Lapsarian Debate." *Scottish Journal of Theology* 62.3 (2009) 299–315.

   Denies that Edwards spoke of the lapsarian debate only so far as it was relevant to the Arminian "denial of unconditional election."

2. Ariail, Austin T. "Jonathan Edwards's Doctrine of Imputed Sin: Nineteenth-Century Southern Presbyterian Accusations Considered." ThM thesis, Dallas Theological Seminary, 2009.

   Portrays Edwards's opinions in *Original Sin* "would fall out of favor with Reformed theologians," particularly Southern Presbyterians, namely, James Henley Thornwell. The primary question is considered in the question, "Is Edwards Harmful or Inadequate with his imputation of sin?"

3. Barshinger, David. "The Only Rule of Our Faith and Practice: Jonathan Edwards' Interpretation of the Book of Isaiah as a Case Study of His Exegetical Boundaries." *Journal of the Evangelical Theological Society* 52.4 (2009) 811–29.

Articulates how Edwards interpreted Isaiah from the "Notes on Scripture" and the "Blank Bible" in harmony with the "conviction that Scripture interprets Scripture" and in the normal way of Protestant exegesis.

4. Bebbington, David W. Review of *Reading Jonathan Edwards: An Annotated Bibliography in Three Parts*, by M. X. Lesser. *Church History: Studies in Christianity and Culture* 78.3 (2009) 693–94.

    Reviews Lesser's book very favorably. Comments, "Altogether this work will be essential for any future work done on Edwards."

5. ———. "Revivals, Revivalism and the Baptist." *Baptistic Theologies* 1.1 (2009) 1–13.

    Defines revival in the nineteenth century as "outpourings of the Spirit, which result in the quickening of the church and the conversion of sinners." Edwards proves a case in point of this explanation.

6. Beck, Peter. *A Short Life of Jonathan Edwards*, by George Marsden. *Fides et Historia* 41.1 (2009) 130–31.

    Commends Marsden—he "has done it again" and "for this book, Marsden is to be congratulated."

7. Biehl, Craig. *The Infinite Merit of Christ: The Glory of Christ's Obedience in the Theology of Jonathan Edwards*. Jackson, MS: Reformed Academic, 2009.

    Contrasts the revisionist interpretations of Edwards's soteriology "as inclusive or Catholic, therefore, [they] are untenable without an overthrow and rewrite of the entirety of Edwards's theology."

8. Bogue, Carl. *Jonathan Edwards and the Covenant of Grace*. Jonathan Edwards Classic Studies Series. Eugene, OR: Wipf & Stock, 2009.

    Contends that Edwards's theology of the covenant of grace was more consistent with the Reformers despite Perry Miller's assertion to the contrary.

9. Bridgers, Lynn. "Emotion, Experience and Enthusiasm: The Growing Divide in US Religion." *Modern Believing* 50.4 (2009) 6–24.

    Explores the "role that emotion, experience and enthusiasm" continue to have in American religion. He focuses on George Whitfield, John Wesley, and Edwards to give proof of this point.

10. Brown, Robert E. "Jonathan Edwards and the Discourses of Nature." In *Nature and Scripture in the Abrahamic Religions*, edited by Jitse

M. van der Meer and Scott Mandelbrote, 2:83–114. Leiden: Brill, 2009.

Suggests that biblical exegesis is fundamental to understanding Edwards's corpus.

11. Bynum, T. "'The Saving Change': New Birth and Conversion in Eighteenth-Century African-American Literature." PhD diss., Johns Hopkins University Press, 2009.

Examines the impact that John Bunyan, George Whitfield, John Donne, and Edwards had on African American devotional religious literature.

12. Cherock, Richard J. Review of *A Short Life of Jonathan Edwards*, by George Marsden. *Stone-Campbell Journal* 12.1 (2009) 84–85.

Calls the "greatest weakness" also the "greatest strength" in Marsden's intention for "brevity." One is left to desire additional information of his "writing, life, and career."

13. Challies, Tim. Review of *The Unwavering Resolve of Jonathan Edwards*, by Stephen J. Lawson. *American Theological Inquiry* 2.2 (2009) 104–5.

Says that this books "finds a niche and fills it well."

14. Choi, Ki Joo. "The Deliberative Practices of Aesthetic Experience: Reconsidering the Moral Functionality of Art." *Journal of the Society of Christian Ethics* 29.1 (2009) 193–218.

Turns specifically to "select themes" treated in the work of "the moral and aesthetical theology of Jonathan Edwards."

15. Clary, Ian Hugh. "Alexander Carson (1776–1844): 'Jonathan Edwards of the Nineteenth Century.'" *American Theological Inquiry* 2.2 (2009) 43–52.

Compares Carson to Edwards because of the description by *Orthodox Presbyterian*, "He has been called 'the Jonathan Edwards of the nineteenth century.'"

16. Crisp, Oliver. "Jonathan Edwards and the Closing of the Table: Must the Eucharist Be Open to All?" *Ecclesiology* 5.1 (2009) 48–68.

Notes that Edwards changed his mind about the membership of his church at Northampton because of his "sacramental theology." This "makes a constructive contribution to ecclesiology."

17. ———. "Jonathan Edwards on the Divine Nature." *Journal of Reformed Theology* 3.2 (2009) 175–201.

    Offers Edwards's doctrine of God differently than "recent literature" that is in keeping with the Reformed scholastic tradition. Ultimately, Crisp makes the argument that he ended up with something tantamount to panentheism.

18. Crisp, Oliver, and Kyle Strobel. *Jonathan Edwards: An Introduction to His Thought*. Edinburgh: T&T Clark, 2009.

    Surveys key "theological and philosophical themes" in Edwards's theology of God, creation, atonement, and soteriology. This book is comprehensive and concise.

19. Danaher, William J. "'Fire Enfolding Itself': Jonathan Edwards, the Merkabah, and Reparative Reasoning." *Journal for Scripture Reasoning* 8.2 (2009). https://digitalcommons.hamline.edu/jsr/vol8/iss2/3/.

    Seeks to "examine Jonathan Edwards's interpretation of the Merkabah (Ezek 1:4–28)" as it is "an exercise in reparative reasoning." This then "helps illustrate the distinctiveness of Edwards's interpretation, but it also sheds light on the different connections made between texts, doctrinal understandings, and hermeneutical practices in the history of biblical interpretation."

20. Edwards, Jonathan. *History of Redemption, to Which Are How* [sic] *Added Notes, Historical, Critical, and Theological, with the Life and Experience of the Author*. N.p.: General Books, 2009.

21. ———. *The Religious Affections*. Vancouver: Eremitical, 2009.

22. ———. *A Treatise Concerning Religious Affections*. Bedford, MA: Applewood, 2009.

23. ———. *An Unpublished Essay of Edwards on the Trinity: With Remarks on Edwards and His Theology*. Edited by George Park Fisher. New York: Scribner's Sons, 2009.

24. ———. *The Works of Jonathan Edwards: With a Memoir of His Life and Character*. Edited by Tryon Edwards. Andover: Allen, Morrill & Wardwell, 2009.

25. ———. *The Works of President Edwards*. 8 vols. Bedford, MA: Applewood, 2009.

26. Edwards, Jonathan, Jr. *The Salvation of All Men Strictly Examined and the Endless Punishment of Those Who Die Impenitent.* Charleston: BiblioLife, 2009.

27. Epstein, A. Review of *A Natural History of Pragmatism: The Fact of Feeling from Jonathan Edwards to Gertrude Stein*, by John Richardson. *Henry James Reviews* 30.1 (2009) 87–90.

    Insists that this book is about "the history of ideas" and particularly about the Puritans and Jonathan Edwards.

28. Fehler, Brian. "Jonathan Edwards on Nature as a Language of God: Symbolic Typology as Rhetorical Presence." In *Religion in the Age of Reason: A Transatlantic Study of the Long Eighteenth Century*, edited by Kathryn Duncan, 181–94. New York: AMS, 2009.

    Portrays Edwards as of a contemplative nature. Describes how types of God in Edwards's sermons and in his preaching launched the Great Awakening.

29. Grasso, Christopher. Review of *The Great Awakening: The Roots of Evangelical Christianity in Colonial America*, by Thomas Kidd. *Reviews in American History* 37.1 (2009) 13–21.

    Opines that Kidd "wants to retain the notion of the Great Awakening as a series of dramatic events within a narrower chronological frame that have some sort of causal for in American history." Kidd indicates that the "Great Awakening *is* the evangelical movement," therefore, "we have something producing itself." This "remains a problem not just of ambiguous labeling but of conceptualization and historical interpretation."

30. Gray, Lauren Davis. "Birthing the New Birth: The Natural Philosophy of Childbirth in the Theology of Jonathan Edwards." MA thesis, Florida State University, 2009.

    Insists Edwards, Wesley, and Zinzendorf had differences in doctrine regarding the new birth; however, this doctrine was surprisingly uniform in that "they all sought to ground the spiritual metaphor of the new birth in the natural philosophy of childbirth."

31. Grigg, John A. *The Lives of David Brainerd: The Making of an American Evangelical Icon.* Oxford: Oxford University Press, 2009.

    Provides a study of David Brainerd who, in 1747, at the age of twenty-nine, died in Edwards's home. In 1749 Edwards published *The Life of David Brainerd*. From Edwards's work, John Wesley published *An Extract of the Life of the Reverend David Brainerd*, which made him "An American Evangelical Icon." Both Edwards and Wesley edited the *Life* to promote their theological agenda, Edwards his Calvinistic agenda and Wesley an Arminian one.

32. Gura, Philip F. "American Primer." *Early American Literature* 44.1 (2009) 179–94.

    Reviews E. Brooks Holifield's *Theology in America* and Mark Noll's *America's God: From Jonathan Edwards to Abraham Lincoln*. Gura makes notes when and how they speak about Edwards.

33. Hall, Brent E. "The Methodology of Persuasion in the Preaching of Jonathan Edwards." ThM thesis, Dallas Theological Seminary, 2009.

    Contends that "the Puritan preacher Jonathan Edwards can certainly provide some helpful insight for effective preaching" as he "ignited" the Great Awakening. Edwards's effective sermons are a "result of his methodology for preaching," and "a view of human psychology." In the last chapter he analyzes *Sinners in the Hands of an Angry God*.

34. Hambrick-Stowe, Charles. Review of *A Short Life of Jonathan Edwards*, by George Marsden. *The Journal of Ecclesiastical History* 60.4 (2009) 853–54.

    Assesses *A Short Life of Jonathan Edwards* favorably as "illuminating . . . blending intellectual history with social science categories."

35. ———. Review of *The Cambridge Companion to Jonathan Edwards*, edited by Stephen J. Stein. *The Journal of Ecclesiastical History* 60.1 (2009) 189–90.

    Values *The Cambridge Companion* the fruit "of many decades and several generations of work."

36. Hanson, Paul D. "The Bible as a Resource for Christian Political Engagement." *Bangalore Theological Forum* 41.1 (2009) 23–36.

    Cites Edwards as an example of how the Bible has been used for political engagement.

37. Holder, Arthur G., ed. "Jonathan Edwards." In *Christian Spirituality: The Classics*, 269–80. London: Routledge, 2009.

    Wishes that anyone desiring to gain the knowledge of *Christian Spirituality* read this book. Includes the experiences of Origen,

Augustine, Thérèse of Lisieux, Thomas Merton, and Jonathan Edwards, etc.

38. Howe, Daniel Walker. *Making the American Self: Jonathan Edwards to Abraham Lincoln*. 1997. Reprint, New York: Oxford University Press, 2009.

    Reprint: M. X. Lesser, *Reading Jonathan Edwards: An Annotated Bibliography in Three Parts, 1729–2005* (Grand Rapids: Eerdmans), 509 [1997.13].

39. Howe, Susan. "Choir Answers to Choir: Notes on Jonathan Edwards and Wallace Stevens." *Chicago Review* 54.4 (2009) 51–61.

    Offers "critical assessment of the poetry of Jonathan Edwards and Wallace Stevens."

40. Hubbard, Larry A. "Using Jonathan Edwards's Treatise Concerning Religious Affections to Equip Selected Members of Riverside Baptist Church, Denham." DMin thesis, New Orleans Baptist Theological Seminary, 2009.

    Purposes to equip "Riverside Baptist Denham Springs, Louisiana, to cultivate authentic faith" in examination of Edwards's *Treatise Concerning Religious Affections* to "define and cultivate authentic faith."

41. Hubers, John. "Making Friends with Locusts: Early ABCFM Missionary Perceptions of Muslims and Islam, 1818–50." *International Bulletin of Missionary Research* 33.3 (2009) 151–54.

    Challenges earlier exegetes for positing that the kingdom would come through "cataclysmic means" or "natural means" as Edwards believed it would come through the pouring out of the Holy Spirit through preaching and teaching.

42. Hutchens, S. M. Review of *Understanding Jonathan Edwards: An Introduction to America's Theologian*, by Gerald R. McDermott. *Touchstone: A Journal of Mere Christianity* 22.4 (2009) 39.

    Reviews McDermott's *Understanding Jonathan Edwards* very briefly.

43. Jacobs, Alan. *Original Sin: A Cultural History*. New York: HarperCollins, 2009.

    Takes a sweeping view of Edwards's *The Great Christian Doctrine of Original Sin Defended*.

44. Jonik, Michael E. "A Natural History of the Mind: Edwards, Emerson, Thoreau, Melville." PhD diss., State University of New York at Albany.

    Examines "how eighteenth-century and nineteenth-century American writers drew on European natural science and philosophy." The author traces four key figures: Edwards, Ralph Waldo Emerson, Henry David Thoreau, and Herman Melville.

45. Kidd, Thomas S. "Evangelicals, the End Times, and Islam." *Historically Speaking* 10.1 (2009) 16–18.

    Harmonizes Edwards with other colonial pastors in viewing "Islam as a demonic force that would be extinguished in the last days."

46. Kimnach, Wilson H. "The Literary Life of Jonathan Edwards." In *Understanding Jonathan Edwards: An Introduction to America's Theologian*, edited by Gerald McDermott, 133–45. New York: Oxford University Press, 2009.

    Views Edwards's literary history on the frontier from which "he derived inspiration" as an author of scientific, philosophic, and theological writing.

47. Kiteley, Brian. *The River Gods*. Tuscaloosa: University of Alabama Press, 2009.

    Recounts a narrative through a "mix of fact and fiction" about Northampton, Massachusetts, "from the eleventh century through the 1990s." One of the speakers, among many, is Jonathan Edwards.

48. Lee, Sang Hyun. "Jonathan Edwards." In *The History of Western Philosophy*, 223–33. New York: Oxford University Press, 2009.

    Attempts to explain what Edwards scholars have postulated as regarding Edwards's dispositional ontology; beauty and relational ontology; imagination, knowledge, and the sense of the heart; and the Trinity and the end for which God created the world.

49. Lesser, M. X., and Patience Ford. "A Transcendentalist Conversion Narrative." *Massachusetts Historical Review* 11 (2009) 153–67.

    Refers to the Transcendental conversion narrative as the "Romantic wing of New England's Unitarians." Edwards in the famed "Personal Narrative" promoted the type of piety that he expected in the conversion experiences of the church at Northampton.

Therefore, he bears some of the guilt in introducing the head-heart "dichotomy" of church membership.

50. Littauer, Allison K. "The Spirit of Reform: St. Augustine and Jonathan Edwards on the Glory of God." DMin thesis, Gordon Conwell Theological Seminary, 2009.

    Unifies Augustine and Edwards, who were separated by 1,400 years, for their shared focus on the depravity of men and their high view of God.

51. Marsden, George. *A Short Life of Jonathan Edwards (Unabridged)*. Narrated by Grover Garder. Audiobook. Escondido, CA: Christianaudio, 2009.

    Records Marsden's *A Short Life of Jonathan Edwards*.

52. McCartney, D. G. Review of *A Short Life of Jonathan Edwards* [Audiobook], by George M. Marsden. *Westminster Theological Journal* 71.1 (2009) 243–44.

    Reviews Marsden's book very favorably, as Edwards is "the most important and creative theologian and Christian philosopher America has ever produced."

53. McCollum, D. "A Study of Evangelicals and Revival Exercises from 1730–1805: Tracing the Development of Exercise Traditions Through the First Great Awakening Period to the Southern Great Revival." PhD diss., Southeastern Baptist Theological Seminary, 2009.

    Studies the Great Awakening in the 1730s–1740s and examines the works of Charles Chauncy and Jonathan Edwards, which "express many of the psychological and theological assumptions about exercises that were held by ministers in the other groups."

54. McDermott, Gerald R., ed. *Understanding Jonathan Edwards: An Introduction to America's Theologian*. Oxford: Oxford University Press, 2009.

    Recruits scholars that explain the most vitally important subjects on Edwards's thinking, which includes "revival, Bible, typology, aesthetics, literature, preaching, philosophy, and world religions."

55. Mickle, Allen R., Jr. Review of *The God-Centered Life: Insights from Jonathan Edwards for Today*, by Josh Moody. *Puritan Reformed Journal* 1.2 (2009) 295–96.

    Provides a "helpful volume" and "has done the church a service."

56. Minkema, Kenneth P. Review of *Communion in the Spirit: The Holy Spirit as the Bond of Union in the Theology of Jonathan Edwards*, by Robert Caldwell III. *The Journal of Ecclesiastical History* 60.4 (2009) 854–55.

    Acknowledges recent studies of the Holy Spirit in Edwards's works (Nichols, 2003; Vlastuin, 2001; Haykin, 2005) and says that Caldwell produces the best and most comprehensive work on the topic.

57. Minor, Mitzi, et al. "Proper Fourteen, Ordinary 19, Pentecost 10: August 9, 2009." *Lectionary Homiletics* 20.5 (2009) 14–20.

    Refers to Edwards's *Treatise on the Will* to interpret John 6, "No one can come to me unless the Father who sent me draw him." Edwards's "compatibilist perspective" is "worthy of consideration."

58. Moore, Darnell L. "Theorizing the 'Black Body' as a Site of Trauma: Implications for Theologies of Embodiment." *Theology & Sexuality* 15.2 (2009) 175–88.

    Refers to Edwards as the "iconic American revivalist and theologian" who unfortunately purchased a slave named Venus.

59. Moorhead, Jonathan. Review of *Jonathan Edwards and the Ministry of the Word: A Model of Faith and Thought*, by Douglas A. Sweeney. *Journal of the Evangelical Society* 52.3 (2009) 661–63.

    Commends this book as biographical mixed with application of "the most important figure in evangelical history."

60. Ohst, Martin. Review of *The Cambridge Companion to Jonathan Edwards*, edited by Stephen J. Stein. *Theologische Literaturzeitung* 134.3 (2009) 379–81.

    Recognizes the experts, "most of whom also worked on complete edition of Edwards' works, present the life, work and aftermath of a man." This "book is definitely worth reading."

61. Parker, David. Review of *A Short Life of Jonathan Edwards*, by George Marsden. *Evangelical Review of Theology* 33.3 (2009) 287.

    Places Edwards "firmly within the social, political, intellectual and religious context of the day, clearly showing why he is such an important figure in American (and evangelical) history."

62. Peters, Nathaniel. Review of *A Short Life of Jonathan Edwards*, by George Marsden. *First Things* 189 (2009) 63.

Encourages readers to grapple with Edwards as an "historical figure," and suggests they would most likely benefit from reading Marsden's book.

63. Pederson, Randall J. Review of *A Short Life of Jonathan Edwards*, by George Marsden. *Puritan Reformed Journal* 1.2 (2009) 298–300.

    Regards Marsden as doing "an exemplary job" and "should be commended."

64. ———. Review of *Reading Jonathan Edwards: An Annotated Bibliography in Three Parts, 1729–2005*, by M. X. Lesser. *Westminster Theological Journal* 71.1 (2009) 244–45.

    Commends Lesser for his work, "which is quite impressive."

65. ———. Review of *Reading Jonathan Edwards: An Annotated Bibliography in Three Parts, 1729–2005*, by M. X. Lesser. *Puritan Reformed Journal* 1.2 (2009) 296–98.

    Observes that Lesser gives a "clear guide to this literary maze" of Jonathan Edwards's bibliography.

66. Rager, Christopher. Review of *A Short Life of Jonathan Edwards*, by George M. Marsden [Audiobook]. *Library Journal* 134.13 (2009) 44.

    Reviews Marsden's audiobook, *A Short Life of Jonathan Edwards*.

67. Rivett, Sarah. Review of *Jonathan Edwards at 300: Essays on the Tercentenary of His Birth*, edited by Harry Stout, Kenneth Minkema, and Caleb Maskell; *Jonathan Edwards: America's Evangelical*, by Philip Gura. *Early American Literature* 44.2 (2009) 423–32.

    Recommends two books for reading: one, the biography of Philip Gura, and a collection of essays "written by some of the most influential recent generations who came together at the tercentenary of Edwards's birth."

68. Rogers, Mark C. "A Missional Eschatology: Jonathan Edwards, Future Prophecy, and the Spread of the Gospel." *Fides et Historia* 41.1 (2009) 23–46.

    Treats the "prophecy of the sixth vial" as a removal of "obstacles to the gospel's spread, accompanied by an outpouring of God's Spirit and resulting in an extraordinary awakening."

69. Ross, Melanie. Review of *The Trinitarian Ethics of Jonathan Edwards*, by William J. Danaher. *Scottish Journal of Theology* 62.4 (2009) 503–5.

Contributes to the "Columbia Series in Reformed Theology" by displaying Edwards's Trinitarian theology. Danaher anticipates the Trinitarian problems that we in the present century struggle with.

70. Sanlon, Peter. "Bringing Emotions to the Surface in Ministry." *Anvil* 26.3–4 (2009) 231–42.

    Reflects on the emotions in the views of several important figures such as Augustine, Richard Sibbes, and Jonathan Edwards and their impact on Sanlon's ministry.

71. Simonson, Harold. *Jonathan Edwards: Theologian of the Heart*. Eugene, OR: Wipf & Stock, 2009.

    Calls Edwards a "theologian of the heart." This is proven if one explores his sermons, treatises, "Miscellanies," "Diary," "Resolutions," and "Personal Narrative." The author believes that he "shares company" with the likes of literary artists such as "Herman Melville, Nathaniel Hawthorne, Emily Dickinson and William Faulkner."

72. Sims, David. *The Child in American Evangelicalism and the Problem of Affluence: A Theological Anthropology of the Affluent American-Evangelical Child in Late Modernity*. Eugene, OR: Pickwick, 2009.

    Employs the term "Affluent American Evangelical Child" (AAEC) from American history, sociology, and economics. In chapter 2 he examines theological anthropologies of Edwards, Horace Bushnell, and Lawrence Richards. In the subsequent chapters he treats other theological figures and concludes with "forecast of possible futures for the AAEC in the twenty-first century."

73. Smith, Craig. "The Resolutions of Jonathan Edwards as a Contemporary Model for Emerging Leaders in the Twenty-First Century." MA thesis, Denver Seminary, 2009.

    Asks "how did God develop Jonathan Edwards into such a powerful leader for his glory?" A part of the answer is in his "framing of the seventy Resolutions," and his diary is "[worthy] of careful scrutiny," offering a "window into the interior life of this great spiritual leader."

74. Stenschke, Christoph W. Review of *The Cambridge Companion to Jonathan Edwards*, edited by Stephen J. Stein. *Religion & Theology* 16.3–4 (2009) 318–19.

    Assesses that this is a "well-written and comprehensive introduction" to Edwards.

75. Stetina, Karin Spiecker. "The Biblical-Experimental Foundation of Jonathan Edwards's Theology of Religious Experience, 1720–1723." *Puritan Reformed Journal* 1.2 (2009) 170–86.

    Asks "What is the nature of true religion?" and answers that this is the question that Edwards asks in 1746 when he wrote *Religious Affections*. Stetina then provides the answers of Edwards and applies it to our day.

76. Strachan, Owen, and Douglas A. Sweeney. *Jonathan Edwards, Lover of God*. Essential Edwards Collection. Chicago: Moody, 2009.

    Contends that Edwards was a "great philosopher, a great preacher, a great theologian." Edwards was a complex and gifted person, "one who defies easy characterization," but more than that, he was a lover of God, and in this book Strachan and Sweeney make that description.

77. ———. *Jonathan Edwards on Beauty*. Essential Edwards Collection. Chicago: Moody, 2009.

    Engages that Edwards sought beauty from beholding the Triune God revealed in creation, Christology, and the church and drafted a "Christian framework for understanding and experiencing the beauty God has planted in His world."

78. ———. *Jonathan Edwards on the Good Life*. Essential Edwards Collection. Chicago: Moody, 2009.

    Explores the thoughts of Edwards on the "good life" as it focuses the "original design for mankind" and the "transformation of conversion" and restored its creational design to love God and love his commandments.

79. Stratton, Gary David. "Jonathan Edwards' Theology of Spiritual Awakening and Spiritual Formation Leadership in American Higher Education." PhD diss., Talbot School of Theology, Biola University, 2009.

    Studies the "twenty-first century college leaders seeking to foster spiritual formation in their students," and suggests they "would be wise to seek to reintegrate Jonathan Edwards' concepts of spiritual awakening with their educational mission."

80. Strobel, Kyle. Review of *Understanding Jonathan Edwards: An Introduction to America's Theologians*, edited by Gerald R. McDermott. *Themelios* 34.1 (2009) 137–38.

Aims to present a "volume for beginners" and "those teaching classes on Edwards will no doubt be grateful."

81. ———. Review of *The Infinite Merit of Christ: The Glory of Christ's Obedience in the Theology of Jonathan Edwards*, by Craig Biehl. *Scottish Bulletin of Evangelical Theology* 27.2 (2009) 218–20.

Accuses Biehl of taking a "polemical posture" from the outset, which "unfortunately give rise to some curious features" that "[restricts] the usefulness and reliability of his work." Strobel applauds the book for filling a "lacuna in the field," but his "failure to engage" with scholars and "cavalier dismissal of Edwards scholarship make this volume unfortunately anemic."

82. Studebaker, Steven M. Review of *Understanding Jonathan Edwards: An Introduction to America's Theologian*, by George McDermott. *Religious Studies Review* 35.3 (2009) 160–61.

Lauds the achievements of this book as producing "essays by leading North American and European Edwards scholars and alternative viewpoint/response essays, mostly by Eastern European non-Edwards specialists."

83. Sweeney, Douglas A. *Jonathan Edwards and the Ministry of the Word: A Model of Faith and Thought*. Downers Grove, IL: IVP Academic, 2009.

Recommends Edwards as a model of Christian faith in his devotion to preaching, pastoring, and teaching. This was the "core and key to Edwards' lasting impact."

84. Tooman, William A. "Edwards's Ezekiel: The Interpretation of Ezekiel in the Blank Bible and Notes on Scripture." *Journal of Theological Interpretation* 3.1 (2009) 17–39.

Studies Ezekiel in the "Blank Bible" and "Notes on Scripture" to uncover Edwards's "exegetical techniques" and "hermeneutical principles."

85. Twomey, Jay. "Antonin Scalia v Jonathan Edwards: Romans 13 and the American Theology of State." In *Sacred Tropes: Tanakh, New Testament, and Qur'an as Literature and Culture*, edited by Roberta Sterman Sabbath, 493–503. Leiden: Brill, 2009.

Asserts that although "contemporary sacred text scholarship," specifically on "the Tanakh, New Testament, and Qur'an," have been well represented in their research fields, yet "no collection combines an examination of all three." The contributions of Edwards as he discusses Romans 13 are assessed.

86. Waddington, Jeffrey C. Review and Responses to *Union with Christ: A Doctrine in Contention*, by J. Todd Billings; *Covenant and Salvation: 'Union' with Christ*, by Michael Horton; and *Life in Christ: Union with Christ and the Twofold Grace in Calvin's Theology*, by Mark A. Garcia. *The Confessional Presbyterian* 5 (2009) 256–69.

Debates chiefly with Michael Horton for depending on the "Korean-American" philosophy of Sang H. Lee that argued "Edwards radically reworked the metaphysical tradition of the West with a disposition ontology." Further, Horton calls into question Edwards's doctrine of justification by faith as departing from the Reformers.

87. Wainwright, William. "Jonathan Edwards." *Stanford Encyclopedia of Philosophy*, edited by Edward N. Zalta. Fall 2009 ed. http://plato.stanford.edu/archives/fall2009/entries/edwards.

Examines the claim that Edwards is America's most significant philosophical theologian. This article considers his notion of the doctrine of the absolute sovereignty of God, theological determinism, occasionalism, idealism, God's end in creation, the nature of true virtue, divine benevolence, and true beauty.

88. Weimer, Adrian Chastain. "Heaven and Heavenly Piety in Colonial American Elegies." In *The Church, the Afterlife, and the Fate of the Soul: Papers Read at the 2007 Summer Meeting and the 2008 Winter Meeting of the Ecclesiastical History Society*, edited by Peter Clarke and Tony Claydon, 258–67. Woodbridge, Suffolk, UK: Boydell, 2009.

Considers Edwards's expressions of afterlife theology as representing that of the Puritans.

89. Wiersbe, Warren W. *Fifty People Every Christian Should Know: Learning from Spiritual Giants of the Faith*. Grand Rapids: Baker, 2009.

Surveys people that every Christian needs to know for their encouragement in Christ. In chapter 4, Edwards is a person to know.

90. Yeager, Jonathan M. "John Erskine (1721–1803): Disseminator of Enlightened Evangelical Calvinism." PhD diss., University of Stirling, 2009.

Discusses John Erskine's relationship with Edwards as the two shared much correspondence. Erskine sent Edwards "countless religious and philosophical works so that he and others could learn about current ideas."

91. Zakai, Avihu. *Jonathan Edwards's Philosophy of History: The Reenchantment of the World in the Age of Enlightenment.* Princeton, NJ: Princeton University Press, 2009.

    Explores time in Edwards's thinking as God's "redemptive activity" in contrast to the Enlightenment reorientation of time as a secular activity. Edwards sought to reestablish time as "God's pre-eminence within the order of time" and "to re-enthrone God as the author and lord of history."

92. ———. "The Theological Origins of Jonathan Edwards's Philosophy of Nature." *The Journal of Ecclesiastical History* 60.4 (2009) 708–24.

    Analysis of the works of Edwards (1703–1758) on natural philosophy and demonstrates how he showed "affinities" with medieval and Reformed scholasticism, Renaissance, and Enlightenment thought.

2010

1. Allen, Alexander V. G. *Jonathan Edwards.* Charleston: Nabu, 2010.
    Reprint. See M. X. Lesser, *Reading Jonathan Edwards: An Annotated Bibliography in Three Parts, 1729–2005* (Grand Rapids: Eerdmans, 2008), 114 [1889.1].

2. Barshinger, David P. Review of *The Preaching of Jonathan Edwards*, by John Carrick. *Themelios* 35.1 (2010) 104–6.

    Asserts that Carrick "does not achieve his stated aim" of dealing extensively with the sermons. By dealing only with the published sermons (158), he does not treat the sermons which have not been published (ca. 1,000).

3. ———. Review of *Jonathan Edwards and the Ministry of the Word: A Model of Faith and Thought*, by Douglas A. Sweeney. *Fides et Historia* 42.1 (2010) 88–90.

    Reviews the volume very favorably as Sweeney "bridges the gap between the academy and the church" and provides a "Christian historian" as an example that takes "history seriously without setting aside our faith."

4. Bawulski, Shawn. "Annihilationism, Traditionalism and the Problem of Hell." *Philosophia Christi* 12.1 (2010) 61–78.

    Examines Edwards's view of hell from a traditional standpoint in contrast with annihilationism.

5. Beck, Peter. "The 'Little Church': Raising a Spiritual Family with Jonathan Edwards." *Puritan Reformed Journal* 2.1 (2010) 342–53.

    Commends Edwards's "spiritual nurture of the family" as God's "little church" and Beck's essay explains this for the "teaching of another generation" that needs to be taken seriously.

6. ———. *The Voice of Faith: Jonathan Edwards's Theology of Prayer*. Ontario, Canada: Joshua, 2010.

    Seeks to establish that Edwards is a "theologian of prayer" in the Triune God. He begins his book by addressing what the Father, the Son, and the Spirit have to do with and in prayer.

7. Biehl, Craig. "The Ceremonial or Moral Law: Jonathan Edwards's Old Perspective of an Old Error." *Puritan Reformed Journal* 2.1 (2010) 120–40.

    Aims to consider how Edwards lines up with the Pauline statement "works of the law." The Reformers assessed that it was the moral works of the law and not simply the ceremonial. Edwards embraces this Reformation principle.

8. ———. *A Study Guide to Jonathan Edwards' Classic The Religious Affections*. Birmingham, AL: Solid Ground Christian, 2010.

    Guides the reader through *A Treatise of Religious Affections*.

9. Brandt, Eric T. Review of *A Short Life of Jonathan Edwards*, by George Marsden. *Presbyterion* 36.1 (2010) 57–58.

    Lauds Marsden for his accomplishment in *Jonathan Edwards: A Life* principally for scholars. In *A Short Life*, he has now accomplished the best biography for "interested general readers."

10. Carpenter, Roy. "La stupidité des damnés: Jonathan Edwards et sa doctrine de l'enfer." In *Les damnés du ciel et de la terre*, 193–215. Limoges: Presses Univ. de Limoges, 2010.

    Reflects on the "stupidity" of the damned in Edwards's doctrine of the damned on heaven and on earth.

11. Carr, Kevin C. "Jonathan Edwards and a Divine and Supernatural Light." *Puritan Reformed Journal* 2.2 (2010) 187–205.

    Relates that the Reformers "focused" on the doctrine of justification, but in the time of the Great Awakening the supreme focus was on the doctrine of regeneration, as indicated by Edwards's sermon *A Divine and Supernatural Light*.

12. Carver, Benjamin T. "The Development of the Redemptive Role of the Holy Spirit in the Reformed Trinitarian Theology of Jonathan Edwards." ThM thesis, Gordon Conwell Theological Seminary, 2010.

    Argues that Edwards's Trinitarian theology in scholarship goes "largely unnoticed"; therefore, he examines the "significance of the theology of the Holy Spirit in the writings of Jonathan Edwards."

13. Cho, Hyun-Jin. "Jonathan Edwards on Justification: Reformed Development of the Doctrine in Eighteenth-Century New England." PhD diss., Trinity International University, 2010.

    Treats Edwards's doctrine of justification and "its continuity with Reformed tradition" in contrast to scholars such as Thomas A. Schafer, Anri Morimoto, and George Hunsinger, who suspect Edwards had "a quasi-Roman Catholic view of salvation including justification due to his use of the scholastic terms and concepts."

14. Choi, Ki Joo. "The Role of Perception in Jonathan Edwards's Moral Thought: The Nature of True Virtue Reconsidered." *Journal of Religious Ethics* 38.2 (2010) 269–96.

    Aims to establish that Edwards's "virtue ethics can be included in and contribute to prevailing approaches to virtue in contemporary theological ethics." Reviews the "moral agency" in his sermons on charity and a new "spiritual sense" in the treatise on *Religious Affections* and then turns toward the significance of Edwards's virtue ethics.

15. Clark, Michael P. "The Eschatology of Signs in Cotter Mather's 'Biblia Americana' and Jonathan Edwards' Cases for the Legibility of Providence." In *Cotton Mather and the Biblia Americana—America's First Bible Commentary: Essays in Reappraisal*, edited by Reiner Smolinski and Jan Stievermann, 413–38. Tübingen: Mohr Siebeck; Grand Rapids: Baker Academic, 2010.

Contrasts Cotton Mather's view of signs with Jonathan Edwards. "Unlike Edwards, who looks *to* nature to read what God communicates of Himself to man, Mather is always 'looking away' from nature, in the expectation of an apocalyptic future where God rescues his elect from nature."

16. Cochran, Elizabeth Agnew. Review of *Jonathan Edwards and the Metaphysics of Sin*, by Oliver Crisp. *Scottish Journal of Theology* 63.2 (2010) 241–43.

    Accuses Crisp of "examining Edwards' writings more or less in isolation from specific works of his contemporaries."

17. Cooley, Paul M. "'Neither Seen nor Heard': The Absent Child in the Study of Religion." *Journal of Childhood and Religion* 1.1 (2010) 1–31.

    Challenges the scholarship which does not take "children" as subjects of religious studies. Cooley offers Edwards and his story of Phebe's conversions in *A Faithful Narrative* as a break of that trend.

18. Cooper, William Henry, Jr. *The Great Revivalists in American Religion, 1740–1944: The Careers and Theology of Jonathan Edwards, Charles Finney, Dwight Moody, Billy Sunday, and Aimee Semple McPherson*. Jefferson, NC: McFarland, 2010.

    Expounds the revival theology of Edwards to Billy Sunday and makes the case that at the close of Sunday's ministry, revivals had become simply entertainment.

19. Crisp, Oliver D. "Jonathan Edwards's Ontology: A Critique of Sang Hyun Lee's Dispositional Account of Edwardsian Metaphysics." *Religious Studies* 46.1 (2010) 1–20.

    Argues that Lee's explanation of Edwards's interpretation of ontology is "flawed in several crucial respects." Crisp offers a response to these misinterpretations.

20. Crisp, Oliver D., and Kyle C. Strobel. *Jonathan Edwards: An Introduction to His Thought*. London: Continuum, 2010.

    See 2009.18.

21. De Witt, John. *Jonathan Edwards: A Study. An Address Delivered at Stockbridge, Massachusetts, October 5, 1903*. Charleston: BiblioLife 2010.

    Reproduces John De Witt's "Jonathan Edwards: A Study" from the *Princeton Theological Review*. See M. X. Lesser, *Reading Jonathan*

Edwards: An Annotated Bibliography in Three Parts, 1729–2005 (Grand Rapids: Eerdmans, 2008), 140 [1904.4].

22. Edwards, Deborah. Review of *A Short Life of Jonathan Edwards*, by George M. Marsden. *Churchman* 124.2 (2010) 187–88.

    Evaluates the volume and commends the book for being short, scholarly, and "entertaining enough to be readable."

23. Edwards, Jonathan. *A Faithful Narrative of the Revival of Religion in New England; With Thoughts on That Revival.* N.p.: Mottelay, 2010.

24. ———. *The Justice of God in the Damnation of Sinners, Explained, Illustrated, and Proved, in a Sermon Upon Romans III:19.* Rev. ed. Charleston: BiblioBazaar, 2010.

25. ———. *Sinners in the Hands of an Angry God. A Sermon, Preached at Enfield, July 8, 1741, at a Time of Great Awakenings; And Attended with Remarkable Impressions on Many of the Hearers.* Farmington Hills: Gale Ecco, 2010.

26. ———. *A Treatise Concerning Religious Affections—In Three Parts.* N.p.: Butler, 2010.

27. Fulton, Joe B. "'Jonathan Edwards, Calvin, Baxter & Co.': Mark Twain and the Comedy of Calvinism." In *John Calvin's American Legacy*, edited by Thomas David, 239–57. New York: Oxford University Press, 2010.

    Offers a treatment of Mark Twain's reading through Edwards's *Freedom of the Will* that contributed to Twain's "comedy of Calvinism."

28. Gardiner, Harry Norman. *Jonathan Edwards: A Retrospect; Being the Addresses Delivered in Connection with the Unveiling of a Memorial in the First Church of Christ in Northampton.* Charleston: BiblioBazaar, 2010.

    Six essays: V. G. Allen, "The Place of Edwards in History"; Egbert C. Smith, "The Influence of Edwards on the Spiritual Life of New England"; George A. Gordon, "The Significance of Edwards To-Day"; George P. Fisber and Alexander T. Ormond, "Greeting"; Henry T. Ross, "Edwards in Northampton"; H. Norman Gardiner, "The Early Idealism of Edwards." Reprint. See M. X. Lesser, *Reading Jonathan Edwards: An Annotated Bibliography in Three Parts, 1729–2005* (Grand Rapids: Eerdmans, 2008), 129–30 [1901.6].

29. Glover, David. "Reconciling the Doctrine of Original Sin with Principles of Moral Responsibility." PhD diss., California State University, Long Beach, 2010.

Examines federalism and realism and decides that the sin of Adam cannot be imputed to his descendants. He reviews the theories of Augustine, Aquinas, and Edwards.

30. Gragg, Rod. *Forged in Faith: How Faith Shaped the Birth of the Nation 1607–1776*. New York: Simon and Schuster, 2010.

Explores the Great Awakening, where Edwards was an instrumental player, in chapter 9.

31. Guyette, Fred. "Jonathan Edwards, the Ethics of Virtue and Public Theology." *International Journal of Public Theology* 4.2 (2010) 158–74.

Investigates Edwards's *The Nature of True Virtue*, where he explains that one must have love for God as the chief end and then the virtue of "common morality" flows from this love; "benevolence, beauty, conscience, justice, love for family and country are all threads in the fabric of a common morality." This is problematic to modern liberal discourses on virtue.

32. ———. Review of *A Short Life of Jonathan Edwards*, by George A. Marsden. *Southwest Journal of Theology* 2.2 (2010) 260–61.

Argues that the *Short Life* is "the first authoritative, yet largely accessible" biography of Edwards.

33. Hannah, John D. Review of *The Preaching of Jonathan Edwards*, by John Carrick. *Bibliotheca Sacra* 167.665 (2010) 125–27.

Criticizes the work as "voluminous quotations" that should have been reduced. Second, there seems "a lack of cohesiveness between the various chapters." However, the book is helpful in understanding his role as a preacher.

34. ———. Review of *The Unwavering Resolve of Jonathan Edwards*, by Stephen J. Lawson. *Bibliotheca Sacra* 167.665 (2010) 127–28.

Reviews the volume positively as "a delight to read" and a "challenge for those who understand the spiritual growth in more than just passive trust; it is an active, assiduous life long endeavor." Edwards is put forth as a "model" of "one's life and ministry."

35. Hastings, W. R. "Discerning the Spirit: Ambivalent Assurance in the Soteriology of Jonathan Edwards and Barthian Correctives." *Scottish Journal of Theology* 63.4 (2010) 437–55.

   Assesses, "in short, Edwards' theology of assurance is, in the end, individualistic and anthropocentric."

36. Hermann, Leslie Allison. "One Alone Cannot Be Excellent: The Theology and Spirituality of Beauty in the Thought." ThM thesis, Regent College, Vancouver, BC, 2010.

   Indicates that one of the "key indicators" that a person is a true Christian in Edwards's *Religious Affections* is that "one could see and love the beauty of God" and "reflect his beauty." Hermann wishes to establish her thesis by examining his metaphysical work, ethics, and Trinitarian theology.

37. Hessel-Robinson, Timothy. "Jonathan Edwards (1703–1758): A Treatise Concerning Religious Affections." In *Christian Spirituality*, edited by Arthur G. Holder, 269–80. London: Routledge, 2010.

   Contains a Christian spiritual classic, Edwards's *Religious Affections*. Hessel-Robinson offers an introduction and a synopsis, treating the influence it had on the New Divinity movement.

38. Howard, Joy A. J. "Jonathan Edwards's Metaphors of Sin in Indian Country." In vol. 2 of *Religion in the Age of Enlightenment*, edited by Brett C. McInelly, 153–76. New York: AMS, 2010.

   Includes Edwards's sermons to the Indians at Stockbridge.

39. Jeroncic, Ante. "'The Architecture of Beneficence': An Account of Nontotalitarian Beauty." *Andrews University Seminary Studies* 48.2 (2010) 287–304.

   Turns to Edwards's "Trinitarian aesthetics" in an "attempt to provide a constructive engagement" with the "Great Controversy" of the Seventh-Day Adventist's "theology and piety."

40. Kreider, Glenn R. Review of *Jonathan Edwards and the Ministry of the Word: A Model of Faith and Thought*, by Douglas A. Sweeney. *Journal of the Evangelical Homiletics Society* 10.2 (2010) 125–27.

   Recommends the volume for "pastors, preachers, and other Christian leaders."

41. Kimnach, Wilson H., et al., eds. *Jonathan Edwards's Sinners in the Hands of an Angry God: A Casebook*. New Haven, CT: Yale University Press, 2010.

Designs to present the "Sinners" in a classroom setting to a twenty-first-century audience. The experts present an "accurate and definitive version of Sinners" as "accompanied by the tools necessary to study and teach this famous American sermon."

42. Knutson, Andrea. "'Something That Is Seen, That Is Wonderful': Jonathan Edwards and the Feeling of Conviction." In *American Spaces of Conversion: The Conductive Imaginaries of Edwards, Emerson, and James*, 54–82. New York: Oxford University Press, 2010.

    Refers to a "dynamic tension," which the following authors display about the unknowable and the knowable God unto "advancements in religious doctrine" by Edwards. Knutson focuses on "literary style" by Ralph Waldo Emerson and "philosophical premise" by William James, which adds to the literary history in America.

43. Madueme, Hans. Review of *Reading Jonathan Edwards: An Annotated Bibliography in Three Parts, 1729–2005*, by M. X. Lesser. *Themelios* 35.1 (2010) 170–71.

    Applauds Lesser for putting scholars, professors, pastors, and theologians "in his debt."

44. Martin, Ryan J. "'Violent Motions of Carnal Affections': Jonathan Edwards, John Owen, and Distinguishing the Work of the Spirit from Enthusiasm." *Detroit Baptist Seminary Journal* 15 (2010) 99–116.

    Compares how Edwards defined "enthusiasm" and contrasted this by the explanation of John Owen. This essay demonstrates how Edwards differed from the Puritans but his views "largely echo his Reformed forebears."

45. McCarthy, Keely. "'A Sweet Union of Souls': The Dangers of Representing the Conversion in Jonathan Edwards' Biography of Missionary David Brainerd." In *Imaging the Other: Essays on Diversity*, 67–81. Lanham, MD: University Press of America, 2010.

    Addresses when "much of the world is in turmoil" how to speak of the "other." "Each essay in this collection stands on its own and grows out of the author's unique discipline and experience; however, these essays intersect with each other in many intriguing ways." This article is on the dangers of approaching David Brainerd's journal as a way of representing the conversion of Edwards.

46. McDermott, Gerald R. "Is Sola Scripture Really Sola? Edwards, Newman, Bultmann, and Wright on the Bible as Religious Authority." In *By What Authority? The Vital Question of Religious Authority in Christianity*, 66–95. Macon, GA: Mercer University Press, 2010.

    Compares what Edwards believed about biblical authority.

47. ———. "Jonathan Edwards: America's Theologian." In *The Great Theologians: A Brief Guide*, 113–33. Downers Grove, IL: InterVarsity, 2010.

    Republishes 2009.54.

48. McDowell, David Paul. "Beyond the Half-Way Covenant: Solomon Stoddard's Understanding of the Lord's Supper as a Converting Ordinance; Its Origins, Development, and Influence in the Connecticut Valley of Western Massachusetts." PhD diss., Trinity Theological Seminary, 2010.

    Poses that Solomon Stoddard has "often been marginalized" for the manner in which the Lord's Supper was for him a "converting ordinance." Then he explores Stoddard's view of communion "as compared to the changing face of Puritanism reflected in the Half-Way Covenant" that Edwards so strongly fought for.

49. McRae, Richard J. "Preaching That Awakens the Heart: As Seen Through the Preaching of Jonathan Edwards and George Whitefield." DMin thesis, Master's Seminary, 2010.

    Considers how these two preachers "persuaded many to believe during the course of their sermons" when they preached the word "that produces faith and repentance. It is the word preached that saves souls."

50. Minkema, Kenneth P. Review of *A Short Life of Jonathan Edwards*, by George Marsden and *Understanding Jonathan Edwards: An Introduction to America's Theologian*, by Gerald R. McDermott. *Theological Studies* 71.3 (2010) 755.

    Appraises the state of Edwards scholarship in North America, Europe, Russia, and beyond as he is read in English, Russian, Korean, etc.

51. Mitchell, Louis. J. "The American Sunday and the Formative Work of Jonathan Edwards." In *Sunday, Sabbath, and the Weekend: Managing Time in a Global Culture*, 179–85. Grand Rapids: Eerdmans, 2010.

Reflects on Edwards and his thoughts on the Sabbath or Lord's Day.

52. Nichols, Stephen J. "More Than Metaphors: Jonathan Edwards and the Beauty of Nature." *The Southern Baptist Journal of Theology* 14.4 (2010) 48–58.

    Discusses the beauty of nature in Edwards's theology. He focuses on Edwards's view of the environment and how he thought about nature in the varying ministries in Northampton, Stockbridge, and Princeton and then relates it to the doctrine to the Reformed thought of general revelation.

53. Nichols, Stephen R. C. "The Relationship of the Old and New Testaments in the Theology of Jonathan Edwards (1703–58)." PhD diss., University of Bristol, 2010.

    Describes the "relationship between the Old and New Testaments in the theology of the New England divine Jonathan Edwards (1703–58)." It follows the "Harmony of the Old and New Testaments" and examines the individual parts of the structure, following the three patterns indicated in his "Harmony" notebook: (1) Prophecy and Fulfillment; (2) Types and Antitypes; and (3) Doctrine of Precept as the Holy Spirit gives a "new sense" and leads to the object contained in the Old and New Testaments of saving faith, namely, the messiah Jesus.

54. Noll, Mark A. *The Rise of Evangelicalism: The Age of Edwards, Whitefield and the Wesleys.* Downers Grove, IL: InterVarsity, 2010.

    Argues that within the last three hundred years, evangelicalism has rapidly been diffused; "theology, hymnody, gender, warfare, politics and science are all taken into consideration." These all began with the revivals of Edwards, Whitefield, and the Wesleys.

55. Ortlund, Dane. "Sanctification by Justification: The Forgotten Insight of Bavinck and Berkouwer on Progressive Sanctification." *Scottish Bulletin of Evangelical Theology* 28.1 (2010) 43–61.

    Compares Edwards's theology of sanctification to Bavinck and Berkouwer's views on the subject.

56. Parton, James. "Jonathan Edwards, the Father of Aaron Burr's Mother." In *The Life and Times of Aaron Burr, Lieutenant-Colonel in the Army of the Revolution, United States Senator, Vice President of the United States*, 25–30. Whitefish, MT: Kessinger, 2010.

Reissues from *The Life and Times of Aaron Burr*, originally published in 1858 and now newly printed by Kessinger. See M. X. Lesser, *Reading Jonathan Edwards: An Annotated Bibliography in Three Parts, 1729–2005* (Grand Rapids: Eerdmans, 2008), 94 [1858.10].

57. Pauw, Amy Plantinga. "Practical Ecclesiology in John Calvin and Jonathan Edwards." In *John Calvin's American Legacy*, edited by Thomas J. Davis, 91–110. Oxford: Oxford University Press, 2010.

    Conducts an analysis of the impact of "Jonathan Edwards's and Calvin's church courts practices."

58. ———. Review of *Understanding Jonathan Edwards: An Introduction to America's Theologian*, by Gerald McDermott. *Theology Today* 66.4 (2010) 502–3.

    Collects essays from an international conference held in Budapest, Hungary, in 2006.

59. Pederson, Randall J. "Puritan Studies in the Twenty-First Century: Preamble and Projections." *Puritan Reformed Journal* 2.2 (2010) 106–20.

    Analyzes Puritan studies in the twenty-first century and says that Puritans "encompass more than Jonathan Edwards" as he "exemplifies two poles within modern studies of Puritanism." The first is the more academic or intellective "venture," and the second is more geared toward practical projects.

60. Peterson, Paul Silas. "'The Perfection of Beauty': Cotton Mather's Christological Interpretation of the Shechinah Glory in the 'Biblia Americana' and Its Theological Contexts." In *Cotton Mather and the Biblia Americana—America's First Bible Commentary: Essays in Reappraisal*, edited by Reiner Smolinski and Jan Stievermann, 383–412. Tübingen: Mohr Siebeck; Grand Rapids: Baker Academic, 2010.

    Compares Cotton Mather's interpretation of the Shechinah Glory with Jewish rabbis, Luther, Calvin, Grotius, Brian Walton, Matthew Poole, Matthew Henry, John and Edward Stillingfleet, and Jonathan Edwards.

61. Rehnman, Sebastian. "Is the Distinction Between Natural and Moral Attributes Good? Jonathan Edwards on Divine Attributes." *History of Philosophy Quarterly* 27.1 (2010) 57–78.

Analyzes "Edwards's distinctions between natural and moral divine attributes" and ends with "attempting to promote historical understanding of philosophical theology by proceeding from a historical issue to philosophical issues."

62. Rivera, Ted. *Jonathan Edwards on Worship: Public and Private Devotion to God*. Eugene, OR: Pickwick, 2010.

    Republishes his dissertation of the same title (2007.48).

63. Sasser, Daryl. "The Weather and Theology: The Influence of the Natural World on Religious Thought in Puritan New England." PhD diss., Presbyterian School of Christian Education, 2010.

    Illustrates "Puritan attitudes to the New England landscape" by focusing on the writing of Increase and Cotton Mather and Samuel Seawall. He concludes with particular interest in Jonathan Edwards.

64. Scalise, Brian T. "Wilderness Beauty: A Means to Resolve Volitional Doubt." *Eleutheria* 1.1 (2010) 2–22.

    Reconstructs Edwards's form of "aesthetic theology" for "resolving volitional doubt."

65. Schweitzer, Don, ed. *Jonathan Edwards as Contemporary: Essays in Honor of Sang Hyun Lee*. New York: Peter Lang, 2010.

    Honors Sang Hyun Lee's contribution in placing Edwards in the context of other philosophical writings as divided into three parts. Part I consists of essays examining Edwards's philosophy: Stephen H. Daniel, "Edwards' Occasionalism"; Avihu Zakai, "The Medieval and Scholastic Dimensions of Edwards' Philosophy of Nature"; Anri Morimoto, "The End for Which God Created"; Don Schweitzer, "Jonathan Edwards' Understanding of Divine Infinity"; Michael J. McClymond, "Hearing the Symphony: A Critique of Some Critics of Sang Lee's and Amy Pauw's Accounts of Jonathan Edwards' View of God"; Paul Helm, "The Human Self and the Divine Trinity"; and the final article of this part is Oliver Crisp, "Jonathan Edwards' Panentheism."

    Part II, "Trinitarian Action in the Incarnation," examines his theology: See-Kong Tam, "Jonathan Edwards and Justification: The Rest of the Story"; Douglas A. Sweeney, "Jonathan Edwards' Ecclesiology"; Amy Plantinga Pauw, "Jonathan Edwards' Ecclesiology"; and Gerald R. McDermott "Revelation as Divine Communication Through Reason, Scripture and Tradition."

Part III examines Edwards in the context of his own time and his contemporary relevance: Wilson H. Kimnach, "Frightful Inspiration, Sweet Elevation: The Application of Homiletics by Jonathan Edwards, Jonathan Mayhew, and Their Successors of the Late Eighteenth Century"; Stephen D. Crocco, "Jonathan Edwards and Princeton"; Kenneth P. Minkema and Harry S. Stout, "Jonathan Edwards Studies During the Career of Sang Hyun Lee"; and Robert Jenson, "How I Stole from Jonathan Edwards."

66. Schweitzer, William M. "An Uncommon Union: Understanding Jonathan Edwards's Experimental Calvinism." *Puritan Reformed Journal* 2.2 (2010) 208–19.

    Suggests that "there are better ways to understand Edwards's experimental Calvinism" than D. G. Hart's explanation that the visible church was made up of people who had "dramatic conversion" experiences. Schweitzer points to the information that this is an unfair representation of "Edwards's definitive public statement on the matter."

67. Sholl, Brian K. Review of *Jonathan Edwards and the Ministry of the Word: A Model of Faith and Thought*, by Douglas A. Sweeney. *The Review of Politics* 72.2 (2010) 354–56.

    Summarizes this book saying Edwards was "a model, albeit with flaws."

68. Smart, Robert Davis. "Jonathan Edwards's Apologetic for the Great Awakening with Particular Attention to Charles Chauncy's Criticisms." PhD diss., Illinois State University, 2010.

    Relies on 2008.68.

69. Snead, Jennifer. "Print, Predestination, and the Public Sphere." *Early American Literature* 45.1 (2010) 93–118.

    Cites part 5 of Edwards, *Some Thoughts Concerning the Present Revivals of Religion in New-England*, as he was familiar with print culture and promoted its publication to be circulated far and wide.

70. Stein, Stephen J. "Cotton Mather and Jonathan Edwards on the Epistle of James: A Comparative Study." In *Cotton Mather and the Biblia Americana—America's First Bible Commentary: Essays in Reappraisal*, edited by Reiner Smolinski and Jan Stievermann, 363–82. Tübingen: Mohr Siebeck; Grand Rapids: Baker Academic, 2010.

Compares the work of Cotton Mather with Edwards on their exegesis of Epistle of James. They commented on similar sources (Poole, Henry, Whitby, and Doddridge, etc.) and similar passages of James so that, in the end, Stein commends them favorably. He said, "Here Mather's and Edwards's understanding of the proper business of religion, or the working of nature of saving faith, led them to a powerful witness to the work of peace."

71. Stetina, Karin Spiecker. "The 'Sense of the Heart': Edwards's Public Expression of His Pietistic Understanding of Religious Experience." *Puritan Reformed Journal* 2.1 (2010) 197–212.

    Examines the "sense of the heart" in three works of Edwards, *A Divine and Supernatural Light*; *A Treatise Concerning Religious Affections*; and *The Nature of True Virtue*.

72. Stewart, Carole Lynn. *Strange Jeremiahs: Civil Religion and the Literary Imaginations of Jonathan Edwards, Herman Melville, and W. E. B. Du Bois*. Albuquerque: University of New Mexico Press, 2010.

    Examines the works of Edwards, who "made use of the jeremiad" in theological discourses, as compared to Herman Melville and W. E. B. Du Bois, who appealed to them with the "implications of the Reconstruction."

73. Storms, C. Samuel, and Justin Taylor, eds. *For the Fame of God's Name: Essays in Honor of John Piper*. Wheaton: Crossway, 2010.

    Centers the ministry of John Piper on "prayer, the sovereignty of God, justification, Jonathan Edwards, Christian Hedonism, and more."

74. Strachan, Owen, and Douglas A. Sweeney. *Jonathan Edwards, Lover of God*. Essential Edwards Collection. Chicago: Moody, 2010.

    Reprint (2009.76).

75. ———. *Jonathan Edwards on Beauty*. Essential Edwards Collection. Chicago: Moody, 2010.

    Reprint (2009.77).

76. ———. *Jonathan Edwards on the Good Life*. Essential Edwards Collection. Chicago: Moody, 2010.

    Reprint (2009.78).

77. ———. *Jonathan Edwards on Heaven and Hell*. Essential Edwards Collection. Chicago: Moody, 2010.

    Queries Edwards's traditional belief in heaven or hell and makes the transition to the modern age.

78. ———. *Jonathan Edwards on True Christianity*. Essential Edwards Collection. Chicago: Moody, 2010.

    Focuses on the non-committed "Christian" in contrast to Edwards, who shows that a true Christian "tenaciously" loves God.

79. Strange, Alan D. Review of *Jonathan Edwards and the Ministry of the Word: A Model of Faith and Thought*, by Douglas A. Sweeney. *Mid-America Journal of Theology* 21 (2010) 172–73.

    Applauds Sweeney for answering the question "Is another book about Edwards really warranted?" with a resounding yes.

80. Strobel, Kyle C. "Jonathan Edwards' Trinitarian Theology of Redemption." PhD diss., University of Aberdeen, 2010.

    Advances "Edwards' theology as fundamentally Trinitarian."

81. Thuesen, Peter J. "Geneva's Crystalline Clarity: Harriet Beecher Stowe and Max Weber on Calvinism and the American Character." In *John Calvin's American Legacy*, 219–37. Oxford: Oxford University Press, 2010.

    Cites Edwards's *Freedom of the Will* as the inspiration of Mark Twain's comedic fashion of describing the fatalism of Calvinism from Edwards's work.

82. Venter, Rian. "Trinity and Beauty: The Theological Contribution of Jonathan Edwards." *Dutch Reformed Theological Journal* 51.3–4 (2010) 185–92.

    Explores Edwards's Trinitarian confessions of God and beauty. Edwards believed the Trinity was "primarily relational" and an "aesthetic" quality. Lastly, Venter considers the study of Edwards and the influence it potentially has "in a South African context."

83. Waddington, Jeffery C. "Must We Believe? Jonathan Edwards and Conscious Faith in Christ." *The Confessional Presbyterian* 6 (2010) 11–21.

    Disputes with Anri Morimoto's *Jonathan Edwards and the Catholic Vision of Salvation* "sympathetically" but "critically."

84. Wainwright, William J. "Jonathan Edwards, God, and 'Particular Minds.'" *International Journal for Philosophy of Religions* 68.1–3 (2010) 201–13.

   Commends Edwards as a "notable exception" from the Reformed tradition in his explanation of the mind, and he presents "novel" description of "humanity's essential ontological, moral, and soteriological dependence on God."

85. Zakai, Avihu. *Jonathan Edwards's Philosophy of Nature: The Re-Enchantment of the World in the Age of Scientific Reasoning*. London: T&T Clark, 2010.

   Aims to place Edwards in the historical context of his time in its natural philosophical and "modern scientific of the early modern period."

86. Zaleski, Carol. "Pilgrim's Progress." *The Christian Century* 127.5 (2010) 35.

   Feels a "kinship" for Solomon Stoddard and Edwards for having lived in the town of Northampton for twenty years and that explains why she is re-reading Bunyan's *The Pilgrim's Progress*.

87. Zylla, Phil. "Virtue and the Hermeneutics of Culture." *Jian Dao* 34 (2010) 71–91.

   Seeks "to explore the theme with the intent to create dialogue about culturally-laden version of virtue theory, especially in connection with the pastoral task of spiritual formation in the congregation." The paper examines the work of Jonathan Edwards on *the Nature of True Virtue* as a "core understanding of true virtue as a basis for refection on this issues."

2011

1. Ashcraft, W. Michael. "Progressive Millennialism." In *The Oxford Handbook of Millennialism*, 44–65. Oxford: Oxford University Press, 2011.

   Explores progressive millennialism in every age, especially English Puritanism, and devotes special attention to Jonathan Edwards.

2. Barshinger, David P. Review of *Jonathan Edwards on Worship: Public and Private Devotion to God*, by Ted Rivera. *Fides et Historia* 43.1 (2011) 90–92.

    Examines Edwards's approach to "public worship, private devotion, and self-examination" and emphasizes "the central place of privation and public worship."

3. Beeke, Joel, and Brian G. Najapfour. *Taking Hold of God: Reformed and Puritan Perspectives on Prayer*. Grand Rapids: Reformation Heritage, 2011.

    Takes six of the Reformers and Puritans, "among them Martin Luther, John Calvin, William Perkins, Matthew Henry, and Jonathan Edwards" by six contemporary scholars as they guide us "to growth in prayer and a more grateful communion with God."

4. Bennett, Miranda. Review of *A Short Life of Jonathan Edwards*, by George M. Marsden. *Religious Studies Review* 37.1 (2011) 75.

    Provides an "engaging look at an important historical character."

5. Bezzant, Rhys Stewart. "Orderly but Not Ordinary: Jonathan Edwards's Evangelical Ecclesiology." ThD diss., Australian College of Theology, 2011.

    Contends that Edwards's context in New England "ossified" his ecclesiology by "the church's dynamic relationship with the created order, history and the nations, and by advocating renewal in ecclesial life through revivals, itinerancy, Concerts of Prayer, and missionary initiatives outside of local congregations, and doctrinal clarification."

6. Bombaro, John J. *Jonathan Edwards's Vision of Reality: The Relationship of God to the World, Redemption History, and the Reprobate*. Eugene, OR: Wipf & Stock, 2011.

    Supports the claim that in history the elect and reprobate give glory to God. "The logic of Edwards's theocentric vision of reality pushes his ideas to the limits of acceptable Reformed orthodoxy, and sometimes beyond those limits."

7. Bolt, John. "The Glory of Spiders and Politics." *Calvin Theological Journal* 46.1 (2011) 72–80.

    Proposes that the spider was more useful to Edwards than just for his sermon "Sinners in the Hands of an Angry God," where he refers to a "loathsome creature dangling over hell." However, "the spider of the young Jonathan Edwards gives us clues to help put politics in a more glorious light," and Bolt explores that.

8. Caldwell, Robert, W., III. "A Brief History of Heaven in the Writings of Jonathan Edwards." *Calvin Theological Journal* 46.1 (2011) 48–71.

    Canvasses what Edwards thought about "high points of heaven's history," including the creation of heaven, the fall of Lucifer, the angels, the saints in the intermediate state, the Days of Judgment, and the last Day.

9. ———. Review of *The Works of Jonathan Edwards: The Catalogue of Books*, edited by Peter J. Thuesen; *Reading Jonathan Edwards: An Annotated Bibliography in Three Parts: 1729–2005*, by M. X. Lesser. *Southwestern Journal of Theology* 54.1 (2011) 101–3.

    Evaluates these two works as "definitely for Edwards specialists which is probably their one main drawback."

10. Campagna-Pinto, S. T. *The Workshop of Being: Religious Affections and Their Pragmatic Value in the Thought of Jonathan Edwards and William James*. Lanham, MD: Lexham, 2011.

    Reprint. See M. X. Lesser, *Reading Jonathan Edwards: An Annotated Bibliography in Three Parts, 1729–2005* (Grand Rapids: Eerdmans, 2008), 586–87 [2004.13].

11. Cheng, Yang-En. "Jonathan Edwards and the First Great Awakening in North America." *Taiwan Journal of Theology* 33 (2011) 27–44.

    Examines Edwards as the "most prominent figure in the First Great Awakening." The author pays considerable attention to *The Distinguishing Marks* and *A Treatise Concerning Religious Affection*.

12. Choiński, Michał. "Rhetoric of the Revival: A Pragma-Rhetorical Analysis of the Language of the Great Awakening Preachers." PhD diss., University of Kraków, Poland, 2011.

    Investigates carefully the sermons of each of the revival preachers to uncover the distinct similarities and differences between each preachers.

13. Clark, Jawanza Eric. "Jonathan Edwards." In *Beyond the Pale: Reading Theology from the Margins*, edited by Miguel A. De La Torre and Stacy M. Floyd-Thomas. Louisville, KY: Westminster John Knox, 2011.

    Gives a short "historical background" for Edwards and describes his "most important contributions."

14. Clark, John C. Review of *Jonathan Edwards and the Ministr of the Word: A Model of Faith and Thought*, by Douglas A. Sweeney. *Calvin Theological Journal* 46.2 (2011) 403–5.

    Applauds the book as "being both authoritative and accessible" but criticizes Sweeney for slipping (only for a moment) into "the genre of hagiography."

15. Cochran, Elizabeth Agnew. "Consent, Conversion, and Moral Formation: Stoic Elements in Jonathan Edwards's Ethics." *Journal of Religious Ethics* 39.4 (2011) 623–50.

    Argues that Edwards's moral ethics "exemplifies major Stoic themes."

16. ———. *Receptive Human Virtues: A New Reading of Jonathan Edwards's Ethics*. University Park: Pennsylvania State University Press, 2011.

    Purports a "new reading" of Edwards's virtue ethics and "considers their importance for contemporary ethics."

17. Crampton, W. Gary. *Interpreting Edwards: An Overview and Analysis of John H. Gerstner's The Rational Biblical Theology of Jonathan Edwards*. Chattanooga, TN: Whitefield, 2011.

    Interprets Edwards through the lens of John Gerstner. Gerstner says that Edwards's theology is by and large consistent with the Westminster Standards. Crampton analyzes this claim and gives an "extensive bibliography."

18. Crisp, Oliver D. Review of *A Short Life of Jonathan Edwards*, by George M. Marsden. *Scottish Journal of Theology* 64.3 (2011) 368–69.

    Shortcoming of this books is in "Edwards' ideas," which is "rather less here than the larger life." That said, Marsden has more historiographic information and it is "the best popular biography of Edwards that we are likely to see for some time." Commends the "honest handling of the darker side of Edwards," such as his use of slave labor.

19. Cuthbert, Christian. Review of *Jonathan Edwards and the Ministry of the Word: A Model of Faith and Thought*, by Douglas A. Sweeney. *Interpretation* 65.2 (2011) 216.

    Values Sweeney's book as achieving "scholarly" rigor yet "accessibility" to general reading in his contribution.

20. Davidson, Bruce W. "Glorious Damnation: Hell as an Essential Element in the Theology of Jonathan Edwards." *Journal of the Evangelical Theological Society* 54.4 (2011) 809–22.

    Considers the doctrine of hell as an important feature for Edwards and states that doctrine is "most typically theocentric."

21. Dussol, Vincent. "Spider and Webs in American Literature." *Transatlantic* 2.2 (2011). https://doi.org/10.4000/transatlantica.5506.

    Proposes that from "Jonathan Edwards to Jorie Graham, spiders are strikingly present in American literature." Makes the case that spiders and webs were most likely inherited from Native American myths in which spiders are a central figure and feminine side of culture.

22. Edgar, William, and K. Scott Oliphint. "Jonathan Edwards." In *From 1500*, 219–38. Vol. 2 of *Christian Apologetics Past and Present: A Primary Source Reader*. Wheaton, IL: Crossway, 2011.

23. Edwards, Jonathan. *The Personal Narrative of Jonathan Edwards and His Seventy Resolutions*. Narrated by Adam Verner. Audiobook. Escondido, CA: Christianaudio, 2011.

24. Gibson, Jonathan. "Jonathan Edwards: A Missionary?" *Themelios* 36.4 (2011) 380–402.

    Explores Edwards's role as an Indian missionary as "consistently overlooked and understated by contemporaries and scholars alike." He contrasts the "retreat" and "exile" missionary for a "New Approach to the Stockbridge Years."

25. Heacock, Clint. "Rhetorical Influences Upon the Preaching of Jonathan Edwards." *Homiletic* 36.2 (2011). https://homiletic.net/index.php/homiletic/article/view/3460.

    Focuses on Edwards's rhetorical influences that shaped his preaching, such as Peter Ramus.

26. Henry, Caleb. "Pride, Property, and Providence: Jonathan Edwards on Property Rights." *Journal of Church & State* 53.3 (2011) 401–20.

    Recalls that when Edwards first read Locke's *Essay Concerning Human Understanding*, he read it with much ecstasy. "Despite his ardent enthusiasm," Edwards pushed beyond Locke by forming a "relational ontology" and "softened" Locke's "epistemology and political theory."

27. Hoggard-Creegan, Nicola. "Vestiges of Trinity." In *Trinitarian Theology After Barth*, edited by Myk Habets and Phillip Tolliday, 377–92. Princeton Theological Monograph 140. Eugene, OR: Pickwick, 2011.

    Assesses Edwards as "a gift of seeing 'images and shadows' of divine things in nature."

28. Johnson, Keith E. Review of *Jonathan Edwards' Social Augustinianism in Historical and Contemporary Perspectives*, by Stephen M. Studebaker. *Evangelical Theological Society* 54.2 (2011) 427–31.

    Assesses this volume as making "an important contribution" to Edwards scholarship and "should be read by everyone who is interested in Edwards's trinitarian thought."

29. Knutson, Andrea. *American Spaces of Conversion: The Conductive Imaginaries of Edwards, Emerson, and James.* New York: Oxford University Press, 2011.

    Approaches three iconic figures—Edwards, Emerson, and James—and examines "how the Puritan legacy, especially the concept of conversion, shaped developments in American literature, theology, and pragmatist philosophy."

30. Korving, Willem Jacob. "The Dynamics of Time and Location in Salvation as Developed by Jonathan Edwards in the History of the Work of Redemption." ThM thesis, Puritan Reformed Theological Seminary, 2011.

    Purports that his paper examines "the dynamics of *time* and *location* in the context of redemption" and examines Edwards's *The History of the Work of Redemption.*

31. Kosits, Russell D. "Whose Psychology? Which Christianity?" *McMaster Journal of Theology and Ministry* 13 (2011–12) 101–95.

    Asks this question in regard to the publication of Eric Johnson's *Psychology and Christianity: Five Views* and highlights Edwards's *Religious Affections* for a Christian psychology.

32. Kreider, Glenn R. Review of *Jonathan Edwards and the Ministry of the Word: A Model of Faith and Thought*, by Douglas A. Sweeney. *Bibliotheca Sacra* 168.670 (2011) 251–53.

    Lauds Sweeney's work that "Scholars of Edwards will be challenged," and "pastors and students will be encouraged to pursue the ministry of the Word of God through Edwards's example."

33. Lane, Belden C. *Ravished by Beauty: The Surprising Legacy of Reformed Spirituality*. New York: Oxford University Press, 2011.

Narrates an exposition of Reformed spirituality. He surveys the "ecological" Calvin that speaks of "earth's beauty" and Edwards's "enjoyment of God's beauty" as "the only real way of knowing God." Lane argues that Reformed theologians can appear drab and prudish but have passionate desires for God's glory in everything that he has made. However, "spirituality of desire can be derailed."

34. ———. "A Reformed Vision of the World: Trinitarian Beauty and Environmental Ethics." In *Spirit and Nature: The Study of Christian Spirituality in a Time of Ecological Urgency*, edited by Timothy Hessel-Robinson and Ray Maria McNamara, 70–97. Eugene, OR: Pickwick, 2011.

Interprets Calvin's and Edwards's trinitarian ethics in view of environmental ethics.

35. Lee, Joseph W. "Jonathan Edwards on Man's Propensity to Sin." ThM thesis, Dallas Theological Seminary, 2011.

Specifies in the doctrine of original sin that "Edwards's rationale for man's propensity to sin is due to a corrupt/depraved nature" and this "natural principle" rules "in consequence of the divine principle."

36. Lucas, Sean Michael. *God's Grand Design: The Theological Vision of Jonathan Edwards*. Wheaton: Crossway, 2011.

Explores the "theology of the Christian life" that begins "with God's glory" and ends with "all creation returning that glory."

37. McClymond, Michael J., and Gerald R. McDermott. *The Theology of Jonathan Edwards*. Oxford: Oxford University Press, 2011.

Analyzes the theology of Edwards, which the authors identify as "five theological constituents," namely, "trinitarian communication, creaturely participation, necessitarian dispositionalism, divine priority, and harmonious constitutionalism." They discuss themes which range from "aesthetics, metaphysics, typology, history of redemption, revival, and true virtue" and extend to thirty-one chapters.

38. McDermott, Gerald R. "My Top 5 Books: On Jonathan Edwards." *Christianity Today* 55.11 (2011) 68.

Cites as his favorites: George M. Marsden, *Jonathan Edwards: A Life*; John E. Smith et al., eds., *A Jonathan Edwards Reader*; Stephen

J. Stein, ed., *The Cambridge Companion to Jonathan Edwards*; Sang Hyun Lee, *The Princeton Companion to Jonathan Edwards*; and John Piper, *God's Passions for His Glory*.

39. McGraw, Ryan M. Review of *The Preaching of Jonathan Edwards*, by John Carrick. *Puritan Reformed Journal* 3.2 (2011) 391–92.

    Recommends that pastors "avail themselves" to Carrick's "labor of love" and this book "will do good service to themselves and to their congregations."

40. Minkema, Kenneth P. "A 'Dordtian Philosophe': Jonathan Edwards, Calvin, and Reformed Orthodoxy." *Church History and Religious Culture* 91.1–2 (2011) 241–53.

    Examines the thought of Edwards with Calvin, especially as Edwards operated generally within a "Calvinist framework of divine sovereignty." However, he also worked "within the context of the Enlightenment," and Minkema explores the differences and discontinuities that extended from his adoption of an enlightenment philosophy.

41. ———. "Informing of the Child's Understanding, Influencing His Heart, and Directing Its Practice: Jonathan Edwards on Education." *Acta Theologica* 31 (2011) 159–89.

    Explores "the role of education" Edwards received from Yale and his ministry as a teacher and preacher to the English colonists and Native American children at Stockbridge. Minkema then compares his philosophy of teaching with the Edwardsean's.

42. Moses, John A. Review of *A Short Life of Jonathan Edwards* by George M. Marsden. *The Journal of Religious History* 35.1 (2011) 132–33.

    Applauds the "great value" of this book as "lucid and sympathetic (certainly not hagiographic) . . . portrayal of Edwards."

43. Niebuhr, Richard R. *Streams of Grace: Studies of Jonathan Edwards, Samuel Taylor Coleridge, and William James*. 1982. Reprint, Eugene, OR: Wipf & Stock, 2011.

    Niebuhr speaks of Edwards's philosophy of "excellency." Reprint. (M. X. Lesser. *Reading Jonathan Edwards: An Annotated Bibliography in Three Parts, 1729–2005* (Grand Rapids: Eerdmans), 373 [1983.28].)

44. Paeth, Scott R. "'You Make All Things New': Jonathan Edwards and a Christian Environmental Ethic." *International Journal of Public Theology* 5.2 (2011) 209–32.

    Examines an Edwardsean theology which "can contribute to the construction of a Christian approach to ecological ethics."

45. Pederson, Randall J. Review of *Understanding Jonathan Edwards: An Introduction to America's Theologian*, by Gerald R. McDermott. *Puritan Reformed Journal* 3.1 (2011) 385–86.

    Recommends this "collection" to "anyone interested in the life, thought, ministry, and relevance of Jonathan Edwards."

46. Price, Christopher. Review of *Jonathan Edwards and the Ministry of the Word: A Model of Faith and Thought*, by Douglas A. Sweeney. *American Theological Inquiry* 4.2 (2011) 89–90.

    Debates the way it "could have been a bit better" by giving a "more in-depth" explanation of the half-way covenant, which led to Edwards's expulsion from Northampton, and *Freedom of the Will*, *Original Sin*, and *Two Dissertations*, which could have been integrated in his time as a missionary to the Indians because that was the precise time that they were produced. Criticism aside, Sweeney "ably accomplishes his goal in writing the book."

47. Ristau, Scott. "Neo-Aristotelean Rhetorical Criticism of Sermons from the Great Awakening." PhD diss., South Dakota State University, 2011.

    Studies the homiletical methods and practices of the Great Awakening as represented by two sermons each by Edwards and Whitefield.

48. Rivett, Sarah. *The Science of the Soul in Colonial New England*. Chapel Hill: University of North Carolina Press, 2011.

    Challenges the "long-standing notions of Puritan provincialism as antithetical to the Enlightenment." Thomas Shepard, John Eliot, Cotton Mather, and Edwards studied the human soul.

49. Schafer, Thomas A. "Jonathan Edwards, 1703–58, American Theologian and Metaphysician." *Columbia Electronic Encyclopedia*. 6th ed. 2011. https://www.britannica.com/biography/jonathan-edwards/dismissal-from-northampton.

    Introduces readers to a basic biography of Edwards by saying that he was "the greatest theologian and philosopher of British

America Puritanism, stimulator of the religious revival known as the 'Great Awakening,' and one of the forerunners of the age of Protestant missionary expansion in the nineteenth century."

50. Smart, Robert Davis. *Jonathan Edwards's Apologetic for the Great Awakening.* Grand Rapids: Reformation Heritage, 2011.
    Reprint (2008.68).

51. Spar, Natalie D. "This Loquacious Soil: Language and Religious Experience in Early America." PhD diss., Washington University in St. Louis, 2011.
    Argues that early American religious leaders coined specific and complex language in "sermons, tracts, letters, diaries, ethnographies, and trials." Spar specifically focuses on Edwards in his Great Awakening diaries.

52. Stetina, Karin S. *Jonathan Edwards' Early Understanding of Religious Experience: His New York Sermons, 1720–1723.* Lewiston, NY: Edwin Mellen, 2011.
    Focuses on Edwards's "earliest sermons and personal writings," which reveal his biblical study and piety.

53. Stewart, Kenneth J. "The Doctrine of Regeneration in Evangelical Theology: The Reformation to 1800." *Journal for Baptist Theology & Ministry* 8.1 (2011) 42–57.
    Disregards the representation that regeneration was rediscovered by the preachers of the Great Awakening as opposed to the Protestant Reformation. He corrects that popular notion by a development of thought through Edwards.

54. Stinson, Susan. "Spider and Fly: Novel Excerpt, August 1735, Northampton, Massachusetts." *Early American Literature* 9.1 (2011) 245–59.
    Fuses the "historic and the imaginative telling" of Edwards's years as "a preacher in eighteenth-century Northampton" from the years 1731 to 1750. Stinson ends with Sarah Edwards, who was assisted by Leah and Saul, both enslaved persons.

55. Stratton, Gary David. "Paparazzi in the Hands of an Angry God: Jonathan Edwards, George Whitfield, and the Birth of American Celebrity Culture." *The Other Journal* (2011) 46–64.

Aims to present Whitefield and Edwards as "using celebrity for the glory of God" and suggests we must pay "careful attention to the lessons" of Edwards.

56. Strobel, Kyle. Review of *Jonathan Edwards as Contemporary: Essays in Honor of Sang Hyun Lee*, edited by Don Schweitzer. *Themelios* 36.3 (2011) 560–62.

    Applauds this as an "archetype of what a *Festschrift* should be."

57. Studebaker, Steven M., and Robert W. Caldwell III. *The Trinitarian Vision of Jonathan Edwards: Text, Context, and Application*. Amherst, NY: Cambria, 2011.

    Strengthens the scholarship that emphasizes the Trinity in Edwards's work according to three parts. In the first part, Edwards's "chief trinitarian writings" are analyzed. The second part sets his doctrine of the Trinity in its historical context. The third part "demonstrates how Edwards employed the Trinity in his sermons, in spiritual formation, and in other areas of doctrine."

58. Sundberg, Walter. Review of *Jonathan Edwards for Armchair Theologians*, by James M. Byrd. *Lutheran Quarterly* 25.2 (2011) 180–81.

    Lauds the "summary of Edwards' position" of the *Freedom of the Will* in "twenty-five pages," saying it is "the best thing in the book" and "I strongly recommend this book."

59. Tyson, Samuel Daley. "The Effect of Social Context and Culture in the Preaching of Jonathan Edwards and Charles Finney." ThM thesis, Dallas Theological Seminary, 2011.

    Details a comparison of "two of America's most famous and influential theology and preachers, Jonathan Edwards and Charles Finney," stating they shared continuity in their sermonic material. However, in contrast to Edwards, "Finney allowed his culture to define his interpretation of Christian beliefs, thereby abandoning historically orthodox doctrine."

60. Van Andel, Kelly, et al., eds. *Jonathan Edwards and Scotland*. Edinburgh: Dunedin Academic, 2011.

    Papers from a conference at the University of Glasgow in 2009.

61. Withrow, Brandon G. *Becoming Divine: Jonathan Edwards's Incarnational Spirituality Within the Christian Tradition*. Eugene, OR: Wipf & Stock, 2011.

Searches how Edwards sought to makes sense of the "unexpected joy" as a "theology of divine participation rooted in the incarnation of Christ."

62. Yoo, Jeongmo. "Jonathan Edwards's Interpretation of the Major Prophets: The Book of Isaiah, Jeremiah, and Ezekiel." *Puritan Reformed Journal* 3.2 (2011) 160–92.

    Discusses Edwards's exegetical and hermeneutical method of the major prophets.

63. Youngs, F. "Jonathan Edwards, A Mystic?" *Perspectives in Religious Studies* 38.1 (2011) 47–60.

    Describes how Edwards defined mystical belief as "bastard religion" but by his own narrative should he not be considered a mystic? Youngs explores that question.

64. Zylla, Phil C. *Virtue as Consent to Being: A Pastoral-Theological Perspective on Jonathan Edwards's Construct of Virtue*. Eugene, OR: Pickwick, 2011.

    Examines the idea of virtue as "consent to being" taken from Edwards's *The Nature of True Virtue*. Edwards uses this as an attempt "to articulate the moral life." This is particularly applied to Edwards's "pastoral theological perspective" and how this can have a "significant contribution" to modern "pastoral theology."

2012

1. Agan, Jimmy. Review of *Signs of the Spirit: An Interpretation of Jonathan Edwards' "Religious Affections,"* by Sam Storms. *Presbyterion* 38.1 (2012) 53–54.

   Recommends this book very highly.

2. Allen, Bob, et al. "Weighing the Evidence: Examining the Fruit of Charles Finney and Jonathan Edwards." DVD. Fayetteville, NC: Dominion, 2012. https://dominionproductionsstudio.blogspot.com.

   Contrasts the theology of Charles Finney and Jonathan Edwards. Finney's was a theology of emotionalism and Edwards's was absolute sovereignty of God in salvation.

3. Allison, C. M. B. "The Methodist Edwards: John Wesley's Abridgement of the Selected Works of Jonathan Edwards." *Methodist History* 50.3 (2012) 144–60.

   Focuses on Wesley's abridgement of the works of Edwards but with an Arminian theological slant.

4. Barshinger, David P. "'So Much of the Gospel . . . Shining in It': Jonathan Edwards' Redemptive-Historical Vision of the Psalms." *Trinity Journal* 33.2 (2012) 285.

   Summarizes Barshinger's dissertation on Edwards and the Psalms.

5. ———. Review of *Jonathan Edwards' Early Understanding of Religious Experience: His New York Sermons, 1720–1723*, by Karin Spiecker Stetina. *Fides et Historia* 44.1 (2012) 124–26.

   Calls into question Locke's role in Edwards's defining religious experience as a "new sense of the heart." The reviewer's criticism is this book comes from a dissertation that came out "over a decade ago" and that it is "somewhat dated" and her "bibliography contains nothing later than 1999."

6. Beck, Peter. Review of *God's Grand Design: The Theological Vision of Jonathan Edwards*, by Sean Michael Lucas. *Themelios* 37.2 (2012) 355–57.

   Commends Lucas's claim that Edwards was a "theologian of the Christian life."

7. Benge, Dustin W., ed. *A Journey Toward Heaven: Daily Devotions from the Sermons of Jonathan Edwards.* Grand Rapids: Reformation Heritage, 2012.

   Submits a "years' worth of daily devotionals drawn from Edwards's sermons, captures the true essence of this great preacher's words and speaks personally to readers' hearts."

8. Bezzant, Rhys S. Review of *The God-Centered Life: Insight from Jonathan Edwards for Today*, by Josh Moody. *The Reformed Theological Review* 71.1 (2012) 70–71.

   Applauds Moody's volume as "a superb introduction." This is a book for Christians "who want to serve the church with a full mind and heart."

9. Biehl, Craig. *Reading "Religious Affections": A Study Guide to Jonathan Edwards' Classic on the Nature of True Christianity*. Birmingham, AL: Solid Ground Christian, 2012.

    Reprint (2010.8).

10. Bombaro, John. *Jonathan Edwards's Vision of Reality: The Relationship of God to the World*. Princeton Theological Monograph 172. Reprint, Princeton, NJ: Princeton University Press, 2012.

    Reprint (2011.6).

11. Boss, Rob. Review of *Understanding Jonathan Edwards: An Introduction to America's Theologian*, by Gerald R. McDermott. *Southwestern Journal of Theology* 54.2 (2012) 237–38.

    Confirms it as a work that "shines" and that the "non-specialist should find" the work an "unintimidating, illuminating, and enjoyable read."

12. Brissett, W. "Jonathan Edwards, Continuity, and Secularism." *Early American Literature* 47.1 (2012) 171–82.

    Reviews the works *The Puritan Origins of the American Self*, by Sacvan Bercovitch; *American Spaces of Conversion: The Conductive Imaginaries of Edwards, Emerson, and James*, by Andrea Knutson; *Reading Jonathan Edwards: An Annotated Bibliography in Three Parts, 1729–2005*, by M. X. Lesser; *A Short Life of Jonathan Edwards*, by George M. Marsden; and *Strange Jeremiahs: Civil Religion and the Literary Imaginations of Jonathan Edwards, Herman Melville, and W. E. B. Du Bois*, by Carole Lynn Stewart.

13. Chamberlain, Ava. *The Notorious Elizabeth Tuttle: Marriage, Murder, and Madness in the Family of Jonathan Edwards*. New York: New York University Press, 2012.

    Appraises the controversy of Elizabeth Tuttle as Chamberlain says, "At best, she is a minor villain in the story of Jonathan Edwards, perhaps the greatest American theologian of the colonial era," at worst, she was Edwards's "crazy grandmother" who committed monstrosities that surely affected her grandson.

14. Cho, Hyun-Jin. *Jonathan Edwards on Justification: Reformed Development of the Doctrine in Eighteenth-Century New England*. Lanham, MD: University Press of America, 2012.

    Republishes his dissertation (2010.13).

15. Chun, Chris. *The Legacy of Jonathan Edwards in the Theology of Andrew Fuller*. Leiden: Brill, 2012.

    Republishes his dissertation (2008.9).

16. Cochran, Elizabeth Agnew. "Bricolage and the Purity of Traditions: Engaging the Stoics for Contemporary Christian Ethics." *The Journal of Religious Ethics* 40.4 (2012) 705–29.

    Responds to Rowe's critique of Cochran's argument as "certain dimensions of Roman Stoic ethics" are perceived in the ethics of Edwards's "moral thought."

17. Cosby, Brian H. "The Christology of John Flavel." *Puritan Reformed Journal* 4.1 (2012) 116–34.

    Says Edwards quotes Flavel as "Holy Mr. Flavel" "more than anyone else in *Religious Affections*" and J. I. Packer "calls Edwards the 'spiritual heir' of Flavel."

18. Crisp, Oliver. *Jonathan Edwards on God and Creation*. New York: Oxford University Press, 2012.

    Considers "two central themes in Edwards's thought—namely, his doctrine of God and his understanding of the created order, and how God and creation interrelate."

19. Crisp, Oliver, and Douglas A. Sweeney, eds. *After Edwards: The Courses of the New England Theology*. New York: Oxford University Press, 2012.

    Collects essay from experts of the "New Divinity" as containing Edwards's ideas as a "movement in colonial New England, to Edwards's impact upon European traditions and modern Asia" and its lasting shape on America.

20. DeHoff, Susan L. "Distinguishing Mystical Religious Experience from Psychotic Experience in the Presbyterian Church (USA)." PhD diss., Boston University, 2012.

    Interviews "twenty members of the Presbytery of Boston of the Presbyterian Church (USA) . . . to explore what clergy consider to be mystical religious experiences and the methods they employ to distinguish such experience from psychotic experience." Historical characters of autobiographical and biographical literature in the Reformed tradition, chiefly Edwards, are considered.

21. Dresdow, Kent H. "Building Great Love Toward God and Neighbor in Selected Northcreek Church Members Using Jonathan Edwards'

Charity and Its Fruit." DMin thesis, Trinity Evangelical Divinity School, 2012.

Guides the reader to examine Edwards's *Charity and Fruits* as an evaluative tool to help to edify the church with more love to God and neighbor.

22. Easley, Toby K. "Jonathan Edwards's Five Stages of Homiletical Development: A Model for Contemporary Preaching." DMin thesis, Southwestern Baptist Seminary, 2012.

Examines the "five homiletical stages that can be extended from his youth from his first pastorate in New York" and "continuing until his death in 1758." He offers Edwards as exemplary for modern preachers.

23. Eddy, G. T. *Dr. Taylor of Norwich: Wesley's Arch Heretic*. Eugene, OR: Wipf & Stock, 2012.

Assesses the controversy of Taylor's doctrine of original sin that received sharp opposition from John Wesley and Edwards.

24. Eden, Jason Edward. Review of *Understanding Jonathan Edwards: An Introduction to America's Theologian*, by Gerald R. McDermott. *The Journal of Religious History* 36.1 (2012) 129–30.

Evaluates the "greatest contribution" of the volume is "making Edwards's ideas and methodologies accessible and relevant for today's theologians and philosophers."

25. Finn, Nathan A. Review of *The Legacy of Jonathan Edwards in the Theology of Andrew Fuller*, by Chris Chun. *Themelios* 37.3 (2012) 536–38.

Assesses that Chun has done "tremendous service" by demonstrating how Fuller appropriated Edwards's theology.

26. Hall, Kenley. "The Great Awakening: Calvinism, Arminianism and Revivalistic Preaching: Homiletical Lesson for Today." *The Journal of Evangelical Homiletics Society* 12.2 (2012) 31–40.

Purposes to analyze the sermons of Edwards, Whitefield, and Wesley in the context of the Great Awakening. He asks two questions: (1) What impact did the preacher's Calvinistic or Arminian theology have on his preaching style, content, and evangelistic appeal? (2) Why did the preacher's preaching spark revival?

27. Harper, George W. Review of *Jonathan Edwards on Worship: Public and Private Devotion to God*, by Ted Rivera. *Evangelical Review of Theology* 36.2 (2012) 188–90.

    Disagrees with Rivera's "critique of Edwards's practice in regard to family devotion" and in turning from public worship to personal devotion "the book loses focus." The second "concern" according to Harper is that Rivera understood the Puritans to hold the "regulative principle of worship" and he chastised him for not appealing to the "normative principle of worship."

28. Haykin, Michael A. G. "The Holy Spirit, the Charismata, and Signs and Wonders: Some Evangelical Perspectives from the Eighteenth Century." *The Southern Baptist Journal of Theology* 16.4 (2012) 54–73.

    Maintains that the "emergence of Pentecostalism" is "*not* the first time in the history of the church" that the Spirit's work has come under "intense and prolonged scrutiny." He suggests at one time the eighteenth-century revivals came under this sort of scrutiny.

29. Heathcock, Clint. "Rhetorical Influences upon the Preaching of Jonathan Edwards." *The Journal of Evangelical Homiletical Society* 12.2 (2012) 11–30.

    Reveals that Edwards inherited the Puritan model of preaching and "never substantially depart[ed] from this tradition," yet he was "no mere slave to convention."

30. Huggins, Jonathan R. "Jonathan Edwards on Justification by Faith Alone: An Analysis of His Thought and Defense of His Orthodoxy." PhD diss., University of Stellenbosch, 2012.

    Expands on his MA thesis (2006.30).

31. Kidd, Thomas S. Review of *The Theology of Jonathan Edwards*, by Michael J. McClymond and Gerald R. McDermott. *The Christian Century* 129.16 (2012) 38–39.

    Contends that the authors' "bridge metaphor" is not helpful because it "suggests" that Edwards "stood (or stands) between other position" whether it be Protestant versus Catholic, etc., but the reviewer sees him as "a pillar grounded in the terra firma of his Reformed, evangelical, theological tradition." However, Kidd says, this book is "a remarkable achievement."

32. Kim, Nam Joon. *Jonathan Edwards and My Ministry*. Seoul: Yullin Church, 2012.

    Evaluates Edwards's influence on Kim's ministry and the Korean church.

33. McClenahan, Michael. *Jonathan Edwards and Justification by Faith*. Farnham, UK: Ashgate, 2012.

    Republishes his dissertation (2007.38).

34. McClymond, Michael J., and Gerald R. McDermott. *The Theology of Jonathan Edwards*. Oxford: Oxford University Press, 2012.

    Traces the theology of Edwards in three parts. The first part includes an historical-sociological setting of Edwards. The second part, which is the longest, divides the theology into four sections. Section 1 is entitled "Method and Strategies." These articles contain seven chapters which involve Edwards's views on revelation, beauty and aesthetics, typology, Scripture, and biblical exegesis. Section 2, divided into seven chapters, focuses on "The Triune God, the Angels, and Heaven." Section 3 considers "Theological Anthropology and Divine Great," which is separated into eight chapters, concerning things like the affections, the divine covenant, free will and original sin, a theology of salvation, grace, faith, conversion, justification, sanctification, and revival. Section 4 explores "Church, Ethics, Eschatology, and Society," and the theology of the church, the ministry, sacraments, preaching, ethics, the missionary enterprises, and eschatology. The third part deals with "Legacies and Affinities: Edwards Disciples and Interpreters," and it is divided into nine chapters which contains the New Divinity, Princeton and Andover Seminaries, and the reactions of the twentieth century to the recovery of Edwards.

35. McDowell, David Paul. *Beyond the Half-Way Covenant: Solomon Stoddard's Understanding of the Lord's Supper as a Converting Ordinance*. Eugene, OR: Wipf & Stock, 2012.

    Republishes his dissertation (2010.48).

36. McMullen, Michael D. "A Previously Unpublished Sermon by Jonathan Edwards (1703–1758) on John 3:36." *Midwestern Journal of Theology* 11.1 (2012) 66–74.

    Publishes a sermon by Edwards to the Stockbridge Indians which had never been published along with the editor's introduction.

37. ———. "A Previously Unpublished Sermon by Jonathan Edwards on 'What It Is to Come to Christ (Matt 11:28).'" *Midwestern Journal of Theology* 11.2 (2012) 46–57.

    Publishes a sermon by Edwards to the Stockbridge Indians which had never been published along with the editor's introduction.

38. Miller, Mark J. "Jonathan Edwards, Affective Conversion, and the Problem of Masochism." *GLQ: A Journal of Lesbian and Gay Studies* 18 (2012) 565–94.

    Traces the "intellectual, historical, and theoretical connections between eighteenth-century religious conversion." Miller focuses on Edwards's account of his religious experience in the "Personal Narrative" as well as other works and demonstration of which led Edwards to masochism.

39. Miller, Rebecca. "Jonathan Edwards Center at Yale University: Website Publishing." *Theological Librarianship* 5.1 (2012) 7.

    Lauds the Jonathan Edwards Center at Yale University for granting to the public the twenty-six volumes of the printed versions of Edwards's works as well as the remaining works that are online.

40. Minkema, Kenneth P., et al., eds. *True and False Christians (On the Parable of the Wise and Foolish Virgins)*. Vol. 1 of *Jonathan Edwards on the Matthean Parables*. Eugene, OR: Cascade, 2012.

    Presents the first volume of previously unpublished sermons of the Matthean Parables.

41. Minkema, Kenneth P., and Adriaan C. Neele, eds. *Divine Husbandmen (On the Parable of the Sower and the Seed)*. Vol. 2 of *Jonathan Edwards on the Matthean Parables*. Eugene, OR: Cascade, 2012.

    Presents the second volume of previously unpublished sermons of the Matthean Parables.

42. ———, eds. *Fish Out of Their Element (On the Parable of the Net)*. Vol. 3 of *Jonathan Edwards on the Matthean Parables*. Eugene, OR: Cascade, 2012.

    Presents the third volume of previously unpublished sermons of the Matthean Parables.

43. Moody, Josh, ed. *Jonathan Edwards and Justification*. Wheaton, IL: Crossway, 2012.

Assembles "a team of internationally reputed Edwards scholars" to address the question of Edwards's view on justification.

44. Neele, Adriaan C. "Jonathan Edwards (1703–1758) and the Nature of Theology." *Studia Historiae Ecclesiasticae* 38.2 (2012) 273–86.

    Expresses that Edwards's "inquiry into the nature of theology" holds continuity with medieval Catholic theologians and Protestants scholasticism in "eighteenth-century New England."

45. ———. "Jonathan Edwards (1703–1758) and the Nature of Theology." *Fides Reformata* 17.2 (2012) 113–28.

    Similar to 2012.44 but in a different journal.

46. Noll, Mark A. "Theology." In *The Columbia Guide to Religion in American History*, edited by Paul Harvey and Edward J. Blum, 105–21. New York: Columbian University Press, 2012.

    Highlights the "high point in American theological history" occurred at the "end of the Puritan era" in Jonathan Edwards as he was "America's most compelling theologian."

47. Park, Hyun Shin. "Toward a Life-Changing Application Paradigm in Expository Preaching." PhD diss., Southern Baptist Theological Seminary, 2012.

    Aims to provide homiletical principles of biblical interpretation which are derived from four historical characters: Chrysostom, Calvin, Edwards, and Broadus. Examines in these individuals "exegetical, doctrinal, homiletical, and transformational" which they intend as transforming the listeners "for the glory of God."

48. Parmenter, Margaret Rose. "Epistolary Physick: Familiar Letters, Friendship, and Self-Preservation in Eighteenth-Century America." PhD diss., University of Chicago, 2012.

    Examines the benefits that can be derived from letter writing and focuses, among others, on Esther Edwards Burr, who wrote many letters to her father, Jonathan Edwards.

49. Pennings, Ray. "Jonathan Edwards and Life's Adverbial Questions." *Comment*, March 1, 2012. https://comment.org/jonathan-edwards-and-lifes-adverbial-questions.

    Summarizes the impact of Edwards's "God-centered theology" and what role it played on Pennings's life and vocation.

50. Phillips, Christopher N. "Cotton Mather Brings Isaac Watts's Hymns to America; or, How to Perform a Hymn with Singing It." *New England Quarterly* 85 (2012) 203–21.

    Reconstructs Cotton Mather's promotion of the publication of "Isaac Watt's hymns into New England." Edwards also encouraged his congregation in Northampton to use Watts's hymns.

51. Prud'homme, Joseph Gilbert, and James Hoitsma Schelberg. "Disposition, Potentiality, and Beauty in the Theology of Jonathan Edwards: A Defense of His Great Christian Doctrine of Original Sin." *American Theological Inquiry* 5.1 (2012) 25–53.

    Reveals that Edwards's *Original Sin* is "brilliantly argued" and should be read "to supply arguments that establish a compelling basis for the tradition account of inherited sin."

52. Robinson, C. Jeffrey. "The Home in an Earthly Kingdom: Family Discipleship Among Reformers and Puritans." *The Journal of Discipleship & Family Ministry* 3.1 (2012) 18–28.

    Aims to defend Edwards as "the last and most noteworthy of the American Puritans" who continued the theme of the Reformers and sought to give an example of how a family ministry ought to be.

53. Rogers, Mark. "Edward Dorr Griffin and the Edwardsian Second Great Awakening." PhD diss., Trinity International University, 2012.

    Articulates how Edwards influenced the life of Edward Dorr Griffin as a "New Divinity pastor, evangelist, theologian, seminary professor, college president, and one of the most successful revivalists of the Second Great Awakening." Griffin was "trained by Jonathan Edwards Jr." He embodied an "Edwardian theology" and "practical piety," and he had revivalist leanings.

54. Russell, Andrew C. "Polemical Solidarity: John Wesley and Jonathan Edwards Confront John Taylor on Original Sin." *Wesleyan Theological Journal* 47.2 (2012) 72–88.

    Recounts that although Edwards (Calvinist) and Wesley (Arminian) were on different sides of the theological vantage point, within a three-month period, they had both written treatises against John Taylor's *Original Sin*.

55. Saunders, Dan. "A Biblical and Theological Critique of Jonathan Edwards' Doctrine of Christian Assurance." *Churchman* 126.2 (2012) 115–46.

Studies Edwards's biblical theological doctrine of assurance and highlights the difference from the Reformers indicated by adopting a Puritan form of assurance which asserts that assurance doesn't necessarily belong to the essence of faith.

56. Schweitzer, William M. *God Is a Communicative Being: Divine Communicativeness and Harmony in the Theology of Jonathan Edwards.* New York: T&T Clark, 2012.

    Suggests that the proper way of reading Edwards is as a Trinitarian theologian. Edwards begins his theological project with his "insight into the Trinitarian life." The Trinity was eternally a communicative being between the Father, Son, and Spirit. This communication is said to produce "harmony."

57. Scott-Coe, Justin M. "Covenant Nation: The Politics of Grace in Early American Literature." PhD diss., Claremont Graduate University, 2012.

    Traces the concept of covenant "in early American literature" and in theological readings of "Edwards's *Freedom of Will* and the essays of Ralph Waldo Emerson," displaying "how the covenant theology of colonial New England dispersed into more 'secular' forms of what may be called an American political theology."

58. Sederholm, Carl. "The Trouble with Grace: Reading Jonathan Edwards's Faithful Narrative." *New England Quarterly* 85 (2012) 326–34.

    Attempts to explain how Edwards "reordered the Northampton revival's chronology in history" by describing that Joseph Hawley's suicide "signified the withdrawal of God's Spirit."

59. Smith, Yvonne S., et al. "The God of the Games: Towards a Theology of Competition." *Christian Scholar's Review* 41.3 (2012) 267–91.

    Sets out to explore the "spiritual assumptions of competition" and give answers to the question "does God approve of competition?" Gives basic answers about pride, judgment, rivalry, and idolatry. The authors use Augustine, Calvin, and Edwards as test cases on the topic.

60. Spurlock, R. Scott. Review of *Jonathan Edwards and Scotland*, edited by K. P. Minkema et al. *The Expository Times* 123.9 (2012) 459–60.

    Represents "an eclectic mix of scholarship."

61. Story, Ronald. *Jonathan Edwards and the Gospel of Love*. Amherst: University of Massachusetts Press, 2012.

Contends that Edwards was not a hell and brimstone preacher but a preacher of love, as revealed in his sermon "Heaven Is a World of Love." The "afterlife" is social "in nature because love is social." He pictures this sermon as having profound impact on his life and ministry.

62. Strobel, Kyle, ed. *Charity and Its Fruits: Living in the Light of God's Love*. Wheaton, IL: Crossway, 2012.

Reprint.

63. ———. "Jonathan Edwards and the Polemics of Theosis." *Harvard Theological Review* 105 (2012) 259–79.

Argues that while Edwards did not use the terminology of theosis, he "invokes the grammar of theosis."

64. ———. *Jonathan Edwards's Theology: A Reinterpretation*. London: T&T Clark, 2012.

Provides "an interpretative key to Jonathan Edwards's theology developed from within his own doctrinal constructs." Strobel begins with acknowledging that Edwards began with the assumption of the Trinity and applies "three key areas of redemption": "spiritual knowledge, regeneration, and religious affection." Strobel speaks in systematic theological terms rather than philosophical terms.

65. Studebaker, Steven M., and Robert W. Caldwell III. *The Trinitarian Theology of Jonathan Edwards: Text, Context, and Application*. Farnham, UK: Ashgate, 2012.

Confirms the scholars "have increasingly recognized the central role that the Trinity played in his [Edwards's] thought," yet none of those academic writing contained the "central texts on the Trinity and interprets and applies them to contemporary theological issues." They speak of this in three parts: Part I, Edwards's "chief trinitarian writings"; part II, Edwards's "trinitarianism in historical context"; and part III "demonstrates how Edwards employed the Trinity in his sermons, in spiritual formation, and in other areas of doctrine."

66. Vondey, Wolfgang. Review of *The Trinitarian Vision of Jonathan Edwards*, by Stephen Studebaker and Robert Caldwell III. *One in Christ* 46.2 (2012) 361–65.

Praises this book as "an exemplary study" that is based on "rigorous historical research" and "systematic theological know-how."

2013

1. Abernathy, Andrew T. "Jonathan Edwards as Multi-Dimension Bible Interpreter: A Case Study from Isaiah 40–55." *Journal of Evangelical Theological Society* 56.4 (2013) 815–30.

    Builds on Barshinger and Yoo in his study on Edwards's "approach to the Bible."

2. Ballan, Joseph N. Review of *Strange Jeremiahs: Civil Religion and the Literary Imaginations of Jonathan Edwards, Herman Melville, and W. E. B. Du Bois*, by Carole Lynn Stewart. *Literature and Theology* 27.2 (2013) 254–56.

    Reads the book critically though not negatively.

3. Barshinger, David P. Review of *The Theology of Jonathan Edwards*, by Gerald R. McDermott and Michael McClymond. *Journal of the Evangelical Theological Society* 56.1 (2013) 205–11.

    Debates "how much of a 'bridge' figure is Jonathan Edwards?" However, this is "a fine work" and is "essential reading for Edwards scholars."

4. ———. Review of *The Trinitarian Theology of Jonathan Edwards: Text, Context, and Application*, by Steven M. Studebaker and Robert W. Caldwell III. *Fides et Historia* 45.1 (2013) 154–56.

    Deserves a "wide reading among Edwards scholars," and historical theologians "interested in the Trinity."

5. Beck, Peter. "Worship God with Our Minds: Theology as Doxology Among the Puritans." *Puritan Reformed Journal* 5.2 (2013) 193–203.

    Surveys "four key Puritan thinkers" that shared a "common goal: a theology that leads to doxology." Beck focused on William Ames, John Owen, Thomas Watson, and Jonathan Edwards.

6. Bräutigam, Michael. Review of *God Is a Communicative Being: Divine Communicativeness and Harmony in the Theology of Jonathan Edwards*, by William M. Schweitzer. *European Journal of Theology* 22.2 (2013) 179–80.

    Reviews this volume as one of "outstanding quality."

7. Brooks, Joshua Barrett. "Was Jonathan Edwards a Christian Hedonist?" STM thesis, Dallas Theological Seminary, 2013.

   Contests that "Christian hedonism is inconsistent with the moral theology of Jonathan Edwards" as defined by John Piper.

8. Caldwell, Robert W. III. "The Ministerial Ideal in the Ordination Sermons of Jonathan Edwards: Four Theological Portraits." *Themelios* 38.3 (2013) 390–401.

   Presents four ordination sermons of Edwards as "portraits of the Christ-like minister."

9. ———. Review of *Jonathan Edwards as Contemporary: Essays in Honor of Sand Hyun Lee*, edited by Don Schweitzer. *Southwestern Journal of Theology* 55.2 (2013) 325–27.

   Honors Sang Hyun Lee for his contribution of Edwards theology and philosophy. This volume is "an excellent resource for scholars."

10. ———. Review of *The Theology of Jonathan Edwards*, by Michael J. McClymond and Gerald R. McDermott. *Fides et Historia* 45.1 (2013) 152–54.

    Recommends this book as accessible for "Edwards enthusiasts" and "indispensable for aspiring specialists."

11. ———. Review of *God Is a Communicative Being: Divine Communicativeness and Harmony in the Theology of Jonathan Edwards*, by William M. Schweitzer. *The Journal of Theological Studies* 64.2 (2013) 796–98.

    Ascertains this as an "important book," both "clearly written" and "easy to understand." The reviewer recommends it to "anyone seeking to grasp the central themes animating Edwards's theology."

12. ———. Review of *After Jonathan Edwards: The Courses of New England Theology*, edited by Oliver D. Crisp and Douglas A. Sweeney. *Themelios* 38.2 (2013) 294–95.

    Recommends this book to anyone "interested in the complex history of theology in America."

13. Chun, Chris. Review of *Sermons by Jonathan Edwards on the Matthean Parables, Vols. 1–3*, edited by Kenneth P. Minkema et al. *Church History and Religious Culture* 93.4 (2013) 619–21.

    Applauds the editors as doing "a splendid service."

14. Coulter, Dale M. Review of *The Theology of Jonathan Edwards*, by Michael J. McClymond and Gerald R. McDermott. *Religious Studies Review* 39.2 (2013) 85.

    Assesses the work of the authors. It is "difficult to imagine another introduction that surpasses this one."

15. Finn, Nathan A. Review of *The Theology of Jonathan Edwards*, by Michael J. McClymond and Gerald R. McDermott. *Southeastern Theological Review* 4.2 (2013) 231–34.

    Establishes the value of the book. "Despite my personal demurrals on some points," it will "certainly become the starting point" of Edwards's theology as much as Marsden's *Jonathan Edwards: A Life* is a preliminary interest of his life.

16. ———. Review of *God Is a Communicative Being: Divine Communicativeness and Harmony in the Theology of Jonathan Edwards*, by William M. Schweitzer. *Themelios* 38.2 (2013) 311–12.

    Recommends this study highly as "a balanced portrait that avoids pitfall of anachronistic or simplistic portraits so common" among both "scholars and popular authors."

17. Friesen, Paul H. Review of *Jonathan Edwards, Religious Affection and the Puritan Analysis of True Piety, Spiritual Sensation and Heart Religion*, by Brad Walton. *Journal of Canadian Church Historical Society* 51.1–2 (2013) 67–69.

    Reviews this as a "careful and narrowly focused book." Some might even say it is "too narrow and careful."

18. Gura, Philip F., ed. *Jonathan Edwards: Writings from the Great Awakening*. Library of America. New York: Literary Classics of the United States, 2013.

    Reprints some of Edwards's well-known treatises, sermons, and letters.

19. Hamilton, Catherine Sider. "Jonathan Edwards on the Atonement." *International Journal of Systematic Theology* 15.4 (2013) 394–415.

    Suggests Edwards adheres to a "*version* of the penal substitution theory of the atonement" and requires "certain metaphysical commitment," arguing Edwards's emphasis is on what has been described as a "realist penal substitution."

20. ———. "Jonathan Edwards, Paul, and the Priority of Holiness: A Variant Reading." *Journal of Theological Interpretation* 7.1 (2013) 1–20.

    Examines Edwards's interesting interpretation of Paul in several sermons. He finds in Paul "a spokesman for the priority and beauty of holiness and for a grace that is in conception more organic, more mystical, than juridical." This "proves a valuable interlocutor in the quest for a full and nuanced understanding of Paul."

21. Hanvey, James. Review of *The Theology of Jonathan Edwards*, by Michael J. McClymond and Gerald R. McDermott. *Theological Studies* 74.4 (2013) 1007–9.

    Exposits this as "a major contribution to the field."

22. Helm, Paul. Review of *The Theology of Jonathan Edwards*, by Michael J. McClymond and Gerald R. McDermott. *The Journal of Ecclesiastical History* 64.3 (2013) 649–50.

    Says this is "without a doubt the Big Mac of Edwards studies." Judges the work favorably.

23. Haykin, Michael, with Ron Baines. *Travel with Jonathan Edwards: A God-Centered Life, an Enduring Legacy*. Leominster, England: Day One, 2013.

    Paints Edwards as seeking the "glory of God, sovereign over this world's empires, and its practical implications for humanity" in every aspect of his life—from his role in the revivals to his role as a husband, father, and a "preacher and theologian."

24. Haykin, Michael, et al. "The SBJT Forum." *The Southern Baptist Journal of Theology* 17.1 (2013) 46–53.

    Discusses how Edwards influenced Andrew Fuller.

25. Huggins, Jonathan. *Living Justification: A Historical-Theological Study of the Reformed Doctrine in the Writings of John Calvin, Jonathan Edwards, and N. T. Wright*. Eugene, OR: Wipf & Stock, 2013.

    Examines the history of justification through the lens of Calvin, Edwards, and Wright. Huggins assesses that these theologians have points of "development, continuity, and discontinuity within the Reformed tradition."

26. ———. Review of *Jonathan Edwards and Justification*, edited by Josh Moody. *Fides et Historia* 45.2 (2013) 147–49.

Presents the volume as a "helpful contribution" to "Edwards studies" and "discussion about the doctrine of justification."

27. Kreider, Glenn R. Review of *Jonathan Edwards and Justification*, edited by Josh Moody. *Bibliotheca Sacra* 170.680 (2013) 503–5.

    Applauds this book as being "packed with excellent content."

28. ———. Review of *God's Grand Design: The Theological Vision of Jonathan Edwards*, by Sean Michael Lucas. *Bibliotheca Sacra* 170.678 (2013) 248–49.

    Suggests that Lucas views Edwards "as a mentor and a model worthy emulating."

29. Johnson, Terrence L. Review of *Strange Jeremiahs: Civil Religions and the Literary Imaginations of Jonathan Edwards, Herman Melville, and W. E. B. Du Bois*, by Carole Lynn Stewart. *The Journal of Southern Religions* 15 (2013). http://jsr.fsu.edu/issues/vol15/johnson.html.

    Uncovers in Edwards an "articulation of the public self that undermined the era's theology" in the insistence "on adhering to the covenant as a central component of salvation." For Edwards, "focus on the conversion through the Holy Spirit signifies an effort to disrupt the narrow public by expanding the range of persons with access and the ability to transform public spheres."

30. Lovi, David S., and Benjamin Westerhoff. *The Power of God: A Jonathan Edwards Commentary of the Book of Romans.* Cambridge: Lutterworth, 2013.

    Takes all of Edwards's writings on the book of Romans, such as his "Blank Bible" and "Notes on Scripture," and wraps them together in the form of a commentary.

31. Martin, Ryan. "'A Soul Inflamed with High Exercises of Divine Love': Affections and Passions in the Theology of Jonathan Edwards." PhD diss., Central Baptist Theological Seminary, 2013.

    Studies the problem of the affections in Christian tradition, surveying Patristic, Medieval, Reformers, Puritan, and Enlightenment figures to see how they deal with the problem. This is done mostly as a segue to Edwards's "affection and passions."

32. Mattei, Tobias A. "Neuroscience and Cognitive Psychology Insights into the Classical Theological Debate About Free Will and Responsibility." *Christian Scholar's Review* 42.2 (2013) 123–47.

Analyzes the positions of Calvin, Edwards, Luther, and the Westminster Confession of Faith as he "exposes how all of them involved a view of human will as 'self-determined' and 'corrupted.'" Mattei "strongly supports" the empirical view of "free will" and a "complex and elaborated 'illusion' of the human mind."

33. McDermott, Gerald R., and Michael J. McClymond. "Jonathan Edwards and the Future of Global Christianity." *Theology Today* 69 (2013) 478–85.

    Investigates the impact Edwards played on world Christianity in the present. "A new agenda needs to be scripturally based, open to vibrant, Spirit-led experience, engaged with non-Christian religions, and ecumenically fruitful." Edwards provides a "bridge" in a four-way discussion between "Catholics and Protestants, the Christian East and West, Charismatics and non-Charismatics, and liberals and conservatives."

34. ———. *The Theology of Jonathan Edwards.* New York: Oxford University Press, 2013.

    Republishes 2012.34.

35. McGraw, Ryan M. Review of *God Is a Communicative Being: Divine Communicativeness and Harmony in the Theology of Jonathan Edwards*, by William M. Schweitzer. *Puritan Reformed Journal* 5.2 (2013) 278–81.

    Demonstrates that this is an "important book that reassesses the big picture of the theology of Jonathan Edwards."

36. McNeill, John. Review of *The Theology of Jonathan Edwards*, by Michael J. McClymond and Gerald R. McDermott. *Theology* 116.4 (2013) 282–83.

    Surveys the works of Edwards "neatly summarizing his thinking on a variety of theological loci grouped under sections." The authors are Edwards scholars and are well known. It serves as an "excellent cross-reference volume rather than as one good read." He commends this work as concerning "America's Augustine."

37. Melton, Frankie, Jr. "The Effect of the Fear Appeals on George Whitefield's Auditors." *Puritan Reformed Journal* 5.1 (2013) 163–82.

    Discusses how Whitfield's preaching impacted Jonathan Edwards but more on Sarah Edwards as recorded in her diary.

38. Moody, Josh W. Review of *Jonathan Edwards and Justification by Faith*, by Michael McClenahan. *Theology* 116.5 (2013) 363–64.

    Brings to the table "an excellent, scholarly, accurate, creative and compelling account of Jonathan Edwards's essential orthodoxy with relation to the doctrine of justification by faith."

39. Morden, Peter J. Review of *The Legacy of Jonathan Edwards in the Theology of Andrew Fuller*, by Chris Chun. *The Baptist Quarterly* 45.2 (2013) 114–15.

    Assesses the book as an "excellent addition to this growing body of secondary literature."

40. Moreland, James P. "Mental vs. Top-Down Causation: Sic et Non: Why Top-Down Causation Does Not Support Mental." *Philosophia Christi* 15.1 (2013) 133–47.

    Criticizes "top-down causation" and suggests there is not "justifying belief in mental causation." Moreland believes there are "no clear examples of top-down causation and there is a persuasive case against it."

41. ———. Review of *The Theology of Jonathan Edwards*, by Gerald R. McDermott and Michael McClymond. *The Master's Seminary Journal* 24.1 (2013) 159–61.

    Reinvents the *Theology of Jonathan Edwards* if one "understands Edwards's Puritan heritage." "Despite the above listed shortcoming," this volume "provides the reader with a wealth of information."

42. Najapfour, Brian G. *Jonathan Edwards: His Doctrine of and Devotion to Prayer*. Caledonia, MI: Biblical Spirituality, 2013.

    Explores Edwards's devotion to prayer.

43. Neele, Adriaan C. "Theological Education of Nineteenth-Century French Missionaries: An Appropriation of the Catholicity of Classical Christian Theology." *Studia Historiae Ecclesiasticae* 39.2 (2013) 149–78.

    Presents the "limited research" on the "theological education of nineteenth-century Christian missionaries." Through manuscripts of the missionaries, Neele finds Edwards significantly shaped their theology.

44. ———. Review of *Jonathan Edwards' Early Understanding of Religious Experience: His New York Sermons, 1720–1723*, by Karin Spiecker Stetina. *Journal of Reformed Theology* 7.1 (2013) 121–22.

Concludes with the preliminary observations: (1) Edwards was not a pastor but an interim preacher; (2) invites further "theological reflection" on the New York era; and (3) offers a "welcome entry point" to the "large sermon corpus of Edwards" available since 2008.

45. Nichols, Stephen R. C. *Jonathan Edwards's Bible: The Relationship of the Old and New Testaments.* Eugene, OR: Pickwick, 2013.

    Republishes his dissertation (2010.53).

46. O'Brien, Brandon J. "The Edwardsean Isaac Backus: The Significance of Jonathan Edwards in Backus's Theology, History, and Defense of Religious Liberty." PhD diss., Trinity Evangelical Divinity School, 2013.

    Studies Isaac Backus, who found in Edwards a synthesis of his own religious thoughts, particularly the defense that Baptists were "true heirs of the New England spiritual tradition."

47. Schultz, Walter J. "Jonathan Edwards' Concept of an Original Ultimate End." *Journal of the Evangelical Theological Society* 56 (2013) 107–22.

    Summarizes his dissertation and supplements introductory and background information "necessary for an appropriate appreciation of the centrality of this concept."

48. Schweitzer, Don. Review of *Sermons by Jonathan Edwards on the Matthean Parables*, vol. 1: *True and False Christians (On the Parable of the Wise and Foolish Virgins)*, by Kenneth P. Minkema et al. *Toronto Journal of Theology* 29.1 (2013) 186–87.

    Commends the importance of these sermons.

49. ———. Review of *Sermons by Jonathan Edwards on the Matthean Parables*, edited by Kenneth P. Minkema and Adriaan C. Neele. *Toronto Journal of Theology* 29.2 (2013) 436–37.

    Commends the importance of these sermons.

50. Stein, Stephen J. Review of *After Jonathan Edwards: The Courses of New England Theology*, edited by Oliver D. Crisp and Douglas A. Sweeney. *The Journal of Religion* 93.4 (2013) 511–12.

    Values the contribution for the "continuing and enduring impact" of the reflection and writing of "Edwards over the course of more than two and a half centuries."

51. Stinson, Susan. *Spider in a Tree: A Novel of the First Great Awakening*. Easthampton, MA: Small Beer, 2013.

    Considers Edwards's "dangling a spider" in his famous sermon "Sinners in the Hands of an Angry God" to what "spiders" might preach back.

52. Strobel, Kyle. *Formed for the Glory of God: Learning from the Spiritual Practices of Jonathan Edwards*. Downers Grove, IL: InterVarsity, 2013.

    Purports that Edwards taught with the "means of grace" that makes us "receptive to God's work in our lives as we learn to abide in Christ."

53. ———. *Jonathan Edwards's Theology: A Reinterpretation*. London: Bloomsbury T&T Clark, 2013.

    Describes three features debated in scholarly literature "spiritual knowledge, regeneration, and religious affections."

54. ———. Review of *Jonathan Edwards on Justification: Reformed Development of the Doctrine of the Eighteenth-Century New England*, by Hyun-Jin Cho. *Themelios* 38.2 (2013) 292–93.

    Commends "overall, this volume is well-done"; however, there "are a handful of weaknesses," and "while none of these points undermines the importance of this volume," it does give the incentive to read "alongside others."

55. Sweeney, Douglas A. "Jonathan Edwards, the Harmony of Scripture, and Canonical Exegesis." *Trinity Journal* 34.2 (2013) 171–207.

    Addresses the "major deficit" regarding Edwards's "approach to the Bible" and his "treaty of interpreting all of Scripture canonically."

56. Thuesen, Peter J. Review of *The Theology of Jonathan Edwards*, by Michael J. McClymond and Gerald R. McDermott. *The Journal of Presbyterian History* 91.2 (2013) 91–92.

    Welcomes this as a "definitive volume" and a "helpful image for comprehending the scope of his theology."

57. Waddington, Jeffrey C. "The Unified Operations of the Human Soul Jonathan Edwards's Theological Anthropology and Apologetic." *The Westminster Theological Journal* 75.2 (2013) 374.

    Questions whether "Edwards's doctrine of man" is "consistent with the picture painted of him by John Gerstner."

58. Wilmoth, Daniel Ray. "Economic Models of Addiction and the Christian View of Temptation." *Faith & Economics* 61–62 (2013) 55–65.

    Illustrates the "Christian view of temptation" by taking a sermon of Edwards as it departs from "prominent economic models of addiction."

59. Yeager, Jonathan M. Review of *The Notorious Elizabeth Tuttle: Marriage, Murder, and Madness in the Family of Jonathan Edwards*, by Ava Chamberlain. *Church History* 82.3 (2013) 732–34.

    Contends that "Edwards's biographers" Ola Elizabeth Winslow, Perry Miller, and George Marsden "propagat[ed] the myth of Edwards's crazy grandmother without properly considering" Elizabeth Tuttle's "side of the story." Yeager says that Chamberlain's thesis, "though sometimes based on conjecture, is plausible given the detailed court records."

2014

1. Aiken, Peter. "Jonathan Edwards on the Justice of God." *Puritan Reformed Journal* 6.2 (2014) 88–102.

    Argues that the justice of God was an integral aspect of Edwards's understanding of the glory of God.

2. Anderson, Owen J. *Reason and Faith in Early Princeton: Piety and the Knowledge of God.* New York: Palgrave Macmillan, 2014.

    Writes as a prequel to the book *Reason and Faith in the Theology of Charles Hodge*. Traces the founding of Princeton and the thought of its formative leaders, including Jonathan Edwards. Advances the thesis that Princeton represents the "highwater mark" of American higher education.

3. Atwood, Christopher S. "Jonathan Edwards's Doctrine of Justification: A New Reading of Edwards's Treatises, Sermons, and *Miscellanies*." PhD diss., Wheaton College, 2014.

    Claims that Edwards taught a doctrine of "*duplex iustitia* that was highly idiosyncratic yet internally coherent." God justifies a person "virtually" on the basis of faith and then "actually" on the basis of works.

4. Bailey, Richard A. Review of *A Novel of the Great Awakening*, by Susan Stinson. *Books & Culture* 20.4 (2014) 37.

   Reviews Susan Stinson's *Spider in a Tree*. Bailey argues that this is the greatest source of reflection on Jonathan Edwards.

5. Barshinger, David P. *Jonathan Edwards and the Psalms: A Redemptive-Historical Vision of Scripture*. New York: Oxford University Press, 2014.

   Offers insights on Edwards's theological engagement with the Psalms in the contexts of interpretation, worship, and preaching and asserts that the history of redemption was Edwards's theological framework for engaging the Psalms.

6. Beeke, Joel, and Brian G. Najapfour. *Taking Hold of God: Reformed and Puritan Perspectives on Prayer*. Seoul: YWAM, 2014.

   Reprint (2011.3). One chapter is devoted to Edwards's doctrine of the Trinity and his thoughts on prayer.

7. Bezzant, Rhys. *Jonathan Edwards and the Church*. Oxford University Press, 2014.

   Presents Edwards's doctrine of the church as it developed over the course of his ministry.

8. ———. Review of *Jonathan Edwards and Justification by Faith*, by Michael McClenahan. *Themelios* 39.1 (2014) 164–66.

   Praises the work as an "extraordinarily rich contribution to present debates on justification in Edwards's corpus."

9. ———. "'Singly, Particularly, Closely': Edwards as Mentor." *Jonathan Edwards Studies* 4.2 (2014) 228–47.

   Demonstrates ways in which Edwards's mentoring relationships contributed to his pastoral ministry.

10. Blaauw, Corné. "Redemptive History as a Paradigm for Jonathan Edwards' Exposition of Miracles." *Jonathan Edwards Studies* 4.1 (2014) 4–20.

    Summarizes 2014.11.

11. ———. "A Whole New World of Philosophy: Jonathan Edwards on Science, Nature and Miracles." ThM thesis, Jonathan Edwards Centre Africa at the University of the Free State, 2014.

    Presents Edwards's theology and defense of miracles.

12. Britz, R. M. Review of *God Is a Communicative Being: Divine Communicativeness and Harmony in the Theology of Jonathan Edwards*, by William Schweitzer. *Journal of Reformed Theology* 8.4 (2014) 418–20.

    Lauds the volume for its extensive use of primary and secondary sources.

13. Brown, R. E. Review of *Jonathan Edwards and the Gospel of Love*, by Ronald Story. *Church History* 83 (2014) 218–19.

    Offers a brief survey of Story's work.

14. Burnell, Joel. "Jonathan Edwards Meets Dietrich Bonhoeffer: True Religion or Non-Religious Christianity?" *Jonathan Edwards Studies* 4.2 (2014) 248–64.

    Argues that Edwards and Bonhoeffer, despite obvious differences in their historical time, traditions, and terminology, share much in common.

15. Caldwell, Robert W., III. Review of *Jonathan Edwards on God and Creation*, by Oliver Crisp. *The Journal of Theological Studies* 65.1 (2014) 340–43.

    Commends the book as "the most important interpretation of Jonathan Edwards's philosophical theology in a generation."

16. Carr, Simonetta. *Christian Biographies for Young Readers: Jonathan Edwards*. Grand Rapids: Reformation Heritage, 2014.

    Offers an illustrated biography to introduce young readers to Edwards's life and thought.

17. Chamberlain, Ava. Review of *After Jonathan Edwards: The Courses of the New England Theology*, edited by Oliver Crisp and Douglas Sweeney. *Church History* 83.1 (2014) 219–21.

    Claims that the authors do not "fully disempower the declension thesis" of Joseph Haroutunian as they had aimed to do.

18. Choiński, Michał. "A Cognitive Approach to the Hermeneutics of Jonathan Edwards's Sermons." *Jonathan Edwards Studies* 4.2 (2014) 215–27.

    Employs cognitive poetics to investigate the language of two Edwards sermons: "Punishment of the Wicked" and "Sinners in the Hands of an Angry God."

19. Chun, Chris. Review of *The Trinitarian Theology of Jonathan Edwards: Text, Context, and Application*, by Steven Studebaker and Robert Caldwell III. *Themelios* 39.3 (2014) 574–75.

    States, "I do not yield to all of the authors' interpretations of Edwards . . . nonetheless, their arguments demonstrate keen awareness of the theological issues involved, and are made with attention to meticulous details, which, in my opinion, ought to be commended."

20. Cooley, Daniel W. "The New England Theology and the Atonement: Jonathan Edwards to Edwards Amasa Park." PhD diss., Trinity International University, 2014.

    Argues that there is "a connected chain of thought" from Edwards to Park on the doctrine of atonement.

21. Crisp, Oliver. "Jonathan Edwards on the Trinity." *Jonathan Edwards Studies* 4.1 (2014) 21–41.

    Presents Edwards's doctrine of the Trinity along with the author's objections to some of Edwards's formulations.

22. ———. "On the Orthodoxy of Jonathan Edwards." *Scottish Journal of Theology* 67.3 (2014) 304–22.

    Discusses Edwards's idealism, occasionalism, and continuous-creationism and argues that these doctrines pose problems for maintaining an orthodox view of God and his relationship to evil.

23. Cunnington, Ralph. "A Critical Examination of Jonathan Edwards's Doctrine of the Trinity." *Themelios* 39.2 (2014) 224–40.

    Analyzes Edwards's doctrine of the Trinity with particular reference to the Holy Spirit. Argues that Edwards's philosophical idealism, use of analogies, and doctrine of perichoresis "created some problems" for his doctrine of the Trinity.

24. Davidson, Bruce W. "Narcissism: The Root of All Hypocrisy in the Theological Psychology of Jonathan Edwards." *Journal of the Evangelical Theological Society* 57.1 (2014) 135–45.

    Discusses Edwards's understanding of the self-deluding nature of self-love.

25. Davis, Oshea. *The Kingdom of the Son of His Love: Jonathan Edwards Sermons on the Christ*. N.p.: Lulu, 2014.

    Introduces readers to the theology of Edwards and offers a series of previously unpublished Edwards sermons on the doctrine of Christ.

26. Detrich, James P. "Sacramental Recital: Christological Use of Scripture in *A History of the Work of Redemption.*" PhD diss., Dallas Theological Seminary, 2014.

    Answers the question of how Jonathan Edwards uses Scripture in his 1739 discourse, *A History of the Work of Redemption*. "This study uniquely examines Edwards's usage of Scripture within a specific theological proposal—a historiographical argument for divine immanence."

27. Dochuk, Darren, et al., eds. *American Evangelicalism: George Marsden and the State of American Religious History.* Notre Dame, IN: University of Notre Dame Press, 2014.

    Honors George Marsden on the occasion of his retirement. Three chapters explore his work on Jonathan Edwards, including his biography, *Jonathan Edwards: A Life.*

28. Farris, Joshua R. Review of *After Jonathan Edwards: The Courses of the New England Theology*, edited by Oliver Crisp and Douglas Sweeney. *Southwestern Journal of Theology* 57.1 (2014) 125–26.

    Praises the volume as a "*tour de force* on matters concerning Edwardsian influence."

29. Finn, Nathan A. Review of *Jonathan Edwards and Justification by Faith*, by Michael McClenahan. *Southeastern Theological Review* 5.2 (2014) 263–65.

    Believes the author ably demonstrates his point.

30. ———. Review of *The Trinitarian Theology of Jonathan Edwards: Text, Context, and Application*, by Steven M. Studebaker and Robert W. Caldwell III. *Journal of the Evangelical Theological Society* 57.4 (2014) 870–74.

    Commends the book as a significant addition to the literature on Edwards's thought.

31. Fisk, Philip J. "Divine Knowledge at Harvard and Yale: From William Ames to Jonathan Edwards." *Jonathan Edwards Studies* 4.2 (2014) 151–78.

    Argues that a "significant shift" occurred in the conception of the doctrines of divine knowledge and freedom during the period between William Ames (1576–1633) and Jonathan Edwards.

32. Gin Lum, Kathryn. *Damned Nation: Hell in America from the Revolution to Reconstruction.* New York: Oxford University Press, 2014.

Tracks the development of the doctrine of hell from the American Revolution through the American Civil War and, prominently, Jonathan Edwards.

33. Hamilton, S. Mark. Review of *Jonathan Edwards and Scotland*, edited by Kenneth P. Minkema et al. *Scottish Journal of Theology* 67.2 (2014) 233–34.

    Says the book is "useful" but also suggests it is "not without some liabilities," including chapters of uneven quality and the absence of two essays presented at the conference upon which the volume was built.

34. Haykin, Michael A. G. Review of *The Legacy of Jonathan Edwards in the Theology of Andrew Fuller*, by Chris Chun. *Church History and Religious Culture* 94.3 (2014) 389–91.

    Believes "Chun clearly demonstrates that Fuller's debt to Edwards as both a missionary statesman and pastor-theologian is enormous."

35. Haykin, Michael A. G., and C. Jeffrey Robinson Sr. *To the Ends of the Earth: Calvin's Missional Vision and Legacy*. Wheaton: Crossway, 2014.

    Addresses long-standing misperceptions about Calvin's missionary vision and legacy. A chapter is devoted to Jonathan Edwards's missionary prayer life.

36. Helm, Paul. "Jonathan Edwards and the Parting of the Ways?" *Jonathan Edwards Studies* 4.1 (2014) 42–60.

    Responds to Richard Muller's "Jonathan Edwards and the Absence of Free Choice: A Parting of Ways in the Reformed Tradition" (2011) by challenging Muller's characterization of Reformed orthodox views on human freedom in general and Edwards's views in particular.

37. ———. "Turretin and Edwards Once More." *Jonathan Edwards Studies* 4.3 (2014) 286–96.

    Expresses appreciation for Muller's article "Jonathan Edwards and Francis Turretin" (2014) and offers a rejoinder.

38. Hordern, Joshua. "Loyalty, Conscience and Tense Communion: Jonathan Edwards Meets Martha Nussbaum." *Studies in Christian Ethics* 27.2 (2014) 167–84.

"Responds to Jeffrey Stout's argument in favor of immanent criticism of religious convictions in public reasoning by examining the affective dimension of religious loyalty and conscience."

39. Howe, Susan. *Spontaneous Particulars: The Telepathy of Archives.* New York: New Directions, 2014.

    Offers facsimiles of manuscripts from a number of writers, including Edwards.

40. Huggins, Jonathan. "Jonathan Edwards and Justification: Embodying a Living Tradition." *Journal of Reformed Theology* 8.2 (2014) 169–202.

    Examines Edwards's doctrine of justification and commends him as a "helpful resource" for contemporary Reformed theological thought.

41. ———. Review of *Edwards on the Christian Life*, by Dane Ortlund. *Jonathan Edwards Studies* 4.3 (2014) 383–85.

    Appreciates Ortlund's introduction to Edwards as a "trustworthy guide" to Edwards's main ideas.

42. Hulse, Erroll. *One in a Thousand: The Calling and Work of a Pastor.* Darlington: EP, 2014.

    Studies the office of pastor from Scripture and church history. Includes sections on "Jonathan Edwards, the Pastor as Theologian"; "The Impact of Jonathan Edwards on Church History"; "Edwards' Most Influential Books"; and "Edwards as an Example to Pastors."

43. Kim, Hyunkwan. "Jonathan Edwards's Reshaping of Lockean Terminology into a Calvinistic Aesthetic Epistemology in His *Religious Affections*." *Puritan Reformed Journal* 6.2 (2014) 103–22.

    Argues against Perry Miller's contention that Edwards's *Religious Affections* was developed within a Lockean framework. Contends that Edwards instead "transformed" Lockean terminology for his own theological purposes.

44. Kimble, Jeremy M. Review of *Jonathan Edwards and the Church*, by Rhys Bezzant. *Themelios* 39.2 (2014) 340–42.

    Praises the book as "an outstanding work on a topic that has not received the attention it rightly deserves."

45. ———. "That Their Souls May Be Saved: The Theology and Practice of Jonathan Edwards on Church Discipline." *Themelios* 39.2 (2014) 251–67.

    Presents the theological convictions which informed Edwards's practice of church discipline and excommunication.

46. Kling, David W. Review of *The Theology of Jonathan Edwards*, by Michael McClymond and Gerald McDermott. *Church History* 83.1 (2014) 216–18.

    Writes that "Edwards's legacy is now indisputable"; but whether he serves as a "bridging figure within the fragmented world of twenty-first-century Christianity" remains to be seen.

47. Knight, Henry H. Review of *The Trinitarian Theology of Jonathan Edwards: Text, Context, and Application*, by Steven Studebaker and Robert Caldwell III. *Wesleyan Theological Journal* 49.2 (2014) 295–97.

    Summarizes the content of the work and leaves it to readers to determine whether the book's thesis is correct. Offers a comparison of Edwards's theology with the Wesleyan tradition.

48. Kornu, Kimbell. "The Beauty of Healing: Covenant, Eschatology, and Jonathan Edwards' Theological Aesthetics: Toward a Theology of Medicine." *Christian Bioethics* 20.1 (2014) 43–58.

    Argues that Edwards's theology provides a "metaethic" for the field of bioethics.

49. Kreider, Glenn R. Review of *Jonathan Edwards's Theology: A Reinterpretation*, by Kyle Strobel. *Bibliotheca Sacra* 171.684 (2014) 500–501.

    Describes Strobel as having "provided an excellent summary introduction of Edwards's theology."

50. Landrum, Douglas Blake. "Jonathan Edwards's Exegetical Reflections of Genesis: A Puritan Literal Hermeneutic?" PhD diss., Mid-America Baptist Theological Seminary, 2014.

    Contends that Edwards generally adhered to Puritan exegetical methods while also being guilty of "typological excess."

51. Lane, Mary M. "What Ever Happened to Martha Root?" *Jonathan Edwards Studies* 4.1 (2014) 104–9.

    Chronicles a "controversial paternity case" late in Edwards's Northampton ministry.

52. Martin, James Alfred. *Beauty and Holiness: The Dialogue Between Aesthetics and Religion.* Princeton, NJ: Princeton University Press, 2014.

    Scans the development of the ideas of beauty and holiness and their use in theories of aesthetics and religion from the Bible to Wittgenstein and from India to Japan, including the ideas of Jonathan Edwards.

53. McDermott, Gerald. "Jonathan Edwards and God's Inner Life: A Response to Kyle Strobel." *Themelios* 39.2 (2014) 241–50.

    Surveys the state of Edwards studies with particular reference to theologians working on Edwards's doctrine of God. Addresses debates over dispositionalism and criticizes the use of analytical philosophy in evaluating Edwards's doctrine of God.

54. ———. Review of *Jonathan Edwards and Justification by Faith*, by Michael McClenahan. *The Journal of Religion* 94.4 (2014) 541–43.

    Believes the author "misses the complexity in Edwards's thought."

55. ———. "The 'Spiritual Music' of a Beautiful Word." *The Behemoth* 3 (2014). https://www.christianitytoday.com/behemoth/2014/issue-3/spiritual-music-of-beautiful-world-jonathan-edwards.html.

    Paraphrases Jonathan Edwards's "Beauty of the World" in contemporary English.

56. Moorhead, Jonathan. Review of *The Theology of Jonathan Edwards*, by Michael McClymond and Gerald McDermott. *The Master's Seminary Journal* 25.1 (2014) 117–19.

    Praises the work as "a significant contribution to Edwardsean studies" yet takes exception to the authors' idea that Edwards is useful as a "theological bridge" for ecumenical and interfaith dialogue. "In short, this is a reinvention of Edwards," the reviewer says.

57. Morimoto, Anri. Review of *The Workshop of Being: Religious Affections and their Pragmatic Value in the Thought of Jonathan Edwards and William James*, by Stephen Thomas Campagna-Pinto. *The Journal of Religion* 94.4 (2014) 548–50.

    Criticizes the book for its lengthy sentences, its lack of introductions and conclusions, and its lack of chapter summaries. "I find myself at a loss to draw any conclusion with which I could either agree or disagree. More than a series of chapters is required to make a book."

58. Muller, Richard A. "Jonathan Edwards and Francis Turretin on Necessity, Contingency, and Freedom of Will. In Response to Paul Helm." *Jonathan Edwards Studies* 4.3 (2014) 266–85.

    Argues, contra Helm, that Edwards's views were more deterministic than the older Reformed orthodox tradition.

59. Oppy, G., and N. N. Trakakis. *Early Modern Philosophy of Religion.* London: Routledge, 2014.

    Surveys leaders in the history of Western thought from the sixteenth to the eighteenth centuries, including leaders of the Protestant Reformation, Catholic Counter-Reformation, and Enlightenment. Edwards is treated in chapter 17 (pp. 223–34).

60. Ortlund, Dane. *Edwards on the Christian Life: Alive to the Beauty of God.* Theologians on the Christian Life. Wheaton, IL: Crossway, 2014.

    Maintains that the concept of beauty stood at the heart of Edwards's theology and permeated his portrait of the Christian life.

61. Pauley, Garth E. "Soundly Gathered Out of the Text? Biblical Interpretation in 'Sinners in the Hands of an Angry God.'" *Westminster Theological Journal* 76.1 (2014) 95–117.

    Posits that while Edwards relied on his Reformed and Puritan interpretive heritage for some of his sermon, Edwards also "neglects the historical and contextual analysis provided for by his interpretive heritage, and sometimes gleans unwarranted theological significance from the language of his text." Edwards also "gives the mistaken impression that his text deals in a central way with the theological topic that is the focus of the sermon."

62. Peterson, Cheryl M. "The Great Awakening as an 'Outpouring of the Spirit' in the Work of Redemption According to Jonathan Edwards: A New Interpretive Framework." *Jonathan Edwards Studies* 4.1 (2014) 61–80.

    Reasons that Edwards understood the Great Awakening revivals as "another in the long progression of outpourings of the Spirit to prepare and revitalize the people of God for the final dispensation, not as events which themselves would inaugurate the millennial reign of Christ."

63. Reklis, Kathryn. *Theology and the Kinesthetic Imagination: Jonathan Edwards and the Making of Modernity.* New York: Oxford University Press, 2014.

    Evaluates Edwards's theology in its eighteenth-century religious context and examines contemporary questions in Christian theology about the role of bodily experience, beauty, and desire as sources and methods for theological inquiry.

64. Robinson, Marilynne. "Jonathan Edwards in a New Light." *Humanities: The Magazine of the National Endowment for the Humanities* 35 (2014) 14–17, 45.

    Robinson said that in college she was assigned to read Edwards's *The Great Christian Doctrine of Original Sin Defended* and found that she was liberated. This is a basic exposition of *Original Sin*.

65. Ruetenik, Tadd. "Beauty, Horror, and Tragedy: The Idea of Hell in Jonathan Edwards and William James." *Philosophy & Theology* 26.1 (2014) 19–37.

    Compares and contrasts Edwards and James on the doctrine of hell. Argues that Edwards remains "aloof" to the suffering of others while James remains "tragically tied" to others' suffering.

66. Schuit, John. Review of *The Power of God: A Jonathan Edwards Commentary on the Book of Romans*, edited by David S. Lovi and Benjamin Westerhoff. *McMaster Journal of Theology and Ministry* 15 (2013–14) 1–5.

    Commends the editors of the volume for demonstrating the relevance of Edwards's thought for the church, not just the academy. Cautions that sometimes Edwards quotes are given without proper consideration of context. Additionally, there is "no reasoned engagement with the current scene on Edwards's behalf."

67. Schultz, Walter J. "Jonathan Edwards' Argument That God's End in Creation Must Manifest His Supreme Self-Regard." *Jonathan Edwards Studies* 4.1 (2014) 81–103.

    Presents Edwards's view that "only God can be God's original ultimate end in creation."

68. ———. "Jonathan Edwards' Philosophical Argument Concerning God's End in Creation." *Jonathan Edwards Studies* 4.3 (2014) 297–326.

Summarizes Edwards's concept of God's purpose and motive in creating the world.

69. Stahle, Rachel S. *The Great Work of Providence: Jonathan Edwards for Life Today*. Eugene, OR: Cascade, 2014.

    Offers a popular-level treatment of Edwards's theology and argues that Edwards's doctrine of the Trinity was the foundation of his entire theological system.

70. Stetina, Karin Spiecker. Review of *Jonathan Edwards and Justification*, edited by Josh Moody. *Trinity Journal* 35.2 (2014) 356–59.

    Applauds the book as a welcome addition to Edwardsean studies.

71. Stievermann, Jan. "Faithful Translations: New Discoveries on the German Pietist Reception of Jonathan Edwards." *Church History* 83 (2014) 324–66.

    Compares and contrasts two German translations, one Lutheran and one Reformed, of Edwards's *Faithful Narrative*, published in 1738.

72. ———. "Studying the History of American Protestantism Through Jonathan Edwards: Versions of 'America's Theologian' at Mid-Century." *Jonathan Edwards Studies* 4.2 (2014) 179–97.

    Suggests that Edwards's national and international reception offer significant potential as interpretive lenses for studying the trajectories of American Protestantism.

73. Stoever, William K. B. "Godly Mind: Puritan Reformed Orthodoxy and John Locke in Jonathan Edwards's Conception of Gracious Cognition and Conviction." *Jonathan Edwards Studies* 4.3 (2014) 327–52.

    Considers Edwards's theory of regenerate cognition and conviction.

74. ———. Review of *Fullness Received and Returned: Trinity and Participation in Jonathan Edwards*, by Seng-Kong Tan. *Themelios* 39.3 (2014) 594–95.

    Warns that the work suffers from "several major drawbacks," including (1) an a-historical reading of Edwards; (2) spending too little time interacting with Edwards scholars and too much time with the broad tradition; and (3) "seem[ing] to ignore" the secondary literature.

75. ———. Review of *Jonathan Edwards and Justification by Faith*, by Michael McClenahan. *The Journal of Theological Studies* 65.1 (2014) 343–45.

　　Reviewer says, "McClenahan accomplishes what no scholar has been able to achieve, which is to outline in great detail the precise polemical context within which Edwards's doctrine of justification was forged, and to show how this forms his view." Also critiques the work for failing to consider questions of development in Edwards's thought.

76. Strunk, Stephen R. "Destiny by Design: Understanding the Doctrine of the Curse in the Thought of Augustine, Martin Luther, Jonathan Edwards, and Karl Barth." ThM thesis, Grand Rapids Theological Seminary, 2014.

　　Explores the doctrine of original sin in the teachings of Jonathan Edwards and others.

77. Tan, Seng-Kong. *Fullness Received and Returned: Trinity and Participation in Jonathan Edwards*, by Seng-Kong Tan. Minneapolis: Fortress, 2014.

　　Argues that human participation in the divine, an idea usually associated with Eastern Orthodoxy, is a central theme in the theology of Edwards as well.

78. VanBrugge, David. "The Full Brightness and Diffused Beams of Glory: Jonathan Edwards' Concept of Beauty and Its Relevance for Apologetics." *Puritan Reformed Journal* 6.1 (2014) 124–42.

　　Presents Edwards's doctrine of divine beauty and contends that "beauty, as Edwards understood it, needs to be rediscovered."

79. Vlastuin, Willem van. "A Retrieval of Jonathan Edwards's Concept of Free Will: The Relevance for Neuroscience." *Jonathan Edwards Studies* 4.2 (2014) 198–214.

　　Argues that Edwards's compatibilist view of determinism and free will may offer a better paradigm than the common view of neuroscience, which uses determinism to deny free will.

80. Whitefield, George. "When Whitefield Met Edwards." *Banner of Truth* 610 (2014) 1.

　　Reflections of Whitefield in his journal when he met Jonathan Edwards. He said, "Their pastor's name is Edwards . . . a solid and excellent Christian. . . . I think I have not seen his fellow [an equal] in all New England." When Edwards opened his pulpit to Whitefield, he said, "both minister and people wept much"; he felt "great satisfaction at the home of Mr. Edwards." As to Sarah he said, "A sweeter couple I have not yet seen."

81. Whitney, Donald S. *Finding God in Solitude: The Personal Piety of Jonathan Edwards and Its Influence on His Pastoral Ministry.* American University Studies 7: Theology and Religion. New York: Peter Lang, 2014.

    Explores Edwards's personal piety and its impact on his public ministry, especially his relationships, preaching, and publications.

82. Winiarski, Douglas L. "New Perspectives on the Northampton Communion Controversy II: Relations, Professions, and Experiences, 1748–1760." *Jonathan Edwards Studies* 4.1 (2014) 110–45.

    Presents documents relating to the controversy that led to Edwards's dismissal from Northampton. The second installment in a five-part series.

83. ———. "New Perspectives on the Northampton Communion Controversy III." *Jonathan Edwards Studies* 4.3 (2014) 353–82.

    Presents documents relating to the controversy that led to Edwards's dismissal from Northampton. The third installment in a five-part series.

84. Woo, B. Hoon. "Is God the Author of Sin? Jonathan Edwards' Theodicy." *Puritan Reformed Journal* 6 (2014) 98–123.

    Summarizes Edwards's theodicy in ten statements: (1) when Adam sinned, God was not the author of sin; (2) all the events in the universe are decreed by wisdom, not by chance; (3) Adam's fall results from the privation of God's active efficiency; (4) the perverted free choice of humanity is the cause of sin; (5) the effect of the secondary cause is reduced to the first cause in regards to being and perfection, but not in regards to defect; (6) the notion of co-causality admits both God's preserving the existence of the will and Adam's sinning; (7) in the revealed will of God, sin is not permitted. In the secret will of God, however, Adam's sin is permitted; (8) those who consider all things, especially the final cause of the Fall, can concede that it was decreed by God for a perfectly wise and holy purpose; (9) the Fall is the occasion of Christ's becoming the head of believers; and (10) Arminian arguments cannot solve this problem.

85. Zakai, Avihu. Review of *After Jonathan Edwards: The Courses of New England Theology*, edited by Oliver Crisp and Douglas Sweeney. *The Journal of Ecclesiastical History* 65.1 (2014) 216–17.

   Commends the book as "a unique interdisciplinary contribution to the reception of Edwardsean ideas."

2015

1. Allen, Russell J. "The Beautiful Mystery: Examining Jonathan Edwards' View of Marriage." *Bound Away: The Liberty Journal of History* 1.1 (2015). http://digitalcommons.liberty.edu/vol1/iss1/3.

   Presents Edwards's theological understanding of the sanctity of marriage.

2. Ball, Carol. *Approaching Jonathan Edwards: The Evolution of a Persona*. Farnham, UK: Ashgate, 2015.

   Explores the inner life of Edwards and his journey from introvert to public intellectual by tracing the development of his persona through the many conflicts in which he was engaged over the course of his life.

3. Barshinger, David P. "Spite or Spirit? Jonathan Edwards on the Imprecatory Language in the Psalms." *Westminster Theological Journal* 77 (2015) 53–69.

   Concludes that Edwards's interpretation suggests Christians should read, pray, and sing these texts while acknowledging the tension of interpreting the Psalms in this way.

4. Beck, Peter. Review of *After Jonathan Edwards: The Courses of the New England Theology*, edited by Oliver Crisp and Douglas Sweeney. *Fides et Historia* 47.1 (2015) 210–12.

   Declares that "Crisp and Sweeney have assembled the best in their fields and crafted a volume of useful, readable works."

5. Boss, Robert L. *God-Haunted World: The Elemental Theology of Jonathan Edwards*. Fort Worth, TX: JESociety, 2015.

   Offers "a visual exploration of the nexus between Scripture and Nature in the theology of Edwards. Methods of data visualization and associative thinking have been used to illustrate the vast network of Edwards' emblematic thought."

6. Bräutigam, Michael. Review of *Jonathan Edwards and the Church*, by Rhys Bezzant. *The Expository Times* 126.11 (2015) 556.

    Assesses the book as "a highly valuable resource for students and professionals" in getting to understand the "person, work and context of Jonathan Edwards in general, and of his nuanced vision of the church in particular."

7. Carpenter, Roy. *Théologie et Lumières: Jonathan Edwards Entre Raison et Réveil*. Paris: Ampelos, 2015.

    Explores the balance Edwards struck between the intellectual heritage of the Enlightenment and revivalist religion and how it impacted his thought on a range of issues.

8. Chamberlain, Ava. Review of *Jonathan Edwards and the Church*, by Rhys Bezzant. *The Journal of Religion* 95.4 (2015) 540–42.

    Commends the book for being the first "synthetic analysis of Edwards's ecclesiology."

9. Chapman, Mark. "Models of Conversion in American Evangelicalism: Jonathan Edwards, Charles Hodge and Old Princeton, and Charles Finney." PhD diss., Marquette University, 2015.

    Considers the appropriateness of identifying "conversionism" as a common feature of evangelicalism by demonstrating the widely diverging views on the topic in the history of the movement.

10. Chun, Chris. Review of *The Theology of Jonathan Edwards*, by Michael McClymond and Gerald McDermott. *International Journal of Systematic Theology* 17.3 (2015) 363–65.

    Welcomes the book as "a force to be reckoned with."

11. Cochran, Elizabeth Agnew. "The Moral Significance of Religious Affections: A Reformed Perspective on Emotions and Moral Formation." *Studies in Christian Ethics* 28.2 (2015) 150–62.

    Uses the works of Edwards as the foundation for a study of emotion from a Reformed perspective. Considers Reformed theology's "singular understanding" of virtue as love for God and neighbor and how it roots the emotions in the human will.

12. Crawford, Brandon James. "Jonathan Edwards: Theologian of God's Glory in Christ." *Puritan Reformed Journal* 7 (2015) 120–42.

    Proposes that Edwards should be remembered first and foremost as a man who championed the God's glory in Christ.

13. Crisp, Oliver. *Jonathan Edwards Among the Theologians.* Grand Rapids: Eerdmans, 2015.

    Surveys Edwards's theological and philosophical thought on such topics as the Trinity, creation, original sin, free will, and preaching and brings Edwards into dialogue with other prominent theologians from church history.

14. ———. Review of *Jonathan Edwards and the Gospel of Love,* by Ronald Story. *International Journal of Systematic Theology* 17.3 (2015) 346–48.

    Commends the book for emphasizing aspects of Edwards's social concerns that have often been overlooked, but worries that it may come at the cost of minimizing the "less appealing aspects of Edwards' visage."

15. ———. Review of *The Theology of Jonathan Edwards,* by Michael McClymond and Gerald McDermott. *Scottish Journal of Theology* 68.3 (2015) 368–70.

    Expresses gratitude for "a monument which begins to do justice to the importance and influence of the Sage of Northampton."

16. DeOliveira, Charles Melo. "The Human Heart in the View of John Calvin, Jonathan Edwards and Wilhelmus a Brakel: With Particular Reference to the Presbyterian Church in Brazil and the Pentecostal Influences Upon Her." ThM thesis, Puritan Reformed Theological Seminary, 2015.

    Explores the constitutional nature of the human heart in Calvin, Edwards, and Brakel, considered in light of Pentecostal influence on the Presbyterian Church in Brazil.

17. Detzler, Wayne A. "Jonathan Edwards, Slavery, and Africa Missions." *Evangelical Review of Theology* 39 (2015) 229–42.

    Posits that Edwards played a key role in the emergence of Protestant missions, which included both the abolition of slavery and the evangelization of Africa.

18. Dever, Mark E. "Believers Only: Jonathan Edwards on Communion." *Bibliotheca Sacra* 172 (2015) 259–67.

    Presents Edwards's doctrine of the visible church and its implications for the sacrament of Communion.

19. Farris, Joshua R. Review of *Jonathan Edwards' Bible: The Relationship of the Old Testament and New Testament*, by Stephen R. C. Nichols. *Southwestern Journal of Theology* 58.1 (2015) 133–35.

    Promotes the book as "an exceptional contribution to Jonathan Edwards's studies and hermeneutics."

20. Fennema, Scott R. Review of *Fullness Received and Returned: Trinity and Participation in Jonathan Edwards*, by Seng-Kong Tan. *Jonathan Edwards Studies* 5.2 (2015) 180–81.

    Believes the greatest scholarly contribution of the book is the author's insight regarding Edwards's "iterative reliance upon the Spirit as being an Augustinian *vinculum amoris*." Yet, the book's value is limited by the author's failure to develop the meaning of the concept.

21. Finn, Nathan. Review of *Jonathan Edwards and the Psalms: A Redemptive-Historical Vision of Scripture*, by David P. Barshinger. *Themelios* 40.2 (2015) 325–26.

    Thinks the book reads too much like a dissertation, but it will still be profitable to a wide audience.

22. Fisk, Philip J. "Jonathan Edwards (1703–58) on Freedom of Perfection: Establishing the Shift Away from the Classic-Reformed Tradition of Freedom of the Will." PhD diss., Evangelische Theologische Faculteit, Leuven, Belgium, 2015.

    Argues that Edwards parted ways with the standard view of Reformed orthodoxy on the issues of freedom of will, contingency, and necessity.

23. Garretson, James M. Review of *After Jonathan Edwards: The Courses of New England Theology*, edited by Oliver Crisp and Douglas Sweeney. *Banner of Truth* 616 (2015) 31–32.

    Assesses although "the book is expensive, the essay are of a high quality and valuable for the historical insights which they provide."

24. Gray, Patrick. Review of *From Jonathan Edwards to Rudolph Bultmann*. Vol. 2 of *History of New Testament Research*, by Christoph Stenschke. *The Catholic Biblical Quarterly* 77.3 (2015) 544–46.

    Appreciates the work for contributing to a greater awareness of the history of biblical interpretation and theology.

25. Hall, Richard A. "Jonathan Edwards on the 'Flying' Spider: A Model of Ecological Thought in Microcosm." *Jonathan Edwards Studies* 5.1 (2015) 3–19.

    Summarizes "Of Insects" and compares this work to other studies in entomology from Edwards's time. Concludes that the work is similar to those of naturalists Ray, Lister, and Leeuwenhoek.

26. Hamilton, S. Mark. "Jonathan Edwards, Anselmic Satisfaction, and God's Moral Government." *International Journal of Systematic Theology* 17.1 (2015) 46–67.

    Presents the Anselmic satisfaction theory of Christ's atonement and the moral government theory and discounts the notions that Edwards articulated the former and gave impetus to the latter.

27. Hastings, W. Ross. *Jonathan Edwards and the Life of God: Toward an Evangelical Theology of Participation.* Minneapolis: Fortress, 2015.

    Expounds on Edwards's doctrine of *theosis* in its three relations: the Trinity, the hypostatic union, and believers with Christ, and brings Edwards into dialogue with patristic and Reformed authors.

28. Hopf, Christopher Jeffrey. "A Grand Juxtaposition: Jonathan Edwards and Charles Finney on Justification in Revival." ThM thesis, Dallas Theological Seminary, 2015.

    Surveys the doctrine of justification in church history, Edwards's doctrine, then Finney's, and finally a comparison of the two.

29. Hoselton, Ryan. "Jonathan Edwards, the Inner Witness of the Spirit, and Experiential Exegesis." *Jonathan Edwards Studies* 5.2 (2015) 90–120.

    Demonstrates the ways in which Edwards drew from the traditions of experimental piety in his Scriptural exegesis. Argues that Edwards's emphasis on the role of the Spirit's inner testimony in biblical interpretation impacted laity in populist evangelical identity.

30. ———. Review of *Jonathan Edwards and the Psalms: A Redemptive-Historical Vision of Scripture*, by David P. Barshinger. *Jonathan Edwards Studies* 5.1 (2015) 80–82.

    Commends the book as "a tremendous resource to Edwards studies and the history of biblical interpretation" while also arguing that its arguments are "strained and overstated" at times.

31. Jung, Peter B. "Jonathan Edwards and New England Arminianism." PhD diss., University of the Free State, South Africa, 2015.

    Presents a history of Arminianism in Dutch, English, and New England Arminianism contexts along with Edwards's critique.

32. Klaassen, Maarten. Review of *Living Justification: A Historical-Theological Study of the Reformed Doctrine of Justification in the Writings of John Calvin, Jonathan Edwards, and N. T. Wright*, by Jonathan Huggins. *Journal of Reformed Theology* 9.4 (2015) 413–15.

    Finds the chapter on Calvin the least convincing, and the work "disappointing" overall for its lack of detailed analysis.

33. Kreider, Glenn R. Review of *Jonathan Edwards and the Church*, by Rhys Bezzant. *Bibliotheca Sacra* 172.686 (2015) 250–51.

    Recommends the book "not just for Edwardsean scholars but also for church leaders, especially those interested in learning from the past how to do ministry in the present and future."

34. Landrum, Doug. *Jonathan Edwards' Exegesis of Genesis: A Puritan Hermeneutic?* Mustang, OK: Tate, 2015.

    Provides a comprehensive treatment of Edwards's exegetical reflections on the book of Genesis and measures them against a Puritan hermeneutic.

35. Lawson, Steven J. "The Life and Legacy of Jonathan Edwards (Part 1)." *Expositor* 8 (2015) 41–43.

    Reflects on the importance of life and ministry on Jonathan Edwards.

36. Lowe, John T. Review of *Finding God in Solitude: The Personal Piety of Jonathan Edwards (1703–1758) and Its Influence on His Pastoral Ministry*, by Donald S. Whitney. *Jonathan Edwards Studies* 5.1 (2015) 85–87.

    Appreciates the book for "providing a well-polished treatment of this pivotal eighteenth-century pastor. . . . This book is a great example of how pastors can learn from Edwards, and why he matters today."

37. McDermott, Gerald R. Review of *Jonathan Edwards and the Church*, by Rhys Bezzant. *Church History* 84.2 (2015) 452–54.

    Calls the work "beautifully written" and "elegantly executed study." Argues that it is pivotal for Edwards studies and Protestant ecclesiology.

38. McDermott, Gerald R., and Ronald Story. *The Other Jonathan Edwards: Selected Writings on Society, Love, and Justice.* Amherst: University of Massachusetts Press, 2015.

    Seeks to provide a corrective to the stereotype of Edwards as a hellfire preacher with selected writings demonstrating Edwards's compassion, social conscience, commitment to love and justice, etc.

39. Minkema, Kenneth P. Review of *Approaching Jonathan Edwards: The Evolution of a Persona*, by Carol Ball. *Jonathan Edwards Studies* 5.2 (2015) 177–79.

    Commends the work as a "useful, 'dirt-moving' study."

40. ———. Review of *Jonathan Edwards and the Life of God: Toward an Evangelical Theology of Participation*, by W. Ross Hastings. *Jonathan Edwards Studies* 5.1 (2015) 83–84.

    Praises the book as a contribution to scholars, specialists, and pastors searching for ministry resources.

41. Nichols, Stephen J. "Jonathan Edwards and Preaching in a Postmodern World." *Expositor* 4 (2015) 30–33.

    Thinks of how Edwards might help preachers today in the age of Postmodernism. "In this regard, Edwards might prove rather helpful." "Three things in particular stand out." Edwards points out that: (1) Christianity is about knowing; (2) Christianity is not reduced to knowing; and (3) preaching is "about imparting to knowledge, but it is not reduced to imparting knowledge."

42. Pauw, Amy Plantinga. Review of *The Trinitarian Theology of Jonathan Edwards: Text, Context, and Application*, by Steven Studebaker and Robert Caldwell III. *Journal of Reformed Theology* 9.1 (2015) 84–85.

    Writes that the book's greatest strength is that it gives historical and theological context for Edwards's Trinitarian thinking and gives several contemporary concerns.

43. Pollock, Darren M. "The Exegetical Basis of Jonathan Edwards' Cessationism." *Jonathan Edwards Studies* 5.2 (2015) 121–37.

    Examines several sermons by Edwards to show the exegetical basis for his belief that the "extraordinary gifts" of the Spirit ceased with the close of the apostolic age.

44. Rainey, David. Review of *Jonathan Edwards and Justification by Faith*, by Michael McClenahan. *The Evangelical Quarterly* 87.2 (2015) 182–83.

    Acclaims the book as a significant contribution to the body of literature on justification by faith as well as a valuable contribution to the ever-increasing number of works on Edwards.

45. Reddinger, William. "'Virtue and 'True Virtue': Competing Ethical Philosophies in the American Founding Era." *The Journal of Church and State* 59.1 (2015) 23–42.

    Suggests that America had "shared language of virtue" (such as Thomas Kidd and Mark Noll maintain) but this overlooks the fact that "many in the American Founding were Edwardsians who opposed a broader, republican conception of virtue."

46. Rehnman, Sebastian. "Towards a Solution to the 'Perennially Intriguing Problem' of the Sources of Jonathan Edwards' Idealism." *Jonathan Edwards Studies* 5.2 (2015) 138–55.

    Contends that Edwards developed his idealism from the sources he relied upon in the fields of logic, ethics, physics, and metaphysics.

47. Rigney, Joe. Review of *Jonathan Edwards on God and Creation*, by Oliver Crisp. *Themelios* 40.3 (2015) 549–51.

    Disagrees with Crisp's interpretation of Edwards on the topic of persistence, yet still believes "Crisp's book offers a comprehensive and careful treatment of his subject."

48. Schmidt, Darren. "'Different Streams . . . into the Same Great Ocean': Jonathan Edwards, Robert Millar, and Transatlantic Influence on a History of the Work of Redemption." *Jonathan Edwards Studies* 5.1 (2015) 20–43.

    Compares Edwards's *History of the Work of Redemption* with Scottish clergyman Robert Millar's *History of the Propagation of Christianity* (3rd ed., 1731), which Edwards owned, and *History of the Church Under the Old Testament* (1730), which Edwards did not own. Believes the similarities reveal appropriation of Millar's writings on the part of Edwards.

49. Schwanda, Tom. Review of *Finding God in Solitude: The Personal Piety of Jonathan Edwards (1703–1758) and Its Influence on Pastoral Ministry*, by Donald S. Whitney. *Spiritus* 15.2 (2015) 255–57.

Suggests the book as a text for undergraduate courses and believes it could help "those more conversant with this subject" to understand the larger context of Edwards's piety.

50. Schweitzer, William M., ed. *Jonathan Edwards for the Church: The Ministry and the Means of Grace.* Welwyn Garden City, UK: EP, 2015.

    Offers the papers presented at the Jonathan Edwards for the Church Conference held in Durham, England, in February 2014. Features articles from Gerald R. McDermott, William M. Schweitzer, Roy Mellor, John D. Payne, John J. Murray, Douglas Sweeney, Stephen R. C. Nichols, Nicholas T. Batzig, Michael Brautigam, and William Macleod.

51. ———. Review of *The Power of God: A Jonathan Edwards Commentary on the Book of Romans*, edited by David S. Lovi and Benjamin Westerhoff. *Reviews in Religion and Theology* 22.1 (2015) 44–46.

    Determines that the work is useful as biblical commentary but not as a scholarly resource as quotations from Edwards are extracted from all of his writings—early and late, public and private—without any apparent consideration given to context.

52. Smith, Ted A. "From Silkworms to Songbirds: Why We No Longer Preach Like Jonathan Edwards." *Commonwealth: A Review of Religion, Politics, and Culture*, Oct. 9, 2015. 16–21.

    Explains the cultural shifts which moved preachers from "typology" to "illustrations" in their sermons.

53. Snoddy, Richard M. Review of *After Jonathan Edwards: The Courses of the New England Theology*, edited by Oliver Crisp and Douglas Sweeney. *Ecclesiology* 11.3 (2015) 403–5.

    Praises the book as "an excellent collection of essays."

54. ———. Review of *Jonathan Edwards and the Church*, by Rhys Bezzant. *Ecclesiology* 11.2 (2015) 268–70.

    Declares the book to be of the "first rank" work of Edwards scholarship, offering fresh readings of familiar texts.

55. Stegeman, Daniel. "The Pastoral Theology of Jonathan Edwards: Reflections from Nine Ordination Sermons." MA thesis, Gordon-Conwell Theological Seminary, 2015.

Answers the question, "What does it mean to be a pastor according to Jonathan Edwards?" by reviewing the contents of his ordination sermons.

56. Stein, Stephen J. Review of *Jonathan Edwards and the Psalms: A Redemptive-Historical Vision of Scripture*, by David P. Barshinger. *Church History* 84.4 (2015) 901–2.

    Commends the work for its treatment of Edwards's exegetical principles.

57. Stetina, Karin Spiecker. Review of *The Trinitarian Theology of Jonathan Edwards: Text, Context, and Application*, by Steven Studebaker and Robert Caldwell III. *Trinity Journal* 36.1 (2015) 142–44.

    Acclaims the book as an "excellent starting point into Edwards's Trinitarian theology."

58. Strobel, Kyle, ed. *The Ecumenical Edwards: Jonathan Edwards and the Theologians*. Farnham, UK: Ashgate, 2015.

    Brings together prominent Catholic, Orthodox, and Protestant theologians to evaluate Edwards's thought. Each chapter places Edwards in dialogue with a specific theological tradition on a specific issue.

59. ———. Review of *Finding God in Solitude: The Personal Piety of Jonathan Edwards (1703–1758) and Its Influence on His Pastoral Ministry*, by Donald S. Whitney. *Themelios* 40.1 (2015) 152–54.

    Disagrees with the book's presuppositions and questions if they will hinder its usefulness.

60. ———. Review of *Jonathan Edwards and the Psalms: A Redemptive-Historical Vision of Scripture*, by David P. Barshinger. *The Journal of Theological Studies* 66.2 (2015) 859–60.

    Believes the author has "developed a reasonable and well-articulated argument for Edwards's exegetical method through the Psalms."

61. Sumner, George. Review of *Living Justification: A Historical-Theological Study of the Reformed Doctrine of Justification in the Writings of John Calvin, Jonathan Edwards, and N. T. Wright*, by Jonathan Huggins. *Anglican Theological Review* 97.4 (2015) 710–11.

    Praises the book for its clear presentation, "though the book is clearly born of a dissertation."

62. Thomas, David R. "'They Cannot Forbear Crying Out'—A Critical Study of Travailing Prayer as a Pattern of Preparedness for Revival, Examining It Historically in the Theology and Practice of Jonathan Edwards and Charles Finney." PhD diss., Asbury Theological Seminary, 2015.

   Identifies twelve characteristics of travailing prayer as advocated and practiced by two "seminal leaders" in American history and explores how travailing prayer has been used in Christian history as preparation for revival.

63. Van Der Knijff, Cornelis, and Willem van Vlastuin. "Why Edwards Did Not Understand Thomas Boston: A Comparison of Their Views on the Covenants." *Jonathan Edwards Studies* 5.1 (2015) 44–57.

   Posits that Edwards did not "understand" Boston's covenant theology in the sense that he did not believe it made theological sense. Edwards, in contrast to Boston, taught a three-fold covenant scheme.

64. Waddington, Jeffery C. "Which Comes First, the Intellect or the Will? Alvin Plantinga and Jonathan Edwards on a Perennial Question." *The Confessional Presbyterian* 11 (2015) 121–28.

   Assesses Edwards's and Plantinga's views and gives a critique of the latter's presentation of the Edwards position.

65. Woznicki, Christopher. "Bad Books and the Glorious Trinity: Jonathan Edwards on the Sexual Holiness of the Church." *McMaster Journal of Theology and Ministry* 16 (2014–15) 151–76.

   Explains how Edwards's doctrine of the Trinity informed his sexual ethics and, specifically, how it informed his decisions regarding the "Bad Book Case."

66. ———. "The Son in the Hands of a Violent God? Assessing Violence in Jonathan Edwards's Covenant of Redemption." *Journal of the Evangelical Theological Society* 58.3 (2015) 583–97.

   Answers that the Covenant of Redemption, as Edwards articulates it, does not meet the criteria for an act of violence as the Son freely consents to entering the covenant in Edwards's system.

67. Yeager, Jonathan. "An Early Printing of a Sermon by Edwards." *Jonathan Edwards Studies* 5.2 (2015) 156–76.

   Reprint of a sermon by Edwards on Revelation 14:2, preached in November 1734, and appearing in the English journal *The Biblical Magazine* in 1801.

68. ———. "Samuel Kneeland and Daniel Henchman: Jonathan Edwards' Chief Printer and Publisher in Boston." *Jonathan Edwards Studies* 5.1 (2015) 58–77.

    Positions Kneeland and Henchmen in the context of the colonial Boston book trade and examines their role in the publication and distribution of Edwards's works.

69. Yong, Amos. Review of *The Other Jonathan Edwards: Selected Writings on Society, Love, and Justice*, by Gerald R. McDermott and Ronald Story. *International Journal of Public Theology* 9.4 (2015) 480–82.

    Thanks the authors for providing a new perspective for those working in the area of public theology.

2016

1. Allen, Russell J. "Holy Children Are Happy Children: Jonathan Edwards and Puritan Childhood." MA thesis, Liberty University, 2016.

    Posits that Edwards bridged Puritan and Enlightenment ideas about childhood as seen in his addresses to children.

2. Beach, Mark J. Review of *Jonathan Edwards Among the Theologians*, by Oliver D. Crisp. *Mid-America Journal of Theology* 27 (2016) 192–93.

    Writes, "Crisp is a keen thinker; and he has given us an insightful book on the keen mind of Jonathan Edwards."

3. Beck, Peter. "Training Up Children in the Way That They Should Go: Jonathan Edwards's Advice to Young Converts." *Puritan Reformed Journal* 8.1 (2016) 225–37.

    Reviews personal letters that Edwards sent to young converts.

4. Bezzant, Rhys S. "Remind, Rebuke, Refocus: Three Correctives After Investigating Edwards's Use of 'Known by God.'" *Evangelical Review of Theology* 40.3 (2016) 217–31.

    Recasts "the vision of Edwards" to "recast our own assumption about epistemology, hermeneutics, and spirituality in light of Edwards's insights."

5. Blaauw, Corné. "'An Holy and Beautiful Soul': Jonathan Edwards on the Humanity of Christ." *Jonathan Edwards Studies* 6.1 (2016) 16–30.

   Contends that a full study of Edwards's Christology that takes into account his exegetical and sermonic material is warranted, which leads to the conclusion that his doctrine of Christ's humanity was both "historic and insightful."

6. Boss, Sarah. "Edwards and Thoreau: Typologies of Lakes." *Augustine Collective*, April 1, 2016. http://augustinecollective.org/augustine/edwards-and-thoreau-typologies.

   Compares Edwards's typology of lakes found in his *Images of Divine Things* to Thoreau's *Walden*. Boss finds that although they come from different backgrounds—Edwards's continuity with Puritan tradition and Thoreau's transcendental context—they both "meditate on the exact same image of water." However, Boss finds that they come to conflicting opinions about the typologies of lakes.

7. Bowden, Zachary M. "The Speckled Bird: Nathanael Emmons, Consistent Calvinism, and the Legacy of Jonathan Edwards." PhD diss., Southwestern Baptist Theological Seminary, 2016.

   Demonstrates that Nathanael Emmons's "theological development" depended on his relationship to Edwards.

8. ———. Review of *Jonathan Edwards and the Church*, by Rhys Bezzant. *The Journal of Theological Studies* 67.2 (2016) 857–59.

   Commends the book as a work of scholarship which "clearly displays the richness of Edwards's ecclesiology."

9. ———. Review of *The Theology of Jonathan Edwards*, by Michael McClymond and Gerald McDermott. *The Journal of Theological Studies* 67.2 (2016) 855–57.

   States that the authors have produced "a comprehensive view" of Edwards's work and the world while also providing "a framework by which to comprehend Edwards's extensive theological project."

10. Brown, Robert E. Review of *Jonathan Edwards and the Psalms: A Redemptive-Historical Vision of Scripture*, by David P. Barshinger. *Trinity Journal* 37.2 (2016) 292–94.

    Declares the book to be a "welcome addition" to a neglected area of Edwards studies, but wishes that more time had been devoted to "analytical engagement with [Edwards's] interlocutors on the Psalms, with contemporary Edwards scholarship, and with Edwards's broader theological corpus."

11. ———. Review of *Jonathan Edwards on God and Creation*, by Oliver Crisp. *Religious Studies Review* 42.2 (2016) 132.

    Contends that the book's contribution is to evaluate the strength and weakness of Edwards's thought. It is not hagiographical for modern theologians to emulate.

12. ———. Review of *Theology and the Kinesthetic Imagination: Jonathan Edwards and the Making of Modernity*, by Kathryn Reklis. *Church History* 85.4 (2016) 849–51.

    Argues that the strength of the book is its attempt to place Edwards's theology of revivals and of the body in historical context.

13. Campos, Heber Carlos de, Jr. "Jonathan Edwards Sobre a Liberdada Humana: Reformado ou Näo?" *Fides Reformata* 21.2 (2016) 67–96.

    Discusses the question of whether Edwards's doctrine of free will is fully consistent with Reformed orthodox teaching.

14. Carpenter, Roy. *Théologie et Lumières: Jonathan Edwards Entre Raison et Réveil*. Paris: Ampelos, 2016.

    Reprint. Introduces the life and work of Jonathan Edwards to a French audience.

15. Choiński, Michał. *The Rhetoric of the Revival: The Language of the Great Awakening Preachers*. Göttingen: Vandenhoeck & Ruprecht, 2016.

    Identifies a series of novel rhetorical techniques employed by Great Awakening preachers which later became standard fare among revivalists. Also explores the impact of these rhetorical techniques on colonial America.

16. Davidson, Bruce W. "Not From Ourselves: Holy Love in the Theology of Jonathan Edwards." *The Journal of the Evangelical Theological Society* 59.3 (2016) 571–84.

    Explains the difference between the modern concept of love and love as Edwards understood it. Develops Edwards's concept of holy love as something that exalts God, pursues ethical purity, values truth, embraces rationality, produces deep humility, and fixes its attention on heavenly realities.

17. De Klerk, Jenny-Lyn. Review of *Formed for the Glory of God: Learning from the Spiritual Practices of Jonathan Edwards*, by Kyle Strobel. *Pneuma Review* 19.2 (2016). http://pneumareview.com/kyle-strobel-formed-for-the-glory-of-god.

    Believes the book is useful for those want to revive "their devotional practices by grounding them in Scripture and learning from the saints of old."

18. Everhard, Matthew. "A Theology of Joy: Jonathan Edwards and Eternal Happiness in the Holy Trinity." DMin thesis, Reformed Theological Seminary, 2016.

    Explores "the universal human quest to find joy." The presupposition of this paper is that one can only find joy in the Triune God, and this thesis "examines the theology of Puritan Jonathan Edwards (1703–1758) on this important topic." He wrote on this subject frequently, and several of "his most important extant works will be considered here."

19. Finn, Nathan A. Review of *Edwards the Exegete: Biblical Interpretation and Anglo-Protestant Culture on the Edge of the Enlightenment*, by Douglas A Sweeney. *Themelios* 41.1 (2016) 150–51.

    Lauds the book as a "first-rate work of historical scholarship that fills a gaping hole in Edwards studies" and "highly recommended."

20. ———. Review of *Finding God in Solitude: The Personal Piety of Jonathan Edwards (1703–1758) and Its Influence on His Pastoral Ministry*, by Donald S. Whitney. *Journal of Spiritual Formation & Soul Care* 9.1 (2016) 135–36.

    Appreciates the academic work represented in the book but also notes that it is "more prescriptive than most historical studies." As such, "Whitney's approach to Edwards is too presentist a strategy to be embraced by most historians," though it might be of interest to contemporary readers regarding the topic of spiritual formation.

21. ———. Review of *Jonathan Edwards Among the Theologians*, by Oliver D. Crisp. *Southeastern Theological Review* 7.2 (2016) 144–47.

    Appreciates the book's "extensive, stimulating, and sometimes vexing interpretations of 'America's theologian.'"

22. ———. Review of *Jonathan Edwards for the Church: The Ministry and the Means of Grace* by Rhys Bezzant. *The Southern Baptist Journal of Theology* 20.1 (2016) 163–65.

Contends that the book is necessary because it combines serious scholarship with a writing style accessible to a lay readership—a rare combination. It does not contain anything that advances Edwards Studies, but that is okay because the book was not written to advance scholarship; it was written to "prompt change in the contemporary church."

23. ———. Review of *The Ecumenical Edwards: Jonathan Edwards and the Theologians*, edited by Kyle Strobel. *Southeastern Theological Review* 7.2 (2016) 144–47.

    Believes the chapters are uneven and do not engage Edwards as well as others.

24. Fisk, Philip J. *Jonathan Edwards's Turn from the Classic-Reformed Tradition of Freedom of the Will*. Göttingen: Vandenhoeck & Ruprecht, 2016.

    Reappraises Edwards's *Freedom of the Will* and seeks to demonstrate, based upon a comparison with Harvard and Yale commencement theses and quaestiones, that Edwards departed from Reformed orthodoxy on the matters of freedom of will, contingency, and necessity.

25. Garretson, James M. Review of *Jonathan Edwards and the Psalms*, by David P. Barshinger. *Banner of Truth* 633 (2016) 32.

    Reflects on Barshinger's important work on the Psalms.

26. Gurr, Nigel A. "A Comparison of Jonathan Edwards and Charles Hodge on the Doctrine of Conversion." ThM thesis, Westminster Theological Seminary, 2016.

    Compares the theology of conversions in the thoughts of Edwards and Hodge. Lists a number of reasons for the comparison: (1) the importance of conversion; (2) the proven value of the teaching of each theologian; and (3) factors related to difference in their calling and historical contexts.

27. Gwon, Gyeongcheol. Review of *Jonathan Edwards Among the Theologians*, by Oliver D. Crisp. *Westminster Theological Journal* 78.2 (2016) 355–57.

    States that the work is "well researched and lucid"; however, he questions the author's decision to place Edwards alongside Anselm, Arminius, and Girardeau given their different contexts. He also wonders why the author chose not to consider Edwards's relationship to Reformed Scholasticism.

28. Hamilton, S. Mark. "Jonathan Edwards, Hypostasis, Impeccability, and Immaterialism." *Neue Zeitschrift für systematische Theologie und Religionsphilosophie* 58.2 (2016) 206–28.

    Unpacks Edwards's understanding of Christ's human nature and demonstrates how it can be used to support the notion of Christ's impeccability without suffering from the liabilities of the soul-body metaphysic known as interactionism.

29. ———. "Jonathan Edwards on the Election of Christ." *Neue Zeitschrift für systematische Theologie und Religionsphilosophie* 58.4 (2016) 525–48.

    Posits that Edwards was supralapsarian in his doctrine of election and explores how this affected his doctrines of union with Christ and atonement. Considers whether Edwards's formulation gave impetus to the doctrine of hypothetical universalism.

30. Hannah, John D. "Jonathan Edwards's Thoughts on Prayer." *Bibliotheca Sacra* 173.689 (2016) 80–96.

    Recounts Edwards's prayer life and discusses how Edwards regarded prayer as a delight more than a duty because, in Edwards's words, "God never begrutches his people anything they desire, or are capable of, as being good to 'em."

31. Hastings, W. Ross. "Jonathan Edwards on the Trinity: Its Place and Its Rich but Controversial Facets." *The Journal of the Evangelical Theological Society* 59.3 (2016) 585–600.

    Summarizes the state of scholarship on Edwards's doctrine of the Trinity and addresses five questions related to his doctrine: (1) the model: does Edwards simply follow the typical western Augustinian model of the Trinity or is his a cobbled mix of Eastern and Western influences? (2) novelty: did Edwards, in accordance with his desire, in fact contribute something new in the tradition? (3) ontology: did Edwards reflect a dispositional ontology in his way of understanding the Godhead? (4) revelation: how does Edwards see the relationship between the immanent and economic Trinity? and (5) pneumatology: does Edwards espouse a new emphasis on pneumatology within the Reformed-Puritan tradition?

32. Haykin, Michael A. G. "A Previously Uncatalogued Letter." *Jonathan Edwards Studies* 6.1 (2016) 81–83.

    Publishes a previously uncatalogued letter found in the Angus Library, Regent's Park College, University of Oxford. The letter comes from Stockbridge, is dated November 21, 1757, and is addressed to Joseph Bellamy. The letter discusses the council of ministers that will convene at Stockbridge to help Edwards determine whether he should accept the offer to become the next president of the College of New Jersey.

33. Helm, Paul. "Jonathan Edwards, John Locke, and the Religious Affections." *Jonathan Edwards Studies* 6.1 (2016) 3–15.

    Demonstrates that Edwards's fascination with Locke wasn't a "mere adolescent infatuation" but was a lifelong interest.

34. Horton, Michael S. "Panentheism and Jonathan Edwards." *Modern Reformation* 25.3 (2016) 66.

    Discusses the differences between pantheism and panentheism and then the varieties of the latter. Claims that Edwards was a panentheist and offers an explanation as to why this is problematic from a confessional Reformed perspective.

35. Hurd, Ryan M. "Jonathan Edwards's View of That Great Act of Obedience: Jesus' Laying Down His Life." *Westminster Theological Journal* 78.2 (2016) 271–86.

    Demonstrates that Edwards viewed Christ's so-called "passive" obedience as his "principle act" of obedience and commends this understanding to the readership—Christ's death should not just be seen as the satisfaction of God's justice but also as an act of righteousness in fulfillment of God's law.

36. Hurh, Paul. *American Terror: The Feeling of Thinking in Edwards, Poe, and Melville*. Stanford, CA: Stanford University Press, 2016.

    Explores "American literature's distinctive tone of terror through a close study of three authors . . . who not only wrote works of terror, but who defended, theorized, and championed it."

37. Hussey, Phillip. "Jesus Christ as the 'Sum of God's Decrees': Christological Supralapsarianism in the Theology of Jonathan Edwards." *Jonathan Edwards Studies* 6.2 (2016) 107–19.

    Argues that Edwards adopted a "form of Christological supralapsarianism" which understands the divine decrees in the following arrangement: (1) the triune God decrees to communicate the fullness of the Godhead through the second person of the Trinity; (2) the decree to communicate God's fullness in the Son is creative; and (3) the creative decree also entails God's desire to draw the creature into fellowship through the Son's taking on creaturely existence, in particular the existence of a human being.

38. ———. Review of *Jonathan Edwards and the Life of God: Toward an Evangelical Theology of Participation*, by W. Ross Hastings. *International Journal of Systematic Theology* 18.3 (2016) 341–43.

   Suggests that the author "would have benefited from more consistent engagement with Edwards's immediate historical context . . . as well as important secondary literature," but does appreciate the pastoral overtones of the work.

39. ———. Review of *Theology and the Kinesthetic Imagination: Jonathan Edwards and the Making of Modernity*, by Kathryn Reklis. *The Journal of Ecclesiastical History* 67.3 (2016) 668–69.

   Says the author's conclusion "fails to convince" as it bifurcates reason and affection, the public and the private, which contradicts the union between them that Edwards labored to maintain in works like *Religious Affections*.

40. James, Nicholas Kyle. "The False Dichotomy of the Laity: Rejuvenating Evangelicalism with Jonathan Edwards' Doctrine of the Priesthood of All Believers." *Journal of Contemporary Theological Studies* 3 (2016) 1–14.

   Exemplifies the priesthood of all believers in the sermons and practical theology of Jonathan Edwards.

41. Kellicut, Jordan. Review of *Jonathan Edwards and the Life of God: Toward an Evangelical Theology of Participation*, by W. Ross Hastings. *Stone-Campbell Journal* 19.2 (2016) 251–52.

   Praises the book for its deeply pastoral concerns. Furthermore, "Edwards, despite his deficiencies, is treated fairly."

42. Kirkland, E. Trevor. "Jonathan Edwards and Psalmody." *Free Church Witness* 10 (2016) 16–18.

   Reviews the main points of Barshinger's *Edwards and the Psalms* and reiterates that Edwards relied exclusively on the psalms for congregational singing in worship while making use of hymns at summer afternoon gatherings.

43. Kreider, Glenn R. Review of *Jonathan Edwards and Justification*, edited by Josh Moody. *Bibliotheca Sacra* 170.680 (2016) 503–5.

    Offers a summary of each chapter and concludes that the work is "packed with excellent contents."

44. ———. Review of *Jonathan Edwards and the Psalms: A Redemptive-Historical Vision of Scripture*, by David P. Barshinger. *Bibliotheca Sacra* 173.289 (2016) 115–16.

    Praises the book for being "comprehensively and competently researched and carefully and clearly written."

45. Lawson, Steven J. "The Life and Legacy of Jonathan Edwards, pt. 2." *Expositor* 9 (2016) 48–51.

    Summarizes the life of Edwards, particularly of his seventy resolutions from the Great Awakening to his untimely death in 1758.

46. Leader, Jennifer L. *Knowing, Seeing, Being: Jonathan Edwards, Emily Dickinson, Marianne Moore and American Typological Interpretation.* Amherst: University of Massachusetts Press, 2016.

    Argues that the eighteenth-century theologian Jonathan Edwards, the nineteenth-century poet Emily Dickinson, and the twentieth-century poet Marianne Moore "share heretofore under-recognized set of religious and philosophical preoccupations." Most commonly, the "Protestant tradition of typology, a rigorous mode of interpreting scripture," and natural "phenomena are read as the fulfillment of prophecy."

47. Lowe, John T. Review of *Jonathan Edwards Among the Theologians*, by Oliver D. Crisp. *Jonathan Edwards Studies* 6.1 (2016) 84–85.

    Says the author provides "a great constructive theological reading of Edwards. His work is concise, right with new insights, and opens new doors to Edwards's theology."

48. Marsden, George M. Review of *The Other Jonathan Edwards: Selected Writings on Society, Love, and Justice*, by Gerald R. McDermott and Ronald Story. *Early American Literature* 51.3 (2016) 701–3.

    Appreciates the work but believes some of the readings could be omitted as "a bit pedestrian." Wishes the authors had included Edwards's sermon "A Divine and Supernatural Light."

49. Masui, Shitsuyo. "Female Piety and Evangelical Ritualization of Death: Abigail Hutchinson's Conversion in 'A Faithful Narrative.'" *Jonathan Edwards Studies* 6.2 (2016) 120–34.

　　Notes that Edwards's "Faithful Narrative" includes two prominent narratives of female converts, Abigail Hutchinson and Phebe Bartlet, which are then treated as exemplars of biblical piety in evangelical publications throughout the nineteenth century.

50. McClymond, Michael. "Analogy: A Neglected Theme in Jonathan Edwards and Its Pertinence to Contemporary Theological Debates." *Jonathan Edwards Studies* 6.2 (2016) 153–75.

　　Posits that the diagrams appearing in Edwards's philosophical writings "contain clues," leading one to conclude that a doctrine of analogy undergirds his whole approach to theology.

51. McDermott, Gerald. "Jonathan Edwards and Islam." *Jonathan Edwards Studies* 6.2 (2016) 93–106.

　　Demonstrates that Edwards knew more about Islam than most in his day, accurately predicting that it would rise to become a dominant world player, and outlines Edwards's theology of religions.

52. Minkema, Kenneth P. Review of *Knowing, Seeing, Being: Jonathan Edwards, Emily Dickinson, Marianne Moore, and the American Typological Tradition*, by Jennifer L. Leader. *Jonathan Edwards Studies* 6.1 (2016) 86–87.

　　Appreciates the book, noting the common Reformed heritage drawn upon by such diverse figures as Edwards, Dickinson, and Moore, and invites the reader to wonder what other figures might share this commonality.

53. Okubo, Masatake. "Tokutaro Takakura's Work Towards the Development of Evangelical Christianity in Japan: With Some References to Jonathan Edwards." *Jonathan Edwards Studies* 6.2 (2016) 135–52.

　　Recounts the ministry of a prominent early twentieth-century Japanese evangelical and the relation of his theology of Edwards.

54. Pass, Bruce. Review of *Jonathan Edwards Among the Theologians*, by Oliver D. Crisp. *Reviews in Religion & Theology* 23.3 (2016) 281–83.

　　Says the author moves "very quickly" from premise to conclusion regarding Edwards's thoughts on divine simplicity and panentheism. Even so, the work is a "fine opus of engaging short essays."

55. Pauw, Amy Plantinga. Review of *Jonathan Edwards and the Psalms: A Redemptive-Historical Vision of Scripture*, by David P. Barshinger. *Journal of Reformed Theology* 10.2 (2016) 183–84.

    Commends the author for recognizing Edwards's concern for moral formation as he expounded the Psalms.

56. ———. Review of *Theology and the Kinesthetic Imagination: Jonathan Edwards and the Making of Modernity*, by Kathryn Reklis. *Scottish Journal of Theology* 69.3 (2016) 372–73.

    Praises the works for (1) setting Edwards in the context of the whole transatlantic world and (2) directing attention to the "kinesthetic imagination," which describes "the complex ways in which cultural memory is transmitted and recreated in bodily performance." Concludes by declaring "this ground-breaking book deserves a wide readership."

57. Payne, Jon D. "Jonathan Edwards: Missionary to the Indians." *The Evangelical Times* 50.2 (2016) 23, 29.

    Tells the story of Edwards's arrival in Stockbridge and surveys an early sermon.

58. Potgieter, Esmari. "Jonathan Edwards and a Reformational View of the Purpose of Education." *In die Skriflig* 50.1 (2016) 1–9.

    Explores three philosophical themes in Edwards which may serve to develop an overall philosophy of education: (1) knowledge as the true perception of relations; (2) human beings as creation's consciousness; and (3) sound morality as arising from true perception.

59. Rempel, Brent Anders. "The Invisible Redemption of God: Justification and Union with Christ in Jonathan Edwards and Seventeenth-Century Puritanism." MA thesis, Providence Theological Seminary, 2016.

    Argues that Edwards reflects mainstream Puritan thought but also adds to the tradition by identifying the infusion of grace at salvation as the Holy Spirit. He posits faith as the bond of this union, and in so doing makes it a non-causal condition of justification.

60. Salladin, James. "Nature and Grace: Two Participations in the Thought of Jonathan Edwards." *International Journal of Systematic Theology* 18.3 (2016) 290–303.

Claims Edwards employed both ontological and soteriological categories of participation but did not embed one into the other, rendering them complementary and facilitating a clear distinction between nature and grace.

61. Schultz, Walter. "The Metaphysics of Jonathan Edwards's *End of Creation*." *Journal of the Evangelical Theological Society* 59.2 (2016) 339–59.

    Identifies the metaphysical commitments of Edwards as dispositionalism, emanationism, idealism, panentheism, anti-platonism, continuous creationism, and occasionalism.

62. Schweitzer, William M. "'A Point of Infinite Consequence': Jonathan Edwards' Experimental Calvinism on Trial." *Banner of Truth Magazine* 635–36 (2016) 44–55.

    Asks the questions "Did Edwards have, and expect that every Christian should have, a 'dramatic' conversion experience of soul-wrenching' proportions?" and "Did Edwards' insistence upon genuine regenerate experience undermine the ordinary means of grace and covenantal Christian nurture?" Answers both questions in the negative.

63. ———. Review of *The Trinitarian Theology of Jonathan Edwards: Text, Context, and Application*, by Steven Studebaker and Robert Caldwell III. *The Journal of Theological Studies* 67.1 (2016) 367–69.

    Champions the book as "a triumph of good scholarship and cogent theological discourse."

64. Song, J. Gaius. Review of *The Power of God: A Jonathan Edwards Commentary on the Book of Romans*, edited by David S. Lovi and Benjamin Westerhoff. *The Expository Times* 127.8 (2016) 411.

    Publishes a "unique compilation" that is a "welcome event." Further, "it may even contribute to" Edwards "contemporary debate on fundament doctrines such as justification by faith, original sin, and covenant theology, among others."

65. Strobel, Kyle. "Jonathan Edwards's Reformed Doctrine of Theosis." *Harvard Theological Review* 109.3 (2016) 371–99.

    Suggests that studying Edwards's doctrine of theosis through the lens of neo-Platonism has led to the false conclusion that Edwards's views were outside the bounds of Reformed orthodoxy. By moving from a philosophical to a theological perspective, however, one is able to discern that Edwards's views "rest on firmly Protestant foundations and result in recognizably Reformed conclusions," while also containing "distinctive" and "innovative elements."

66. ———. Review of *Approaching Jonathan Edwards: The Evolution of a Persona*, by Carol Ball. *The Journal of Theological Studies* 67.1 (2016) 366–67.

    Writes, "it could be that Ball overstates some of the aspects of Edwards's experience and agenda to generate and control a persona, and makes these a bit too central to Edwards's life and ideology." Yet, "her work is also helpful in that it shine[s] a light on this feature of his thought."

67. Sutanto, Nathaniel Gray. Review of *Jonathan Edwards Among the Theologians*, by Oliver D. Crisp. *International Journal of Systematic Theology* 18.3 (2016) 353–55.

    Offers two negative critiques of the work: (1) "the impetus behind reading two thinkers in tandem is at times unclear" and (2) "one may wish that a greater measure of constructive and normative considerations had been brought to bear in the monograph."

68. Sweeney, Douglas A. *Edwards the Exegete: Biblical Interpretation and Anglo-Protestant Culture on the Edge of the Enlightenment*. Oxford: Oxford University Press, 2016.

    Reconstructs the historical context of Edwards's exegesis and then describes his place within his tradition. Summarizes Edwards's four main approaches to biblical exegesis as (1) canonical; (2) Christological; (3) redemptive-historical; and (4) pedagogical. Also compares Edwards's exegetical work to that of his partners in debate.

69. Thuesen, Peter J. Review of *The Notorious Elizabeth Tuttle: Marriage, Murder, and Madness in the Family of Jonathan Edwards*, by Ava Chamberlain. *The Journal of Religion* 96.3 (2016) 392–94.

    Lauds the work as "one of the best social histories of colonial New England published in a generation."

70. Van Wyk, John. "'To Understand Things as Well as Word': An Examination of Jonathan Edwards as an Educator and His Pedagogical Methodology." PhD diss., Trinity Evangelical Divinity School, 2016.

    Seeks to reveal Edwards as an educator as much as a minister, theologian, and philosopher. Considers Edwards's pedagogical methodology, which worked to move students from passive recipients to active participants in the learning process. Also considers the impact of this pedagogical method on the development of the New Divinity.

71. Vlastuin, Willem van. "Jonathan Edwards' *Spiritualis*: Towards a Reconstruction of His Theology of Spirituality." *Journal for the History of Reformed Pietism* 2.1 (2016) 23–46.

    Considers Edwards's spirituality and develops a fourfold framework for understanding his doctrine: (1) spiritual union with Christ is the basis for all spiritual blessings which flow to the Christian; (2) spiritual union with Christ is the means by which Christians participate in the divine nature; (3) Edwards's spirituality is "pneumatocentric"; and (4) the anthropocentric parts of his spirituality are grounded in his theocentric outlook.

72. Willemsen, Gerald F. Review of *Theology and the Kinesthetic Imagination: Jonathan Edwards and the Making of Modernity*, by Kathryn Reklis. *Journal of Reformed Theology* 10.1 (2016) 92–93.

    Believes the author may confuse Edwards's understanding of passions and affections and may have erred in developing her argument using performance discourse, which would have been "foreign to Edwards's self-understanding." Nevertheless, says the author has produced a "pleasantly written, readable study of Edwards."

73. Winiarski, Douglas L. *Darkness Falls on the Land of Light: Experiencing Religious Awakening in Eighteenth-Century New England*. Chapel Hill: University of North Carolina Press, 2016.

    Examines the spiritual experiences of ordinary people in eighteenth-century New England, drawing principally from letters, diaries, and personal testimonies.

74. ———. "New Perspectives on the Northampton Communion Controversy IV: Experience Mayhew's Dissertation on Edwards's Humble Inquiry." *Jonathan Edwards Studies* 6.1 (2016) 31–80.

    Publishes a newly discovered manuscript relating to the communion controversy, which ultimately drove Edwards from his Northampton parish. "Mayhew remained convinced that the standards for membership in New England's Congregational churches should encompass a broad range of knowledge and experience."

75. Yeager, Jonathan M. *Jonathan Edwards and Transatlantic Print Culture*. Oxford: Oxford University Press, 2016.

Tells the story of how Edwards's works were published, including the personalities involved, the process of editing, printing, and publishing the works, details such as the paper, binding, formats, etc., and how these factors shaped the reception of Edwards's published works.

76. Yeo, Ray S. *Renewing Spiritual Perception with Jonathan Edwards: Contemporary Philosophy and the Theological Psychology of Transforming Grace.* Transcending Boundaries in Philosophy and Theology Series. London: Routledge, 2016.

    Revisits Edwards's doctrine of spiritual perception, incorporating insights from recent work in the field of philosophy of emotions. Concludes that Christocentric wisdom is the heart of transforming grace and Christian virtue formation.

77. Zhu, Victor. Review of *The Ecumenical Edwards: Jonathan Edwards and the Theologians*, edited by Kyle Strobel. *The Expository Times* 127.11 (2016) 569–70.

    Summarizes how these essays "present a much-needed study of Edwards's theology in an ecumenical context . . . despite the fact that around half of the contributors are not Edwardsian scholars."

2017

1. Barshinger, David P. Review of *Jonathan Edwards and Transatlantic Print Culture*, by Jonathan Yeager. *Fides et Historia* 49.2 (2017) 105–7.

    Quibbles with Yeager's claim that the positive reception Edwards's books received had "just as much" to do with the marketing and packaging of the books as it did with the thinking and writing abilities of the author, but praises the work overall as a valuable contribution to the field.

2. Bezzant, Rhys S., ed. *The Global Edwards: Papers from the Jonathan Edwards Congress Held in Melbourne, August 2015.* Australian College of Theology Monographs. Eugene, OR: Wipf & Stock, 2017.

    Collects essays exploring Edwards's worldwide impact. Includes chapters on Edwards's legacy in Britain, Australia, China, and Poland. Other chapters include explorations of various doctrines held by Edwards and how his theology has been interpreted by others.

3. ———. Review of *Jonathan Edwards Among the Theologians*, by Oliver Crisp. *Theology Today* 73.4 (2017) 402–3.

Offers high praise for the book as "Crisp's philosophical steel-trap mind pulls apart Edwards's own words to uncover tensions, convergences and even possible contradictions in Edwards's speculative theological project, which pulls out the rug from under the feet of many of Edwards's homeboys." Nevertheless, he critiques the book for its "eccentric" selection of theologians to place in conversation with Edwards and for its lack of discussion on historical contexts.

4. Boss, Robert L. *Bright Shadows of Divine Things: The Devotional World of Jonathan Edwards.* Fort Worth, TX: JESociety, 2017.

Introduces readers to a devotional frame of mind, including how to be attentive to spiritual things in everyday life. Offers a general introduction to Edwards and then moves to a series of chapters that explore Revelation, the Trinity, Creation, Providence and Purpose, Suprahuman Beings, Humanity, the Church, and Last Things from a devotional perspective.

5. Brown, Robert E. Review of *Edwards the Exegete: Biblical Interpretation and Anglo-Protestant Culture on the Edge of the Enlightenment*, by Douglas A. Sweeney. *Church History* 86.3 (2017) 904–6.

Lauds the book as "a welcome addition to the field" which will be of particular interest to intellectual historians, Edwards scholars, and those interested in the history of biblical interpretation.

6. Caldwell, Robert W. *Theologies of the American Revivalists: From Whitefield to Finney.* Downers Grove, IL: IVP Academic, 2017.

Presents the theological views of leading revival preachers, including Edwards, Wesley, Bellamy, Hopkins, and Finney. Includes discussions of the New Divinity, Taylorism, Baptist revival theology, Princeton theology, and the Restorationist movement.

7. Chang, Nathan W. "The Legacy of Jonathan Edwards in the Founder of American Deaf Education: An Historical Theology of Thomas Hopkins Gallaudet." PhD diss., Trinity International University, 2017.

Surveys the doctrines taught to Thomas Hopkins Gallaudet during his time at Yale and Andover and considers how he appropriated Edwards's thought.

8. Cochran, Joseph T. Review of *Jonathan Edwards Among the Theologians*, by Oliver Crisp. *Themelios* 42.1 (2017) 180–82.

   Submits that the author "misconstrues Edwards at times." For example, "Edwards would be appalled to be considered a panentheist."

9. ———. Review of *Jonathan Edwards and the Church*, by Rhys Bezzant. *Trinity Journal* 38.1 (2017) 123–25.

   Praises the author's diachronic approach but believes his "attempt to repristinate Edwards as a moderate is not convincing" and perhaps even contradictory of the author's main thesis.

10. Congrove, Mark J. "The Presence and Priority of the Spiritual Disciples in the Sermons of Jonathan Edwards." DMin thesis, Dallas Theological Seminary, 2017.

    Articulates that Edwards "established the practice of promoting spiritual exercise that has come to shape his earlier years as a young man and disciple" and evaluated "seven hundred sermons" "searching for the presence and application of these particular spiritual exercises."

11. Crawford, Brandon James. *Jonathan Edwards on the Atonement: Understanding the Legacy of America's Greatest Theologian*. Eugene, OR: Wipf & Stock, 2017.

    Traces the development of the doctrine of atonement from the Apostolic Fathers to Jonathan Edwards. Concludes that Edwards's doctrine of atonement brings penal substitution and moral government together into a single, coherent theory.

12. Crisp, Oliver D. "Moral Character, Reformed Theology, and Jonathan Edwards." *Studies in Christian Ethics* 30.3 (2017) 262–77.

    Offers Edwards as a counter-example to the theory that Reformed theology is "antipathetic" to virtue theory.

13. Crocco, Stephen D. Review of *The Other Jonathan Edwards: Selected Writings on Society, Love, and Justice*, by Gerald McDermott and Ronald Story. *The Journal of Presbyterian History* 95.2 (2017) 81–82.

    Summarizes the book and then asks why Edwards continues to be caricatured as a hellfire preacher when scholars have been showing the "other" Edwards for so long. Answers that "Edwards's unwavering belief in judgment, damnation and hell . . . gives people reasons to caricature and ignore him, the other Edwardses notwithstanding."

14. Dominski, Lolly. "The Religious Affections in Presbyterian Church (USA) Liturgy." PhD diss., Garrett-Evangelical Theological Seminary, 2017.

    Considers how the liturgy of the Presbyterian Church (USA) as outlined in the *Book of Common Prayer* "encourages a range of religious affections that reflect the Reformed understanding of Christian character." Includes a discussion on Jonathan Edwards, who coined the term "religious affections."

15. Doyle, Peter Reese, et al., eds. *Jonathan Edwards on the New Birth in the Spirit: An Introduction to the Life, Times, and Thought of America's Greatest Theologian.* Durham, NC: Torchflame, 2017.

    Develops Edwards's doctrine of the "new birth," which includes a sense of the glory of God, a sense of one's own sinfulness, and a humble acceptance of the sacrifice of Christ.

16. Every, Samuel Stephen. "An Exploration of the Diary as a Medium: During the Seventeenth and Eighteenth Centuries." BS thesis, Vassar College, 2017.

    Explores American diaries from the 1600s and 1700s to explore the unique contribution of diaries as a literary genre. Considers how diaries function, for whom they are written, their place in manuscript culture, and the kinds of people who kept diaries.

17. Farris, Joshua R., and Ryan A. Brandt. "Ensouling the Beatific Vision: Motivating the Reformed Impulse." *Perichoresis: The Theological Journal of Emanuel University* 15.1 (2017) 67–84.

    Surveys the beatific vision and has three parts: (1) introducing relevant biblical material; (2) developing a theological interpretation of those passages; and (3) presenting the history of the doctrine in both medieval and Reformed theology, of which Edwards is a part of that theological tradition.

18. Fennema, Scott. "George Berkley and Jonathan Edwards on Idealism: Considering an Old Question in Light of New Evidence." *Intellectual History Review*, November 7, 2017. http://dx.doi.org/10.1080/17496977.2017.1388030.

    Argues, contrary to the commonly accepted view, that Edwards developed his Idealism from the writings of George Berkeley.

19. Finn, Nathan A., and Jeremy Kimble, eds. *A Reader's Guide to the Major Writings of Jonathan Edwards.* Wheaton, IL: Crossway, 2017.

    Offers beginning readers of Edwards an introduction to his historical context, suggests reading strategies, and offers contemporary applications of Edwards's thought. Contents include chapters on spiritual writings and revival writings as well as introductions to *Justification by Faith Alone*; *Religious Affections*; *The Life of David Brainerd*; *Freedom of the Will*; *Original Sin*; and *A History of the Work of Redemption*. An appendix by John Piper considers his own personal journey with Edwards.

20. Fitzgerald, Frances. *The Evangelicals: The Struggle to Shape America.* New York: Simon & Schuster, 2017.

    Follows the rise and development of American evangelicalism from its beginning at the Great Awakening, through the North/South split in the nineteenth century, to the fundamentalist/modernist conflict in the early twentieth century, and then to the revival of evangelicalism under Billy Graham, its politicization under Jerry Falwell and Pat Robertson, and its current state.

21. Friend, Nathan. "Inventing Revivalist Millennialism: Edwards and the Scottish Connection." *Journal of Religious History* 41.1 (2017) 1–20.

    Argues that the 1740s stand as a unique decade in that Jonathan Edwards and other ministers created a synthesis between revival, social progress, and millennialism—a synthesis which would characterize religious movements throughout the nineteenth and twentieth centuries.

22. Geissler, Suzanne. Review of *Jonathan Edwards Among the Theologians*, by Oliver Crisp. *Anglican and Episcopal History* 86.1 (2017) 112–14.

    States that the book is not for the casual reader as it requires deep familiarity with Edwards's thought in order to follow its development. Also wonders why the author chose the historical individuals he did and why they are not presented in chronological order. Nevertheless, the book "belongs on the shelf of the serious Edwards scholar."

23. Gierer, Emily Dolan. "Monstrous Confessions: Early American Women and the Dangers of Divine Revelation." *Jonathan Edwards Studies* 7.1 (2017) 2–25.

   Describes the religious experiences of Sarah Edwards in 1742 and how they were moderated by Edwards in his published account. Describes the public confessions of women in general and gives particular attention to the words and influence of Anne Hutchinson.

24. Griffith, Christopher Ryan. "Promoting Pure and Undefiled Religion: John Ryland, Jr. (1753–1825) and Edwardsean Evangelical Biography." PhD diss., Southern Baptist Theological Seminary, 2017.

   Explains how Edwards and his heirs used biography as a vehicle for teaching Christian doctrine and piety. Argues specifically that John Ryland Jr. purposefully adopted Edwards's biographical methods when composing his biography of Andrew Fuller.

25. Gullotta, Daniel N. Review of *Jonathan Edwards and Transatlantic Print Culture*, by Jonathan Yeager. *Wesley and Methodist Studies* 9.2 (2017) 191–92.

   Explores print culture in colonial America, and Yeager's book "does not disappoint as the first systematic study of the intersection of print culture." It is a "must-read" for those "interested in Jonathan Edwards and how books were produced in colonial America."

26. Halambiec, Kamil M. "Jonathan Edwards and Charles Finney on the Theology and Methodology of Religious Revivals." STM thesis, Yale Divinity School, 2017.

   Intends to compare the methodology of "Edwards' and Finney's theology in historical-biographical context."

27. Hall, Kevin David. "Jonathan Edwards and Sanctification: The Pursuit of Happiness Found in Union and Obedience." PhD diss., Southern Baptist Theological Seminary, 2017.

   Suggests that Edwards supplies an element to sanctification often missing in contemporary evangelicalism, namely, an emphasis on happiness rooted in one's union with Christ.

28. Hamilton, S. Mark. "Re-Thinking Atonement in Jonathan Edwards and New England Theology." *Perichoresis: The Theological Journal of Emanuel University* 15.1 (2017) 85–99.

   Argues against those who claim Edwards embraced penal substitution while his followers embraced moral government. Suggests a more nuanced perspective that begins with a consideration of their respective views on the nature and demands of divine justice.

29. ———. Review of *The Ecumenical Edwards: Jonathan Edwards and the Theologian*, edited by Kyle Strobel. *Southwestern Journal of Theology* 59.2 (2017) 255–57.

    Extols the collection of essays as "strong, technical, and . . . accessible."

30. ———. *A Treatise on Jonathan Edwards, Continuous Creation and Christology*. Fort Worth, TX: JESociety, 2017.

    Tackles Edwards's understanding of the relationship between God and the universe and how it bears upon his doctrine of Christ.

31. Hamilton, Stephen James. *Born Again: A Portrait and Analysis of the Doctrine of Regeneration Within Evangelical Protestantism*. Göttingen: Vandenhoeck & Ruprecht, 2017.

    Explains the doctrine of regeneration with an exposition of Scripture texts as well as "close readings" of Philipp Jakob Spener, Jonathan Edwards, Friedrich Schleiermacher, and Charles Finney.

32. Hancock, C. Layne. "Edwards' Copy of William Ames' Medulla." *Jonathan Edwards Studies* 7.1 (2017) 55–61.

    Describes the author's discovery of Edwards's copy of Ames's *Medulla* in the stacks of the Beinecke Rare Book and Manuscript Library at Yale University. Offers images and descriptions of the volume.

33. ———. Review of *Jonathan Edwards Among the Theologians*, by Oliver Crisp. *The Journal of Religion* 97.4 (2017) 558–60.

    Extols the work as "a benchmark in the career of one of the most important Edwards scholars today." It plows "new and controversial ground in the field while remaining ever charitable, constructive, and thought provoking."

34. Hannafey, Francis T. Review of *Jonathan Edwards Among the Theologians*, by Oliver Crisp. *Theological Studies* 78.1 (2017) 245–46.

    Says the book is a "wealth of insight," offering "a thoughtful introduction to and careful analysis of Edwards's theology."

35. Hannah, John D. Review of *Jonathan Edwards and the Life of God: Toward an Evangelical Theology of Participation*, by W. Ross Hastings. *Bibliotheca Sacra* 174.694 (2017) 252–56.

Concludes the book is a model of serious scholarly research "regardless of one's evaluation of the validity of the assertions," such as the author's claim that evangelicalism's anthropocentrism is owing to Edwards while the solution to it is Barth.

36. Higgins, J. August. "The Aesthetic Foundations of Religious Experience in the Writings of Jonathan Edwards and Ralph Waldo Emerson." *American Journal of Theology & Philosophy* 38 (2017) 152–66.

    Brings Edwards and Emerson into conversation with one another as it relates to the tension between individual and community in the experience of God. Posits that the two men "provide distinct yet complementary models for recovering a more robust and fruitful notion of the human experience of God."

37. Hoselton, Ryan. "Jonathan Edwards and the Beauty of Christ." *Tabletalk* 41.8 (2017) 62.

    Provides a brief biographical sketch of Edwards and suggests that Edwards "was able to grasp the exquisite loveliness of Christ as few others could" precisely because he also understood the reality of God's justice.

38. ———. Review of *Jonathan Edwards Among the Theologians*, by Oliver Crisp. *Theologische Literaturzeitung* 142.12 (2017) 1364–65.

    Considers that "not all readers will be satisfied" with Crisp's interpretations, but he "initiates and advances the conversation" and is a "formidable and creative thinker" of Edwardsean scholarship.

39. Jung, Peter. "Thomas Reid's Reading Notes on Edwards' *Freedom of the Will*." *Jonathan Edwards Studies* 7.1 (2017) 62–71.

    Reveals the thoughts of a leading Edwards detractor, Thomas Reid, as he interacted with Edwards's *Freedom of the Will*.

40. Kellicut, Jordan. Review of *Jonathan Edwards and the Life of God: Toward an Evangelical Theology of Participation*, by W. Ross Hastings. *Stone-Campbell Journal* 20.1 (2017) 93–94.

    Says the author has written a work of "both breadth and depth." It is not for theological beginners, but it also exhibits strong pastoral concern.

41. Kemeny, Paul C. Review of *The Rhetoric of Revival: The Language of the Great Awakening Preachers*, by Michał Choiński. *The Journal of Ecclesiastical History* 68.3 (2017) 645–46.

Believes the author provides a compelling analysis of revival preaching but wishes the author had included the full text of the sermons he analyzed within the volume.

42. Kerley, Tyler. "The Beauty of the Cross: Retrieving Penal Substitutionary Atonement on Jonathan Edwards' Aesthetic Basis." *Jonathan Edwards Studies* 7.2 (2017) 79–102.

    Attempts to retrieve the doctrine of penal substitution for the present day by moving past debates about whether to ground the doctrine on a legal or moral basis and suggesting instead that it be grounded on the beauty of the Trinity as Edwards allegedly does.

43. Kim, Sun Wook. "Evaluating the Revival Experience of Korean Missionary Robert A. Hardie (1865–1949) in View of Jonathan Edwards' Religious Affections." *The Expository Times* 128.9 (2017) 427–40.

    Investigates Jonathan Edwards's "Religious Affections" and the "Distinguishing Marks" for judging the genuineness of the revival ministry of the Korean missionary Robert Hardie.

44. Knutson, Andrea. Review of *Knowing, Seeing, Being: Jonathan Edwards, Emily Dickinson, Marianne Moore and the American Typological Tradition*, by Jennifer Leader. *Religion & Literature* 49.3 (2017) 191–93.

    Declares the work an "original, sophisticated study."

45. Kreider, Glenn R. "'The Death of Christ Was a Murder': Jonathan Edwards and Blame for Christ's Death." *Bibliotheca Sacra* 174.696 (2017) 424–44.

    Examines the sermon "The True and Voluntary Suffering and Death of Christ" preached by Edwards in April 1736, in which he blames the soldiers for killing Jesus but also explains that Christ's death was a voluntary act which provided an atoning sacrifice for sin.

46. Labosier, Jeremy W. Review of *The Ecumenical Edwards: Jonathan Edwards and the Theologians*, edited by Kyle Strobel. *Christian Librarian* 60.1 (2017) 82–83.

    Applauds the work as a "welcome integration of Edwardsian scholarship." Further, "librarians should consider this acquisition to support graduate-level discussions."

47. Lee, Jeong. "The Vision of the Fullness of the Church: Jonathan Edwards' Interpretation of Zechariah 8 and 12–14." PhD diss., Torch Trinity Graduate University, 2017.

    Studies Edwards's hermeneutical methods for interpreting OT prophecy with particular reference to passages from Zechariah. Demonstrates Edwards's use of literal and historical interpretive methods as well as the use of typology.

48. Leidenhag, Joanna. Review of *Fullness Received and Returned: Trinity and Participation in Jonathan Edwards*, by Seng-Kong Tan. *Reviews in Religion and Theology* 24.2 (2017) 379–81.

    Summarizes the contents of the work and concludes that *exitus-reditus* is a strong theme in Edwards's writing, but perhaps not the "integrating motif" as per Tan. Because the work is a published dissertation it cannot be recommended to undergraduates, but scholars in the field could benefit from the book.

49. Madaras, Larry. "From Jonathan Edwards to Billy Graham." *America* 217.3 (2017) 1–4.

    Reviews Frances Fitzgerald's *The Evangelicals*. Criticizes it for not including the story of African-American evangelicals, for focusing on big personalities rather than the lives and experiences of "ordinary" church members, and for neglecting the evangelical movement within Roman Catholicism.

50. McCleery, Jennifer Reagan. "A Profile of the Northampton Minority." *Jonathan Edwards Studies* 7.1 (2017) 26–35.

    Explores that portion of Edwards's congregation which did not vote for his dismissal. Concludes that they sided with Edwards because they shared the same desire as him—to have a regenerate church membership. Also considers the contribution that age, economic status, pew seating, military service, personal connections, geographic proximity, and kinship had on their decision to support Edwards.

51. Minkema, Kenneth P. "A Chronology of Edwards's Life and Writings." Jonathan Edwards Center at Yale University, 2017. http://edwards.yale.edu/files/JE%20Chronology.pdf.

    Outlines Edwards's major writings and life events.

52. Mizell, Stephen. Review of *Jonathan Edwards Among the Theologians*, by Oliver Crisp. *Journal for Baptist Theology & Ministry* 14.2 (2017) 82–84.

    Declares that "Crisp has produced a superb, well-researched, and engaging work," though he misrepresents Arminius as a Molinist.

53. Neele, Adriaan C. "*A History of the Work of Redemption* by Jonathan Edwards (1739/1788)." *The Banner of Sovereign Grace Truth* 25.6 (2017) 247.

    Offers a brief, popular-level explanation of the historical context and details of the sermons later published as *A History of the Work of Redemption*.

54. ———. "*A Treatise Concerning Religious Affections* by Jonathan Edwards (1746)." *The Banner of Sovereign Grace Truth* 25.6 (2017) 246.

    Offers a brief, popular-level explanation of the historical context and details of Edwards's famous treatise.

55. ———. Review of *De ruimte van sovereine genade. Zeven preken*. *Jonathan Edwards Studies* 7.1 (2017) 74.

    Expresses satisfaction at seeing the sermons of Jonathan Edwards being published for Dutch speakers.

56. Pierpont, James, Jr. "The First Devinity Lecture Made by Me James Pierpont & Published in Yale College," edited and introduced by Kenneth P. Minkema. *Jonathan Edwards Studies* 7.2 (2017) 139–68.

    Publishes, for the first time, a manuscript in the Edwards Family Papers from Andover Newton Theological School. Contains lectures delivered by Pierpont to students at Yale College in the fourth year of the school's operation.

57. Reklis, Kathryn. Review of *The Ecumenical Edwards: Jonathan Edwards and the Theologians*, edited by Kyle Strobel. *Journal of Reformed Theology* 11.4 (2017) 441–42.

    Cites "its lack of diversity in both authors and topics engaged" as an "obvious weakness" of the book. "It is not hard to imagine how this work could animate pressing contemporary discussions about race, patriarchy, empire, and capitalism." Even so, the book deserves a wide readership.

58. Richardson, Herbert. *Jonathan Edwards' Precocious Childhood, Oedipal Conflict, Mid-Life Identity Crisis, and Old Age Radicalization:*

Psychological Factors Shaping the Development of His Theology. Lewiston, NY: Mellen, 2017.

Attempts to understand Edwards's thought as it developed through various phases of his life.

59. Rosario, Jeffrey. "The Edwardsean Roots of Manifest Destiny." *Jonathan Edwards Studies* 7.2 (2017) 103–19.

    Traces the connections between Edwards's millennial doctrine and the idea of manifest destiny along three lines: (1) an east to west geographical progression; (2) a mission to eradicate heathenism from the land; and (3) the interpretation of military conflict as divinely ordained.

60. Salladin, James. "Essence and Fullness: Evaluating the Creator-Creature Distinction in Jonathan Edwards." *Scottish Journal of Theology* 70.4 (2017) 427–44.

    Reflects on how Edwards develops the concept of *theosis* without obliterating the Creator-creature distinction.

61. Schutter, David H. "Jonathan Edwards's Preaching of Romans 8: Presenting and Evaluating Two Previously Unpublished Sermons." MA thesis, Westminster Theological Seminary, 2017.

    Publishes previously unpublished sermons with annotations on Romans 8:22; 8:29–30.

62. Schweitzer, William M. Review of *Theology and the Kinesthetic Imagination: Jonathan Edwards and the Making of Modernity*, by Kathryn Reklis. *Interpretation* 71.2 (2017) 237–38.

    Disparages the book as one which does not make a serious contribution to Edwards scholarship as it fails to display the kind of research and analysis required in a work of historical theology.

63. Sherron, Tyler P. "Jonathan Edwards and Roger Sherman on True Self-Love." ThM thesis, Dallas Theological Seminary, 2017.

    Evidences that Roger Sherman, founder of Connecticut, "found his concept of social order in the writings of Jonathan Edwards."

64. Stanton, Allen. "He Was 'Altogether Peculiar': Samuel Miller's Cautious Appreciation of Jonathan Edwards." *Jonathan Edwards Studies* 7.2 (2017) 120–38.

    Considers the reception of Jonathan Edwards by Samuel Miller, one of the faculty members at Princeton Seminary.

65. Stout, Harry S., et al., eds. *The Jonathan Edwards Encyclopedia.* Grand Rapids: Eerdmans, 2017.

    References work on the life, times, and thought of Jonathan Edwards. Contains nearly 400 entries from 169 scholars.

66. Todd, Obbie. "The Influence of Jonathan Edwards on the Missiology and Conversionism of Richard Furman (1755–1825)." *Jonathan Edwards Studies* 7.1 (2017) 36–54.

    Offers a comparison of Edwards's *A Divine and Supernatural Light* with Furman's *Conversion Essential to Salvation*, revealing the latter's appropriation of the former and the role he played in moving Edwards's thought beyond into the American South.

67. Trocchio, Rachel Donegan. "American Puritanism and the Cognitive Style of Grace." PhD diss., University of California, Berkley, 2017.

    Plots a correspondence between acts of creative thinking and the Puritan concept of grace to show that the Puritans established a distinctive art, or "cognitive style," which mediated intellection, representation, and belief.

68. Valeri, Mark R. Review of *Jonathan Edwards Among the Theologians*, by Oliver Crisp. *Interpretation* 71.3 (2017) 345–46.

    States the book will be useful for those who can wade through the author's dense material and terminology.

69. Waddington, Jeffrey C. Review of *Jonathan Edwards Among the Theologians*, by Oliver Crisp. *Fides et Historia* 49.1 (2017) 157–59.

    Writes that "while Crisp is able to ascertain where Edwards falls short or goes beyond the Reformed tradition, he is freer in his own formulations or correctives to Edwards than I believe is appropriate." Further, Edwards becomes "abstracted from [his] original historical contexts" in the author's work.

70. Wigginton, Jesse C. Review of *Jonathan Edwards on Worship: Public and Private Devotion to God*, by Ted Rivera. *Artistic Theologian* 5 (2017) 106–7.

    States the book is a "great addition to anyone interested in the worship practices of Jonathan Edwards and how self-evaluation played a role in his worship services."

71. Wolosky, Shira. Review of *Knowing, Seeing, Being: Jonathan Edwards, Emily Dickinson, Marianne Moore and the American*

Typological Tradition, by Jennifer Leader. *Christianity and Literature* 66.2 (2017) 329–33.

Praises the book for emphasizing the importance of religion to these authors at a time when this area is often neglected.

72. Yeager, Jonathan M. Review of *Finding God in Solitude: The Personal Piety of Jonathan Edwards (1703–1758) and Its Influence on His Pastoral Ministry*, by Donald S. Whitney. *The Catholic Historical Review* 103.1 (2017) 155–56.

Declares the book to be essential reading for those interested in Edwards's spiritual practices.

73. Zerra, Luke. Review of *Theology and the Kinesthetic Imagination: Jonathan Edwards and the Making of Modernity*, by Kathryn Reklis. *Reviews in Religion & Theology* 24.4 (2017) 783–85.

Believes the book is "a story about religion in the Atlantic World as much as it is a book about Edwards. This allows Reklis to see Edwards within the broader movement of trans-Atlantic revivalism, show how he was affected by modernity's tendencies toward universality, and discuss the role of the slave trade in modern subjectivity." Wishes the book would have included a discussion of how Edwards's ideas could be applied in contemporary times.

2018

1. Adkins, Tucker. Review of *Jonathan Edwards and Scripture: Biblical Exegesis in British North America*, edited by David Barshinger and Douglas Sweeney; Review of *The Jonathan Edwards Encyclopedia*, edited by Harry S. Stout et al. *The New England Quarterly* 91.4 (2018) 683–88.

Assesses that "two new works have entered the challenge this year." The first is *The Jonathan Edwards Encyclopedia* that has produced "almost 400 entries written by 169 authors." The "most recent work" edited by Doug Sweeney and David Barshinger is *Jonathan Edwards and Scripture*. "Both books will help scholars engage with Edwards's intellectual output" as well as push the scope of the conversation.

2. Bannon, Brad. *Jonathan Edwards, Samuel Taylor Coleridge, and the Supernatural Will in American Literature.* London: Routledge, 2018.

Explores Samuel Taylor Coleridge's interactions with the theology of Jonathan Edwards and their combined influence on writers like Poe, Emerson, Melville, and Crane.

3. Barone, Marco. "The Relationship Between God's Nature, God's Image in Man, and Freedom in the Philosophy of Jonathan Edwards." *Jonathan Edwards Studies* 8.1 (2018) 37–51.

    Begins with Jack Davidson's statement that G. W. Leibniz is the only philosopher known to him to suggest that a proper definition of human freedom must begin by understanding God's freedom, for the one must reflect the other. Contends that Edwards is another thinker who developed this connection. Explores Edwards's theology of the divine nature, of human nature, and how, for Edwards, human free agency reflects God's free agency.

4. Barshinger, David P., and Douglas A. Sweeney, eds. *Jonathan Edwards and Scripture: Biblical Exegesis in British North America*. Oxford: Oxford University Press, 2018.

    Addresses a long-neglected aspect of Edwards's ministry: his engagement with Scripture. Includes essays from a number of authors and addresses topics including Edwards's historical context, case studies in Edwards's exegetical methods, and his use of Scripture in developing his theology. Comparisons between Edwards and other exegetes are also made.

5. Benge, Dustin Wayne. "'Nobles and Barons in the Court of Heaven': A Survey of Angelology from the Patristic Era to the Eighteenth Century with Particular Emphasis Given to Jonathan Edwards." PhD diss., Southern Baptist Theological Seminary, 2018.

    Rediscovers the contribution of Jonathan Edwards on the subject of angels, arguing that he is one of the most important thinkers on the topic in the Christian tradition.

6. Black, Griffin. "Hampshire County Ministerial Association Minutes, 1731–47." *Jonathan Edwards Studies* 8.2 (2018) 115–20.

    Transcribes a photocopy of the original document found at Forbes Library, Northampton, Massachusetts. Includes topics like a case of fornication and whether the repentant individual's child may receive baptism, rules for the association's library, and suggestions to reform the morals of the county.

7. ———. "'Spectator' of Shadows: The Human Being in Jonathan Edwards's 'Images of Divine Things.'" *Jonathan Edwards Studies* 8.2 (2018) 82–95.

    Explains how "types" were traditionally understood as OT foreshadowings of NT truths. But under Edwards, "types" became earthly "shadows" of divine realities. For example, by studying the sun, a tree, or a silkworm, one could learn more about God himself. Explores the "typological language" of Edwards.

8. Bruce, Dustin Blane. "'The Grand Encouragement': Andrew Fuller's Pneumatology as a Reception of and Advancement on Orthodox, Puritan, and Evangelical Perspectives on the Holy Spirit." PhD diss., Southern Baptist Theological Seminary, 2018.

    Includes a study of the pneumatology of Jonathan Edwards as part of the backdrop to his presentation of Fuller's doctrine.

9. Cavalier, Adam Gabriel. Review of *A Reader's Guide to the Major Writings of Jonathan Edwards*, edited by Nathan Finn and Jeremy Kimble. *Southwestern Journal of Theology* 61.1 (2018) 108–10.

    Writes that the book offers an "outstanding introduction to Edwards's major works." Wishes that the list of contributors had been indexed so readers could more easily connect each contributor to the article(s) they wrote.

10. ———. Review of *The Jonathan Edwards Encyclopedia*, edited by Harry Stout et al. *Criswell Theological Review* 15.2 (2018) 90–92.

    Declares the book a "broad yet comprehensive analysis of Edwards's life and theology."

11. Chamberlain, Ava. Review of *Jonathan Edwards and Transatlantic Print Culture*, by Jonathan Yeager. *Church History* 87.1 (2018) 256–59.

    Appreciates the insights into print culture offered by this volume.

12. Cochran, Elizabeth Agnew. "Relational Consent: Reflections on Disability and Jonathan Edwards's Aesthetics." *Journal of Disability & Religion* 22.2 (2018) 177–86.

    Retrieves Edwards's understanding of "consent" in aesthetics as a framework for thinking through political participation by the intellectually disabled. Edwards's concept means that human flourishing is fundamentally grounded in relationships; therefore,

Edwards's aesthetic can be used to argue that intellectual disability, of itself, ought not to hinder civic participation.

13. Cochran, Joseph T. Review of *Jonathan Edwards and Scripture: Biblical Exegesis in British North America*, edited by David Barshinger and Douglas Sweeney. *Themelios* 43.3 (2018) 488–89.

    Praises the work and believes "pastors and interested lay-readership will find comfort and encouragement from Edwards's traditional yet innovative interpretive work."

14. ———. Review of *Jonathan Edwards and the Psalms: A Redemptive-Historical Vision of Scripture*, by David P. Barshinger. *Fides et Historia* 50.1 (2018) 163–65.

    Admires the author for "attentively and convincingly" demonstrating his thesis and for providing "an exemplary model for intellectual historians who wish to pursue the pioneering enterprise of constructing histories of exegesis."

15. ———. Review of *Jonathan Edwards and Transatlantic Print Culture*, by Jonathan Yeager. *Themelios* 43.2 (2018) 304–6.

    Writes that the work "demonstrates the positive contribution that social history and print culture studies provide to the construction of evangelical history."

16. Crisp, Oliver D. "Jonathan Edwards on God's Relation to Creation." *Jonathan Edwards Studies* 8.1 (2018) 2–16.

    Explores the question of God's relation to the physical universe; namely, is God related to his creation in the same way that a parent is related to his child? Considers the implications for the doctrine of divine aseity.

17. Crisp, Oliver D., and Kyle C. Strobel. *Jonathan Edwards: An Introduction to His Thought*. Grand Rapids: Eerdmans, 2018.

    Provides a brief introduction to the distinctive themes in Edwards's writings. Includes chapters on his doctrine of the Trinity, God and creation, the atonement, and salvation.

18. Delph, Joseph Michael. "George Whitefield's Preaching: An Evangelical Response to the Enlightenment." PhD diss., Southern Baptist Theological Seminary, 2018.

    Considers the preaching ministry of Whitefield as a precursor to presuppositional apologetics. Also explores the works of Wesley and Edwards and their efforts to confront the rationalism of their day.

19. Easterling, Joe M. "From the Pulpit to the People: A Comparative Survey of Jonathan Edwards' Pastoral Leadership in Northampton and Stockbridge." *Theology of Leadership Journal* 1.2 (2018) 30–39.

Argues that Edwards had a more effective pastorate in Stockbridge than in Northampton and grounds the success of Stockbridge to a shift in Edwards's pastoral leadership style from being pulpit-centered to being people-centered.

20. Ericson, John. "When God Ceased Winking: Jonathan Edwards the Younger's Evolution on the Problem of Slavery." *Connecticut History Review* 57.1 (2018) 7–32.

Probes the sermon on Mark 12 in which he cried for the abolition of slavery as the duty of "national moral regeneration." This sermon in 1791 was "undeniably his greatest."

21. Everhard, Matthew. "Jonathan Edwards: The Theologian of Joy." *Modern Reformation* 27.5 (2018) 34–43.

Introduces three themes related to joy found in Edwards's works: (1) joy is an attribute of God; (2) humanity was created with a great capacity for joy; and (3) heaven will be the great domain in which joy is most fully realized.

22. ———. *A Theology of Joy: Jonathan Edwards and Eternal Happiness in the Holy Trinity*. Fort Worth, TX: JESociety, 2018.

Surveys the sermons and treatises of Edwards and attempts to systematize them into a theology of joy. Edwards's theology of joy is grouped into categories: Trinity, salvation, the holy life, and the believer's final state in heaven.

23. Fisk, Philip J. Review of *Jonathan Edwards Among the Theologians*, by Oliver Crisp. *Journal of Reformed Theology* 12.2 (2018) 210–11.

Appreciates the "cumulative work" in Edwards studies that Oliver Crisp has contributed. But in this volume, he "unapologetically critiques America's Theologian . . . examining the Trinity, creation, free will, and the atonement."

24. Garcia, John J. Review of *Jonathan Edwards and Transatlantic Print Culture*, by Jonathan Yeager. *Early American Literature* 53.2 (2018) 595–99.

Believes the title is deceptive as the book is more of a "biography of Edwards's publications from the point of view of the commercial book trade." Wishes more time had also been spent exploring the broader context of the book trade during that period and why Edwards's popularity as an author appeared to decline as the eighteenth century wore on.

25. Goodman, Russel B. *American Philosophy Before Pragmatism*. Oxford: Oxford University Press, 2018.

    Traces the development of philosophy in America during the eighteenth and nineteenth centuries with special focus on the thought of Jonathan Edwards, Benjamin Franklin, Thomas Jefferson, the writers of *The Federalist*, and the transcendentalists Emerson and Thoreau. The theme of slavery and its morality is also unpacked from the writings of these men.

26. Gowler, Steve. "Radical Orthodoxy: William Goodell and the Abolition of American Slavery." *The New England Quarterly* 91.4 (2018) 592.

    Explores the impact of New Divinity theology on abolitionist William Goodell, who claimed that the writings of Jonathan Edwards Jr. and Samuel Hopkins provided the "moral foundation of immediate abolitionism."

27. Hamilton, S. Mark. "Jonathan Edwards, Dispositionalism and Spirit Christology." *Scottish Bulletin of Evangelical Theology* 38.2 (2018) 122–42.

    Advances the thesis that Edwards's Spirit Christology is inseparably bound up in his doctrine of the Trinity, and that a dispositional reading of Edwards on the Trinity presents "worrisome consequences for the metaphysics that underpin Edwards' Christology, and those that underpin his Spirit Christology in particular."

28. Hamilton, S. Mark, and Joshua R. Farris. "A Biographical Sketch and Documentary History of the Reverend Maltby Gelston (1766–1856)." *Jonathan Edwards Studies* 8.1 (2018) 52–76.

    Explores Gelston's private notebook, *A Systematic Collection of Questions and Answers in Divinity*, arguing that it gives insight into the development of New England theology on par with Bellamy's *True Religion Delineated* (1750) and Hopkins's *System of Doctrines* (1793).

29. Helm, Paul. "Francis Turretin and Jonathan Edwards on Compatibilism." *Journal of Reformed Theology* 12.4 (2018) 335–55.

Responds to Richard Muller's book *Divine Will and Human Choice: Freedom, Contingency, and Necessity in Early Modern Reformed Thought*, which concluded that the Reformed Orthodox were not compatibilists. Argues that Muller's claim is false by working through the relevant passages in Turretin's and Edwards's works and showing that a careful reading of those documents presents insurmountable challenges to Muller's view.

30. ———. *Human Nature from Calvin to Edwards.* Grand Rapids: Reformation Heritage, 2018.

    Traces the faculty psychology through the patristic and medieval theologians, John Calvin, John Locke, Jonathan Edwards, and ending up at Herman Bavinck.

31. Higgins, J. August. Review of *The Spirit of Early Evangelicalism: True Religion in a Modern World*, by D. Bruce Hindmarsh. *Spiritus* 18.2 (2018) 283–85.

    Trusts that the great contribution of the book is the "critical alternative" it provides "for defining and capturing the spirit of the evangelical movement in its formative years in a way that is still relevant for interpreting contemporary evangelicalism"—namely, its call for people to be "born again."

32. Hindmarsh, D. Bruce. *The Spirit of Early Evangelicalism: True Religion in a Modern World.* Oxford: Oxford University Press, 2018.

    Tells the story of the emergence of evangelical spirituality in the eighteenth century with a special focus on four of evangelicalism's early leaders: George Whitefield, John and Charles Wesley, and Jonathan Edwards. Concludes that the uniqueness of evangelicalism is in its emphasis on the conversion experience.

33. Hooks, James Michael. "The Spiritual and the Moral Sense: The Role of Theology and British Moral Sense Philosophy in Jonathan Edwards's 'True Virtue.'" MATS thesis, Regent College, 2018.

    Argues that Edwards's "treaties *On the Nature of True Virtue* is a synthesis between British moral sense philosophy" and "Edwards's broader theological perspective."

34. Hussey, Phillip. Review of *Jonathan Edwards's Turn from the Classic-Reformed Tradition of Freedom of the Will*, by Philip Fisk. *Journal of Reformed Theology* 12.1 (2018) 73–74.

Proposes, "Edwards departs from the 'classic-Reformed' tradition on the freedom of the will because Edwards's theological assertions, specifically in his *Freedom of the Will*, replace an ontology of true contingency and it corresponding scholastic distinction with a necessitarian framework." This thesis is simple. However, "the argument to defend his thesis" is "not so simple."

35. Kim, Ji-Jyuk. "Jonathan Edwards' Theocentric Ethics: Analysis and Implications for Christian Ethics." 한국기독교신학논총 109 (2018) 199–223.

    Contemplates the ways in which Edwards's ethics can be applied to contemporary issues like pluralism, political liberalism, and ecological problems. Argues that the sovereignty of God was at the heart of Edwards's thought and that his theocentric perspective shaped his political theory and social ethics.

36. Komline, David. Review of *Jonathan Edwards and Transatlantic Print Culture*, by Jonathan Yeager. *The Journal of Religion* 98.3 (2018) 433–34.

    Complements the book on its transatlantic scope and emphasis on relationships in the publication of Edwards's works.

37. Kreider, Glenn R. Review of *Jonathan Edwards Among the Theologians*, by Oliver Crisp. *Bibliotheca Sacra* 175.699 (2018) 382–83.

    Determines the book is a "helpful contribution" to the study of Edwards but will be more useful to scholars than to laypersons as it assumes a great deal of knowledge about Edwards's context and writings.

38. Lee, Joseph W. "Jonathan Edwards, Samuel Hopkins, and Theological Ethics of Social Concern." PhD diss., Dallas Theological Seminary, 2018.

    Explores the virtue theories of Edwards and Hopkins to demonstrate the congruence between them. Argues that Hopkins was more consistent than Edwards by applying his theory to the abolition of slavery.

39. Lengyel, Thomas Grant. "Recovering the Disciplines: A Comparative Study on the Spiritual Disciplines as Expressed in the Lives, Teaching and Ministry of Jonathan Edwards, Charles Finney and Richard Foster." DMin thesis, Duke University, 2018.

Makes two assertions: (1) the spiritual disciplines have always been important within the evangelical tradition, and (2) the spiritual disciplines still have a role to play in the life and practice of the church today. Chooses Edwards, Finney, and Foster as representatives of evangelicalism in the eighteenth, nineteenth, and twentieth centuries, respectively.

40. Lowe, John T. Review of *The Global Edwards: Papers from the Jonathan Edwards Congress Held in Melbourne*, edited by Rhys S. Bezzant. *Jonathan Edwards Studies* 8.1 (2018) 77–78.

    Praises the work as a "must-have for any Edwards reader" as it offers a glimpse into the research being conducted on Edwards all over the world.

41. Martin, Ryan J. *Understanding Affections in the Theology of Jonathan Edwards: "The High Exercises of Divine Love."* London: T&T Clark, 2018.

    Argues that Edwards's term "affections" differs markedly from the contemporary term "emotions" and that Edwards's understanding of the term derived almost entirely from the Christian tradition rather than from John Locke or the pressures of the Great Awakening. Traces the use of the term "affections" and how it was distinguished from "passions" in early, medieval, and post-medieval Christianity and then through the writings of Edwards.

42. McDermott, Gerald R. *Everyday Glory: The Revelation of God in All Reality*. Grand Rapids: Baker Academic, 2018.

    Aims to "recapture a Christian vision of all reality: that the world is full of divine signs that are openings into God's glory." Includes insights from Edwards, Newman, and Barth.

43. ———. "Jonathan Edwards on Property, Liberty, and the National Covenant." *Journal of Markets and Morality* 21.2 (2018) 259–70.

    Inspects Edwards's ideas about property and liberty and the role of government in securing them. Concludes Edwards's views are best read within the national covenant tradition.

44. ———. "Types in Nature: Jonathan Edwards on Typology." *Bibliotheca Sacra* 175.699 (2018) 271–83.

    Provides a litany of examples of the ways in which Edwards found types of divine things in the created order "outside us" and "inside us."

45. Miller, Paul. "Jonathan Edwards and the Beauty of God." *Touchstone* 36.3 (2018) 6–13.

    Looks for a way that Edwards's thinking could be relevant for the modern world and finds it in Edwards's teaching on beauty. Edwards found beauty in creation, the gospel, and ultimately God himself, whose love is the greatest expression of true beauty.

46. Neele, Adriaan C. *Before Jonathan Edwards: Sources of New England Theology*. Oxford: Oxford University Press, 2018.

    Balances the attention given to developments in theology *after* Edwards with a work exploring Edwards's use of Reformed orthodox and Protestant scholastic primary sources and how he employed them in the formulation of his own theology.

47. Nichols, Stephen J. "Jonathan Edwards and the First Great Awakening." *Tabletalk* 42.7 (2018) 21–23.

    Tells the story of the First Great Awakening in a concise manner and offers devotional thoughts for contemporary Christians.

48. Phillips, Charles. *Edwards Amasa Park: The Last Edwardsean*. New Directions in Jonathan Edwards Studies. Göttingen: Vandenhoeck & Ruprecht, 2018.

    Demonstrates that Park is incorrectly labeled a "Taylorite" and a "proto-liberal" and should rather be thought of as a modified Hopkinsian who "conserved the substance and prolonged the influence" of New England theology through the nineteenth century.

49. Rosenbeck, Craig. Review of *Jonathan Edwards's Turn from the Classic-Reformed Tradition of the Freedom of the Will*, by P. J. Fisk. *The Christian Librarian* 61.1 (2018) 69.

    Asserts that this is an "immense resource" as a "scholarly resource." This book "contributes" to the conversation of whether or not Edwards truly abandoned the Reformed tradition in his comments on the will. Fisk says that he does.

50. Ryu, Gilsun. "The Federal Theology and the History of Redemption in Jonathan Edwards's Biblical Exegesis." *The Journal of the Evangelical Theological Society* 61.4 (2018) 785–803.

    Examines the relationship between Edwards's federal theology and biblical exegesis. Argues that Edwards developed the former on the basis of the latter.

51. ———. "Jonathan Edwards' Federal Theology in Exegetical Perspective: The Doctrinal Harmony of Scripture as a Framework for Interpreting the History of Redemption." PhD diss., Trinity Evangelical Divinity School, 2018.

    Considers similarities and differences between Edwards's federal theology and that of other Reformed thinkers. Believes Edwards's thinking represents a development in the Reformed tradition as he made the history of redemption an inseparable element of his biblical exegesis.

52. Schultz, Walter J. "Is Jonathan Edwards a Neoplatonist? The Concept of Emanation in the End of Creation." *Jonathan Edwards Studies* 8.1 (2018) 17–36.

    Argues that the term "Neoplatonist," commonly attributed to Jonathan Edwards since the 1850s, is inappropriate.

53. Schweitzer, Cameron. Review of *Jonathan Edwards's Turn from the Classic-Reformed Tradition of Freedom of the Will*, by Philip J. Fisk. *Jonathan Edwards Studies* 8.2 (2018) 125–28.

    Says this book "will surely help to place Fisk among the well-respected authors in the philosophical studies of Northampton's Pastor, among the likes of Oliver Crisp and Sang Hyun Lee."

54. Schweitzer, Don. Review of *Jonathan Edwards's Turn from the Classic-Reformed Tradition of Freedom of the Will*, by Philip J. Fisk. *Toronto Journal of Theology* 34.1 (2018) 148.

    Believes the book will be useful to anyone interested in the theological and philosophical issues surrounding the question of the freedom of the will.

55. Smith, John H. Review of *The Rhetoric of Revival: The Language of the Great Awakening*, by Michał Choiński. *Church History* 87.2 (2018) 585–87.

    Declares that the book is "a much needed, important, and fascinating study, though one that will likely appeal only to a narrow readership of specialists in early American religious history and culture."

56. Smith, Phillip. "'A Shadow of Death': Jonathan Edwards and the Book of Job." *Jonathan Edwards Studies* 8.2 (2018) 96–114.

    Considers Edwards's interpretation and use of the biblical book of Job.

57. Strachan, Owen. *Always in God's Hands: Day by Day in the Company of Jonathan Edwards*. Carol Stream, IL: Tyndale Momentum, 2018.

   Gives attention to Edwards daily, offering quotes from Edwards's letters and sermons along with devotional thoughts by the author.

58. Strachan, Owen, and Douglas A. Sweeney. *The Essential Jonathan Edwards: An Introduction to the Life and Teaching of America's Greatest Theologian*. Chicago: Moody, 2018.

   Provides a concise introduction to the life and thought of Edwards with excerpts of primary sources. Explores his daily life and notions of beauty, true Christianity, heaven, hell, and the good life.

59. Sweeney, Douglas A. Review of *Edwards Amasa Park: The Last Edwardsean*, by Charles Phillips. *Jonathan Edwards Studies* 8.2 (2018) 121–24.

   Notes that the book is not a biography *per se*, but a work examining Park's defense of Edwards's Calvinism. Even so, this book "is now the go-to book on its subject's life and thought."

60. Todd, Obbie Tyler. "Purchasing the Spirit: A Trinitarian Hermeneutic for Jonathan Edwards's Doctrine of the Atonement." *Puritan Reformed Journal* 10.2 (2018) 148–67.

   Explores Edwards's teaching that Christ purchased the Holy Spirit for his people in the atonement.

61. ———. "What Is a Person? Three Essential Criteria for Jonathan Edwards' Doctrine of Personhood." *Journal of the Evangelical Theological Society* 61.1 (2018) 121–35.

   Attempts to understand how Edwards understood personhood, especially as it relates to the persons of the Trinity. Says Edwards explained personhood as relational, reflexive, and redemptive.

62. Torseth, Robb. "Jonathan Edwards and Reformed Ethico-Teleology: Locating Continuities in a Theological Tradition." MA thesis, Yale Divinity School, 2018.

   Suggests that Edwards's *The End for Which God Created the World* is usually read from a philosophical perspective; however, it is best understood as a product of his Calvinist theological heritage.

63. Tyrpak, Joseph Kirk. "The Spirituality of David Brainerd: A Summary and Critique." PhD diss., Southern Baptist Theological Seminary, 2018.

Discusses Edwards's most popular work, *Life of Brainerd*, and then offers a critical examination of Brainerd's spirituality from extant sources. Specific topics include Brainerd's view of conversion, love as the essence of spirituality, and evangelical humiliation as the daily experience of spirituality.

64. Underhill, Tom. "Does Jonathan Edwards' Concept of Virtue as 'Love to Being in General' Explain the Governmentalism Found in His Son Jonathan Edwards Jr.?" MA thesis, Puritan Reformed Theological Seminary, 2018.

   Believes Edwards's concept of virtue was appropriated by his son in a way that encouraged his son to adopt governmentalism.

65. Valeri, Mark R. Review of *Jonathan Edwards and Transatlantic Print Culture*, by Jonathan Yeager. *The Journal of Ecclesiastical History* 69.2 (2018) 442–44.

   Appreciates the insights of the book but believes the title itself is a bit misleading since the book does not actually connect print history to religious affairs at large. "We read little of what the accumulated data about print runs and various publishers means for understanding Edwards, Evangelical culture, or eighteenth-century religious issues." For example, what explains the wild popularity of *Life of Brainerd*? Or, what was it about the 1750s that made *Freedom of the Will* so popular? "These questions go unasked." The book also reveals little about transatlantic print culture, focusing exclusively on Edwards and his works.

66. Waddington, Jeffrey C. Review of *The Jonathan Edwards Encyclopedia*, edited by Harry S. Stout et al. *Ordained Servant* 27 (2018) 84–85.

   Explains that the quality of the articles may be uneven because of the various skill levels and theological perspectives of the authors, but it is still the best single-volume source for the many topics it addresses.

67. Willson, Cory B. "A Little Exercise for Those New to Interfaith Dialogue: Lessons on Spiritual Formation from Jonathan Edwards and Helmut Thielicke." *Calvin Theological Journal* 53.2 (2018) 351–69.

   Argues that Christian approaches to mission and interfaith dialogue need to pay proper attention to spiritual formation. Suggests ways in which the works of Edwards and Thielicke may be used to frame interfaith dialogue along these lines.

68. Zhu, Xinying. "A Beautiful Vision of Glory: Jonathan Edwards's Use of Scripture in His Aesthetic Approach to God's End of Creation." MA thesis, Trinity Evangelical Divinity School, 2018.

Analyzes God's end in creation from Edwards's perspective and posits that Edwards considered the subject from an aesthetic standpoint. Believes this approach offers a fresh perspective on our perceptions of God, our relationship to him, and our purpose in life.

2019

1. Adkins, Tucker. "'Craved Reality': Perry Miller, Sinclair Lewis, and Puritanism." *Jonathan Edwards Studies* 9.2 (2019) 1–27.

    Considers a eulogy published in the December 10, 1963, issue of *The Harvard Crimson* for Perry Miller (1905–1963) and then outlines the life and legacy of the man who sparked the modern renaissance in Edwards studies.

2. Bannon, Brad. *Jonathan Edwards, Samuel Taylor Coleridge, and the Supernatural Will in American Literature.* New York: Routledge, 2019.

    Reprint. Examines Samuel Taylor Coleridge's reception of the theology of Jonathan Edwards and shows how the thinking of both men influenced the literature of the nineteenth century.

3. Barone, Marco. "'Edwards Saw More Perspicaciously': R. L. Dabney's Edwardsean Philosophy of Free-Agency." *Jonathan Edwards Studies* 9.1 (2019) 2–24.

    Contends that Dabney, despite opposing many aspects of Edwards's theology, did appropriate some of Edwards's thoughts on free-agency. Offers a comparative analysis of the two men to prove the thesis.

4. ———. "G. W. Leibniz and Jonathan Edwards on Free-Agency." PhD diss., Queens University Belfast, 2019.

    George Marsden claimed that "Leibniz . . . was in some ways like Edwards without the Calvinism" (*Jonathan Edwards: A Life*, 462). Barone's work is a comparative study that expounds striking philosophical similarities between Leibniz and Edwards on the topics of freedom and necessity. The dissertation also highlights their deep theological differences, the consideration of which encourages further discussion on the relationship between faith and reason and the role of theological commitments in philosophy.

5. Beck, Peter. "'Dear Mr. Edwards': Theological Dialogue About Seeking God." *Puritan Reformed Journal* 11.1 (2019) 151–67.

    Answers the questions, "How can we reconcile that assumption [that Calvinism stifles evangelism] with the seminal roles played by Calvinists in the First Great Awakening and the Modern Missionary Movement?" and "Can one consistently hold to the tenets of Calvinism and remain wholeheartedly evangelistic?" by looking at the theology of Jonathan Edwards, who "held comfortably in tension the doctrines of man's responsibility and God's sovereignty."

6. Beynon, Graham. "Tuning the Heart: A Historical Survey of the Affections in Corporate Worship, with Special Reference to Jonathan Edwards." *Foundations* 76 (2019) 84–109.

    Defines the "affections" as "something that is 'felt' in corporate worship: the subjective experience of emotion." Presents a brief survey of the concept from Augustine to Edwards.

7. Bezzant, Rhys S. *Edwards the Mentor.* Oxford: Oxford University Press, 2019.

    Explores how Edwards mentored young men into ministry and in the ministry. Considers the historical practice of mentorship as well as Edwards's own method, rationale, and mentoring legacy. Notes the "affective turn" that Edwards's mentorship took. His focus on informality, friendship, and conversation were modern, yet he still resisted the pressures of Enlightenment thinking on his task.

8. Boss, Robert, and Sarah Boss, eds. *The Miscellanies Companion.* Fort Worth, TX: JESociety, 2019.

    Provides a series of essays from various authors on themes found in Jonathan Edwards's *Miscellanies* notes.

9. Boyd, Adam Newcomb. *Jonathan Edwards, Beauty, and Younger Evangelicals.* Fort Worth, TX: JESociety, 2019.

    Explores the dynamics of a healthy, biblical faith, using Jonathan Edwards's *Religious Affections* as the paradigm. Then applies insights to the development of church youth ministry.

10. Bray, Gerald L. Review of *The Jonathan Edwards Encyclopedia*, edited by Harry Stout et al. *Churchman* 133.2 (2019) 175–76.

Appears "at a key moment in the study" of Edwards's thought. "There is now a body of scholarship available that is too much for any one individual to master." Students "will need to acquire this volume, which is remarkably cheap considering its intrinsic scholarly value."

11. Cavalier, Adam G. "'Salvation Shall Spread Through All the Tribes and Ranks of Mankind': Jonathan Edwards and World Mission." PhD diss., Southwestern Baptist Theological Seminary, 2019.

    Makes the case that Edwards had a "coherent theology of world mission." His theology of mission included an emphasis on the sovereignty of God, the universal depravity of humankind, the ability and inability of humankind, the method of mission as the proclamation of the gospel, and conversion.

12. Cochran, Joseph T. Review of *Before Jonathan Edwards: Sources of New England Theology,* by Adriaan C. Neele. *Fides et Historia* 51.2 (2019) 198–200.

    Praises the author for his "mastery of Latin, familiarity with Reformed orthodox and Protestant scholastics, and expertise on Edwards's New England contemporaries." Says that "each of Neele's assertions is meticulously supported with corroborating evidence. This study rounds out the modern depiction of Jonathan Edwards and displays how he is a complex historical figure worthy of continuous engagement and study."

13. ———. Review of *Jonathan Edwards: An Introduction to His Thought,* by Oliver Crisp and Kyle Strobel. *Themelios* 44.3 (2019) 591–92.

    Declares that the authors "provide a lucid portrayal of Edwards while welcoming readers into a churchly reading of Edwards."

14. Conley, Stephen Mark. "Imitation as a Means for Strengthening Pastoral Perseverance." DMin thesis, Southern Baptist Theological Seminary, 2019.

    Addresses the problem of perseverance in pastoral ministry by considering the value of imitation as a means of persevering. The historical examples of Jonathan Edwards and Charles Spurgeon are given careful consideration.

15. Craun, Joy. "We Are Them: The Golden Rule as a Theological Impetus in the Anti-Slavery and Abolitionist Movement." *Jonathan Edwards Studies* 9.1 (2019) 25–48.

Presents a sermon by Jonathan Edwards Jr. in which he uses the Golden Rule as the basis for supporting abolition. "Once the golden rule brought African Americans to the status of neighbors, slavery became a sin; once slavery became a sin, it had to be purged from both individuals and the nation at large."

16. Crawford, Brandon James. "Divine Love as the Organizing Principle of Jonathan Edwards's Doctrine of Atonement." *Journal of the Evangelical Theological Society* 62.3 (2019) 563–81.

    Follows Edwards's doctrine of atonement in its logical order with a representative sampling of Edwards's writings in each section. Particular attention is given to Edwards's views on the mechanics of the atonement and the distinctive role that love played in his thinking on the subject. Concludes that for Edwards, love was not only a divine motive for the atonement, but part of the actual mechanism which makes it effectual for the elect.

17. Crocco, Stephen D. "Perry Miller and Yale's Proudest Moment." *Jonathan Edwards Studies* 9.2 (2019) 83–97.

    Explores the question of when Perry Miller first developed a serious interest in Jonathan Edwards.

18. Daniel, Curt. "Jonathan Edwards on the Love of God." *Banner of Truth* 670 (2019) 19–22.

    Argues that divine love was at the heart of Edwards's theological system.

19. Dillard, Peter S. Review of *Jonathan Edwards Among the Theologians*, by Oliver Crisp. *Heythrop Journal* 60.2 (2019) 315–16.

    Extols the work as "a model of rigorous, historically informed philosophical theology."

20. Engelsma, Esther. "The Journal of Esther Edwards Burr." *The Banner of Sovereign Grace Truth* 27.6 (2019) 248–49.

    Ponders the spiritual lessons that can be gleaned from the diary of Jonathan Edwards's daughter.

21. Everhard, Matthew, and Robert Boss. *A Collection of Essays on Jonathan Edwards*. Fort Worth, TX: JESociety, 2019.

    A collection of essays by various authors, ranging from the devotional to the technical, on the life, times, and thought of Jonathan Edwards. Featuring J. T. Holderman, Sarah Boss, Matthew

Everhard, Obbie Tyler Todd, David Luke, Toby K. Easley, Chris Woznicki, Jonathan S. Marko, Robert Boss, and Zachary Hopkins.

22. Forster, Greg. "Economic Ethics as a Gospel Priority in the Pastoral Ministry of Jonathan Edwards." *Jonathan Edwards Studies* 9.1 (2019) 49–62.

    Believes that matters like generosity, witness against greed, justice for the oppressed, and economic development were vitally connected to the gospel in Edwards's thought. Reviews three periods from Edwards's career to demonstrate that he prioritized economic ethics throughout his ministry.

23. Geissler, Suzanne. Review of *Jonathan Edwards: An Introduction to His Thought*, by Oliver Crisp and Kyle Strobel. *Anglican and Episcopal History* 88.1 (2019) 112.

    Notes that the book advertises itself as an introduction to Edwards's "thought," but it is almost entirely devoted to his theology. Also notes that the book bills itself as a volume for newcomers, but the themes discussed require a "significantly high level of knowledge in theology and philosophy."

24. Hamilton, Ian. "The Importance and Advantage of a Thorough Knowledge of Divine Truth." *Banner of Truth* 666 (2019) 1–4.

    Offers a devotional thought based on the above-named Edwards sermon.

25. Han, Dongsoo. "Jonathan Edwards in Korea: A History of the Reception of Jonathan Edwards." PhD diss., Trinity Evangelical Divinity School, 2019.

    Traces the development of Korean Edwardsean scholarship through three periods: (1) early reception at the end of the nineteenth century, which was spearheaded by American missionaries; (2) active reception in mid-twentieth century when Edwards's writings began to be translated into Korean and the first Korean Edwardseans appeared; and (3) the present era, in which numerous dissertations, journal articles, and essays on Edwards are being produced.

26. Hunter, Drew. "Hebrews and the Typology of Jonathan Edwards." *Themelios* 44.2 (2019) 339–52.

    Examines Edwards's reflections on Hebrews and what they reveal about his typological interpretation of the Old Testament scriptures.

27. Jeon, Heejoon. "The Role of Sanctification in the Ethics of Jonathan Edwards." PhD diss., Trinity International University, 2019.

    Asserts that most studies of Edwards's ethics fail to take into account his doctrine of sanctification, and seeks to offer a corrective. Considers the "epistemological question," the "methodological question," and Edwards's perspective on contemporary social issues.

28. Kim, Isaac. Review of *Jonathan Edwards: An Introduction to His Thought*, by Oliver Crisp and Kyle Strobel. *Religion & Theology* 26.3 (2019) 405–8.

    Declares the book is "an expansive and accessible introduction to Jonathan Edwards. This book stands out in its ability to clearly and concisely communicate the central features of Edwards's theology and philosophy. It contains both deep knowledge of Edwards and a strong pedagogical bent: the authors repeat key claims and regularly provide concise summaries."

29. Kling, David W. Review of *Jonathan Edwards: An Introduction to His Thought*, by Oliver Crisp and Kyle Strobel. *Theology Today* 76.2 (2019) 174–76.

    Concedes that "readers may dispute the authors' interpretations of Edwards's philosophical and theological shortcomings," but believes the work is a "splendid introduction" to Edwards's thought.

30. Kreider, Glenn R. Review of "Jonathan Edwards, Dispositionalism, and Spirit Christology," by S. Mark Hamilton. *Bibliotheca Sacra* 176.703 (2019) 369–70.

    States that "this article is not an easy read. Nonphilosophers and readers with little understanding of Edwards's thought will struggle to follow the article's argument. Yet the issues raised deserve serious and thoughtful engagement."

31. ———. Review of *The Essential Jonathan Edwards: An Introduction to the Life and Teaching of America's Greatest Theologian*, by Owen Strachan and Douglas A. Sweeney. *Bibliotheca Sacra* 176.701 (2019) 125–26.

    Recommends the work for its accessibility to scholars and newcomers alike.

32. ———. Review of *The Jonathan Edwards Encyclopedia*, edited by Harry S. Stout et al. *Bibliotheca Sacra* 176.702 (2019) 255–56.

Praises the work for its value as a reference tool for students of Edwards and American evangelicalism.

33. Lowe, John T., and Daniel N. Gullotta, eds. *Jonathan Edwards Within the Enlightenment: Controversy, Experience, and Thought.* New Directions in Jonathan Edwards Studies. Göttingen: Vandenhoeck & Ruprecht, 2019.

    Brings together a group of emerging Edwards scholars who tackle some of the neglected aspects of Edwards's life and thought. Topics include slavery, colonialism, racism, gender, populism, violence, pain, and witchcraft.

34. Madureira, Jonas. "A Graca Dos Santos É O Alvorecer Da Glória: Uma Nota Sobre Affection Como Sensation of the Mind em Religious Affections de Jonathan Edwards." *Fides Reformata* 24.1 (2019) 39–49.

    Explores the meaning of the term "affection" in Edwards's work *Religious Affections*.

35. Mather, Nicholas S. "Greening America's Virtues." PhD diss., California Institute of Integral Studies, 2019.

    Contends that "there is an American tradition of virtue that can be utilized to inform a uniquely American environmental virtue ethic." Includes an analysis of writings from Jonathan Edwards, Benjamin Franklin, Thomas Jefferson, Alexis de Tocqueville, and others.

36. McDermott, Gerald R. Review of *Jonathan Edwards: An Introduction to His Thought*, by Oliver Crisp and Kyle Strobel. *Scottish Journal of Theology* 72.4 (2019) 441–43.

    Summarizes the book as "provides insightful overviews" on Edwards's thinking. But he criticizes "its coverage of Edwards' moral ontology and metaphysics raises as many questions as it answers."

37. McGraw, Ryan M. Review of *Before Jonathan Edwards: Sources of New England Theology* by Adriaan Neele. *Puritan Reformed Journal* 11.2 (2019) 250–52.

    Says a few areas could have benefited from "expansion and refinement," such as the section on Edwards's method of preaching. Even so, it provides "an exceedingly high model for historical research."

38. Minkema, Kenneth P. "Jonathan Edwards Reads John Owen." *Studies in Puritanism & Piety* 1.1 (2019) 97–108.

Discusses the availability of Owen's works in colonial New England and their reception by Jonathan Edwards. Minkema gives particular attention to those areas in which Edwards believed he "resonated" with Owen.

39. ———. "A New Edwards Document: Receipt for a Slave." *Jonathan Edwards Studies* 9.2 (2019) 98–99.

    Presents a newly acquired manuscript: a sales receipt for Titus, a three-year-old "Negro" slave purchased by Jonathan Edwards.

40. ———. "The Pilgrim's Progress and Jonathan Edwards." *Bunyan Studies* 23 (2019) 62–75.

    Explores the influence of Bunyan's *Pilgrim's Progress* on Jonathan Edwards. Discovers similarities between Edwards and Bunyan on the nature of the Christian life as well as "literary echoes" between Bunyan's work and some of Edwards's writings.

41. Minkema, Kenneth P., and Adriaan C. Neele. "Complaints, Declarations, and Testimonies: Sources of Contention in Stockbridge, 1753–1756." *Jonathan Edwards Studies* 9.1 (2019) 84–93.

    Offers transcriptions of four documents highlighting the conflicts between Jonathan Edwards and the Williams family over control of the boarding schools at Stockbridge and the Williams's absenteeism from church. Their content indicates that they were meant for either the Stockbridge church committee or the Massachusetts General Assembly.

42. Minkema, Kenneth P., et al., eds. *Sermons by Jonathan Edwards on the Epistle to the Galatians.* Eugene, OR: Cascade, 2019.

    Contains previously unpublished sermons by Edwards on the book of Galatians. Introductory chapters discuss Edwards's preaching style, method, and the historical context for these sermons.

43. Minkema, Kenneth P., et al., eds. *Sermons by Jonathan Edwards on the Church.* Vol. 1: *How Christians Are Come to Mt. Sion.* Eugene, OR: Cascade, 2019.

    Offers two introductory chapters describing Edwards's preaching style, method, and historical context. The remainder of the volume contains the previously unpublished discourse "Christians Coming to Mt. Zion," which was preached at the dawn of the Great Awakening.

44. Moga, Dinu. "Jonathan Edwards and His Methodology Promoting Concern for Revival." *Perichoresis* 17.1 (2019) 71–89.

    Explains how Edwards merged the ministries of pastor and evangelist.

45. ———. "Jonathan Edwards and His Theology of Revival." *Perichoresis* 17.1 (2019) 55–70.

    Presents the case that Edwards's theology of revival was grounded in his doctrine of divine sovereignty. In other words, "the engine of any true revival movement is the sovereign work of God and not the work of man and his endeavours to produce revival."

46. ———. "Jonathan Edwards and His Understanding of Revival." *Perichoresis* 17.1 (2019) 37–54.

    Explains how Edwards developed an "explicitly and consistently Calvinistic theology of revival."

47. Monescalchi, Michael John, Jr. "A Disinterested Republic: Reform and New Divinity Theology in Early America." PhD diss., State University of New Jersey, 2019.

    Asserts that the concept of "disinterestedness" was central in early American reform literature. Includes an examination of the writings of Jonathan Edwards Jr. and Samuel Hopkins.

48. Moots, Glenn A. Review of *Jonathan Edwards and Scripture: Biblical Exegesis in British North America*, edited by David Barshinger and Douglas Sweeney. *Religious Studies Review* 45.2 (2019) 224.

    Acclaims the book for being "well organized" with "clearly identified" conclusions.

49. Najapfour, Brian G. Review of *The Emergence of Evangelical Spirituality: The Age of Edwards, Newton, Whitefield*, by Tom Schwanda. *Puritan Reformed Journal* 2 (2019) 232–39.

    Garnishes Schwanda as an authority on the evangelical spirituality and his book as "destined to be a standard" moving forward. Yet Najapfour has criticisms "notwithstanding these critiques," this is a "fine introduction to eighteenth-century evangelical spirituality."

50. Neele, Adriaan C. *Before Jonathan Edwards: Sources of New England Theology.* Oxford: Oxford University Press, 2019.

    Balances the recent academic attention on the development of theology after Edwards with a work considering the Reformed orthodox and Protestant scholastic sources employed by Jonathan Edwards in his writings.

51. ———. "Jonathan Edwards's 'Diary.'" *The Banner of Sovereign Grace Truth* 27.6 (2019) 246–47.

    Summarizes the contents of Edwards's diary and shares the insights it provides into the mind and heart of its author.

52. ———. Review of *Reformed Scholasticism: Recovering the Tools of Reformed Theology*, by Ryan McGraw. *Jonathan Edwards Studies* 9.1 (2019) 94–95.

    Believes the book will help those interested in the relationship between Edwards and his predecessors by establishing the intellectual tools needed to study Reformed scholasticism.

53. Njoto, Ricky F. "The Lord's Supper in the Hands of a Sensitive Preacher: The Bible in Edwards' Sermons on 1 Corinthians 10." *Jonathan Edwards Studies* 9.2 (2019) 28–59.

    Demonstrates how Edwards had a multifaceted view of the Lord's Supper, though the overriding theme in his sermons was union with Christ—in covenantal, marriage, familial, spiritual, eschatological, in righteousness, and in remembrance.

54. Nossaman, Lucas. Review of *Approaching Jonathan Edwards: The Evolution of a Persona* by Carol Ball. *Christianity and Literature* 68.4 (2019) 694–97.

    Complains that the book can be repetitive at times but appreciates the review of Edwards's career.

55. Pino, Ryan. "'America's Theologian' Enters the Middle Kingdom: Uncovering the Earliest Chinese Reception of Jonathan Edwards." *Jonathan Edwards Studies* 9.2 (2019) 60–82.

    Finds a footnote in *A Century of Protestant Missions in China* (1907) which references a missionary to China who translated Edwards's "Resolutions" into Chinese. Determines, through historical investigation, that this occurred toward the end of the nineteenth century. Believes this is likely the first entrance of Edwards's works into China.

56. Raley, Matthew. "A Rational and Spiritual Worship: Comparing J. S. Bach and Jonathan Edwards." *Journal of the Evangelical Theological Society* 62.3 (2019) 583–97.

Contends that Edwards's and Bach's doctrine of creation can be useful in the spiritual formation of modern people facing the "onslaught of information and entertainment."

57. Rivera, Anthony. Review of *The Jonathan Edwards Encyclopedia*, edited by Harry Stout et al. *Religion & Theology* 26.1 (2019) 163–65.

    Welcomes the resource as a unique contribution, bringing scholars from all over the world together into a single volume. It is also "highly functional and easy to use."

58. Ruetenik, Tadd. "Jonathan Edwards and the Vegan Elect: An Unconventional Calvinist Reading." *Journal for Cultural and Religious Theory* 18.3 (2019) 551–62.

    Attempts to apply the thinking of Edwards, especially on the topic of conversion, to the question of the morality of eating animal flesh. Argues that the move toward veganism can be understood as a conversion experience.

59. Ryu, Gilsun. "Jonathan Edwards's Doctrine of the Covenant of Redemption Within the Framework of the History of Redemption." *Westminster Theological Journal* 81.1 (2019) 71–91.

    Contends that Edwards used the history of redemption as an interpretive framework for understanding the Godhead and the covenant of redemption.

60. Snoeberger, Mark A. Review of *Understanding Affections in the Theology of Jonathan Edwards*, by Ryan J. Martin. *Detroit Baptist Seminary Journal* 29 (2019) 163–64.

    Believes "this volume and its conclusions are both erudite and compelling."

61. Steffaniak, Jordan L. "Participation in the Divine: The Method and Content of the Religious Epistemology of Jonathan Edwards." *Jonathan Edwards Studies* 9.1 (2019) 63–83.

    Frames Edwards's religious epistemology with his "idealistic phenomenalism." Explains the content of his epistemology as "divine communication of fullness." Contends that Edwards blends Eastern and Western elements in his system.

62. Strachan, Owen. Review of *Jonathan Edwards Among the Theologians*, by Oliver Crisp. *Scottish Journal of Theology* 72.1 (2019) 115–17.

Praises the book as a "worthy, weighty, and mind-taxing work of scholarly inquiry. It leaves us pondering what it means to be biblical; what it means to be confessional; what it means to base one's intellectual life on scripture; and where we are called to embrace mystery, instead of thinking twenty thoughts not expressly laid down in holy writ."

63. Strobel, Kyle. Review of *Before Jonathan Edwards: Sources of New England Theology*, by Adriaan Neele. *Themelios* 44.2 (2019) 384–85.

    Believes the work is "essential reading" for students of post-Reformation Reformed theology as well as for students of Edwards.

64. ———. Review of *Jonathan Edwards and Scripture: Biblical Exegesis in British North America*, edited by David Barshinger and Douglas Sweeney. *The Journal of Theological Studies* 70.1 (2019) 467–69.

    Explains that the essays vary in quality and focus, but it is still an excellent volume that contributes to our understanding of evangelical hermeneutics.

65. Strobel, Kyle, et al., eds. *Jonathan Edwards: Spiritual Writings*. New York: Paulist, 2019.

    Compiles writings from the Edwards corpus that focus on his spiritual theology.

66. Studebaker, Steven M., and Amos Yong. *Pentecostal Theology and Jonathan Edwards*. London: T&T Clark, 2019.

    Presents a critical conversation between Edwards and modern Pentecostalism on the topics of revival, pneumatology, religious affections, church and culture, mission, and witness.

67. Todd, Obbie Tyler. "An Edwardsean Evolution: The Rise and Decline of Moral Governmental Theory in the Southern Baptist Convention." *Journal of the Evangelical Theological Society* 62.4 (2019) 789–802.

    Explores the development of the doctrine of atonement in the Southern Baptist Convention. Shows that the SBC's first president embraced the moral government view while today the view is virtually absent in SBC life. Nevertheless, "the twin pillars of glory and goodness still remain."

68. ———. "The Grammar of Revival: The Legacy of Jonathan Edwards's Teleological Language in Religion Affections (1746)." *Calvin Theological Journal* 54.1 (2019) 35–56.

Defines Edwards's *Religious Affections* as a "revival spirituality in terms of its end, purpose, or goals." His "investigation into 'true religion' was imbued with overtly teleological language." This is "the story of a common grammar put to several different uses."

69. Valeri, Mark R. Review of *Understanding Affections in the Theology of Jonathan Edwards: "The High Exercises of Divine Love,"* by Ryan Martin. *Theology* 122.5 (2019) 393–94.

    Studies helpfully through the affection in Puritan theology and in Edwards. "It is overall an instructive and sound survey of Edwards on the affections with a modest argument."

70. Waddington, Jeffrey C. Review of *The Other Jonathan Edwards: Selected Writings on Society, Love, and Justice,* edited by Gerald McDermott and Ronald Story. *Fides et Historia* 51.1 (2019) 188–90.

    Hopes this book will encourage people to read the full text of the primary sources cited and develop a fully orbed view of Edwards.

71. Wilkening, Ann-Catherine. Review of *Jonathan Edwards and Scripture: Biblical Exegesis in British North America,* by David Barshinger and Douglas Sweeney. *Church History* 88.1 (2019) 243–44.

    Lauds the work for breaking new ground but laments that "none of the volume's case studies thoroughly investigate how Edwards's use of scripture informed and relate to his constructions of gender and race."

72. Woznicki, Christopher. "The Metaphysics of Jonathan Edwards's 'Personal Narrative': Continuous Creation, Personal Identity, and Spiritual Development." *Neue Zeitschrift für Systematische Theologie und Religionsphilosophie* 61.2 (2019) 184.

    Notes that "conversionism" is central to evangelical piety. Explores Edwards's "Personal Narrative" for its contribution to this concept. Special attention is given to his doctrines of continuous creation and "One-Subject Criterion" and how the two may be reconciled.

73. Yazawa, Reita. *Covenant of Redemption in the Trinitarian Theology of Jonathan Edwards: The Nexus Between the Immanent Trinity and the Economic Trinity.* Eugene, OR: Wipf & Stock, 2019.

    Demonstrates the practical value of studying the immanent Trinity through a study of Edwards's thinking on the topic. Shows how Edwards rooted believers' redemption in the covenant of redemption, which was conceived within the Trinity.

74. Zhu, Xinping. "Jonathan Edwards's Judeo-Centric and Cosmic Vision of the Millennial Kingdom." PhD diss., University of Edinburgh, 2019.

Explores Edwards's teaching on the Millennium as "a Christ-reigning, Judeo-centric and cosmic kingdom arriving on earth in the distant future." Contends that Edwards's doctrine departed from others in that it minimized the significance of England and New England in the millennial age.

2020

1. Banks, John S. "By the Same Spirit: Edwardsean Pneumatology in the Younger Edwards." PhD diss., Southern Baptist Theological Seminary, 2020.

Pushes back against the notion that Edwards Jr. was a "spiritless preacher" compared to his father, Edwards Sr. Looks closely at Edwards Jr.'s Sermon on the Mount manuscripts to show their debt to Edwards Sr.'s thought, especially as expressed in *Religious Affections*.

2. ———. "Jonathan Edwards Jr.'s Relish for True Religion: The Advance of the New England Theology in the Sermon on the Mount." *Evangelical Quarterly* 91.1 (2020) 66–92.

Pushes back against the narrative that Edwards Jr. was a "spiritless preacher" by exploring his forty-six sermons on the Sermon on the Mount and demonstrating the similarities in style and emphasis between Edwards Sr. and Edwards Jr., especially as found in Edwards Sr.'s *Religious Affections*.

3. ———. Review of *A Theology of Joy: Jonathan Edwards and Eternal Happiness in the Holy Trinity*, by Matthew Everhard. *Evangelical Quarterly* 91.2 (2020) 189–90.

Says the book is "a handy survey of Edwards's theology of joy" and "useful from a pastoral perspective."

4. Barone, Marco. "Jonathan Edwards on Necessity and Contingency: A Reconsideration." *Jonathan Edwards Studies* 10.1 (2020) 2–19.

Delves into the debate between Richard Muller and Paul Helm on the question of Edwards's relationship to the broader Reformed tradition on the doctrines of necessity, contingency, and freedom of the will. Believes that several key Edwardsean texts have been omitted from the debate—texts which would make an important contribution to the conversation.

5. Bezzant, Rhys. "A Providential Plumbline for Pastoral Practice: Edwards's Exposition of the Kingdom of God." *Jonathan Edwards Studies* 10.2 (2020) 129–36.

    Considers Edwards's thoughts on the doctrine of the Kingdom of God.

6. Breimaier, Thomas. Review of *The Spirit of Early Evangelicalism: True Religion in a Modern World*, by D. Bruce Hindmarsh. *Church History* 89.1 (2020) 210–11.

    Appreciates the book for incorporating well-known evangelical leaders like Jonathan Edwards as well as lesser-known leaders like Augustus Toplady.

7. Britz, Dolf. "Jonathan Edwards on the Cape of Good Hope." *Jonathan Edwards Studies* 20.2 (2020) 137–49.

    Shows that Edwards was familiar with the Cape of Good Hope and its indigenous population and explains how that was possible, namely, through the travel literature available to Edwards at the time.

8. Burnell, Joel, and Wojciech Szczerba. "After Ten Years: The Jonathan Edwards Center Poland—Past, Present and Future." *Jonathan Edwards Studies* 10.2 (2020) 208–15.

    Looks back at the establishment of JEC-Poland in 2009 and provides an account of its present and planned activities.

9. Caldwell, Robert W., III. Review of *Understanding Affections in the Theology of Jonathan Edwards: "The High Exercises of Divine Love,"* by Ryan Martin. *The Journal of Theological Studies* 71.1 (2020) 394–96.

    Believes the work makes a compelling case for asserting that Edwards drew his concept of "affections" from the Christian tradition as opposed to receiving it from Enlightenment sources.

10. Chun, Chris. "Regeneration, Revival, and Creation." *Jonathan Edwards Studies* 20.2 (2020) 150–56.

Discusses the establishment and inaugural conference of the Jonathan Edwards Center at Gateway Seminary in Ontario, California.

11. Clark, David J. Review of *Jonathan Edwards and Scripture: Biblical Exegesis in British North America*, edited by David P. Barshinger and Douglas A Sweeney. *Journal for the Study of the Old Testament* 44.5 (2020) 72.

    Summarizes the book as only marginally covering the Old Testament, "which will lower its appeal to JSOT reader," but it "remains an interesting reflection on the life and personality of a serious and devoted biblical scholar."

12. Cochran, Joseph T. "Jonathan Edwards's Harmonic Interpretation of Hebrews 12:22–24." *Jonathan Edwards Studies* 10.1 (2020) 20–47.

    Describes the three principle elements of Edwards's "harmonic" (or canonical) exegetical method using Hebrews 12:22–24 as a case study. Those three elements include (1) the prophetic nature of Scripture and prophetic fulfillment, (2) typology, and (3) the harmony of doctrine and precept between the two testaments.

13. Crawford, Brandon James. Review of *Jonathan Edwards: An Introduction to His Thought*, by Oliver Crisp and Kyle Strobel. *Detroit Baptist Seminary Journal* 25 (2020) 155–57.

    Summarizes the contents of the book and concludes that it is not a book for beginners as the authors claim in the introduction; even so, it does make a useful contribution to the field.

14. DeBruyn, David. "Jonathan Edwards's Synthesis of Definitions of Beauty." *Artistic Theologian* 8 (2020) 75–98.

    Explores four ideas related to the definition of beauty and asserts that Edwards's perspective offers the best synthesis of these ideas.

15. Deeter, Justin Baine. "Communion with God and the Means of Grace in the Spirituality of Jonathan Edwards." PhD diss., Southeastern Baptist Theological Seminary, 2020.

    Examines the transition from Puritan spirituality to evangelical spirituality through careful consideration of the piety of Jonathan Edwards.

16. Farrow, Holly. "The Union of Theology and Doxology: A Comparative Study of Jonathan Edwards and Anne Dutton." *Artistic Theologian* 8 (2020) 47–74.

    Offers a comparative study of the spiritual writings of Edwards and Dutton and demonstrates the similarities between the two in content, depth, and intensity of writing.

17. Ferreira, Franklin. "'They Are Precious Gifts of Heaven': Jonathan Edwards's Works in Brazil." *Jonathan Edwards Studies* 10.2 (2020) 157–66.

    Summarizes the reception of Edwards and his writings in Brazil.

18. Finn, Nathan. Review of *Jonathan Edwards: Spiritual Writings*, edited by Kyle Strobel et al. *Themelios* 45.2 (2020) 438–39.

    Acclaims the work as "a signal contribution."

19. Fisk, Philip. "Jonathan Edwards and Samuel Clarke on Liberty and Necessity: A Manner of Distinction, and Why It Matters." *Jonathan Edwards Studies* 10.2 (2020) 167–79.

    Proposes that the background to Edwards's use of the term "moral necessity" is found in the writings of Samuel Clarke (1675–1729) and his work *A Demonstration of the Being and Attributes of God*.

20. Garretson, James M. Review of *Edwards the Mentor*, by Rhys Bezzant. *The Banner of Truth* (UK) 683–84 (2020) 62–63.

    Affirms the book as "a rich and historically informed study with suggestive application to the present moment."

21. Gribben, Crawford. "Andrew Fuller and the Millennium." *Jonathan Edwards Studies* 10.2 (2020) 180–92.

    Discusses the millennial debates among the English Baptists and how the developing evangelical consensus affected their expectations for the conversion of the world and of the missionary work required to bring this about.

22. Hamilton, S. Mark. Review of *Before Jonathan Edwards: Sources of New England Theology*, by Adriaan C. Neele. *International Journal of Systematic Theology* 22.4 (2020) 576–77.

    Comments that few books have "the potential to change the entire field of research" and Neele's book "is certainly one of them."

23. Han, Dongsoo. "Jonathan Edwards on the Work of the Holy Spirit in the Godly Life of the Saint." 한국개혁신학 65 (2020) 10–50.

    Dwells on Edwards's view that the grace of God imparted to the sinner at salvation is the Holy Spirit himself. Considers the workings of the Holy Spirit in the life of the believer.

24. Hancock, C. Layne. Review of *Human Nature from Calvin to Edwards*, by Paul Helm. *Jonathan Edwards Studies* 10.1 (2020) 112–14.

    Describes the work as "difficult yet rewarding."

25. Hart, Matthew J. Review of *Human Nature from Calvin to Edwards*, by Paul Helm. *Unio cum Christo* 6.1 (2020) 246–50.

    Describes the book as "a leisurely jaunt through theological anthropology," but with two weaknesses: (1) "Helm gave too little time to analysis and assessment of the various positions canvassed" and (2) the table of contents lacks sub-chapters, making it difficult to know exactly who and what is covered in each chapter at a glance.

26. Haykin, Michael A. G. "Jonathan Edwards on the Typology of Green." *Barnabas* 12.4 (2020) 12.

    Shares Edwards's thoughts on the color green, which he believed to be the loveliest of all colors and a "most fit emblem of divine grace," as it is the color of "life, flourishing, prosperity, and happiness."

27. ———. Review of *Edwards the Mentor*, by Rhys Bezzant. *Church History and Religious Culture* 100.2–3 (2020) 418–20.

    Shows appreciation for a book that breaks fresh ground on a vital topic.

28. ———. Review of *Jonathan Edwards: Spiritual Writings*, edited by Kyle Strobel, Adriaan C. Neele and Kenneth P. Minkema. *Evangelical Quarterly* 91.2 (2020) 183–84.

    Praises the volume as a "great collection of representative texts of Edwards's spirituality."

29. Helm, Paul. "Edwards: Ethics for Both the Vulgar and the Learned." *Unio cum Christo* 6.1 (2020) 149–65.

    Explores the articulation of Edwards's ethics in his roles as a pastor and a theorist.

30. Hussey, Phillip. Review of *Before Jonathan Edwards: Sources of New England Theology*, by Adriaan C. Neele. *The Journal of Ecclesiastical History* 71.4 (2020) 874–76.

Fills a "lacuna" in the secondary sources as he "meticulously" points to the primary sources.

31. Kay, William K. Review of *Pentecostal Theology and Jonathan Edwards*, edited by Steven M. Studebaker and Amos Yong. *Theology* 123.6 (2020) 459–60.

    Applauds the book for having "no dud chapters." This volume is an "interesting and well-constructed book."

32. Kemp, Raymond A. Review of *The Great Awakening: A History of the Revival of Religion in the Time of Whitefield and Edwards*, by Joseph Tracy. *Free Church Witness*, May 2020. 17–18.

    Writes that "this retypeset, tightly-printed work by the Banner will serve as the standard work on the Great Awakening for many. A delightful read, highly commended to all."

33. Kling, David W. "Jonathan Edwards, Petitionary Prayer, and the Cognitive Science of Religion." *Theology and Science* 18.1 (2020) 113–36.

    Reviews the modern presuppositions of cognitive science with regard to religion: (1) religion is a natural evolutionary development and (2) it involves a two-system model of reasoning that moves from basic beliefs in God to an elaboration of those beliefs. Examines the writings of Edwards on the subject of petitionary prayer to show how moving from the first stage to the second stage in religious development can be fraught with tension and even contradiction.

34. Lowe, John T. Review of *Before Jonathan Edwards: Sources of New England Theology*, by Adriaan Neele. *Jonathan Edwards Studies* 10.1 (2020) 115–16.

    Praises the work as "invaluable and a key to understanding Edwards's theology. The unmatched thoroughness of Neele's prose coupled with the sea of detailed footnotes along prove this work is commendable."

35. Lumpkin, Aaron. "Reading the Gospels with Jonathan Edwards: Interpretive Practices of America's Greatest Theologian." PhD diss., Southeastern Baptist Theological Seminary, 2020.

    Examines Edwards's interpretation of the biblical gospels, beginning with historical foundations and then moving into his doctrine of Scripture, the major influences on his hermeneutic, his use of typology, and his emphasis on the harmony of Scripture, the kingdom of God, and the person and work of Christ.

36. Marsden, George. "Old, Rested, and Reformed: Reflections on the Recovery of Edwards." *Jonathan Edwards Studies* 10.2 (2020) 120–28.

    Offers personal anecdotes about the author's early encounters with Edwards's writings as well as a historical survey of the revival of interest in Edwards. Traces the revival to two sources: (1) the Reformed evangelical rediscovery of Edwards through the ministries of Ligonier and Banner of Truth, and (2) the mainline and neo-orthodox Protestant rediscovery through Perry Miller and others, which resulted in the *Works of Jonathan Edwards* project at Yale University. Edwards was popularized in subsequent years by men like Richard Lovelace, Tim Keller, John Piper, and Mark Noll. Eventually, the two streams of Edwards scholars merged through Edwards conferences. The Edwards website at Yale finally turned Edwards into a global phenomenon.

37. McDermott, Gerald. "The Saints in Heaven as Spectators of Providence: Edwards and the Tradition." *Jonathan Edwards Studies* 10.2 (2020) 193–201.

    Outlines Jonathan Edwards's teachings regarding the intermediate state and concludes that (1) Edwards was not novel in believing that the saints in heaven have some awareness of what is taking place on earth; (2) Edwards was unique in believing that the "main business" of the saints in heaven was to monitor the progress of the church on earth; and (3) while Edwards believed that the saints in heaven could see both the saints on earth and the suffering in hell, he was more interested in emphasizing the former than the latter.

38. Morimoto, Anri. "The Passions and the Interests: An Edwardsean Understanding of Populism." *Jonathan Edwards Studies* 10.2 (2020) 202–7.

    Contends that the modern world is being "ripped apart" by populism, which the author roots in peoples' desire "to be a meaningful part of something." Believes that Edwards disdained populism, being more concerned with divine justice than human, and rooting virtue in "benevolence to Being in general" rather than in one's own partisan interests. Offers Edwards as a corrective to modern populist thinking.

39. Neele, Adriaan C. Review of *Edwards the Mentor*, by Rhys Bezzant. *Puritan Reformed Journal* 12.1 (2020) 214–15.

    Says that "Bezzant has given not only Edwardsean scholarship but those in theological education and church ministry the fruit of historical and careful research, scholarly expertise, and practical application for the church and academy today."

40. Noll, Mark. "Jonathan Edwards in Scotland: An Alternative History." *Jonathan Edwards Studies* 10.2 (2020) 227–50.

    Provides a humorous counter-factual history of Edwards's career in Scotland and how his interactions there "almost changed the course of American history."

41. Painter, Jeremy. "'Made for Other Worlds': The Preacher and the Imagination." PhD diss., Regent University, 2020.

    Situates the imagination in preaching and considers four exemplary models: Chrysostom, Bernard of Clairvaux, Jonathan Edwards, and J. T. Pugh.

42. Paul, Roy M. *Jonathan Edwards and the Stockbridge Mohican Indians: His Mission and Sermons.* Peterborough, Ontario, Canada: H&E, 2020.

    Tells the story of Edwards's ministry in Stockbridge and examines several sermons from that period.

43. Pendergrass, Aaron. "The Everlasting Mediation of the Son of God: A Case Study of the Enduring Mediatorial Office of Christ in Calvin and the Reformed Tradition." PhD diss., Trinity International University, 2020.

    Examines the mediatorial office of Christ in the writings of Calvin, Ambrose, Goodwin, Owen, Turretin, Edwards, and Kuyper.

44. Schultz, Walter J. *Jonathan Edwards' Concerning the End for Which God Created the World: Exposition, Analysis, and Philosophical Implications.* New Directions in Jonathan Edwards Studies. Göttingen: Vandenhoeck & Ruprecht, 2020.

    Identifies and discusses the assumptions undergirding Edwards's famous treatise and provides an exposition of the thesis proper. Also considers the philosophical implications of Edwards's thought. Specific topics addressed include Edwards on exemplarism, dispositionalism, emanationism, idealism, continuous creationism, panentheism, and occasionalism.

45. Schwanda, Tom. Review of *Jonathan Edwards: Spiritual Writings*, edited by Kyle Strobel et al. *The Journal of Spiritual Formation & Soul Care* 13.1 (2020) 139–41.

    Commends the book as a "masterly overview"; however, "what is lacking in this otherwise work" is the biographical background of Edwards, particularly for the "non-protestant readers."

46. Scorgie, Glen G. Review of *The Emergence of Evangelical Spirituality: The Age of Edwards, Newton and Whitefield*, by Tom Schwanda. *Spiritus* 20.2 (2020) 277–80.

    Expresses pleasure that the work not only covers the "great men" of the past but also more than forty lesser-known men and women of early evangelicalism.

47. Shin, Joyce Sue-Mee. "Faith in an Age of Cultural Pluralism: An Aesthetic Approach to Transformation." PhD diss., University of Chicago, 2020.

    Proposes that "attending to the formal and emotional qualities of faith is precisely what distinguishes an aesthetic approach from other approaches [to integrating faith and culture] and further, that such an aesthetic approach is necessary for addressing the question of faith and culture in a globalized cultural context." Jonathan Edwards, John Dewey, and H. Richard Niebuhr are drawn upon as models.

48. Shrader, Matthew C. "New England Baptist Alvah Hovey: A Later Chapter in Baptist Edwardsianism." *Jonathan Edwards Studies* 10.1 (2020) 48–64.

    Explores the Edwardsean themes found in the writings of Alvah Hovey, professor and president of Newton Theological Institute during the second half of the nineteenth century.

49. Steven, Brian. "Jonathan Edwards (1703–1758) On the Book of Genesis." ThM thesis, Puritan Reformed Theological Seminary, 2020.

    Considers Edwards's exegesis of the book of Genesis and the theological conclusions he reached from Genesis.

50. Strobel, Kyle. "Barth and Edwards." In *Barth in Dialogue*, edited by George Johnson and Keith L. Hunsinger, 495–506. Vol. 2 of *The Wiley Blackwell Companion to Karl Barth*. Hoboken, NJ: Wiley-Blackwell, 2020.

    Brings Barth into dialogue with Edwards on the topics of creation, revelation, and the divine attributes.

51. Strobel, Kyle, and Chris Chun, eds. *Regeneration, Revival, and Creation: Religious Experience and the Purposes of God in the Thought of Jonathan Edwards.* Eugene, OR: Pickwick, 2020.

    Contains many of the papers presented at the inaugural conference of the Jonathan Edwards Center at Gateway Seminary (JEC West), focusing mostly on the themes of regeneration, revival, and creation.

52. Swan, Nick. Review of *Covenant of Redemption in the Trinitarian Theology of Jonathan Edwards: The Nexus Between the Imminent Trinity and the Economic Trinity*, by Reita Yazawa. *Trinity Journal* 41.1 (2020) 53–66.

    Applauds the work as not only relaying the covenant of redemption but also "illumines his Trinitarian and covenantal theology" as well as several other points of theology.

53. Underhill, Thomas. "Discovering Naaman's Hypocrisy: A Genealogical Account of Jonathan Edwards's Exegesis of 2 Kings 5." *Jonathan Edwards Studies* 10.1 (2020) 65–88.

    Recounts the passage from *Religious Affections* in which Edwards uses Naaman as an example of counterfeit affections and explores Edwards's lifelong interactions with the Naaman story as well as the history of interpretation related to Naaman and his conversion.

54. Vargas, Kristin. "Positive Mimesis in Jonathan Edwards's *Charity and Its Fruits*." *Jonathan Edwards Studies* 10.1 (2020) 89–111.

    Compares the thinking of Edwards with the twentieth-century French intellectual René Girard on the topic of the teleological pattern of nature.

55. Vlastuin, Willem van. "Jonathan Edwards in Amsterdam." *Jonathan Edwards Studies* 10.2 (2020) 216–26.

    Surveys translations of Edwards's works in the Netherlands and reflects on the academic conversation about Edwards in that nation.

56. ———. Review of *Edwards the Mentor*, by Rhys Bezzant. *Journal of Reformed Theology* 14.3 (2020) 286–87.

    Says that he really "enjoyed this book, especially because" it "sheds new light on Edwards's theology and spirituality."

57. Welch, Shawn. "Justified: The Pragmaticization of American Evangelicalism from Jonathan Edwards to the Social Gospel." PhD diss., University of Michigan, 2020.

   Tracks the "pragmatic attitudes" found in evangelicalism and explores the three major "epistemological underpinnings" of these attitudes: (1) the privileging of direct experience; (2) the practical identification of essence and praxis; and (3) belief in God's pervasive affection toward creation.

58. York, Alwyn. "Sereno Edwards Dwight, Biographer of Jonathan Edwards." *The Banner of Truth* 677 (2020) 11–13.

   Offers a brief biography of Sereno Dwight as Edwards's first biographer.

2021

1. Banks, John S. *The Forgotten Edwards: A New Examination of the Life and Thought of Jonathan Edwards Junior.* Fort Worth, TX: JESociety, 2021.

   Makes the case the Jonathan Edwards Jr. has been largely overlooked. In this book, primary sources are utilized to set the record straight.

2. Barone, Marco. Review of *Pentecostal Theology and Jonathan Edwards*, by Steven Studebaker and Amos Yong. *Jonathan Edwards Studies* 11.1 (2021) 97–98.

   Reveals the primary goal of the book is to employ some of Pentecostalism's best theologians to draw on themes present in Edwards thinking and consider it within the scope of wider contemporary theology.

3. Benge, Dustin W. "The Angelology of Jonathan Edwards." *The Southern Baptist Journal of Theology* 25.2 (2021) 105–23.

   Indicates that for Edwards angelology was a "corollary of Christology."

4. Borgman, Brian. *Jonathan Edwards on Genesis: Hermeneutics, Homiletics, and Theology.* Eugene, OR: Wipf & Stock, 2021.

   Offers a specifically focused approach to Edwards the exegete of Genesis. Edwards includes with paramount importance devotion to Genesis 1–2 and the expression of the image of God.

5. Boss, Robert L., and Sarah B. Boss, eds. *The Jonathan Edwards Miscellanies Companion*. Vol. 1. Fort Worth, TX: JESociety, 2021.

    Collects authors who contribute to the overall discussion of Edwards's theological "Miscellanies."

6. ———, eds. *The Jonathan Edwards Miscellanies Companion*. Vol. 2. Fort Worth, TX: JESociety, 2021.

    Collects authors who contribute to the overall discussion of Edwards's theological "Miscellanies."

7. Brown, Cullin R. "Natures Converts: Reading the Land and Nature in Early American Conversion, 1727–1831." PhD diss., University of Mississippi, 2021.

    Studies clergymen from 1727 to 1836 who were in favor of clearing off wilderness to provide prosperous farms. However, equally Protestants embodied anxiety for land cultivation to produce a godly society. One such minister was Jonathan Edwards.

8. Brown, Geoffrey Todd. "Exegetical Soundness Regarding Race: How White American Evangelicals Were Influenced by Contemporary Racial Opinions of Their Day Rather Than Consistent with Application of Biblical Hermeneutics." PhD diss., Southeastern Baptist Theological Seminary, 2021.

    Analyzes four white evangelicals—Jonathan Edwards, Richard Furman, Charles Hodge, and Bob Jones Sr.—and assesses that they were more influenced by racial opinion of their day than the Bible. After a brief biography of Edwards, Brown evidences his conclusions by presenting "Receipt for a Slave Girl Venus" and Edwards's "Draft on Slavery," among others.

9. Boyden, Michael. *Predicting the Past: The Paradoxes of American Literary History*. Leuven: Leuven University Press, 2021.

    Concentrates on themes such as "Anglocentric" theories of American literature and concludes it is inherently racist. When viewing Edwards, Boyden indicates the way institutions play a part in genealogical misrepresentations, such as Perry Miller, who compared Edwards to Emerson and hence made Puritan studies relevant.

10. Caldwell, Robert W., III. Review of *A Treatise on Jonathan Edwards, Continuous Creation and Christology*, by S. Mark Hamilton. *Themelios* 46.1 (2021) 215–16.

Forges a "new framework" of metaphysics, ontology, and Christology, and weds them together to deal with this thorny question.

11. Campbell, Benjamin Scott. "For Faithful Narratives: Why Pastors Should Journal." *Puritan Reformed Journal* 13.2 (2021) 161–78.

    Examines the diaries of David Brainerd, John Elliot, Jonathan Edwards, and Samuel Ward.

12. Cavalier, Adam G. *"Salvation Shall Spread to All the Tribes and Ranks of Mankind": Edwards and World Mission*. Fort Worth, TX: JESociety, 2021.

    Suggests that a biblical-theological-historical analysis of Edwards's philosophy of missions would fill a "lacuna in Edwards studies."

13. Choi, Paul. "The Agony and the Eschatology: Apocalyptic Thought in New England Evangelical Calvinism from Jonathan Edwards to Lyman Beecher." PhD diss., Boston University, 2021.

    Traces the apocalyptic thinking within the theology of Jonathan Edwards and Lyman Beecher. This dissertation covers Edwards as a representative of the First Great Awakening of the eighteenth century and Second Great Awakening of the nineteenth century. He says that Edwards is a precursor of a distinctly Calvinistic form of apocalypticism.

14. Cochran, Joseph T. "Jonathan Edwards and Hebrews: A Harmonic Interpretation of Scripture." PhD diss., Trinity International University, 2021.

    Focuses Edwards exegesis on the Epistle to the Hebrews as recorded in the "Blank Bible"; "Notes on Scripture"; "Miscellanies"; "Typological Notebooks"; and "Harmony Notebooks" as well as his sermons on Hebrews. Edwards drew on Reformed interpreters such as Phillip Doddridge, John Owen, and Matthew Poole and Enlightenment philosophers such as Isaac Newton, John Locke, and Francis Hutcheson. This is the first survey of Edwards on Hebrews.

15. ———. Review of *The Oxford Handbook of Jonathan Edward*, edited by Douglas A. Sweeney and Jan Stievermann. *Fides et Historia* 53.1 (2021) 74–78.

    Surveys the contributions of scholars that made an impact on Edwards studies from Perry Miller in 1953 until the *Oxford Handbook*. He considers the contributors in the anthology. Describes

Edwards's global influence in North America, Asia, Australia, Africa, and Latin America as having only begun to be analyzed. The *Oxford Handbook* is only the first fruit of this endeavor.

16. ———. Review of *A Great and Remarkable Analogy: The Onto-Typology of Jonathan Edwards*, by Lisanne Winslow. *Jonathan Edwards Studies* 11.2 (2021) 183–84.

    Articulates Edwards's natural theology and indicates that God's glory is revealed through nature.

17. Crampton, W. Gary. *Interpreting Edwards: An Overview and Analysis of John H. Gerstner's The Rational Biblical Theology of Jonathan Edwards*. Lakeland, FL: Whitefield, 2021.

    Assesses John Gerstner's three-volume interpretation in *The Rational Biblical Theology of Jonathan Edwards*. Crampton gives an overview and analysis of this extensive research by Gerstner.

18. Davidson, Bruce W. "Unholy Hate: The Essence of Human Evil in the Theology of Jonathan Edwards." *The Journal of the Evangelical Theological Society* 64.4 (2021) 643–55.

    Edwards's idea of the hostility of God is summed up in self-love or in self-deception.

19. Davis, Holly. "The Interconnectedness of Jonathan Edwards's Ontology and Trinitarianism." MA thesis, University of Arkansas, 2021.

    Defends Edwards's ontology and trinitarianism in its historical, philosophical, and theological context.

20. Everhard, Matthew V. *Holy Living: Jonathan Edwards's Seventy Resolutions for Living the Christian Life*. Peabody, MA: Hendrickson, 2021.

    Argues that Edwards's *Resolutions* should shape the Christian life in the present. These *Resolutions* concentrate on "Holy Living" in three main categories: existential, ethical, and eschatological.

21. Fesko, J. V. "Who Lurks Behind Geerhardus Vos? Sources and Predecessors." *Reformed Faith and Practice* 6.2 (2021) 3–9.

    Contends that scholars should no longer consider Vos the "father of Reformed biblical theology" because his biblical theology is not unique to others in the Reformed tradition. Jonathan Edwards's *History of the Work of Redemption* is a case in point.

22. Field, Brady Paul. "Speaking Up and Out: The Subversion of Puritan Rhetorical Forms in the Writing of Lemuel Haynes." MA thesis, Emporia State University, 2021.

    Contributes to the ongoing discussions in scholarship by studying the Black preacher Lemuel Haynes, who was a theological descendent of Edwards and the Edwardseans.

23. Golding, D. Robert. "Making Sense of Hell." *Themelios* 46.1 (2021) 145–62.

    Assesses that the doctrine of hell is a logically necessary conclusion of Christianity. He examines hell in the theology of Edwards and relies on this conception.

24. Gordon, Bruce, and Carl R. Trueman, eds. *The Oxford Handbook of Calvin and Calvinism*. Oxford: Oxford University Press, 2021.

    Argues that Edwards played a significant role in shaping evangelicalism (pp. 641–56).

25. Griffith, Christopher Ryan. *The Life of Andrew Fuller: A Critical Edition of John Ryland's Biography*. Berlin: de Gruyter, 2021.

    Studies the profound influence Edwards had on Fuller.

26. Hoehner, Paul J. *The Covenant Theology of Jonathan Edwards: Law, Gospel, and Evangelical Obedience*. Eugene, OR: Pickwick, 2021.

    Contends that covenant theology has often been missed by Edwards scholars, but his theology is bound up with the covenant of redemption, works, and grace. Hoehner argues that this is the "internal scaffolding that gave shape to the biblical story of redemption."

27. Huggins, Jonathan. Review of *Understanding Affections in the Theology of Jonathan Edwards: "The High Exercises of Divine Love,"* by Ryan Martin. *Stellenbosch Theological Journal* 7.1 (2021) 1–3.

    Discusses how the affections shape the theology of Edwards but common misinterpretation persists. "Those with academic interests will need to reckon with this work."

28. Jeon, Heejoon. "The Third Use of the Law: John Calvin and Jonathan Edwards." *Journal of Reformed Theology* 15.1–2 (2021) 110–34.

    Contends that despite misunderstanding from some modern scholars, Edwards holds the same view of the third use of the law as Calvin.

29. Johnson, Dana E. "The Categories of Jonathan Edwards' Natural Philosophy Applied to Organic Chemistry: An Integrative Example." *Religion* 12.3 (2021) 151.

    Refers to the "Spider" papers and connects them to organic chemistry as applying to the modern field natural science.

30. Jones, Zachary. "Recognizing Revelation: Illuminating the Epistemology Context of Biblical Worship." PhD diss., Southeastern Baptist Theological Seminary, 2021.

    Adopts Edwards as case study of epistemological apprehension of God's glory.

31. Juchno, Andrew J. "Beyond Salem and Secularism: Jonathan Edwards and Satan in Early America." *Jonathan Edwards Studies* 11.1 (2021) 73–94.

    Discusses Edwards's diabology as compares favorably to Cotton Mather's against such historians who view the Salem witch trials as representative of the colonial understanding of Satan.

32. Kim, Song. "Mysticism in Jonathan Edwards's Theology of Spirituality: A Comparison Between Edwards's and Bernard of Clairvaux's Understanding of Union and Communion with Christ." *Jonathan Edwards Studies* 11.1 (2021) 1–28.

    Compares the concepts of union and communion with God between Edwards and Bernard. He reveals that there are many mystical portions in the spirituality of both Edwards and Bernard. Kim speaks of continuities and discontinuities between them.

33. Kitanov, Severin V. Review of *Seeing God: The Beatific Vision in the Christian Tradition*, by Hans Boersma. *Anglican and Episcopal History* 90.4 (2021) 411–13.

    Argues that theologians of historic Christianity have had a concept of the Beatific Vision, including Edwards.

34. Liem Yoe Gie, Jonathan. "Teresa of Avila and Jonathan Edwards on Prayer and Spirituality." *Veritas* 20.2 (2021) 219–35.

    Contends that Teresa of Avila and Jonathan Edwards compare very favorably on mystical prayer.

35. Lowe, John T. Review of *Jonathan Edwards and Scripture: Biblical Exegesis in British North America*, edited by David P. Barshinger and Douglas A. Sweeney. *Journal of Reformed Theology* 15.1–2 (2021) 158–60.

Collects authors to write about Edwards's "biblical exegesis."

36. Marini, Amelia. "Very Two, Very One: Reading as Friendship." PhD diss., City University of New York, 2021.

    Suggests that by looking at Edwards, Ralph Waldo Emerson, and the poet Susan Howe, one can find friendship in reading sacred texts and poetry.

37. Matalu, Muriwali Yanto. Review of *Pentecostal Theology and Jonathan Edwards*, edited by Steven M. Studebaker and Amos Yong. *European Journal of Theology* 30.2 (2021) 380–82.

    Argues that the book was written mostly by Pentecostal attempts to connect Edwards's theology to Pentecostalism, which is an important achievement. However, the idea that Edwards is "proto-Pentecostal" fails to persuade.

38. McClymond, Michael L. "Agape, Self-Sacrifice, and Mutuality: An Exploration into the Thought of Jonathan Edwards and the Theme of Godly Love." In *The Science and Theology of Godly Love*, edited by Matthew T. Lee and Amos T. Yong, 33–55. Ithaca, NY: Cornell University Press, 2021.

    Explains the "love and mutuality" in the thoughts of Jonathan Edwards. But McClymond also spends time in the "vexation of self-love" and the consequences of this self-love.

39. McGee, Iain. "Revelation and Religions: Towards a More 'Harmonious' Jonathan Edwards." *Themelios* 46.3 (2021) 620–40.

    Argues against McDermott's reading of the "Deist Context" and suggests his own article has certain advantages in presenting a more balanced reading of Edwards's thought.

40. McGlothlin, James C. "A Profoundly Theological Ethical Philosophy." *Criswell Theological Review* 19.1 (2021) 67–82.

    Investigates the first two chapters of Edwards's *Nature of True Virtue*, highlighting a robust ethical system that conceives of a philosophical agenda of a God-centered approach to ethics.

41. Meilaender, Gilbert. "Natural Morality or Splendid Vice? The Case of Paul Ramsey." *Pro Ecclesia* 30.2 (2021) 244–57.

    Claims that Ramsey's *Basic Christian Ethics*, first published in 1950, was a reworking of themes found in Jonathan Edwards *Ethical Writing* to which Ramsey was a major contributor.

42. Minkema, Kenneth P. "'If Thou Reckon Right': Angels from John Calvin to Jonathan Edwards via John Milton." In *Oxford Handbook of Calvin and Calvinism*, edited by Bruce Gordon and Carl Trueman, 393–407. Oxford: Oxford University Press, 2021.

    Offers a sweeping account of angels from the Protestant Reformation to the post Reformation era.

43. Minkema, Kenneth P., et al. "Agitations, Convulsions, Leaping, and Loud Talking: The 'Experiences' of Sarah Pierpont Edwards." *William and Mary Quarterly* 78 (2021) 491–536.

    Offers new insights on the spiritual experiences of Sarah Edwards after her own account.

44. Miyagi, Ken. "Jonathan Edwards's View of Sympathy as It Relates to His Socio-Ethical Perspective." *Jonathan Edwards Studies* 11.2 (2021) 100–116.

    Explores Edwards's view of sympathy and links it to others in the seventeenth century.

45. Neville, Jonathan E. *Infinite Goodness: Joseph Smith, Jonathan Edwards, and the Book of Mormon*. Salt Lake City: Digital Legends, 2021.

    Proposes that during his early years, Joseph Smith spent time reading Christian theology, "particularly the works of Jonathan Edwards." Therefore, the book of Mormon has been shaped by Jonathan Edwards.

46. Nichols, Stephen J. *The Spirit of Truth: The Holy Spirit and the Apologetics of Jonathan Edwards*. Phillipsburg, NJ: P&R, 2021.

    Reprint. See M. X. Lesser, *Reading Jonathan Edwards: An Annotated Bibliography in Three Parts, 1729–2005* (Grand Rapids: Eerdmans, 2008), 577 [2003.74].

47. Njoto, Ricky F. "The Redemption Discourse and Edwards the Missionary." *Journal of Reformed Theology* 15.1–2 (2021) 48–69.

    Offers redemption discourse to interpret Edwards's thought as a missionary.

48. Oesterling, Jason. "Casuistic Book-Lending: Jonathan Edwards' Use of Daniel Defoe's Religious Courtship." *Jonathan Edwards Studies* 11.1 (2001) 45–72.

    Catalogues the books that Edwards owned. Daniel Defoe's *Religious Courtship* was one that he regularly lent out.

49. Petrou, Irene. "Knowledge and Reason Versus Experience and Practice: Jonathan Edwards and the Patristic Doctrine of Deification." In *From the Fifth Century Onwards (Latin Writers); Female Power and Its Propaganda; Theologizing Performance in the Byzantine Tradition; Nachleben*, edited by Markus Vinzent et al., 489–502. Vol. 27 of *Papers Presented at the Eighteenth International Conference on Patristic Studies Held in Oxford 2019*. Studia Patristica 130. Leuven: Peeters, 2021.

   Contends that Edwards noted how Protestantism was growing increasingly rationalistic. Edwards breaks down the dichotomy of knowledge and practice as a false dichotomy. Petrou says it was "the patristic doctrine of deification" or theosis that allowed Edwards to do this.

50. Rehnman, Sebastian. *Edwards on God*. London: Routledge, 2021.

    Questions whether one should refer to Edwards as one of America's greatest philosophical-theologians because his proofs of God and God's attributes have been soundly refuted. But he asks, How should we perceive Edwards's philosophy of God? Rehnman endeavors to provide three values philosophers make use of: history, logic, and wisdom. He evaluates Edwards by these three values.

51. Ryu, Gilsun. *The Federal Theology of Jonathan Edwards: An Exegetical Perspective*. Bellingham, WA: Lexham, 2021.

    Maintains that scholars have not dealt with Edwards's federal theology particularly on the headship of Christ or Christ and the covenants. He fills this void.

52. Schweitzer, Cameron. "Does Edwards Have a 'Thoroughgoing "Feminine" Ecclesiology'? A Response to Benjamin Wayman in a Reconsideration of the Evidence from *The Blank Bible*." *Jonathan Edwards Studies* 11.2 (2021) 147–82.

    Evaluates whether the doctrine of the church is feminine, as Benjamin Wayman says, or this is just another type of Edwards's biblically robust ecclesiology. When one gathers all the relevant material on this subject, Schweitzer says, it requires Wayman to reassess.

53. ———. "'Everything . . . Was Typical of Gospel Things!' A Reconsideration of Jonathan Edwards's Biblical Typology: A Study of His 'Blank Bible.'" *Studies in Puritanism and Piety Journal* 3.1 (2021) 27–60.

Surveys his typological writings as recorded in the "Blank Bible" in the confirmation of Edwards's statement that everything was typical of gospel things.

54. ———. Review of *Regeneration, Revival, and Creation: Religious Experience and the Purposes of God in the Thought of Jonathan Edwards*, edited by Chris Chun and Kyle C. Strobel. *Calvin Theological Journal* 56.1 (2021) 135–38.

    Essays at Gateway Seminary in 2019 devoted to Edwards's theology of regeneration and revival and types in nature.

55. Schweitzer, Don. Review of *How Christians Are Come to Mt. Sion*. Vol. 1 of *Sermons by Jonathan Edwards on the Church*, edited by Kenneth Minkema et al. *Touchstone* 39.2 (2021) 72–74.

    Collects eight sermons that Edwards preached in 1740 on Hebrews 12:22–24. Schweitzer warned modern preachers should not emulate his preaching, yet they give us insight into his homiletical method and his theology of sermonizing.

56. ———. Review of *Understanding Affections in the Theology of Jonathan Edwards: "The High Exercises of Divine Love,"* by Ryan J. Martin. *Religious Studies and Theology* 40.1 (2021) 135–36.

    Endorses Martin's book and says that the psychology which was impressed on Edwards is consistent with William Ames and Johannes Wollebius concerning religious affections to God.

57. Schultz, Walter J. "Contingency in the Late Metaphysics of Jonathan Edwards." *Jonathan Edwards Studies* 11.2 (2021) 117–49.

    Appeals that there are three reasons for the importance of the question of whether the universe is contingent: (1) it determines the Christian metaphysic; (2) it frames one's relation between the decrees of God in providence to the moral choice and actions of the creatures; and (3) it is important to the history of theology and philosophy, as Jonathan Edwards demonstrated by writing the *Freedom of the Will*.

58. Shukla, Abhishek. "The System of Being: A Study of the Metaphysics of Jonathan Edwards." PhD diss., University of Rochester, 2021.

    Contends that scholarly neglect surrounds Edwards's theological ontology. He seeks to make this the main argument of his dissertation, examining Edwards's concept of being as this bears on his epistemology, aesthetics, and ethics.

59. Smolinski, Reiner, and Jan Stievermann, eds. *Cotton Mather and the Biblia Americana—America's First Bible Commentary: Essays in Reappraisal.* Grand Rapid: Baker, 2021.

    Advocates that Cotton Mather is often overshadowed by Edwards. Nevertheless, with the publication of Mather's *Biblia Americana*, scholars and laypeople alike will benefit from his biblical knowledge.

60. Stanton, Allen M. "Samuel Miller (1769–1850): Reformed Orthodoxy, Jonathan Edwards, and Old Princeton." PhD diss., Puritan Reformed Theological Seminary, 2021.

    Makes the case that Miller's lecture on Ecclesiastical History compares favorably to Edwards's *History of the Work of Redemption.*

61. Stevens, Chris S. Review of *The Federal Theology of Jonathan Edwards: An Exegetical Perspective,* by Gilsun Ryu. *McMaster Journal of Theology and Ministry* 23 (2021–22) R1–6.

    Points to two primary outcomes of reading this book: (1) Edwards is situated in the federal theology of the sixteenth- and seventeenth-centuries Reformed theologians, and (2) Edwards faced the rationalistic philosophy but did not resort to polemics.

62. Story, F. Allan. *Utmost Endeavor: An Introduction to Jonathan Edwards on Revival.* Six Mile, SC: F. Allan Story Jr., 2021.

    Focuses of preparation and method for revival.

63. Strobel, Kyle. "Gratitude to God: Jonathan Edwards and the Opening of the Self." *Scientia et Fides* 9.2 (2021) 115–31.

    Enters the views of Jonathan Edwards's "theological anthropology and development of natural and supernatural gratitude."

64. Sweeney, Douglas A., and Jan Stievermann, eds. *The Oxford Handbook of Jonathan Edwards.* Oxford: Oxford University Press, 2021.

    Collects impressive articles by internationally well-reputed Edwards scholars. In these essays, discussed in four parts, the authors contribute to the historical, philosophical, literary, exegetical, and theological contexts of Edwards. In part I, the articles consist in the topic of "Edwards's backgrounds, sources, and context" which are discussed in five essays. In the first essay by Ava Chamberlain, she discusses Edwards's family life. Chamberlain makes the case that he was raised in Puritan fashion with the expectation that he would become the head of his household. This has implications for his own family as he wed Sarah Pierpont, and she was expected to be a helpmeet for Edwards. This has special relevance for Edwards's ministry at Northampton, the primary context of their thirty-one years of marriage. In Harry Stout's essay, "Parish Ministry," he challenged the popularity of writing on Edwards's theology or philosophy and not his enduring vocation of his life which are found in his biblical expositions and pastoral life. This is what Samuel Hopkins and Joseph Bellamy were most impressed with. Stout covered Edwards's four congregations in New York, Bolton, Northampton, and Stockbridge.

George Marsden's article covered the "Historical and Ecclesiastical Contexts" of his day. He says that Edwards's life "took shape in the midst of a web of interwoven contexts" (33). Marsden says that the contents of his essay cover the historical context of New England, political, social, economic, ecclesiastical, and familial life of Edwards.

In David W. Kling's essay, "Edwards in the Context of International Revivals and Missions," he said that Edwards came on the international scene in authoring the *Narrative of the Surprising Work of God* and a *Humble Attempt.* He continued to write on revival throughout his pastoral career and he believed that it was the "primary means by which the Gospel would spread to the ends of earth" (51).

In the last article of part I, Peter J. Thuesen writes "Sources of Edwards's Thought." As Edwards was the son and grandson of pastors (Timothy Edwards and Solomon Stoddard) he was groomed to go into pastoral ministry. He had access to some of the greatest minds in the theological world plus biblical commentators. Yet as a college student, he had access to the philosophical world of Newton, Locke, Malebranche, and Descartes, which he enjoyed reading.

Part II, "Edwards's Intellectual Labors," is by far the longest part containing twenty-six articles. It begins with an article on the being of God entitled "Ontology," by William J. Wainwright. The second article of this section contains "Epistemology," authored by Paul Helm. The third, "The Nature of God and the Trinity," by Kyle C. Strobel; "The Person of Christ," by S. Mark Hamilton; "Pneumatology," by Robert W. Caldwell III; "Revelation," by Stephen R. C. Nichols; "Federalism and Reformed Scholasticism," by Willem van

Vlastuin; "Creation and Predestination," by Phillip Hussey and Michael McClymond; "History, Providence, and Eschatology," by Jan Stievermann; "Sin and Evil," by David P. Barshinger; "Anthropology, Affection, and Free Will," by Seng-Kong Tan; "Ecclesiology and Sacrament," by Rhys Bezzant; "Ethics," by Elizabeth Agnew Cochran; "Aesthetics," by William Dyrness and Christi Wells; "Imagination and Hermeneutics," by Kathryn Reklis; "The Natural Sciences and Philosophy of Nature," by Avihu Zakai; and lastly, "Idealism and Aetiology," by Sebastian Rehnman. These put Edwards's intellectual labors in context consistent with his themes and are well-represented by scholarship.

Part III, "Edwards's Religious and Social Practices," consists of seven essays beginning with his "Spiritual and Devotion," by Charles E. Hambrick-Stowe; "Biblical Exegesis," by Robert E. Brown; "Writing and Preaching Sermons," by Kenneth P. Minkema; "Education," by Esmari Potgieter; "Mission," by John A. Grigg; "Ministry to the Bound and Enslaved," by John Saillant; and "Politics and Economics," by Mark Valeri.

Part IV, "Edwards's Global Reception," consists of several articles where scholars focus on several continents which they have researched just how far Edwards has influenced in those particular countries. James P. Byrd has written on "North America," Jonathan Yeager focuses on "Britain and Europe," Sandra M. Gustafson concentrates on "Edwards's Place and Importance in Anglo-American Literature." Dongsoo Han provides his essay on "Asia"; Stuart Piggin, on "Australia"; and an article on "Africa" is contributed by Adriaan C. Neele. An essay on "Latin America," was written by Heber Carlos de Campos, Jr. and lastly, and the final contribution to the *Oxford Handbook* is an essay from Douglas A. Sweeney entitled "Edwards Studies Today."

Overall, modern research is well represented to the thinking and context of Jonathan Edwards and its global impact. Sweeney and Stievermann collected the finest scholars for representing the best of scholarship of the past and current generations.

65. Tarnasky, Will. Review of *The Covenant Theology of Jonathan Edwards: Law, Gospel, and Evangelical Obedience*, by Paul J. Hoehner. *Jonathan Edwards Studies* 11.2 (2021) 180–82.

Sees Edwards as a constituent of Reformed orthodoxy versus scholars who think that he tended to a more Roman Catholic view of salvation. Hoehner argues that Edwards does not break from Reformed covenant theology.

66. Todd, Obbie Tyler. "From Puritans to Patriots: The Republicanization of American Theology, 1750–1835." *Journal of the Evangelical Theological Society* 64.2 (2021) 341–55.

    Argues that Edwards and the New Divinity illustrated the state of the English colonies with their thoughts on disinterested benevolence.

67. Torseth, Robb L. "Jonathan Edwards and the Image of God in Relation to Reformed Orthodoxy and the Flacian Controversy." *Jonathan Edwards Studies* 11.1 (2021) 29–44.

    Complains that Edwards's view of the image of God is seldom explored in the scholarly sources. Edwards speaks of the image of God discontinuously from the other Reformed theologians and is especially concerned with his use of "image of Satan." Torseth compares this with the Flacian controversy.

68. Walls, Taylor. "Why Are We Here? A Biblical and Trinitarian Perspective on Man's End." *Puritan Reformed Journal* 13.1 (2021) 131–39.

    Examines Edwards's discussion of why we are present in the world, which he states in *Concerning the End for Which God Made the World*.

69. Wigginton, Caroline, and Abram Van Engen. *Feeling Godly: Religious Affections and Christian Contact in Early North America*. Amherst: University of Massachusetts Press, 2021.

    Stems from reflection on Edwards's "Treatise Concerning Religious Affection" (1746). The authors ask how early American communities perceived the affections in ways consistent with Edwards or not. Historians and literary scholars respond to this question in early American, Native American, and African American communities.

70. Vető, Miklós. *The Thought of Jonathan Edwards*. Eugene, OR: Wipf & Stock, 2021.

Republishes Vető's dissertation. See M. X. Lesser, *Reading Jonathan Edwards: An Annotated Bibliography in Three Parts, 1729–2005* (Grand Rapids: Eerdmans, 2008), 403 [1987.32].

71. Vlastuin, Willem van. Review of *Jonathan Edwards Within the Enlightenment: Controversy, Experience, and Thought*, edited by John T. Lowe and Daniel N. Gullotta. *Journal of Reformed Theology* 15.1–2 (2021) 156–57.

    Accumulates scholarly essays to examine how Edwards spoke sometimes in Enlightenment philosophical concepts and classical Christian terms. How did they affect each other and in what ways? The common assumption of these authors is that Edwards was a classical theologian, but he changed his concepts where his culture had changed.

72. Yeager, Jonathan M. "Faith, Free Will, and Biblical Reasoning in the Thought of Jonathan Edwards and John Erskine." In *Every Leaf, Line, and Letter: Evangelicals and the Bible from the 1730s to the Present*, edited by Timothy Larsen, 55–67. Downers Grove, IL: InterVarsity, 2021.

    Discusses Jonathan Edwards's (and John Erskine's) interpretations of the Bible, especially as it displayed modernity. Edwards embraces science but only insofar as it could be proven from the Bible.

2022

1. Austad, Torleiv. Review of *Jonathan Edwards and Deification: Reconciling Theosis and the Reformed Tradition*, by James Salladin. *European Journal of Theology* 31.2 (2022) 313–15.

    Asserts that the thesis of Salladin's book is that God pours out his Spirit on intelligent creatures by means of a theosis and this compares with the Eastern orthodox church. Austad is not convinced that Edwards holds this notion.

2. Bezzant, Rhys S., ed. *Edwards, Germany, and Transatlantic Contexts*. Göttingen: Vandenhoeck & Ruprecht, 2022.

    Claims that Edwards has had a long history with Germany through his spirituality and missional approach, but his impact on Germany was largely absent in scholastic writing. This book begins to correct that.

3. Brown, Audrey. "Jonathan Edwards and the New World: Exploring the Intersection of Puritanism and Settler Colonialism." *Transactions of the Charles S. Pierce Society* 58.2 (2022) 114–37.

   Extends the argument of Hatch and Stout that Edwards's stern Calvinism was compatible with shaping a new nation.

4. Caldwell, Robert W., III. Review of *The Federal Theology of Jonathan Edwards: An Exegetical Perspective*, by Gilsun Ryu. *Southwest Journal of Theology* 64.2 (2022) 135–37.

   Explains how Ryu admirably approached his subject in one of the most neglected areas of study, situating this work in the scholastic context of the post-Reformed theologians. Caldwell comments that Ryu's work is very important.

5. Chun, Chris. "Wealth and Poverty in the Life and Thought of Jonathan Edwards." *Journal for Baptist Theology & Ministry* 19.2 (2022) 381–92.

   Discusses Edwards's views of poverty within the context of Northampton, where his congregation was one of the wealthiest and influential in Massachusetts, until he transitioned to Stockbridge, where Edwards was in the wilderness and surrounded by poverty.

6. Cochran, Joseph. T. "Imitating the Virtue Ethic of Jonathan Edwards and William James." *Bulletin of Ecclesial Theology* 9.2 (2022) 19–42.

   Compares the connection between Edwards and psychologist William James. Both had similar views of habit, ethics, and virtue.

7. Dunnington, Kent. "The Distinctive of Christian Gratitude: A Theological Survey." *Religions* 13.10 (2022) 1–15.

   Expresses that scholars haven't done justice on the common theme of gratitude. In this work, Dunnington believes that he makes a scholarly contribution as he surveys six theologians, one of which is Jonathan Edwards.

8. Edwards, Jonathan. "Sinners in the Hands of an Angry God." In *The Schlager Anthology of Early America: A Student's Guide to Essential Primary Sources*, edited by Christine Eisel, 288–91. Dallas: Schlager, 2022.

9. Fischer, John Martin. "An Actual-Sequence Theology." *Roczniki Filozoficzne/Annals of Philosophy* 70.1 (2022) 49–78.

   Defends Edwards's *Freedom of the Will* in part.

10. Gilpin, W. Clark. Review of *A Great and Remarkable Analogy: The Onto-Typology of Jonathan Edwards*, by Lisanne Winslow. *The Journal of Religion* 103.3 (2022) 438–39.

    Identifies Winslow's significant training in marine biology before she studied theology and how this contributed to the shape of the book, which Gilpin views quite favorably.

11. Hamilton, S. Mark, and C. Layne Hancock. "Confessionalism and Causation in Jonathan Edwards (1703–1758)." In *The Routledge Handbook of Idealism and Immaterialism*, edited by Joshua Farris and Benedikt Paul Göcke, 191–209. New York: Routledge, 2022.

    Concerns the confessional implications of Edwards's idealism in the Reformed tradition. Hamilton and Hancock acknowledge the seriousness of Oliver Crisp's charge that he could not have been consistent with the Reformed tradition since he believed in continuous creationism.

12. Hancock, C. Layne. "Eudaimonia After Edwards: Or, What's 'New' About the New Divinity?" *Jonathan Edwards Studies* 12.1–2 (2022) 1–17.

    Questions "what is new about the New Divinity?" The traditional answer to this question has been that they followed Edwards. Hancock locates two primary sources that present the case that they didn't follow Edwards's ethics.

13. Harder, Michael. "True Excellency: The Missional Preaching of Jonathan Edwards." PhD diss., Southeastern Baptist Theological Seminary, 2022.

    Observes Edwards's style and method changing his approach to preaching to white colonials and his preaching to Native Americans in Stockbridge. Harder seeks to account for this change.

14. Hasker, William. "Introduction—Sketches from an Album." *Roczniki Filozoficzne/Annals of Philosophy* 70.1 (2022) 7–14.

    Says that human free will is incompatible with foreknowledge and deals sharply with Edwards's *Freedom of the Will*.

15. Hoffman, Paul A. Review of *Revival Preaching: Twelve Lessons from Jonathan Edwards*, by Ernest Eugene Kassen. *The Journal of the Evangelical Homiletics Society* 22.2 (2022) 140–41.

    States that this volume could have benefited from "tighter editing" and Hoffman found the biography of Edwards unnecessary.

But if the reader looks past these "foibles," the author provides important information of the revival preaching of Edwards.

16. Hoselton, Ryan P., et al., eds. *The Bible in Early Transatlantic Pietism and Evangelicalism.* University Park: Pennsylvania State University Press, 2022.

    Proposes that Edwards had been influenced by pietism and was a main player in evangelism of the eighteenth-century.

17. Huggins, Jonathan. "Proceed with Caution: Lessons from Saint Augustine, Jonathan Edwards, and Miroslav Volf." In *Technē: Christian Visions of Technology*, edited by Gerald Hiestand and Todd A. Wilson, 92–108. Eugene, OR: Cascade, 2022.

    Claims that "Christians have an increasingly complex and often complicated relationship with technology." Huggins cautions us with lessons from Augustine, Edwards, and Volf.

18. Johnson, Daniel M. "Doing All Things for God's Glory, Acting So That It Is God Who Acts: Kierkegaard, Edwards, and the Problem of Total Devotion." *Religious Studies* 58.1 (2022) 197–216.

    Explores two things: (1) it defends the problem of total devotion in Kierkegaard and Edwards, and (2) it "extends that solution by advancing an interpretation" of doing all things to the glory of God (1 Cor 10:31).

19. ———. "For Glory and for Sport: Jonathan Edwards and the Vedanta School on God's Motive." *Philosophy East & West* 72.2 (2022) 375–95.

    Considers the philosophy of the Vedanta school that says God created the world for sport in contrast to Edwards, who says that God created the world for his glory.

20. Jones, Barry. *Dictionary of World Biography.* Canberra, Australia: ANU, 2022.

    Summarizes a biography of Edwards.

21. Juchno, Andrew. Review of *The Oxford Handbook of Jonathan Edwards*, edited by Douglas A. Sweeney and Jan Stievermann. *Studies in Puritanism and Piety* 4 (2021) 136–38.

    Assesses the *Oxford Handbook* very favorably and gives no critique.

22. Kearney, John. "Ignatius of Loyola, Jonathan Edwards, and Indifference." *Heythrop Journal* 63.1 (2022) 76–83.

    Argues that Edwards's *Freedom of the Will* in comparison with Ignatius and Isaac Watts is open to a "straw man objection."

23. Kennedy, Rick. Review of *The Federal Theology of Jonathan Edwards: An Exegetical Perspective*, by Gilsun Ryu. *Church History* 91.3 (2022) 690–91.

    Applauds this book as "excellent and intricately argued."

24. Kling, David W. Review of *Before Jonathan Edwards: Sources of New England Thought*, by Adriaan Neele. *The Journal of Religion* 102 (2022) 146–48.

    Asks whether Neele has not made too much of the influence of Petrus van Mastricht on Edwards.

25. Kraus, Spencer. "Jonathan Edwards's Unique Role in an Imagined Church History." *Interpreter* 52 (2022) 65–101.

    Reviews Neville's work on *Infinite Goodness, Joseph Smith, Jonathan Edwards, and the Book of Mormon* and says that his findings are "superficial and weak," "the scenario contradicts the historical record," and Neville "uses the sources disingenuously to impose his idiosyncratic and wholly modern worldview onto Joseph Smith."

26. Lee, Dongjun. "The Background of Jonathan Edwards' Dismissal." *Theological Forum* 110 (2022) 155–87.

    Entails the "Bad Book" incident, the issues of the honorarium, the eucharistic controversy, ministry without visitation, and the conflicts with and without the church led to the expulsion of Edwards from the Northampton.

27. Lowe, John Thomas, "Abolitionism as an Expression of Benevolence in Edwardsean Thought." *Jonathan Edwards Studies* 12.1–2 (2022) 18–27.

    Asks how the "slave-owning Edwards" could be linked to the Edwardseans who were abolitionists.

28. ———. "'The Practice That Prevails': Jonathan Edwards, Slavery, and Race." PhD diss., Vrije Universiteit Amsterdam, 2022.

    Engages many scholars who have gotten wrong ideas about Jonathan Edwards and slavery. They operated under this false presupposition that the seventeenth century was not concerned about slavery and race but the Edwardseans in the latter half of the century were instrumental in the rhetoric to abolish slavery. Lowe contends that many scholars embrace this false presupposition, but Edwards was concerned with race as he was a Mohican missionary at Stockbridge. In his writings, he demonstrated that he was concerned about race, and he defended slavery as a God ordained institution.

29. Muller, Richard A. *Providence, Freedom, and the Will in Early Modern Reformed Theology*. Grand Rapids: Reformation Heritage, 2022.

    Refers to his ongoing debate with Paul Helm. Muller says that Edwards parts ways from the Reformed tradition in his work on the *Freedom on the Will* with his notions of contingency and necessity.

30. Nichols, Stephen J. *The Spirit of Truth: The Holy Spirit and the Apologetics of Jonathan Edwards*. Phillipsburg, NJ: P&R, 2022.

    Reprint. See M. X. Lesser, *Reading Jonathan Edwards: An Annotated Bibliography in Three Parts, 1729–2005* (Grand Rapids: Eerdmans, 2008), 577 [2003.74].

31. Perkins, Harrison. Review of *Approaching the Atonement: The Reconciling Work of Christ*, by Oliver D. Crisp. *Anglican and Episcopal History* 91.1 (2022) 131–32.

    Employs Crisp's view of the atonement that this necessarily affects how he deals with Edwards's assessments.

32. Penner, Bradley M. Review of *The Oxford Handbook of Jonathan Edwards*, edited by Douglas A. Sweeney and Jan Stievermann. *Reviews in Religion and Theology* 22.3 (2022) 185–87.

    "Makes for an excellent reference work in a personal or institutional library or even as a textbook for an advance seminar on the life and thought of Edwards." Penner has one "slight disappointment" that in Edwards's "most (in)famous 1741 sermon, *Sinners in the Hand of an Angry God*" because of its influence in "Anglo-Evangelical circles," he would have like to have seen more "sustained interaction with and evaluation of, not only the theology of the sermon but also its initial and continuing influence."

33. Rehnman, Sebastian. "Learning to Love Wisdom from Masters: The Value of Jonathan Edwards' Philosophical Theology." *Jonathan Edwards Studies* 12.1–2 (2022) 28–35.

    Questions whether scholars should refer to Edwards as being one of America's greatest philosophical-theologians given that his proofs of God or God's attributes have been soundly refuted.

34. Ritter, Luke. Review of *The Oxford Handbook of Jonathan Edwards*, edited by Douglas A. Sweeney and Jan Stievermann. *The Journal of Ecclesiastical History* 73.1 (2022) 194–95.

    Overviews the *Handbook* without criticism.

35. Rogers, Tony A. Review of *Jonathan Edwards and Deification: Reconciling Theosis and the Reformed Tradition*, by James R. Salladin. *Jonathan Edwards Studies* 12.1–2 (2022) 48–50.

    Reviews Salladin's book very favorably, saying that he makes a compelling case that theosis arose from the Reformed tradition. Believes this volume will prove useful to systematic and historical theologians.

36. Salladin, James R. *Jonathan Edwards and Deification: Reconciling Theosis and the Reformed Tradition.* Downers Grove, IL: InterVarsity, 2022.

    Considers the role of Edwards's deification and reflects on his soteriology as it compares with others in the Reformed tradition.

37. Schultz, Walter J. "An Augustinian-Edwardsian Metaphysics of Possibility for the Barcan Formula." *Philosophia Christi* 24.2 (2022) 195–215.

    Formulates an "alternative metaphysics of possibility that follows Augustine's" and Edwards's "suggestion that God's plan is the only one of a ranges of alternative histories for creation."

38. Schweitzer, Cameron. "Towards a Clearer Understanding of Jonathan Edwards's Biblical Typology: A Case Study in the *Blank Bible*." PhD diss., Gateway Seminary, 2022.

    Focuses on Edwards's biblical typology in his *Blank Bible*. He uses "new evidence" to clarify terms in the debates regarding how to best describe his biblical typology. He contends that one should not describe his biblical typology as "conservative" or "Christological" but as "spiritual," "teleological," and "eschatological."

39. Sherron, Tyler. "Jonathan Edwards' Self-Love Theory: A Revision." *Jonathan Edwards Studies* 12.1–2 (2022) 36–47.

    Articulates how Samuel Hopkins and Jonathan Edwards Jr. disagreed about the concepts of "self-love" and "disinterested benevolence."

40. Simut, Cornelius, C. "'They Will Reign in Love': Spiritual Formation as Sanctified Affection in Jonathan Edwards." *Spiritual Formation* (2022) 71–76.

    Argues that for Edwards, there is a spiritual pilgrimage to heaven or hell. This clear destination urges us to learn if we have faith and if we pursue Christ.

41. Smith, Philip P. "'Good News from a Far Country': Old Testament Wisdom Literature and the Concept of Wisdom in the Theology of Jonathan Edwards." PhD diss., Southeastern Baptist Theological Seminary, 2022.

    Articulates how Edwards's exegesis of wisdom literature shaped his spiritual and pastoral theology.

42. Spiegel, James S., et al. "Christian Metaphysics and Idealism." In *Four Views on Christian Metaphysics*, edited by Timothy M. Mosteller, 71–102. Eugene, OR: Cascade, 2022.

    Considers how the idealism of Jonathan Edwards was inherited from Rene Descartes, George Berkeley, and Samuel Johnson (among others).

43. Stanton, Allen M. *Samuel Miller (1769–1850): Reformed Orthodoxy, Jonathan Edwards, and Old Princeton*. New York: Peter Lang, 2022.

    Comes from a dissertation of the same title (2021.60).

44. Stetina, Karin Spiecker. Review of *A Great and Remarkable Analogy: The Onto-Typology of Jonathan Edwards*, by Lisanne Winslow. *International Journal of Systematic Theology* 24.1 (2022) 128–30.

    Recommends the volume, yet critiques how it "tends to gloss over some of Edwards' inconsistencies."

45. Světlíková, Anna. "Jonathan Edwards, John Dennis, and the Religious Sublime: A Consideration of Edwardsean Terror." In *New Perspectives in English and America Studies*, edited by Michał Choiński and Małgorzata Cierpisz, 323–36. Kraków: Jagiellonian University Press, 2022.

    Recounts Edwards's conversion experience as recorded in his *Personal Narrative*. Before he converted, Edwards said nothing had been so terrifying to him as thunder, but after he was converted, he said it was a sweet sound that pointed to the glory of God.

46. Todd, Obbie Tyler. *Southern Edwardseans: The Southern Baptist Legacy of Jonathan Edwards.* Göttingen: Vandenhoeck & Ruprecht, 2022.

   The founders of the Southern Baptist Convention were deeply influenced by Puritan theologian Jonathan Edwards and his followers. Although Southern Baptists had a different theological background than Presbyterians or Congregationalists and lived in a distinctly Southern environment, they felt a strong connection to Edwards. They shared his revivalistic spirit, Calvinistic beliefs, loose confessionalism, and commitment to practical divinity. In the nineteenth century, while many Presbyterians and Methodists criticized Edwards, Baptists embraced him. By the first Southern Baptist Convention in 1845, Edwards's theology had significantly shaped their foundation.

47. Uche, Anizor, and Kyle C. Strobel. *Reformed Dogmatics in Dialogue: The Theology of Karl Barth and Jonathan Edwards.* Studies in Historical and Systematic Theology. Bellingham, WA: Lexham Academic, 2022.

   Engages the theology of Edwards and Karl Barth, bringing them into conversation through religious topics, e.g., theology proper, the atonement, and ecclesiology.

48. Vlastuin, Willem van. Review of *Jonathan Edwards and Deification: Reconciling Theosis and the Reformed Tradition*, by James R. Salladin. *Journal of Reformed Theology* 16.3 (2022) 278–79.

   Commends the volume as "a great pleasure to read . . . for three reasons": (1) it allows pieces of Edwards to fall into place, (2) "Edwards's concepts of participation and deification help us in our current reflection," and (3) the book has a spiritual focus.

49. Welty, Kyle. Review of *Darkness Falls on the Land of Light: Experiencing the Religious Awakenings in Eighteenth-Century New England*, by Douglas L. Winiarski. *Anglican and Episcopal History* 91.3 (2022) 371–73.

   Focuses of Edwards's role in the Awakenings of the eighteenth century and how he attempted to stifle religious enthusiasm.

50. Wiess, James M. Review of *Multiple Reformation? The Many Faces and Legacies of the Reformation*, edited by Jan Stievermann and

Randall C. Zachman. *Anglican and Episcopal History* 91.3 (2022) 401–2.

Contains a single essay from Douglas Sweeney on "Jonathan Edwards's Exegetical Practice."

51. Willborn, C. N. "Robert Lewis Dabney and the Problem of Original Sin." *The Confessional Presbyterian* 18 (2022) 55–66, 266–67.

    Examines Dabney's continuities and discontinuities of Edwards's *Great Christian Doctrine of Original Sin Defended*, published in 1758.

52. William, Charles Scott. "*Imago Dei* in Jonathan Edwards: The Locus of Divine Activity for the Glorification of the Triune God in the End of Creation." PhD diss., University of Edinburgh, 2022.

    Concerns the *imago Dei* as the "centrifugal force" of Edwards's view of the Triune God working in humankind.

53. Wood, Timothy L. "Losing Interest: Roger Sherman, Samuel Hopkins, and the Contest Between Disinterested Benevolence and Self-Love." *Fides et Historia* 54.2 (2022) 1–22.

    Treats Edwards's doctrine of disinterested benevolence and self-love, which was inherited by Samuel Hopkins. Hopkins defended these in an article and correspondence to Sherman, who disagreed with Hopkins's views and found no biblical basis for the denial of loving oneself.

54. Woodyard, Jonathan D. "A Faith Disposed Towards Jesus: The Relationship Between Love and Faith in Jonathan Edwards and the Reformed Tradition." PhD diss., Midwestern Baptist Theological Seminary, 2022.

    Aligns Edwards with the Reformed tradition by connecting love and faith.

55. Zhu, Victor. *America's Theologian Beyond America: Jonathan Edwards, Israel, and China*. Oxford: Oxford University Press, 2022.

    Contends that Jonathan Edwards's life and ministry extend beyond America even to this day.

2023

1. Albanese, Catherine L. "Jonathan Edwards: Latter-Day Puritan and Metaphysician." In *The Delight Makers: Anglo-American Metaphysical Religion and the Pursuit of Happiness*, 43–68. Chicago: University of Chicago Press, 2023.

    Unravels a "theology of desire tying Jonathan Edwards to Ralph Waldo Emerson to the religious unaffiliated today." This stresses philosophically that "natural beauty and spiritual fulfillment" are one and the same.

2. Bates, James Jordan. "Benjamin Whichcote's Theology of Deification in Historical Context." MCH thesis, Trinity International University, 2023.

    Conceptualizes the historical context of deification, "normally associated with Eastern Orthodoxy"; however, deification has often been discussed in the context of Martin Luther, John Calvin, John Wesley, and Jonathan Edwards.

3. Baysa, Michael. "Printing, Publics, and Pudding: Charles Chauncy's Universal Salvation and the Material Transformation of New England Orthodoxy." *Church History* 92 (2023) 291–311.

    Focuses on Charles Chauncy but makes passing mentions of Edwards because Edwards wrote contrasting Chauncy's positions on the revival and vice versa. He spends considerable time on Edwards's son, Jonathan Edwards Jr.

4. Boss, Robert L., ed. *The Jonathan Edwards Miscellanies Companion.* Vol. 3. Fort Worth, TX: JESociety, 2023.

    Recruits scholars that focus on the theological developments of the "Miscellanies."

5. ———. *Thunder God, Wonder God: Exploring the Emblematic Vision of Jonathan Edwards.* Fort Worth, TX: JESociety, 2023.

    Explores the typology of Edwards in nature.

6. Carter, Jonathan M. Review of *Jonathan Edwards and Deification: Reconciling Theosis and the Reformed Tradition*, by James Salladin. *International Journal of Systematic Theology* 25.4 (2023) 648–50.

    Criticizes the work as it "suffers from being verbose" and the "significant difference of opinion amongst Reformed orthodox puritans" is "lacking . . . analysis." Still, Salladin's work "remains a

31. Lumpkin, Aaron L. "'Some Agreeable Conversation': Jonathan Edwards Among Early American Baptists." *Perichoresis (Oradea)* 21.2. (2023) 34–49.

    Explores how North American Baptists drew from Edwards's scriptural theology and piety.

32. Manger, Edward. Review of *Southern Edwards: The Southern Baptist Legacy of Jonathan Edwards*, by Obbie Tyler Todd. *Theologische Literaturzeitung* 148.4 (2023) 367–68.

    Applauds Todd for finding a new avenue to write in Edwards studies. Manger said that Tyler's book was an "enjoyable contribution to the fields of Edwards studies and Southern Baptist history."

33. Marquette, Richard C. H. "The Reverend Jonathan Edwards: An American Radical." MA thesis, Southern Connecticut State University, 2023.

    Examines how Edwards should be considered an "American Radical" because he discarded the "prevailing religious thoughts [that] shaped the way New Englanders" viewed the sacraments of baptism and communion.

34. Marsden, George M. *An Infinite Fountain of Light: Jonathan Edwards for the Twenty-First Century*. Downer Grove, IL: InterVarsity, 2023.

    Considers how Edwards can be received in the twenty-first century, how he compares to Benjamin Franklin, and how we inherited the evangelical church from Whitefield and Edwards. Marsden also exposits the *Religious Affections*.

35. McGlothlin, James C. Review of *The Oxford Handbook of Jonathan Edwards*, edited by Douglas A. Sweeney and Jan Stievermann. *Themelios* 48.1 (2023) 222–23.

    Applauds book as a "superb addition to the ongoing academic research on Edwards."

36. McGraw, Ryan M. Review of *The Oxford Handbook of Jonathan Edwards*, edited by Douglas A. Sweeney and Jan Stievermann. *Puritan Reformed Journal* 15.1 (2023) 215–17.

    Writes "this collection of essays is both an ideal entry point into scholarship on Edwards and an important step forward into new areas of research."

37. Neele, Adriaan C. "The Dutch Reception of the History of Jonathan Edwards." *Puritan Reformed Journal* 15.1 (2023) 51–76.

Considers the Dutch reception of Edwards and concludes that it was a "mixed reception."

38. Njoto, Ricky F. "Idealism and Edwards the Preacher." *Journal of Reformed Theology* 17.3–4 (2023) 278–97.

    Suggests that "the preaching of the Word had a significant place in Edwards's idealisms" because of his "theologies of sin, faith, and preaching in new metaphysical and relation terms that allow him to place such theologies in his idealism."

39. Nuenke, Jonathan. "Puritan Involvement with Slavery." *Puritan Reformed Journal* 15.1 (2023) 189–200.

    Introduces this article on slavery with Edwards's purchasing and owning slaves.

40. Quinn, Philip L. "Disputing the Augustinian Legacy: John Locke and Jonathan Edwards on Romans 5:12–19." In *The Augustinian Tradition*, edited by Gareth B. Matthews, 233–50. Los Angeles: University of California Press, 2023.

    Exposits Edwards's view of Romans 5:12–19 in defense of the Augustinian tradition against Arminianism and confirmed his Calvinism.

41. Ramini, Ashwin. "Revive Us Again: Evaluating a Sermon Series on Revival." PhD diss., Asbury Theological Seminary, 2023.

    Proposes the project is to review and examine "the biblical foundation for revival" and the "theological foundations explores the ministry of the Holy Spirit in revival" by taking "insights from three revival leaders—Jonathan Edwards, Charles Finney, and Martyn Lloyd-Jones."

42. Rathel, David. "John Gill and the Rule of Faith: A Case Study in the Baptist Retrieval of Tradition." *Southeastern Theological Review* 14.2 (2023) 55–72.

    Citations of John Gill "appear in the writing of Jonathan Edwards."

43. Schweitzer, Cameron M. Review of *The Federal Theology of Jonathan Edwards: An Exegetical Perspective*, by Gilsun Ryu. *Studies in Puritanism and Piety* 4.1 (2023) 112–14.

    Makes an "important contribution to our understanding of one of the church's most influential theologians."

44. Sexton, Jeremy. "Postmillennialism: A Biblical Critique." *Themelios* 43.3 (2023) 551–72.

    Introduces Edwards's "postmillennial hope" which was "pronounced dead" when R. J. Rushdoony provoked its comeback. The author says that postmillennialists often "keep textual details" in the "belief that the prophecies of worldwide righteousness" will be fulfilled "on earth *before* rather than *at* the second coming."

45. Strobel, Kyle. "'As in a Mirror': Jonathan Edwards, Self-Love and Enlarging to Receive Another." *International Journal of Systematic Theology* 25.2 (2023) 249–66.

    Aims for the reader to acknowledge the unique contribution of Edwards's anthropological theology. By explaining that humans are "constituted through sight" and regenerated as they contemplate the Son who is given as "a vision of the Father in the Son by the Spirit of illumination," Strobel relates this to a common conception of Thomas Aquinas.

46. ———. "Jonathan Edwards's Affective Anthropology." *Journal of Spiritual Formation and Soul Care* 16.1 (2023) 31–49.

    Argues that emotions are a "reduction of Edwards's view." This article "addresses Edwards's use of the term 'emotion' alongside of his understanding of affections and passions within both the unregenerate and the regenerate frame."

47. Strom, Jonathan. "How the Priesthood of All Believers Became American." *Lutheran Quarterly* 37.4 (2023) 424–58.

    Addresses this query through the lens of Cotton Mather and Jonathan Edwards. Edwards delivered a sermon on 1 Peter 2:9 that is "probably the longest treatment of the common priesthood in early America."

48. Timpe, Kevin. "The Inevitability of Sin." *TheoLogica* 7.2 (2023) 1–28.

    Reflects on the doctrine of original sin that leads to actual sin in Edwards's *Original Sin*.

49. Todd, Obbie Tyler. "Almost Baptists: Baptistic Pedobaptist in American History (1650–1950)." *Journal for Baptist Theology & Ministry* 20.1 (2023) 19–29.

    Mentions Timothy Dwight was the grandson of "the famed Puritan Jonathan Edwards."

50. Walker, E. W. "'It Would Be Heaven to Hear Him Adored': Praying Payson of Portland and Revival in Nineteenth-Century Maine." *Puritan Reformed Journal* 15.2 (2023) 107–18.

    Cites in a couple of footnotes that Edwards was instrumental in the First Great Awakening and that Payson had read Edwards's *Freedom of the Will* and his treatise *Original Sin*.

51. Whitlark, Jason A. "Struggling with God's Will: Jesus' Piety in Mark's Account of the Gethsemane in Light of Virgil's Aeneas." *Perspectives in Religion Studies* 50.2 (2023) 181–94.

    Compares Virgil's Aeneas with Edwards on account of Jesus' struggle in the Garden of Gethsemane.

52. Woodbridge, John D. "Biblical Authority and Christian Higher Education." *Evangelical Review of Theology* 47.3 (2023) 211–25.

    Imparts Edwards as a pastoral model who accounted for the "deep delight" as he meditated on Scripture and applied the "Distinguishing marks of the Holy Spirit" and he assists us in "our ministry [and] can help us discern if what we are doing is pleasing to the Lord."

53. Woznicki, Christopher. "Population Genomics, Confessionalism, and the Metaphysics of Original Sin." *The Expositor Times* 135.3 (2023) 89–97.

    Proposes Edwards's account of "personal identity" in original sin as "a possible account of how Christians" who are confessional "might continue to speak of the sins of an original pair if the most prevalent scientific account of human origins is correct."

54. Vlastuin, Willem van. Review of *Pentecostal Theology and Jonathan Edwards*, edited by Steven M. Studebaker and Amos Yong. *Journal of Reformed Theology* 17.3–4 (2023) 374–75.

    Points out that "it is striking that Pentecostals are inspired by Jonathan Edwards's theology and spirituality." Edwards's teaching on "indwelling of the Holy Spirit" and "the importance of the affection" in his spirituality are apparently what inspire Pentecostals to study Edwards.

Appendix I

Sources Prohibited

1. Kuklick, Bruce. Review of *Virtue Reformed: Rereading Jonathan Edwards's Ethics*, by Steven A. Wilson. *British Journal for the History of Philosophy* 14.2 (2006) 358–60.

2. Wright, Frank. "The Full Counsel of God." *NRB* 38 (2006) 4.

3. Atkinson, M. C. "Religious Thought After the Period of Revivalism in Eighteenth-Century New England, c. 1739–1800." PhD diss., University of Cambridge, 2007.

4. Hall, Timothy D. Review of *Jonathan Edwards: America's Evangelical*, by Philip F. Gura. *Historian* 69.2 (2007) 331–32.

5. Hewitson, James. "'As Ordered and Governed by Divine Providence': Jonathan Edwards' Use of the Machine as Master Metaphor." *Interdisciplinary Humanities* 24.1 (2007) 6–20.

6. Kaufman, Matt. "Whee! The People." *Focus on the Family Citizen* 21.14 (2007).

7. Dixon, Christine. "The Concept of the Heart in the Experience of Augustine and Edwards." PhD diss., Macquarie University, 2008.

8. Harris, John. "Jonathan Edwards and the Development of American Democracy." Unpublished paper presented at the 66th Annual Meeting of the Midwest Political Science Association (MPSA), Chicago, April 4, 2008.

9. Scott, David. "A Church Without a View: Jonathan Edwards and Our Current Life View Discipleship Crisis." *Christian Apologetics Journal* 7.2 (2008) 23–40.

10. Habets, Myk. Review of *Jonathan Edwards for Armchair Theologians*, by James Byrd. *The Pacific Journal of Theological Research* 5.2 (2009) 71–74.

11. Jaeger, John. Review of *Jonathan Edwards and the Ministry of the Word: A Model of Faith and Thought*, by Douglas A. Sweeney. *Library Journal* 134.14 (2009) 121.

12. McDermott, Gerald R. Review of *Jonathan Edwards on the Christian Life*, by Dane Ortlund. *Journal of Lutheran Ethics* 9.11 (2009). https://learn.elca.org/jle/jonathan-edwards-on-the-christian-life.

13. Twomey, Jay. "Is Naomi a Liberal Pluralist? The Politics of Loss and Renewal in Jonathan Edwards's Sermon 'Ruth's Resolution.'" In *Women of the Hebrew Bible and Their Afterlives*, edited by Peter S. Hawkins and Lesleigh Cushing Stahlberg, 141–58. Vol. 1 of *From the Margins*. Sheffield, England: Sheffield Phoenix, 2009.

14. Wood, Dustin A. "Rhetoric of Revival: An Analysis of Exemplary Sermons from America's Great Awakenings." MA thesis, University of Cincinnati, 2009.

15. Hamilton, S. Mark. "Jonathan Edwards on Justification: A Reassessment." MA thesis, Southwestern Baptist Theological Seminary, 2010.

16. Karcher, Justin G. "The Queer Jeremiad: Jonathan Edwards, City upon a Hill, and City of Night." MA thesis, State University College at Buffalo, 2010.

17. Luke, D. N. "The Doctrine of Sanctification in the Theology of Jonathan Edwards." PhD diss., Queen's University, Belfast, 2010.

18. Marini, Stephen A. "Cosmology." In *Religion in American History*, edited by Amanda Porterfield and John Corrigan, 109–3. Malden, MA: Oxford, Wiley-Blackwell, 2010.

19. St. John, Thomas. "Brattleboro History: 'Sinners in the Hands of an Angry God.'"

20. Campeau, Gregory J. "'This Awful Affair': Cousins, Communion, and the Collapse of Covenant Society in Jonathan Edwards's Northampton." BA thesis, Amherst College, 2011.

21. Hockfield, Victoria. *Famous Jonathan's, Including Jonathan Edwards, Jonathan Livingston Seagull, Jonathan Brandis, and More.* N.p.: Webster's Digital Services, 2011.

22. Rolski, L. Benjamin. "Edwards and the Enlightenment: Mapping the Secular Within the Covenanted Community." *Religion, Education and the Arts* 7 (2011). http://rea.materdei.ie/pages/journal-issues/issue-7.php.

23. Shea, William M. Review of *A Short Life of Jonathan Edwards*, by George M. Marsden. *Horizons* 38.2 (2011) 366–67.

24. Světlíková, Anna. "Typology as Rhetoric: Reading Jonathan Edwards." PhD diss., Charles University, Prague, Czech Republic, 2012.

25. Cho, Seong, II. "A Study of Jonathan Edwards' Application of Preaching to Aid in Conversion." *Preaching* 5 (2013) 51–70.

26. O'Brien, Jill. Review of *Jonathan Edwards on God and Creation*, by Oliver D. Crisp. *Toronto Journal of Theology* 29.1 (2013) 196–98.

27. Schweitzer, William M. Review of *The Theology of Jonathan Edwards*, by Michael J. McClymond and Gerald R. McDermott. *Scottish Bulletin of Evangelical Theology* 31.1 (2013) 88–91.

28. Strobel, Kyle. Review of *Jonathan Edwards' Social Augustinian Trinitarianism in Historical and Contemporary* Perspectives, by Steven M. Studebaker. *Scottish Bulletin of Evangelical Theology* 31.1 (2013) 91–93.

29. Tay, Edwin E. M. Review of *Jonathan Edwards and Justification by Faith*, by Michael McClenahan. *Scottish Bulletin of Evangelical Theology* 31.2 (2013) 240–42.

30. Gallo, Lou. "Jonathan Edwards." *Pennsylvania Literary Journal* 6.3 (2014) 120, 144.

31. Moye, Jerry. Review of *Jonathan Edwards and the Church*, by Rhys Bezzant. *Hill Road* 17.1 (2014) 161–67.

32. Sharanksy, Rachel D. "Emotional Communities: Nathan Cole and the Separate Movement in Massachusetts and Connecticut, 1740–70." MA thesis, Hebrew University of Jerusalem, 2014.

33. Hawkins, Justin. "The Medieval Puritan: Three Case Studies of Scholastic Themes in Jonathan Edwards." MA thesis, Yale Divinity School, 2015.

34. Kimble, Jeremy. Review of *Edwards on the Christian Life: Alive to the Beauty of God*, by Dane Ortlund. *Trinity Journal* 36.2 (2015) 306–8.

35. Mallèvre, Michel. Review of *Jonathan Edwards and the Church*, by Rhys Bezzant. *Istina* 60.2–3 (2015) 351.

36. Burnell, Joel. "Jonathan Edwards and the Beauty of Work: A Colonial American Argument for Social Responsibility in the Workplace." In *Literature*, edited by Magdalena Bleinert-Coyle et al., 183–99. Vol. 1 of *Beyond Words: Crossing Borders in English Studies*. Krakow, Poland: Tertium, 2016.

37. Larsen, Christian N. "The Glory of the Son in Jonathan Edwards' Christology." PhD diss., University of St. Andrews, 2016.

38. Schuman, Andrew. "The Contemporary Crisis in Higher Education: An Edwardsean Response." MAR thesis, Yale Divinity School, 2016.

39. Korving, Willem J. "Eternal Covenant: An Exploration of Jonathan Edwards' View on Covenant Theology." MA thesis, Free University Amsterdam, 2017.

40. Mallèvre, Michel. Review of *The Ecumenical Edwards: Jonathan Edwards and the Theologians. Istina* 62.1 (2017) 133–34.

41. Keller, Michael S. "Experiencing God in Words: Rhetoric, Logic, Imaginative Languages, and Emotion in Jonathan Edwards' Sermons: A Computational Analysis." PhD diss., Free University Amsterdam, 2018.

42. Thomforde, James Henry. "Defending Happiness: Jonathan Edwards's Enduring Pursuit of a Reformed Teleology of Happiness." PhD diss., University of Edinburgh, 2018.

43. Willi, Nora Lee. "Looking Back to Bellamy: American Political Theory for a New Guilded Age." PhD diss., University of Illinois, Chicago, 2018.

44. Babatunde, Timothy. "The Curse of Adam's Transgression: Jonathan Edwards and John Wesley Against the Theological Writings of John Taylor." *Augustine Collegiate Review* 3.1 (2019) 115–25.

45. Trementozzi, David. Review of *Pentecostal Theology and Jonathan Edwards*, edited by Steven M. Studebaker and Amos Yong. *Journal of Pentecostal and Charismatic Christianity* 42.1 (2022) 87–88.

Index

Abernathy, Andrew T., 2013.1
"Abolitionism as an Expression of Benevolence in Edwardsean Thought," 2022.27
"Accommodating Conscience and Culture: Mary Lyon's Appropriation of Jonathan Edwards in Personal Devotion and Public Evangelism," 2008.2
"An Actual-Sequence Theology," 2022.9
Adams, John C., 2007.1
Adams, Kimberly V., 2006.1
Adkins, Tucker, 2018.1, 2019.1
"The Aesthetic Foundations of Religious Experience in the Writings of Jonathan Edwards and Ralph Waldo Emerson," 2017.36
"Aesthetics," 2021.64
"The Aesthetics of Jonathan Edwards as Seen in His Biblical Theology," 2023.25
"Africa," 2021.64
After Edwards: The Courses of the New England Theology, 2012.19
Review of *After Jonathan Edwards: The Courses of the New England Theology*, 2013.12, 2013.50, 2014.17, 2014.28, 2014.85, 2015.4, 2015.23, 2015.53
"After Ten Years: The Jonathan Edwards Center Poland—Past, Present and Future," 2020.8

Agan, Jimmy, 2012.1
"Agape, Self-Sacrifice, and Mutuality: An Exploration into the Thought of Jonathan Edwards and the Theme of Godly Love," 2021.38
"Agitations, Convulsions, Leaping, and Loud Talking: The 'Experiences' of Sarah Pierpont Edwards," 2021.43
"The Agony and the Eschatology: Apocalyptic Thought in New England Evangelical Calvinism from Jonathan Edwards to Lyman Beecher," 2021.13
Aiken, Peter, 2014.1
Albanese, Catherine L., 2023.1
"Alexander Carson (1776–1844): 'Jonathan Edwards of the Nineteenth Century,'" 2009.15
Allen, Alexander Viets Griswold, 2007.2, 2008.1, 2010.1, 2010.2, 2010.28
Allen, Bob, 2012.2
Allen, Deborah W, 2008.2
Allen, Michael, 2009.1
Allen, Russell J., 2015.1, 2016.1
Allison, C. M. B., 2012.3
"Almost Baptists: Baptistic Pedobaptist in American History (1650–950)," 2023.49

Always in God's Hands: Day by Day in the Company of Jonathan Edwards, 2018.57
American Evangelicalism: George Marsden and the State of American Religious History, 2014.27
American Philosophy Before Pragmatism, 2018.25
"American Primer," 2009.32
"American Puritanism and the Cognitive Style of Grace," 2017.67
American Spaces of Conversion: The Conductive Imaginaries of Edwards, Emerson, and James, 2011.29, 2012.12
"American Spaces of Conversion: The Conductive Imaginaries of Jonathan Edwards, Ralph Waldo Emerson, and William James," 2006.34
"The American Sunday and the Formative Work of Jonathan Edwards," 2010.51
American Terror: The Feeling of Thinking in Edwards, Poe, and Melville, 2016.36
America's Evangelical, 2007.33
Review of *America's God: From Jonathan Edwards to Abraham Lincoln*, 2006.14, 2007.43
America's God: From Jonathan Edwards to Abraham Lincoln, 2009.32
America's Theologian Beyond America: Jonathan Edwards, Israel, and China, 2022.55
"'America's Theologian' Enters the Middle Kingdom: Uncovering the Earliest Chinese Reception of Jonathan Edwards," 2019.55
"Amidst the Great Darkness: The Practical Missiology of Jonathan Edwards at Stockbridge, 1751–1758," 2008.54
"Analogy: A Neglected Theme in Jonathan Edwards and Its Pertinence to Contemporary Theological Debates," 2016.50
"An Analysis of the Doctrine of Seeking in Jonathan Edwards's Conversion Theology as Revealed Through Representative Northampton Sermons and Treatises," 2006.27
Anderson, Owen J., 2014.2
"Andrew Fuller and the Millennium," 2020.21
Andrews, Edward E, 2006.2
"The Angelology of Jonathan Edwards," 2021.3
"Annihilationism, Traditionalism and the Problem of Hell," 2010.4
"Anthropology, Affection, and Free Will,," 2021.64
"Antonin Scalia v Jonathan Edwards: Romans 13 and the American Theology of State," 2009.85
Approaching Jonathan Edwards: The Evolution of a Persona, 2015.2
Review of *Approaching Jonathan Edwards: The Evolution of a Persona*, 2015.39, 2016.66, 2019.54
Review of *Approaching the Atonement: The Reconciling Work of Christ*, 2022.31
"'The Architecture of Beneficence': An Account of Nontotalitarian Beauty," 2010.39
Ariail, Austin T., 2009.2
"Art and Objecthood: Michael Fried and Jonathan Edwards," 2023.22
"The Arts," 2007.19
"'As in a Mirror': Jonathan Edwards, Self-Love and Enlarging to Receive Another," 2023.45
"'As Ordered and Governed by Divine Providence': Jonathan Edwards' Use of the Machine as Master Metaphor., SP.5
Ashcraft, W. Michael, 2011.1
"Asia," 2021.64
"Aspects of God's Relationship to the World in the Theologies of

Jürgen Moltmann, Bonaventure and Jonathan Edwards," 2007.51, 2007.52
Atherstone, Andrew, 2007.3
Atkinson, M. C., SP.3
Atwood, Christopher S., 2014.3
"An Augustinian-Edwardsian Metaphysics of Possibility for the Barcan Formula," 2022.37
Austad, Torleiv, 2022.1
"Australia," 2021.64
"Awakened to the Holy: 'Sinners in the Hands of an Angry God' in Ritualized Context," 2008.74

Babatunde, Timothy, SP.44
"The Background of Jonathan Edwards' Dismissal," 2022.26
"Bad Books and the Glorious Trinity: Jonathan Edwards on the Sexual Holiness of the Church," 2015.65
Bademan, R. Bryan, 2006.3
Bailey, Richard A., 2006.5, 2014.4
Baines, Ron, 2013.23
Baines, Ronald S, 2006.4
Baird, William, 2006.66
Ball, Carol, 2015.2, 2015.39, 2016.66, 2019.54
Ballan, Joseph N., 2013.2
Banks, John S., 2020.1, 2020.2, 2020.3, 2021.1
Bannon, Brad, 2018.2, 2019.2
Barone, Marco, 2018.3, 2019.3, 2019.4, 2020.4, 2021.2
Barshinger, David P., 2009.3, 2010.3, 2011.2, 2012.4, 2012.5, 2013.3, 2013.4, 2014.5, 2015.3, 2015.21, 2015.30, 2015.56, 2015.60, 2016.10, 2016.25, 2016.42, 2016.44, 2016.55, 2017.1, 2018.1, 2018.4, 2018.13, 2018.14, 2019.48, 2019.64, 2019.71, 2020.11, 2021.35, 2021.64
"Barth and Edwards," 2020.50
Bates, James Jordan, 2023.2
Bawulski, Shawn, 2010.4
Baxter, Tony, 2006.5

Baysa, Michael, 2023.3
Beach, Mark J., 2016.2
"Beatific Satisfaction," 2023.29
"The Beautiful Mystery: Examining Jonathan Edwards' View of Marriage," 2015.1
"A Beautiful Vision of Glory: Jonathan Edwards's Use of Scripture in His Aesthetic Approach to God's End of Creation," 2018.68
"Beauty, Benevolence, and Virtue in Jonathan Edwards's *The Nature of True Virtue*," 2007.14
"Beauty, Horror, and Tragedy: The Idea of Hell in Jonathan Edwards and William James," 2014.65
Beauty and Holiness: The Dialogue Between Aesthetics and Religion, 2014.52
"The Beauty of God the Holy Spirit," 2007.54
"The Beauty of Healing: Covenant, Eschatology, and Jonathan Edwards' Theological Aesthetics: Toward a Theology of Medicine," 2014.48
"The Beauty of the Cross: Retrieving Penal Substitutionary Atonement on Jonathan Edwards' Aesthetic Basis," 2017.42
"The Beauty of the Redemption of the World: The Theological Aesthetics of Maximus the Confessor and Jonathan Edwards," 2008.27
"Beauty Seize Us," 2008.47
Bebbington, David W. (Wayne), 2009.4, 2009.5
Beck, Peter, 2006.6, 2007.4, 2009.6, 2010.5, 2010.6, 2012.6, 2013.5, 2015.4, 2016.3, 2019.5
Becoming Divine: Jonathan Edwards's Incarnational Spirituality Within the Christian Tradition, 2011.61
"Becoming One Self: A Critical Retrieval of 'Choice Biography,'" 2007.32

Beeke, Joel, 2011.3, 2014.6
Review of *Before Jonathan Edwards: Sources of New England Theology*, 2019.12, 2019.37, 2019.63, 2020.22, 2020.30, 2020.34, 2022.24
Before Jonathan Edwards: Sources of New England Theology, 2018.46, 2019.50
"Believers Only: Jonathan Edwards on Communion," 2015.18
Belt, Thomas G., 2006.60
Benge, Dustin W., 2012.7, 2018.5, 2021.3
"Benjamin Whichcote's Theology of Deification in Historical Context," 2023.2
Bennett, M. Jay, 2006.7
Bennett, Miranda, 2011.4
Bercovitch, Sacvan, 2012.12
The Best of Jonathan Edwards' Sermons, 2007.26
Beynon, Graham, 2019.6
"Beyond Salem and Secularism: Jonathan Edwards and Satan in Early America," 2021.31
Beyond the Half-Way Covenant: Solomon Stoddard's Understanding of the Lord's Supper as a Converting Ordinance, 2012.35
"Beyond the Half-Way Covenant: Solomon Stoddard's Understanding of the Lord's Supper as a Converting Ordinance; Its Origins, Development, and Influence in the Connecticut Valley of Western Massachusetts," 2010.48
Bezzant, Rhys S. (Stewart), 2007.5, 2011.5, 2012.8, 2014.7, 2014.8, 2014.9, 2014.44, 2015.6, 2015.8, 2015.33, 2015.37, 2015.54, 2016.4, 2016.8, 2016.22, 2017.2, 2017.3, 2017.9, 2018.40, 2019.7, 2020.5, 2020.20, 2020.27, 2020.39, 2020.56, 2021.64, 2022.2, SP.31, SP.35

"The Bible as a Resource for Christian Political Engagement," 2009.36
The Bible in Early Transatlantic Pietism and Evangelicalism, 2022.16
"A Biblical and Theological Critique of Jonathan Edwards' Doctrine of Christian Assurance.," 2012.55
"Biblical Authority and Christian Higher Education," 2023.52
"Biblical Exegesis,," 2021.64
Biehl, Craig, 2008.3, 2009.7, 2009.81, 2010.7, 2010.8, 2012.9
Billings, J. Todd, 2009.86
Biografía de Jonathan Edwards: Su Vida, Obra y Pensamiento, 2023.10
"A Biographical Sketch and Documentary History of the Reverend Maltby Gelston (1766– 1856)," 2018.28
Review of "Bipolar Disorder: Head and Heart American Christianities,," 2008.71
"Birthing the New Birth: The Natural Philosophy of Childbirth in the Theology of Jonathan Edwards," 2009.30
Blaauw, Corné, 2014.10, 2014.11, 2016.5
Black, Griffin, 2018.6, 2018.7
The Blank Bible. Vol. 24 of The Works of Jonathan Edwards., 2006.20
Blore, Erick J., 2007.6
Blum, Edward J., 2012.46
Boersma, Hans, 2021.33
Bogue, Carl, 2009.8
Bolt, John, 2011.7
Bombaro, John J., 2011.6, 2012.10
Borgman, Brian, 2021.4, 2023.12
Born Again: A Portrait and Analysis of the Doctrine of Regeneration Within Evangelical Protestantism, 2017.31
Boss, Robert L., 2012.11, 2015.5, 2017.4, 2019.8, 2019.21, 2021.5, 2021.6, 2023.4, 2023.5
Boss, Sarah B., 2016.6, 2019.8, 2019.21, 2021.5, 2021.6
Bowden, Zachary M., 2016.7, 2016.8, 2016.9

Boyd, Adam Newcomb, 2019.9
Boyd, Gregory A., 2006.60
Boyden, Michael, 2021.9
Brandt, Eric T., 2010.9, 2013.5
Brandt., Ryan A., 2017.17
"Brattleboro History: 'Sinners in the Hands of an Angry God,'" SP.19
Bräutigam, Michael, 2013.6, 2015.6
Bray, Gerald L., 2019.10
Breimaier, Thomas, 2020.6
Brekus, Catherine A., 2006.40
"Bricolage and the Purity of Traditions: Engaging the Stoics for Contemporary Christian Ethics," 2012.16
Bridgers, Lynn, 2009.9
"A Brief History of Heaven in the Writings of Jonathan Edwards," 2011.8
Bright Shadows of Divine Things: The Devotional World of Jonathan Edwards, 2017.4
"Bringing Emotions to the Surface in Ministry," 2009.70
Brissett, W., 2012.12
"Britain and Europe,," 2021.64
Britz, Dolf, 2020.7
Britz, R. M., 2014.12
Brooks, Joshua Barrett, 2013.7
Brown, Audrey, 2022.3
Brown, Cullin R., 2021.7
Brown, Geoffrey Todd, 2021.8
Brown, R. E., 2014.13
Brown, Robert E., 2006.3, 2008.4, 2009.10, 2015.5, 2016.10, 2016.11, 2016.12, 2017.5, 2021.64
Bruce, Dustin Blane, 2018.8
"Building Great Love Toward God and Neighbor in Selected Northcreek Church Members Using Jonathan Edwards' Charity and Its Fruit," 2012.21
Burnell, Joel, 2014.14, 2020.8, SP.36
Bush, Alfred L, 2006.8
"By the Same Spirit: Edwardsean Pneumatology in the Younger Edwards," 2020.1

Bynum, T., 2009.11
Byrd, James P., 2008.5, 2008.61, 2008.62, 2011.58, 2021.64, SP.10

Caldwell, Robert W., III, 2006.9, 2006.10, 2008.57, 2009.56, 2011.8, 2011.9, 2011.57, 2012.65, 2012.66, 2013.4, 2013.8, 2013.9, 2013.10, 2013.11, 2013.12, 2014.15, 2014.19, 2014.30, 2014.47, 2015.42, 2015.57, 2016.63, 2017.6, 2020.9, 2021.10, 2021.64, 2022.4
Calfano, Brian R., 2008.6
"A Call to Gospel Integrity: The Nature of True Christianity in Jonathan Edwards and Thomas Boston," 2007.46
Review of *The Cambridge Companion to Jonathan Edwards*, 2007.17, 2007.20, 2008.12, 2008.15, 2008.34, 2008.41, 2008.75, 2009.35, 2009.60, 2009.74
The Cambridge Companion to Jonathan Edwards, 2007.58, 2011.38
Campagna-Pinto, Stephen Thomas, 2011.10, 2014.57
Campbell, Benjamin Scott, 2021.11
Campeau, Gregory J., SP.20
Campos, Heber Carlos de, Jr., 2016.13, 2021.64
Carpenter, Roy, 2010.10, 2015.7, 2016.14
Carr, Kevin C., 2010.11
Carr, Simonetta, 2014.16
Carrick, John, 2008.7, 2010.2, 2010.33, 2011.39
Carter, Jonathan M., 2023.6
Carver, Benjamin T., 2010.12
"Casuistic Book-Lending: Jonathan Edwards' Use of Daniel Defoe's Religious Courtship," 2021.48
Catalogues of Books. Vol. 26 of The Works of Jonathan Edwards, 2008.19
"The Categories of Jonathan Edwards' Natural Philosophy Applied

to Organic Chemistry: An
Integrative Example," 2021.29
Cavalier, Adam G., 2018.9, 2018.10,
2019.11, 2021.12
Cayton, Mary K., 2006.11
"The Ceremonial or Moral Law:
Jonathan Edwards's Old
Perspective of an Old Error,"
2010.7
Challies, Tim, 2009.13
Chamberlain, Ava, 2007.7, 2007.8,
2007.58, 2012.13, 2013.59,
2014.17, 2015.8, 2016.69,
2018.11, 2021.64
Chang, Nathan W., 2017.7
Chapman, Mark, 2015.9
Charity and Its Fruits: Living in the Light of God's Love, 2012.62
Charry, Ellen T, 2007.9
Cheng, Yang-En, 2011.11
Cherock, Richard J., 2009.12
The Child in American Evangelicalism and the Problem of Affluence: A Theological Anthropology of the Affluent American Evangelical Child in Late Modernity, 2009.72
Cho, Hyun-Jin, 2010.13, 2012.14, 2013.54
Cho, Seong, II, SP.25
Choi, Ki Joo, 2006.12, 2008.7, 2009.14, 2010.14
Choi, Paul, 2021.13
Choiński, Michal, 2011.12, 2014.18, 2016.15, 2017.41, 2018.55
"Choir Answers to Choir: Notes on Jonathan Edwards and Wallace Stevens," 2009.39
"Christ-Centered, Bible-Based, and SecondRate? 'Right Reason' as the Aesthetic Foundation of Christian Education," 2007.27
Christian Biographies for Young Readers: Jonathan Edwards, 2014.16
"Christian Metaphysics and Idealism," 2022.42
"Christianity and the Common Good: Generating Benevolence and Pursuing the Decent Equilibrium in International Fieldwork," 2008.6
"Christological Arguments for Compatibilism in Reformed Theology," 2023.19
"The Christology of John Flavel," 2012.17
"A Chronology of Edwards's Life and Writings," 2017.51
Chun, Chris, 2006.13, 2008.8, 2008.10, 2012.15, 2012.25, 2013.13, 2013.39, 2014.19, 2014.34, 2015.10, 2020.10, 2020.51, 2021.54, 2022.5
"A Church Without a View: Jonathan Edwards and Our Current Life View Discipleship Crisis," SP.9
Clark, David J., 2020.11
Clark, Jawanza Eric, 2011.13
Clark, John C., 2008.11, 2011.14
Clark, Michael P., 2010.15
Clary, Ian Hugh, 2009.15
"Claudius Buchanan: Scotland's First Missionary to the Jews," 2007.49
Cochran, Elizabeth Agnew, 2007.10, 2010.16, 2011.15, 2011.16, 2012.16, 2015.11, 2018.12, 2021.64
Cochran, Joseph T., 2017.8, 2017.9, 2018.13, 2018.14, 2018.15, 2019.12, 2019.13, 2020.12, 2021.14, 2021.15, 2021.16, 2022.6
"A Cognitive Approach to the Hermeneutics of Jonathan Edwards's Sermons," 2014.18
Coleman, Mary, 2008.12
A Collection of Essays on Jonathan Edwards, 2019.21
The Columbia Guide to Religion in American History, 2012.46
Communion in the Spirit: The Holy Spirit as the Bond of Union in the Theology of Jonathan Edwards., 2006.9, 2006.10
Review of *Communion in the Spirit: The Holy Spirit as the Bond of Union*

in the Theology of Jonathan Edwards, 2008.57, 2009.56
"Communion with God and the Means of Grace in the Spirituality of Jonathan Edwards," 2020.15
"A Comparison of Jonathan Edwards and Charles Hodge on the Doctrine of Conversion," 2016.26
"Complaints, Declarations, and Testimonies: Sources of Contention in Stockbridge, 1753–1756," 2019.41
"The Concept of the Heart in the Experience of Augustine and Edwards," SP.7
"Confessionalism and Causation in Jonathan Edwards (1703–1758)," 2022.11
Congrove, Mark J., 2017.10
Conley, Stephen Mark, 2019.14
"Consent, Conversion, and Moral Formation: Stoic Elements in Jonathan Edwards's Ethics," 2011.15
"The Contemplative Foundations of Genuine Religious Experience in the Life and Pastoral Ministry of Jonathan Edwards," 2007.22
"The Contemporary Crisis in Higher Education: An Edwardsean Response," SP.38
"Contingency in the Late Metaphysics of Jonathan Edwards," 2021.57
The Contribution of Jonathan Edwards to American Culture and Society: Essays on America's Spiritual Founding Father, 2008.30
A Conversation with Jonathan Edwards, 2006.15
Cooley, Daniel W., 2014.20
Cooley, Paul M., 2010.17
Cooper, William Henry, Jr., 2010.18
Cope, Kevin L., 2006.24
"Copley and Edwards: Self, Consciousness, and Thing," 2008.60
Cosby, Brian H., 2012.17

"Cosmology," SP.18
"Cotton Mather and Jonathan Edwards on the Epistle of James: A Comparative Study," 2010.70
Cotton Mather and the Biblia Americana—America's First Bible Commentary: Essays in Reappraisal, 2021.59
"Cotton Mather Brings Isaac Watts's Hymns to America; or, How to Perform a Hymn with Singing It," 2012.50
Coulter, Dale M., 2013.14
Review and Response to Covenant and Salvation: 'Union' with Christ, 2009.86
"Covenant Nation: The Politics of Grace in Early American Literature," 2012.57
Covenant of Redemption in the Trinitarian Theology of Jonathan Edwards: The Nexus Between the Immanent Trinity and the Economic Trinity, 2019.73
Review of Covenant of Redemption in the Trinitarian Theology of Jonathan Edwards: The Nexus Between the Imminent Trinity and the Economic Trinity, 2020.52
The Covenant Theology of Jonathan Edwards: Law, Gospel, and Evangelical Obedience, 2021.26
Review of The Covenant Theology of Jonathan Edwards: Law, Gospel, and Evangelical Obedience, 2021.65
Craig, William Lane, 2023.7
Crain, Chris T., 2006.14
Crampton, W. Gary, 2006.15, 2007.11, 2011.17, 2021.17
Craun, Joy, 2019.15
"'Craved Reality': Perry Miller, Sinclair Lewis, and Puritanism," 2019.1
Crawford, Brandon James, 2015.12, 2017.11, 2019.16, 2020.13, 2023.8
"Creation and Predestination,", 2021.64

Review of *The Creation of the British Atlantic World*, 2006.2
"Creaturely Virtues in Jonathan Edwards: The Significance of Christology on the Moral Life," 2007.10
Creegan, Nicola Hoggard, 2007.12
Crisp, Oliver D., 2007.13, 2007.23, 2008.13, 2008.14, 2008.15, 2008.16, 2008.26, 2008.28, 2009.16, 2009.17, 2009.18, 2010.16, 2010.19, 2010.20, 2010.65, 2011.18, 2012.18, 2012.19, 2013.12, 2013.50, 2014.15, 2014.17, 2014.21, 2014.22, 2014.28, 2014.85, 2015.4, 2015.13, 2015.14, 2015.15, 2015.23, 2015.47, 2015.53, 2016.2, 2016.11, 2016.21, 2016.27, 2016.47, 2016.54, 2016.67, 2017.3, 2017.8, 2017.12, 2017.22, 2017.33, 2017.34, 2017.38, 2017.52, 2017.68, 2017.69, 2018.16, 2018.17, 2018.23, 2018.37, 2018.53, 2019.13, 2019.19, 2019.28, 2019.29, 2019.36, 2019.62, 2020.13, 2022.11, 2022.31
"A Critical Examination of Jonathan Edwards's Doctrine of the Trinity," 2014.23
"A Critique of the Taxonomy of Educational Objectives by Jonathan Edwards," 2007.47
Crocco, Stephen D., 2010.65, 2017.13, 2019.17
Cunnington, Ralph, 2014.23
"The Curse of Adam's Transgression: Jonathan Edwards and John Wesley Against the Theological Writings of John Taylor," SP.44
Cuthbert, Christian, 2011.19

Damned Nation: Hell in America from the Revolution to Reconstruction, 2014.32

Danaher, James P., 2007.14, 2007.15, 2007.16
Danaher, William J., Jr, 2006.16, 2006.45, 2006.65, 2007.8, 2007.57, 2009.19, 2009.69
D'Andrea-Winslow, Lisanne, 2023.9
Daniel, Curt, 2019.18
Daniel, Stephen H., 2007.58, 2010.65
Darkness Falls on the Land of Light: Experiencing Religious Awakening in Eighteenth-Century New England, 2016.73
Review of *Darkness Falls on the Land of Light: Experiencing the Religious Awakenings in Eighteenth-Century New England*, 2022.49
Davidson, Bruce W., 2008.17, 2011.20, 2014.24, 2016.16, 2021.18
Davidson, Edward H., 2008.18
Davies, Ronald E., 2006.17, 2007.17, 2007.18
Davis, Holly, 2021.19
Davis, Oshea, 2014.25
De Klerk, Jenny-Lyn, 2016.17
De La Cruz, Juan Carlos, 2023.10
Review of *De ruimte van soevereine genade*, 2017.55
De Witt, John, 2010.21
"'Dear Mr. Edwards': Theological Dialogue About Seeking God," 2019.5
"'The Death of Christ Was a Murder': Jonathan Edwards and Blame for Christ's Death," 2017.45
DeBruyn, David, 2020.14
Deeter, Justin Baine, 2020.15
"Defending Happiness: Jonathan Edwards's Enduring Pursuit of a Reformed Teleology of Happiness," SP.42
DeHoff, Susan L., 2012.20
"The Deliberative Practices of Aesthetic Experience: Reconsidering the Moral Functionality of Art," 2008.7, 2009.14
Delph, Joseph Michael, 2018.18
"Democracy and Virtue: Optimism or Faith?" 2006.48

Review of *Democratic Faith: Accepting Limits*, 2007.31
Deneen, Patrick J., 2007.31
DeOliveira, Charles Melo, 2015.16
"Destiny by Design: Understanding the Doctrine of the Curse in the Thought of Augustine, Martin Luther, Jonathan Edwards, and Karl Barth," 2014.76
"Determining Duty: The Fate of Anglo-Protestant Indian Missions After the Great Awakening," 2007.50
Detrich, James P., 2014.26
Detzler, Wayne A., 2015.17
"The Development of the Redemptive Role of the Holy Spirit in the Reformed Trinitarian Theology of Jonathan Edwards," 2010.12
Dever, Mark E., 2015.18
"'A Diamond in the Sun': The Idea of 'Glory' in the Teleology of Jonathan Edwards," 2006.62
Dictionary of World Biography, 2022.20
"'Different Streams . . . into the Same Great Ocean': Jonathan Edwards, Robert Millar, and Transatlantic Influence on a History of the Work of Redemption," 2015.48
Dillard, Peter S., 2019.19
"Discerning the Spirit: Ambivalent Assurance in the Soteriology of Jonathan Edwards and Barthian Correctives," 2010.35
"Discovering Naaman's Hypocrisy: A Genealogical Account of Jonathan Edwards's Exegesis of 2 Kings 5," 2020.53
"A Disinterested Republic: Reform and New Divinity Theology in Early America," 2019.47
"Disposition, Potentiality, and Beauty in the Theology of Jonathan Edwards: A Defense of His Great Christian Doctrine of Original Sin," 2012.51
"Disputing the Augustinian Legacy: John Locke and Jonathan Edwards on Romans 5:12–19," 2023.40

"The Distinctive of Christian Gratitude: A Theological Survey," 2022.7
"Distinguishing Mystical Religious Experience from Psychotic Experience in the Presbyterian Church (USA)," 2012.20
Ditmore, Michael G, 2006.18
"Divine Beauty and Excellency: Some Lessons from Jonathan Edwards," 2008.13
Divine Husbandmen (On the Parable of the Sower and the Seed), 2012.41
"Divine Knowledge at Harvard and Yale: From William Ames to Jonathan Edwards," 2014.31
"Divine Light and Holy Love: Genuine Conversion in the Works of Jonathan Edwards," 2023.16
"'Divine Light, Holy Heat': Jonathan Edwards, the Ministry of the Word, and Spiritual Formation," 2008.49
A Divine Light: The Spiritual Leadership of Jonathan Edwards, 2007.62
"Divine Love as the Organizing Principle of Jonathan Edwards's Doctrine of Atonement," 2019.16
Divine Will and Human Choice: Freedom, Contingency, and Necessity in Early Modern Reformed Thought, 2018.29
Dixon, Christine, SP.7
Dochuk, Darren, 2014.27
"The Doctrine of Regeneration in Evangelical Theology: The Reformation to 1800," 2011.53
"The Doctrine of Sanctification in the Theology of Jonathan Edwards," SP.17
"The Doctrine of Scripture in the Theology of Jonathan Edwards," 2008.64
"Does Edwards Have a 'Thoroughgoing "Feminine" Ecclesiology'? A Response to Benjamin Wayman in a Reconsideration of the Evidence from The Blank Bible," 2021.52

"Does Jonathan Edwards' Concept of Virtue as 'Love to Being in General' Explain the Governmentalism Found in His Son Jonathan Edwards Jr.?" 2018.64

"Does Pentecostalism Have Reformed Roots? An Analysis of the Argument of W. W. Menzies," 2007.67

"Doing All Things for God's Glory, Acting So That It Is God Who Acts: Kierkegaard, Edwards, and the Problem of Total Devotion," 2022.18

"Domestic Piety in New England," 2007.7

Dominski, Lolly, 2017.14

Dooley, Adam B, 2006.19

"A 'Dordtian Philosophe': Jonathan Edwards, Calvin, and Reformed Orthodoxy," 2011.40

Doyle, Peter Reese, 2017.15

Dr. Taylor of Norwich: Wesley's Arch Heretic, 2012.23

Dresdow, Kent H., 2012.21

Dunnington, Kent, 2022.7, 2023.11

Dussol, Vincent, 2011.21

"The Dutch Reception of the History of Jonathan Edwards," 2023.37

"The Dynamics of Time and Location in Salvation as Developed by Jonathan Edwards in the History of the Work of Redemption," 2011.30

Dyrness, William A., 2007.19, 2021.64

"The Early Idealism of Edwards," 2010.28

Early Modern Philosophy of Religion, 2014.59

"An Early Printing of a Sermon by Edwards," 2015.67

Easley, Toby K., 2012.22, 2019.21

Easterling, Joe M., 2018.19

"Ecclesiology and Sacrament,," 2021.64

"Economic Ethics as a Gospel Priority in the Pastoral Ministry of Jonathan Edwards," 2019.22

"Economic Models of Addiction and the Christian View of Temptation," 2013.58

"An Ecospirituality of Nature's Beauty: A Hopeful Conversation in the Current Climate Crisis," 2023.9

The Ecumenical Edwards: Jonathan Edwards and the Theologians, 2015.58

Review of *The Ecumenical Edwards: Jonathan Edwards and the Theologians*, 2016.23, 2016.77, 2017.29, 2017.46, 2017.57

Eddy, G. T., 2012.23

Eddy, Nathan, 2023.12

Eden, Jason Edward, 2012.24

Edgar, William, 2011.22

"Education,," 2021.64

"The Educational Philosophy of Jonathan Edwards: An Analysis and Application of His Calvinistic Psychology," 2007.6

"Edward Dorr Griffin and the Edwardsian Second Great Awakening," 2012.53

Edwards, Deborah, 2010.22

Edwards, Germany, and Transatlantic Contexts, 2022.2

Edwards, Jonathan, 2006.20, 2006.21, 2006.22, 2008.19, 2008.20, 2008.21, 2008.22, 2009.20, 2009.21, 2009.22, 2009.23, 2009.24, 2009.25, 2010.23, 2010.24, 2010.25, 2010.26, 2011.23, 2022.8

"Edwards, Jonathan." In *Dictionary of Major Biblical Interpreters?* 2007.61

Edwards, Jonathan, Jr., 2009.26

Edwards Amasa Park: The Last Edwardsean, 2018.48

Review of *Edwards Amasa Park: The Last Edwardsean*, 2018.59

"Edwards and Eve: Finding Feminist Strains in the Great Awakening's Patriarch," 2008.40

"Edwards and Indians: Inclusivism or Evangelism?" 2006.6

"Edwards and the Enlightenment: Mapping the Secular Within the Covenanted Community," SP.22

Edwards and the Psalms, 2016.42

"Edwards and Thoreau: Typologies of Lakes," 2016.6

"Edwards' Copy of William Ames' Medulla," 2017.32

"Edwards: Ethics for Both the Vulgar and the Learned," 2020.29

"Edwards' Freedom of the Will: A Review and Analysis," 2007.11

"Edwards in Northampton," 2010.28

"Edwards in the Context of International Revivals and Missions,," 2021.64

"Edwards' Occasionalism," 2010.65

"The Edwards of History and the Edwards of Faith," 2006.3

"Edwards on Education: A Content Analysis of the Philosophy of Education of Jonathan Edwards with Implication from Christian Educators," 2023.28

Edwards on God, 2021.50

Review of *Edwards on the Christian Life: Alive to the Beauty of God*, 2014.41, SP.34

Edwards on the Christian Life: Alive to the Beauty of God, 2014.60

"'Edwards Saw More Perspicaciously': R. L. Dabney's Edwardsean Philosophy of Free-Agency," 2019.3

"Edwards Studies Today," 2021.64

Review of *Edwards the Exegete: Biblical Interpretation and Anglo-Protestant Culture on the Edge of the Enlightenment*, 2016.19, 2017.5

Edwards the Exegete: Biblical Interpretation and Anglo-Protestant Culture on the Edge of the Enlightenment, 2016.68

Review of *Edwards the Mentor*, 2020.20, 2020.27, 2020.39, 2020.56

Edwards the Mentor., 2019.7

"An Edwardsean Evolution: The Rise and Decline of Moral Governmental Theory in the Southern Baptist Convention," 2019.67

"The Edwardsean Isaac Backus: The Significance of Jonathan Edwards in Backus's Theology, History, and Defense of Religious Liberty," 2013.46

"The Edwardsean Roots of Manifest Destiny," 2017.59

"Edwards's Ezekiel: The Interpretation of Ezekiel in the Blank Bible and Notes on Scripture," 2009.84

"Edwards's Place and Importance in Anglo-American Literature," 2021.64

"The Effect of Social Context and Culture in the Preaching of Jonathan Edwards and Charles Finney," 2011.59

"The Effect of the Fear Appeals on George Whitefield's Auditors," 2013.37

Eisel, Christine, 2022.8

Review of *The Emergence of Evangelical Spirituality: The Age of Edwards, Newton and Whitefield*, 2019.49, 2020.46

"Emily Dickinson's Ecocentric Pastoralism," 2007.55

"Emotion, Experience and Enthusiasm: The Growing Divide in US Religion," 2009.9

"Emotional Communities: Nathan Cole and the Separate Movement in Massachusetts and Connecticut, 1740–70," SP.32

"The 'Emotionally Relevant' Congregations," 2006.31

"The End for Which God Created," 2010.65

Engaging with Barth: Contemporary Evangelical Critiques, 2008.26
Engelsma, Esther, 2019.20
"Ensouling the Beatific Vision: Motivating the Reformed Impulse," 2017.17
"Epistemology,," 2021.64
"Epistemology and Terror in American Literature: Edwards, Poe, Melville," 2008.39
"Epistolary Physick: Familiar Letters, Friendship, and Self-Preservation in Eighteenth-Century America," 2012.48
Epstein, A., 2009.27
Ericson, John, 2018.20
"The Eschatology of Signs in Cotter Mather's 'Biblia Americana' and Jonathan Edwards' Cases for the Legibility of Providence," 2010.15
"Essence and Fullness: Evaluating the CreatorCreature Distinction in Jonathan Edwards," 2017.60
The Essential Jonathan Edwards: An Introduction to the Life and Teaching of America's Greatest Theologian, 2018.58
Review of *The Essential Jonathan Edwards: An Introduction to the Life and Teaching of America's Greatest Theologian*, 2019.31
"Eternal Covenant: An Exploration of Jonathan Edwards' View on Covenant Theology," SP.39
"Ethics,," 2021.64
"Eudaimonia After Edwards: Or, What's 'New' About the New Divinity?" 2022.12
"Evaluating the Revival Experience of Korean Missionary Robert A. Hardie (1865–1949) in View of Jonathan Edwards' Religious Affections," 2017.43
The Evangelicals, 2017.49
"Evangelicals, the End Times, and Islam," 2009.45
The Evangelicals: The Struggle to Shape America, 2017.20
Everhard, Matthew, 2016.18, 2018.21, 2018.22, 2019.21, 2020.3, 2021.20
"The Everlasting Mediation of the Son of God: A Case Study of the Enduring Mediatorial Office of Christ in Calvin and the Reformed Tradition," 2020.43
"Everlasting Punishment and the Goodness of God: Some Contribution to the Current Debate from Jonathan Edwards," 2006.29
Every, Samuel Stephen, 2017.16
Every Leaf, Line, and Letter: Evangelicals and the Bible from the 1730s to the Present, 2021.72
Everyday Glory: The Revelation of God in All Reality, 2018.42
"'Everything . . . Was Typical of Gospel Things!' A Reconsideration of Jonathan Edwards's Biblical Typology: A Study of His 'Blank Bible'," 2021.53
"The Excellency of Minds: Jonathan Edwards's Theological Style," 2008.67
"The Exegetical Basis of Jonathan Edwards' Cessationism," 2015.43
"Exegetical Soundness Regarding Race: How White American Evangelicals Were Influenced by Contemporary Racial Opinions of Their Day Rather Than Consistent with Application of Biblical Hermeneutics," 2021.8
"The Expanding World of Jacob Norton: Reading, Revivalism, and the Construction of a 'Second Great Awakening' in New England, 1787–1804," 2006.11
"Experience," 2007.9
"Experiencing God in Words: Rhetoric, Logic, Imaginative Languages, and Emotion in

Jonathan Edwards' Sermons: A Computational Analysis," SP.41
"An Exploration of the Diary as a Medium: During the Seventeenth and Eighteenth Centuries," 2017.16

"Faith, Free Will, and Biblical Reasoning in the Thought of Jonathan Edwards and John Erskine," 2021.72
"A Faith Disposed Towards Jesus: The Relationship Between Love and Faith in Jonathan Edwards and the Reformed Tradition," 2022.54
"Faith in an Age of Cultural Pluralism: An Aesthetic Approach to Transformation," 2020.47
A Faithful Narrative of the Revival of Religion in New England; With Thoughts on That Revival, 2010.23
"Faithful Translations: New Discoveries on the German Pietist Reception of Jonathan Edwards," 2014.71
"The Fall of Man and the Failure of Jonathan Edwards," 2007.4
"The False Dichotomy of the Laity: Rejuvenating Evangelicalism with Jonathan Edwards' Doctrine of the Priesthood of All Believers," 2016.40
"Family Influences on 'The Minister's Wooing' and 'Oldtown Folks': Henry Ward Beecher and Calvin Stowe," 2006.1
Famous Jonathan's, Including Jonathan Edwards, Jonathan Livingston Seagull, Jonathan Brandis, and More, SP.21
Farris, Joshua R., 2014.28, 2015.19, 2017.17, 2018.28
Farrow, Holly, 2020.16
Fea, John, 2007.20
"The Federal Theology and the History of Redemption in Jonathan Edwards's Biblical Exegesis," 2018.50
The Federal Theology of Jonathan Edwards: An Exegetical Perspective, 2021.51
Review of *The Federal Theology of Jonathan Edwards: An Exegetical Perspective*, 2021.61, 2022.4, 2022.23, 2023.15, 2023.43
"Federalism and Reformed Scholasticism,", 2021.64
Feeling Godly: Religious Affections and Christian Contact in Early North America, 2021.69
Fehler, Brian, 2009.28
"Female Piety and Evangelical Ritualization of Death: Abigail Hutchinson's Conversion in 'A Faithful Narrative," 2016.49
Fennema, Scott R., 2015.20, 2017.18
Ferreira, Franklin, 2020.17
Fesko, J. V., 2021.21, 2023.13
Field, Brady Paul, 2021.22
Fifty People Every Christian Should Know: Learning from Spiritual Giants of the Faith, 2009.89
Review of *Finding God in Solitude: The Personal Piety of Jonathan Edwards (1703–1758) and Its Influence on His Pastoral Ministry*, 2015.36, 2015.49, 2015.59, 2016.20, 2017.72
Finding God in Solitude: The Personal Piety of Jonathan Edwards and Its Influence on His Pastoral Ministry, 2014.81
Finn, Nathan A., 2012.25, 2013.15, 2013.16, 2014.29, 2014.30, 2015.21, 2016.19, 2016.20, 2016.21, 2016.22, 2016.23, 2017.19, 2018.9, 2020.18
"'Fire Enfolding Itself': Jonathan Edwards, the Merkabah, and Reparative Reasoning," 2009.19
"The First Devinity Lecture Made by Me James Pierpont & Published in Yale College," 2017.56
Fisber, George P., 2010.28

Fischer, John Martin, 2022.9
Fish Out of Their Element (On the Parable of the Net), 2012.42
Fisk, Philip J., 2007.21, 2008.23, 2014.31, 2015.22, 2016.24, 2018.23, 2018.34, 2018.49, 2018.53, 2018.54, 2020.19, 2023.14
Fitzgerald, Frances, 2017.20, 2017.49
"For Faithful Narratives: Why Pastors Should Journal," 2021.11
"For Glory and for Sport: Jonathan Edwards and the Vedanta School on God's Motive," 2022.19
For the Fame of God's Name: Essays in Honor of John Piper, 2010.73
Ford, Patience, 2009.49
Forged in Faith: How Faith Shaped the Birth of the Nation 1607–1776, 2010.30
"Forgiveness: From the Puritans to Jonathan Edwards," 2006.69
The Forgotten Edwards: A New Examination of the Life and Thought of Jonathan Edwards Junior, 2021.1
Formed for the Glory of God: Learning from the Spiritual Practices of Jonathan Edwards, 2013.52
Review of *Formed for the Glory of God: Learning from the Spiritual Practices of Jonathan Edwards*, 2016.17
Forster, Greg, 2019.22
"The Four Faces of Self-Love in the Theology of Jonathan Edwards," 2008.17
"Francis Turretin and Jonathan Edwards on Compatibilism," 2018.29
Frayne, Darryl R., 2007.22
Freedom of the Will, 2008.20
Friend, Nathan, 2017.21
Friesen, Paul H., 2013.17
"Frightful Inspiration, Sweet Elevation: The Application of Homiletics by Jonathan Edwards, Jonathan Mayhew, and Their Successors of the Late Eighteenth Century," 2010.65
"From Edwards to Emerson," 2007.42
"From Emerson to Edwards," 2007.42
"From Jonathan Edwards to Billy Graham," 2017.49
Review of *From Jonathan Edwards to Rudolph Bultmann. Vol. 2 of History of New Testament Research,*, 2015.24
Review of *From Nature to Experience: The American Search for Cultural Authority*, 2008.31
"From Puritans to Patriots: The Republicanization of American Theology, 1750–835," 2021.66
"From Silkworms to Songbirds: Why We No Longer Preach Like Jonathan Edwards," 2015.52
From the Fifth Century Onwards (Latin Writers); Female Power and Its Propaganda; Theologizing Performance in the Byzantine Tradition; Nachleben, 2021.49
"From the Pulpit to the People: A Comparative Survey of Jonathan Edwards' Pastoral Leadership in Northampton and Stockbridge," 2018.19
"The Full Brightness and Diffused Beams of Glory: Jonathan Edwards' Concept of Beauty and Its Relevance for Apologetics," 2014.78
"The Full Counsel of God," SP.2
"'Full of Wondrous and Glorious Things': The Exegetical Mind of Jonathan Edwards in His Anglo-American Cultural Context," 2007.64
Review of *Fullness Received and Returned: Trinity and Participation in Jonathan Edwards*, 2014.74, 2015.20, 2017.48
Fullness Received and Returned: Trinity and Participation in Jonathan Edwards, 2014.77

Fulton, Joe B., 2010.27

"G. W. Leibniz and Jonathan Edwards on Free-Agency," 2019.4
Gallo, Lou, SP.30
Ganski, Christopher, 2007.23
Garcia, John J., 2018.24
Garcia, Mark A., 2009.86
Garcia, Samuel, 2023.15
Garcia, Yvette D., 2007.24
Gardiner, H. Norman, 2010.28
Garretson, James M., 2015.23, 2016.25, 2020.20
Geissler, Suzanne, 2017.22, 2019.23
"Geneva's Crystalline Clarity: Harriet Beecher Stowe and Max Weber on Calvinism and the American Character," 2010.81
George, Christian, 2008.24
"George Berkley and Jonathan Edwards on Idealism: Considering an Old Question in Light of New Evidence," 2017.18
Gerstner, John, 2006.23, 2008.36
Geschiere, Charles L., 2008.25
"Getaway Sermon," 2007.37
Gibson, David, 2008.26
Gibson, Jonathan, 2011.24
Gibson, Michael D., 2008.27
Gierer, Emily Dolan, 2017.23
Gilpin, W. Clark, 2008.28, 2022.10
Gin Lum, Kathryn, 2014.32
Review of *The Global Edwards: Papers from the Jonathan Edwards Congress Held in Melbourne,* 2018.40
The Global Edwards: Papers from the Jonathan Edwards Congress Held in Melbourne, August 2015, 2017.2
"Glorious Damnation: Hell as an Essential Element in the Theology of Jonathan Edwards," 2011.20
Review of *The Glory and Honor of God: Volume Two of the Previously Unpublished Sermons of Jonathan Edwards,* 2006.36

"The Glory of Spiders and Politics," 2011.7
"The Glory of the Son in Jonathan Edwards' Christology," SP.37
Glover, David, 2010.29
God Is a Communicative Being: Divine Communicativeness and Harmony in the Theology of Jonathan Edwards, 2012.56
Review of *God Is a Communicative Being: Divine Communicativeness and Harmony in the Theology of Jonathan Edwards,* 2013.6, 2013.11, 2013.16, 2013.35, 2014.12
"The God of the Games: Towards a Theology of Competition," 2012.59
Review of *The God-Centered Life: Insights from Jonathan Edwards for Today,* 2007.3, 2007.18, 2009.55, 2012.8
The God-Centered Life: Insights from Jonathan Edwards for Today, 2006.53, 2007.45
God-Haunted World: The Elemental Theology of Jonathan Edwards., 2015.5
"Godly Mind: Puritan Reformed Orthodoxy and John Locke in Jonathan Edwards's Conception of Gracious Cognition and Conviction," 2014.73
God's Grand Design: The Theological Vision of Jonathan Edwards, 2011.36
Review of *God's Grand Design: The Theological Vision of Jonathan Edwards,* 2012.6, 2013.28
God's Passions for His Glory, 2011.38
Golding, D. Robert, 2021.23
"'Good News from a Far Country': Old Testament Wisdom Literature and the Concept of Wisdom in the Theology of Jonathan Edwards," 2022.41
Goodman, Russel B., 2018.25

Gordon, Bruce, 2021.24, 2021.42
Gordon, George A., 2010.28
Gowler, Steve, 2018.26
"A Graca Dos Santos É O Alvorecer Da Glória: Uma Nota Sobre Affection Como Sensation of the Mind em Religious Affections de Jonathan Edwards," 2019.34
Gragg, Rod, 2010.30
Graham, Kenneth W, 2006.24
"The Grammar of Revival: The Legacy of Jonathan Edwards's Teleological Language in Religion Affections (1746)," 2019.68
"'The Grand Encouragement': Andrew Fuller's Pneumatology as a Reception of and Advancement on Orthodox, Puritan, and Evangelical Perspectives on the Holy Spirit," 2018.8
"A Grand Juxtaposition: Jonathan Edwards and Charles Finney on Justification in Revival," 2015.28
Grasso, Christopher, 2009.29
Gratitude to God, 2023.11
"Gratitude to God: Jonathan Edwards and the Opening of the Self," 2021.63
Gray, Lauren Davis, 2009.30
Gray, Patrick, 2015.24
Gray, Robin, 2023.16
Review of *A Great and Remarkable Analogy: The Onto-Typology of Jonathan Edwards*, 2021.16, 2022.10, 2022.44
Review of *The Great Awakening: A History of the Revival of Religion in the Time of Whitefield and Edwards*, 2020.32
"The Great Awakening as an 'Outpouring of the Spirit' in the Work of Redemption According to Jonathan Edwards: A New Interpretive Framework," 2014.62
"The Great Awakening: Calvinism, Arminianism and Revivalistic Preaching: Homiletical Lesson for Today," 2012.26
The Great Awakening: The Roots of Evangelical Christianity in Colonial America, 2007.29
Review of *The Great Awakening: The Roots of Evangelical Christianity in Colonial America*, 2009.29
The Great Revivalists in American Religion, 1740–944: The Careers and Theology of Jonathan Edwards, Charles Finney, Dwight Moody, Billy Sunday, and Aimee Semple McPherson, 2010.18
The Great Work of Providence: Jonathan Edwards for Life Today, 2014.69
"The Greatest Instruction Received from Human Writings: The Legacy of Jonathan Edwards in the Theology of Andrew Fuller," 2008.8
"Greening America's Virtues," 2019.35
"Greeting," 2010.28
Gribben, Crawford, 2020.21
Griffith, Christopher Ryan, 2017.24, 2021.25
Grigg, John A., 2009.31, 2021.64
Gubbins, James P., 2008.29
Guelzo, Allen C., 2006.68, 2007.25, 2007.56, 2007.60, 2008.11, 2008.16, 2008.43, 2008.56
Gullotta, Daniel N., 2017.25, 2019.33, 2021.71
Gura, Philip F., 2006.3, 2006.18, 2006.44, 2007.33, 2007.58, 2009.32, 2009.67, 2013.18, 2023.17, SP.4
Gurr, Nigel A., 2016.26
Gustafson, Sandra M., 2021.64
Guyette, Fred, 2010.31, 2010.32
Gwon, Gyeongcheol, 2016.27

Habets, Myk, SP.10
Halambiec, Kamil M., 2017.26
Hall, Brent E., 2009.33
Hall, David D., 2007.58
Hall, Kenley, 2012.26
Hall, Kevin David, 2017.27

Hall, Richard A., 2015.25
Hall, Richard A. S., 2008.30
Hall, Timothy D., SP.4
Hambrick-Stowe, Charles E., 2007.25, 2009.34, 2009.35, 2021.64
Hamilton, Catherine Sider, 2013.19, 2013.20
Hamilton, Ian, 2019.24
Hamilton, S. Mark, 2014.33, 2015.26, 2016.28, 2016.29, 2017.28, 2017.29, 2017.30, 2018.27, 2018.28, 2019.30, 2020.22, 2021.10, 2021.64, 2022.11, SP.15
Hamilton, Stephen James, 2017.31
"Hampshire County Ministerial Association Minutes, 1731–47," 2018.6
Han, Dongsoo, 2019.25, 2020.23, 2021.64
Hancock, C. Layne, 2017.32, 2017.33, 2020.24, 2022.11, 2022.12
Hannafey, Francis T., 2017.34
Hannah, John D., 2010.33, 2010.34, 2016.30, 2017.35
Hanson, Paul D., 2009.36
Hanvey, James, 2013.21
Harder, Michael, 2022.13
Harper, George W, 2012.27
Harris, John, SP.8
Harrison, Douglas, 2006.25
Harriss, M. Cooper, 2008.31
Harrod, Joseph C., 2008.32
Hart, D. G., 2006.43
Hart, Matthew J., 2020.25
Hart, Richard E., 2008.33
Harvey, Paul, 2012.46
Hasker, William, 2022.14
Hastings, W. Ross, 2008.34, 2010.35, 2015.27, 2015.40, 2016.31, 2016.38, 2016.41, 2017.35, 2017.40
Hawkins, Justin, SP.33
Haykin, Michael A. G., 2006.26, 2007.41, 2009.56, 2012.28, 2013.23, 2013.24, 2014.34, 2014.35, 2016.32, 2020.26, 2020.27, 2020.28

"He Was 'Altogether Peculiar': Samuel Miller's Cautious Appreciation of Jonathan Edwards," 2017.64
Heacock, Clint, 2011.25
Head and Heart: American Christianities, 2007.63
"Hearing the Symphony: A Critique of Some Critics of Sang Lee's and Amy Pauw's Accounts of Jonathan Edwards' View of God," 2010.65
"'A Heart Uncommonly Devoted to God': Theology and Piety in Jonathan Edwards' Funeral Sermon for His Daughter Jerusha," 2008.32
Heath, David Cochran., 2007.26
Heathcock, Clint, 2012.29
Heaven, a World of Love, 2008.21
"Heaven and Heavenly Piety in Colonial American Elegies., 2009.88
Heaven on Earth: Capturing Jonathan Edwards' Vision of Living in Between, 2006.56
Review of *Heaven on Earth: Capturing Jonathan Edwards' Vision of Living in Between*, 2008.44
"Hebrews and the Typology of Jonathan Edwards," 2019.26
Heejoon, Jeon, 2021.28
Helm, Paul, 2010.65, 2013.22, 2014.36, 2014.37, 2016.33, 2018.29, 2018.30, 2020.4, 2020.24, 2020.25, 2020.29, 2021.64
Helseth, Paul Kjoss, 2007.27
Henard, William D., 2006.27
Henry, Caleb, 2011.26
Herdt, Jennifer A., 2008.35
Hermann, Leslie Allison, 2010.36
Hessel-Robinson, Timothy, 2010.37
Hewitson, James, SP.5
Higgins, J. August, 2017.36, 2018.31
Hindmarsh, D. Bruce, 2018.31, 2018.32, 2020.6
"Historical and Ecclesiastical Contexts," 2021.64
"History, Providence, and Eschatology,," 2021.64

Review of *History of New Testament Research, Volume Two: From Jonathan Edwards to Rudolf Bultmann*, 2006.66
History of Redemption, to Which Are How [sic] Added Notes, Historical, Critical, and Theological, with the Life and Experience of the Author, 2009.20
History of the Propagation of Christianity, 2015.48
"A History of the Work of Redemption by Jonathan Edwards (1739/1788)," 2017.53
Hockfield, Victoria, SP.21
Hodges, Igou, 2008.36
Hoehner, Paul J., 2021.26, 2021.65
Hoffman, Paul A., 2022.15
Hoggard-Creegan, Nicola, 2011.27
Holder, Arthur G, 2009.37
Holderman, J. T., 2019.21
Holifield, E. Brooks, 2006.28, 2007.58, 2009.32
"Holistic Spiritual Formation in Dialogue with Jonathan Edwards' Theology of Spiritual Sense," 2023.20
Holloway, Charles S., 2008.37
Holmes, Stephen R., 2006.29
"'An Holy and Beautiful Soul': Jonathan Edwards on the Humanity of Christ," 2016.5
"Holy Children Are Happy Children: Jonathan Edwards and Puritan Childhood," 2016.1
Holy Living: Jonathan Edwards's Seventy Resolutions for Living the Christian Life, 2021.20
"The Holy Spirit, the Charismata, and Signs and Wonders: Some Evangelical Perspectives from the Eighteenth Century.," 2012.28
"The Home in an Earthly Kingdom: Family Discipleship Among Reformers and Puritans," 2012.52

"The Homiletical Theology of Jonathan Edwards, Gilbert Tennent, and Samuel Davies," 2008.37
Hooks, James Michael, 2018.33
Hopf, Christopher Jeffrey, 2015.28
Hopkins, Zachary, 2019.21
Hordern, Joshua, 2014.38
Horton, Michael S., 2009.86, 2016.34
Hoselton, Ryan P., 2015.29, 2015.30, 2017.37, 2017.38, 2022.16
Hostetter, Xon, 2008.38
Review of *How Christians Are Come to Mt. Sion. Vol. 1 of Sermons by Jonathan Edwards on the Church*, 2021.55
"How I Stole from Jonathan Edwards," 2010.65
"How the Priesthood of All Believers Became American," 2023.47
Howard, Joy A. J., 2010.38
Howe, Daniel Walker, 2009.38
Howe, Susan, 2009.39, 2014.39
Hubbard, Larry A., 2009.40
Hubers, John, 2009.41
Huggins, Jonathan, 2006.30, 2012.30, 2013.25, 2013.26, 2014.40, 2014.41, 2015.32, 2015.61, 2021.27, 2022.17
Hulse, Erroll, 2014.42
"Human and Divine Love," 2007.15
"The Human Heart in the View of John Calvin, Jonathan Edwards and Wilhelmus a Brakel: With Particular Reference to the Presbyterian Church in Brazil and the Pentecostal Influences Upon Her," 2015.16
Human Nature from Calvin to Edwards, 2018.30
Review of *Human Nature from Calvin to Edwards*, 2020.24, 2020.25
"The Human Self and the Divine Trinity," 2010.65
Hunter, Drew, 2019.26
Hunter, George G., 2006.31
Hurd, Ryan M., 2016.35
Hurh, John P., 2008.39
Hurh, Paul, 2016.36

Hussey, Phillip, 2016.37, 2016.38, 2016.39, 2018.34, 2020.30, 2021.64
Hutchens, S. M., 2009.42
Hutchins, Zachary, 2008.40

"Idealism and Aetiology,," 2021.64
"Idealism and Edwards the Preacher," 2023.38
"'If Thou Reckon Right': Angels from John Calvin to Jonathan Edwards via John Milton," 2021.42
"Ignatius of Loyola, Jonathan Edwards, and Indifference," 2022.22
"Imagination and Hermeneutics,," 2021.64
Review of *Imagining the Sciences: Expressions of New Knowledge in the "Long" Eighteenth Century*, 2006.24
"*Imago Dei* in Jonathan Edwards: The Locus of Divine Activity for the Glorification of the Triune God in the End of Creation," 2022.52
"Imitating the Virtue Ethic of Jonathan Edwards and William James," 2022.6
"Imitation as a Means for Strengthening Pastoral Perseverance," 2019.14
"The Importance and Advantage of a Thorough Knowledge of Divine Truth," 2019.24
"'In Love with the Image': Transitive Being and Typological Desire in Jonathan Edwards," 2006.38
"The Inevitability of Sin," 2023.48
An Infinite Fountain of Light: Jonathan Edwards for the Twenty-First Century, 2023.34
Infinite Goodness: Joseph Smith, Jonathan Edwards, and the Book of Mormon, 2021.45, 2022.25
The Infinite Merit of Christ: The Glory of Christ's Obedience in the Theology of Jonathan Edwards, 2009.7
Review of *The Infinite Merit of Christ: The Glory of Christ's Obedience in the Theology of Jonathan Edwards*, 2009.81
"The Influence of Edwards on the Spiritual Life of New England," 2010.28
"The Influence of Jonathan Edwards on Andrew Fuller," 2008.58
"The Influence of Jonathan Edwards on the Missiology and Conversionism of Richard Furman (1755–1825)," 2017.66
"Informing of the Child's Understanding, Influencing His Heart, and Directing Its Practice: Jonathan Edwards on Education," 2011.41
An Inquiry into the Prevailing Notions of the Freedom of the Will, 2008.22
"The Integral Relation of Impeccability and Freedom to the Projects of Four Theologians: Cyril of Alexandria, John Calvin, Petrus van Mastricht, and Jonathan Edwards," 2008.23
"The Interconnectedness of Jonathan Edwards's Ontology and Trinitarianism," 2021.19
Interpreting Edwards: An Overview and Analysis of John H. Gerstner's The Rational Biblical Theology of Jonathan Edwards, 2011.17, 2021.17
"Interpreting the Dutch Great Awakening (1749–1755)," 2008.46
"Interpreting the Harmony of Reality: Jonathan Edwards' Theology of Revelation," 2008.65
"Introduction—Sketches from an Album," 2022.14
"Inventing Revivalist Millennialism: Edwards and the Scottish Connection," 2017.21
"The Invisible Redemption of God: Justification and Union with Christ in Jonathan Edwards and Seventeenth Century Puritanism," 2016.59

"Is God the Author of Sin? Jonathan Edwards' Theodicy," 2014.84
"Is God's Moral Perfection Reducible to His Love?" 2023.7
"Is Jonathan Edwards a Neoplatonist? The Concept of Emanation in the End of Creation," 2018.52
"Is Naomi a Liberal Pluralist? The Politics of Loss and Renewal in Jonathan Edwards's Sermon 'Ruth's Resolution,'" SP.13
"Is Sanctification Real? Empirical Evidence for and Against Christian Moral Transformation," 2023.27
"Is Sola Scripture Really Sola? Edwards, Newman, Bultmann, and Wright on the Bible as Religious Authority," 2010.46
"Is the Distinction Between Natural and Moral Attributes Good? Jonathan Edwards on Divine Attributes," 2010.61
"'It Would Be Heaven to Hear Him Adored': Praying Payson of Portland and Revival in Nineteenth-Century Maine," 2023.50

Jackson, Brian, 2007.28
Jacobs, Alan, 2009.43
Jaeger, John, SP.11
James, Nicholas Kyle, 2016.40
Jenson, Robert, 2010.65
Jeon, Heejoon, 2019.27
Jeroncic, Ante, 2010.39
"Jesus Christ as the 'Sum of God's Decrees': Christological Supralapsarianism in the Theology of Jonathan Edwards," 2016.37
Jin, Hyun H., 2023.18
John Corrigan, 2008.52
"John Erskine (1721–1803): Disseminator of Enlightened Evangelical Calvinism," 2009.90

"John Gill and the Rule of Faith: A Case Study in the Baptist Retrieval of Tradition," 2023.42
Johnson, Dana E., 2021.29
Johnson, Daniel M., 2022.18, 2022.19
Johnson, Eric, 2011.31
Johnson, Keith E., 2011.28
Johnson, Randall K., 2023.19
Johnson, Terrence L., 2013.29
"Jonathan Edwards," 2008.52, 2008.55, 2009.37, 2009.48, 2009.87, 2011.13, 2011.22, SP.30
Jonathan Edwards, 2007.2, 2010.1
"Jonathan Edwards, 1703–58, American Theologian and Metaphysician," 2011.49
"Jonathan Edwards (1703–58) on Freedom of Perfection: Establishing the Shift Away from the Classic-Reformed Tradition of Freedom of the Will," 2015.22
"Jonathan Edwards (1703–1758): A Treatise Concerning Religious Affections," 2010.37
"Jonathan Edwards (1703–1758) and the Nature of Theology," 2012.44, 2012.45
"Jonathan Edwards (1703–1758) On the Book of Genesis," 2020.49
Review of *Jonathan Edwards: A Life*, 2006.35, 2006.46, 2007.39
Jonathan Edwards: A Life, 2006.3, 2007.33, 2011.38
"Jonathan Edwards: A Missionary?" 2011.24
"Jonathan Edwards, A Mystic?" 2011.63
Jonathan Edwards: A Retrospect; Being the Addresses Delivered in Connection with the Unveiling of a Memorial in the First Church of Christ in Northampton, 2010.28
"Jonathan Edwards: A Study," 2010.21
Jonathan Edwards: A Study. An Address Delivered at Stockbridge, Massachusetts, October 5, 1903, 2010.21
"Jonathan Edwards: Advice to Weary Theologians," 2006.63

"Jonathan Edwards, Affective
    Conversion, and the Problem of
    Masochism," 2012.38
Jonathan Edwards: America's Evangelical,
    2006.3
Review of *Jonathan Edwards: America's
    Evangelical*, 2006.18, 2006.44,
    2009.67, SP.4
"Jonathan Edwards: America's
    Theologian," 2010.47
*Jonathan Edwards Among the
    Theologians*, 2015.13
Review of *Jonathan Edwards Among the
    Theologians*, 2016.2, 2016.21,
    2016.27, 2016.47, 2016.54,
    2016.67, 2017.3, 2017.8,
    2017.22, 2017.33, 2017.34,
    2017.38, 2017.52, 2017.68,
    2017.69, 2018.23, 2018.37,
    2019.19, 2019.62
Jonathan Edwards: An American Genius,
    2008.24
*Jonathan Edwards: An Introduction to
    His Thought*, 2009.18, 2010.20
Review of *Jonathan Edwards: An
    Introduction to His Thought*,
    2019.13, 2019.23, 2019.28,
    2019.29, 2019.36, 2020.13
"Jonathan Edwards and a Divine and
    Supernatural Light," 2010.11
"Jonathan Edwards and a Reformational
    View of the Purpose of
    Education," 2016.58
"Jonathan Edwards and Alfred North
    Whitehead: The Possibility of
    a Constructive Dialogue in
    Metaphysics," 2006.47
"Jonathan Edwards and Charles
    Finney on the Theology and
    Methodology of Religious
    Revivals," 2017.26
Review of *Jonathan Edwards and
    Deification: Reconciling Theosis
    and the Reformed Tradition*,
    2022.1, 2022.48, 2023.6
*Jonathan Edwards and Deification:
    Reconciling Theosis and the
    Reformed Tradition*, 2022.36

"Jonathan Edwards and Francis Turretin
    on Necessity, Contingency, and
    Freedom of Will. In Response to
    Paul Helm," 2014.58
"Jonathan Edwards and God's Inner
    Life: A Response to Kyle
    Strobel," 2014.53
"Jonathan Edwards and Hebrews: A
    Harmonic Interpretation of
    Scripture," 2021.14
"Jonathan Edwards and His
    Methodology Promoting
    Concern for Revival," 2019.44
"Jonathan Edwards and His Theology of
    Revival., 2019.45
"Jonathan Edwards and His
    Understanding of Revival,"
    2019.46
"Jonathan Edwards and Islam," 2016.51
Jonathan Edwards and Justification,
    2012.43
Review of *Jonathan Edwards and
    Justification*, 2013.26, 2013.27,
    2014.70, 2016.43
*Jonathan Edwards and Justification by
    Faith*, 2012.33
Review of *Jonathan Edwards and
    Justification by Faith*, 2013.38,
    2014.8, 2014.29, 2014.54,
    2014.75, 2015.44, SP.29
"Jonathan Edwards and Justification:
    Embodying a Living Tradition,"
    2014.40
"Jonathan Edwards and Justification:
    The Rest of the Story," 2010.65
"Jonathan Edwards and Life's Adverbial
    Questions," 2012.49
Jonathan Edwards and My Ministry,
    2012.32
"Jonathan Edwards and New England
    Arminianism," 2015.31
"Jonathan Edwards and Preaching in a
    Postmodern World," 2015.41
"Jonathan Edwards and Princeton,"
    2010.65
"Jonathan Edwards and Psalmody,"
    2016.42

"Jonathan Edwards and Reformed Ethico-Teleology: Locating Continuities in a Theological Tradition," 2018.62
"Jonathan Edwards and Samuel Clarke on Liberty and Necessity: A Manner of Distinction, and Why It Matters," 2020.19
"Jonathan Edwards and Sanctification: The Pursuit of Happiness Found in Union and Obedience," 2017.27
Jonathan Edwards and Scotland, 2011.60
Review of *Jonathan Edwards and Scotland*, 2012.60, 2014.33
Review of *Jonathan Edwards and Scripture: Biblical Exegesis in British North America*, 2018.1, 2018.13, 2019.48, 2019.64, 2019.71, 2020.11, 2021.35
Jonathan Edwards and Scripture: Biblical Exegesis in British North America, 2018.4
"Jonathan Edwards and the Beauty of Christ," 2017.37
"Jonathan Edwards and the Beauty of God., 2018.45
"Jonathan Edwards and the Beauty of Work: A Colonial American Argument for Social Responsibility in the Workplace," SP.36
Jonathan Edwards and the Bible, 2006.3
Jonathan Edwards and the Catholic Vision of Salvation, 2010.83
"Jonathan Edwards and the Christian Education of Today's Young People," 2006.32
Jonathan Edwards and the Church, 2014.7
Review of *Jonathan Edwards and the Church*, 2014.44, 2015.6, 2015.8, 2015.33, 2015.37, 2015.54, 2016.8, 2017.9, SP.31, SP.35
"Jonathan Edwards and the Closing of the Table: Must the Eucharist Be Open to All?" 2009.16

Jonathan Edwards and the Covenant of Grace, 2009.8
"Jonathan Edwards and the Development of American Democracy," SP.8
"Jonathan Edwards and the Discourses of Nature," 2008.4, 2009.10
Review of *Jonathan Edwards and the Enlightenment: Knowing the Presence of God*, 2006.41
"Jonathan Edwards and the First Great Awakening," 2018.47
"Jonathan Edwards and the First Great Awakening in North America," 2011.11
"Jonathan Edwards and the Future of Global Christianity," 2013.33
Jonathan Edwards and the Gospel of Love, 2012.61
Review of *Jonathan Edwards and the Gospel of Love*, 2014.13, 2015.14
"Jonathan Edwards and the Image of God in Relation to Reformed Orthodoxy and the Flacian Controversy," 2021.67
"Jonathan Edwards and the Lapsarian Debate," 2009.1
Jonathan Edwards and the Life of God: Toward an Evangelical Theology of Participation, 2015.27
Review of *Jonathan Edwards and the Life of God: Toward an Evangelical Theology of Participation*, 2015.40, 2016.38, 2016.41, 2017.35, 2017.40
Review of *Jonathan Edwards and the Metaphysics of Sin*, 2007.23, 2008.28, 2010.16
Jonathan Edwards and the Ministry of the Word: A Model of Faith and Thought, 2011.14
Review of *Jonathan Edwards and the Ministry of the Word: A Model of Faith and Thought*, 2009.59, 2009.83, 2010.3, 2010.40, 2010.67, 2010.79, 2011.19, 2011.32, 2011.46, SP.11

"Jonathan Edwards and the New World: Exploring the Intersection of Puritanism and Settler Colonialism," 2022.3

"Jonathan Edwards and the Parting of the Ways?" 2014.36

"Jonathan Edwards and the Polemics of Theosis," 2012.63

Jonathan Edwards and the Psalms: A Redemptive-Historical Vision of Scripture, 2014.5

Review of *Jonathan Edwards and the Psalms: A Redemptive-Historical Vision of Scripture*, 2015.21, 2015.30, 2015.56, 2015.60, 2016.10, 2016.25, 2016.44, 2016.55, 2018.14

Jonathan Edwards and the Stockbridge Mohican Indians: His Mission and Sermons, 2020.42

"Jonathan Edwards and the Theology and Practice of Congregational Song in Puritan New England: Jonathan Edwards's Singing Lecture Sermon," 2006.54

"Jonathan Edwards and the Vegan Elect: An Unconventional Calvinist Reading," 2019.58

Jonathan Edwards and Transatlantic Print Culture, 2016.75

Review of *Jonathan Edwards and Transatlantic Print Culture*, 2017.1, 2017.25, 2018.11, 2018.15, 2018.24, 2018.36, 2018.65

"Jonathan Edwards, Anselmic Satisfaction, and God's Moral Government," 2015.26

"Jonathan Edwards' Argument That God's End in Creation Must Manifest His Supreme Self-Regard," 2014.67

Review of *Jonathan Edwards as Contemporary: Essays in Honor of Sand Hyun Lee*, 2013.9

Jonathan Edwards as Contemporary: Essays in Honor of Sang Hyun Lee, 2010.65

Review of *Jonathan Edwards as Contemporary: Essays in Honor of Sang Hyun Lee*, 2011.56

"Jonathan Edwards as Multi-Dimension Bible Interpreter: A Case Study from Isaiah 40–55," 2013.1

Review of *Jonathan Edwards at 300: Essays on the Tercentenary of His Birth*, 2009.67

Review of *Jonathan Edwards at Home and Abroad: Historical Memories, Cultural Movements, Global Horizon*, 2006.70

"Jonathan Edwards, Beauty, and Apologetics," 2007.65

Jonathan Edwards, Beauty, and Younger Evangelicals, 2019.9

Review of *Jonathan Edwards' Bible: The Relationship of the Old Testament and New Testament*, 2015.19

"'Jonathan Edwards, Calvin, Baxter & Co.': Mark Twain and the Comedy of Calvinism," 2010.27

The Jonathan Edwards Center at Yale University, 2006.21

"Jonathan Edwards Center at Yale University: Website Publishing," 2012.39

"Jonathan Edwards' Concept of an Original Ultimate End," 2013.47

Jonathan Edwards' Concerning the End for Which God Created the World: Exposition, Analysis, and Philosophical Implications, 2020.44

"Jonathan Edwards, Continuity, and Secularism," 2012.12

"Jonathan Edwards, Dispositionalism and Spirit Christology," 2018.27

Review of "Jonathan Edwards, Dispositionalism, and Spirit Christology,", 2019.30

"Jonathan Edwards' Doctrine of Justification in the Period up to the Great Awakening," 2007.38

Jonathan Edwards' Early Understanding of Religious Experience: His New York Sermons, 1720–723, 2011.52

Review of *Jonathan Edwards' Early Understanding of Religious Experience: His New York Sermons, 1720–723*, 2012.5, 2013.44
"Jonathan Edwards' Ecclesiology," 2010.65
"Jonathan Edwards' Ecological and Ethical Vision of Nature," 2007.12
The Jonathan Edwards Encyclopedia, 2017.65
Review of *The Jonathan Edwards Encyclopedia*, 2018.1, 2018.10, 2018.66, 2019.10, 2019.32, 2019.57
Jonathan Edwards' Exegesis of Genesis: A Puritan Hermeneutic? 2015.34
"Jonathan Edwards' Federal Theology in Exegetical Perspective: The Doctrinal Harmony of Scripture as a Framework for Interpreting the History of Redemption," 2018.51
Jonathan Edwards for Armchair Theologians, 2008.5
Review of *Jonathan Edwards for Armchair Theologians*, 2008.62, 2011.58, SP.10
Jonathan Edwards for the Church: The Ministry and the Means of Grace, 2015.50
Review of *Jonathan Edwards for the Church: The Ministry and the Means of Grace*, 2016.22
"Jonathan Edwards, God, and 'Particular Minds,'" 2010.84
"Jonathan Edwards Goes to Hell (House): Fear Appeals in American Evangelism," 2007.28
Jonathan Edwards: His Doctrine of and Devotion to Prayer, 2013.42
"Jonathan Edwards, Hypostasis, Impeccability, and Immaterialism," 2016.28
"Jonathan Edwards in a New Light," 2014.64
"Jonathan Edwards in Amsterdam," 2020.55
"Jonathan Edwards in Korea: A History of the Reception of Jonathan Edwards," 2019.25
"Jonathan Edwards in Scotland: An Alternative History," 2020.40
"Jonathan Edwards, John Dennis, and the Religious Sublime: A Consideration of Edwardsean Terror," 2022.45
"Jonathan Edwards, John Locke, and the Religious Affections," 2016.33
"Jonathan Edwards Jr.'s Relish for True Religion: The Advance of the New England Theology in the Sermon on the Mount," 2020.2
"Jonathan Edwards: Latter-Day Puritan and Metaphysician," 2023.1
Jonathan Edwards, Lover of God, 2009.76, 2010.74
"Jonathan Edwards Meets Dietrich Bonhoeffer: True Religion or Non-Religious Christianity?" 2014.14
The Jonathan Edwards Miscellanies Companion. Vol. 1, 2021.5
The Jonathan Edwards Miscellanies Companion. Vol. 2, 2021.6
The Jonathan Edwards Miscellanies Companion. Vol. 3, 2023.4
"Jonathan Edwards: Missionary to the Indians," 2016.57
Jonathan Edwards on Beauty, 2009.77, 2010.75
"Jonathan Edwards on Election," 2023.14
Jonathan Edwards on Genesis: Hermeneutics, Homiletics, and Theology, 2021.4
Review of *Jonathan Edwards on Genesis: Hermeneutics, Homiletics, and Theology*, 2023.12
Review of *Jonathan Edwards on God and Creation*, 2014.15, 2015.47, 2016.11, SP.26
Jonathan Edwards on God and Creation, 2012.18

"Jonathan Edwards on God's Relation to Creation," 2018.16
Jonathan Edwards on Heaven and Hell, 2010.77
"Jonathan Edwards on Justification: A Reassessment," SP.15
"Jonathan Edwards on Justification by Faith," 2008.63
"Jonathan Edwards on Justification by Faith Alone: An Analysis of His Thought and Defense of His Orthodoxy," 2006.30, 2012.30
"Jonathan Edwards on Justification by Faith—More Protestant or Catholic?" 2008.53
"Jonathan Edwards on Justification: Reformed Development of the Doctrine in Eighteenth-Century New England," 2010.13
Jonathan Edwards on Justification: Reformed Development of the Doctrine in Eighteenth-Century New England, 2012.14
Review of *Jonathan Edwards on Justification: Reformed Development of the Doctrine of the Eighteenth-Century New England*, 2013.54
"Jonathan Edwards on Man's Propensity to Sin," 2011.35
"Jonathan Edwards on Nature as a Language of God: Symbolic Typology as Rhetorical Presence," 2009.28
"Jonathan Edwards on Necessity and Contingency: A Reconsideration," 2020.4
"Jonathan Edwards on Property, Liberty, and the National Covenant," 2018.43
"Jonathan Edwards on the Atonement," 2013.19
Jonathan Edwards on the Atonement: Understanding the Legacy of America's Greatest Theologian, 2017.11
"Jonathan Edwards on the Cape of Good Hope," 2020.7

Review of *Jonathan Edwards on the Christian Life*, SP.12
"Jonathan Edwards on the Election of Christ," 2016.29
"Jonathan Edwards on the 'Flying' Spider: A Model of Ecological Thought in Microcosm," 2015.25
Jonathan Edwards on the Good Life, 2009.78, 2010.76
"Jonathan Edwards on the Justice of God," 2014.1
"Jonathan Edwards on the Love of God," 2019.18
Jonathan Edwards on the Matthean Parables, Vol. 1, 2012.40
Jonathan Edwards on the Matthean Parables, Vol. 2, 2012.41
Jonathan Edwards on the Matthean Parables, Vol. 3, 2012.42
Jonathan Edwards on the New Birth in the Spirit: An Introduction to the Life, Times, and Thought of America's Greatest Theologian, 2017.15
"Jonathan Edwards on the Trinity," 2014.21
"Jonathan Edwards on the Trinity: Its Place and Its Rich but Controversial Facets," 2016.31
"Jonathan Edwards on the Typology of Green," 2020.26
"Jonathan Edwards on the Work of the Holy Spirit in the Godly Life of the Saint," 2020.23
Jonathan Edwards on True Christianity, 2010.78
"Jonathan Edwards on Worship: Public and Private Devotion to God," 2007.48
Jonathan Edwards on Worship: Public and Private Devotion to God, 2010.62
Review of *Jonathan Edwards on Worship: Public and Private Devotion to God*, 2011.2, 2012.27, 2017.70
"Jonathan Edwards' Panentheism," 2010.65

"Jonathan Edwards, Paul, and the Priority of Holiness: A Variant Reading," 2013.20
"Jonathan Edwards, Petitionary Prayer, and the Cognitive Science of Religion," 2020.33
"Jonathan Edwards' Philosophical Argument Concerning God's End in Creation," 2014.68
Review of *Jonathan Edwards: Philosophical Theologian*, 2006.51
Jonathan Edwards' Precocious Childhood, Oedipal Conflict, Mid-Life Identity Crisis, and Old Age Radicalization: Psychological Factors Shaping the Development of His Theology, 2017.58
"Jonathan Edwards: Puritan or Pluralist?" 2007.33
A Jonathan Edwards Reader, 2011.38
"Jonathan Edwards Reads John Owen," 2019.38
Review of *Jonathan Edwards, Religious Affection and the Puritan Analysis of True Piety, Spiritual Sensation and Heart Religion*, 2013.17
"Jonathan Edwards, Samuel Hopkins, and Theological Ethics of Social Concern," 2018.38
Jonathan Edwards, Samuel Taylor Coleridge, and the Supernatural Will in American Literature, 2018.2, 2019.2
"Jonathan Edwards' Self-Love Theory: A Revision," 2022.39
"Jonathan Edwards, Slavery, and Africa Missions," 2015.17
"Jonathan Edwards Sobre a Liberdada Humana: Reformado ou Näo?" 2016.13
Jonathan Edwards' Social Augustinian Trinitarianism in Historical and Contemporary Perspectives, 2008.72
Review of *Jonathan Edwards' Social Augustinian Trinitarianism in Historical and Contemporary Perspectives*, 2011.28, SP.28
Jonathan Edwards: Spiritual Writings, 2019.65
Review of *Jonathan Edwards: Spiritual Writings*, 2020.18, 2020.28, 2020.45
"Jonathan Edwards' Spiritualis: Towards a Reconstruction of His Theology of Spirituality," 2016.71
"Jonathan Edwards Studies During the Career of Sang Hyun Lee," 2010.65
"Jonathan Edwards, the Ethics of Virtue and Public Theology," 2010.31
"Jonathan Edwards, the Father of Aaron Burr's Mother," 2010.56
Jonathan Edwards: The First Critical Biography, 1889, 2008.1
"Jonathan Edwards, the Great Awakening, and 'Sinners in the Hands of an Angry God,'" 2007.2
"Jonathan Edwards, the Harmony of Scripture, and Canonical Exegesis," 2013.55
Jonathan Edwards, The Holy Spirit in Revival: The Lasting Influence of the Holy Spirit in the Heart of Man, 2006.26
Review of *Jonathan Edwards: The Holy Spirit in Revival: The Lasting Influence of the Holy Spirit in the Heart of Man*, 2007.41, 2008.42
"Jonathan Edwards, the Inner Witness of the Spirit, and Experiential Exegesis," 2015.29
Jonathan Edwards: The Narrative of a Puritan Mind, 2008.18
"Jonathan Edwards: The Theologian of Joy," 2018.21
"Jonathan Edwards' Theocentric Ethics: Analysis and Implications for Christian Ethics," 2018.35
"Jonathan Edwards: Theologian of God's Glory in Christ," 2015.12
Jonathan Edwards: Theologian of the Heart, 2009.71

"Jonathan Edwards' Theology of Spiritual Awakening and Spiritual Formation Leadership in American Higher Education," 2009.79

"Jonathan Edwards' Trinitarian Theology of Redemption," 2010.80

"Jonathan Edwards, Trinity, and Worship Theology: The Practical Value of Edwards' Trinitarian Covenant Theology for Christian Worship," 2023.18

"Jonathan Edwards' Understanding of Divine Infinity," 2010.65

Jonathan Edwards Within the Enlightenment: Controversy, Experience, and Thought, 2019.33

Review of *Jonathan Edwards Within the Enlightenment: Controversy, Experience, and Thought*, 2021.71

Jonathan Edwards: Writings from the Great Awakening, 2013.18

"Jonathan Edwards's Affective Anthropology," 2023.46

Jonathan Edwards's Apologetic for the Great Awakening, 2011.50

"Jonathan Edwards's Apologetic for the Great Awakening with Particular Attention to Charles Chauncy's Criticisms," 2008.68, 2010.68

Jonathan Edwards's Bible: The Relationship of the Old and New Testaments, 2013.45

"Jonathan Edwards's 'Diary,'" 2019.51

"Jonathan Edwards's Doctrine of Imputed Sin: Nineteenth-Century Southern Presbyterian Accusations Considered," 2009.2

"Jonathan Edwards's Doctrine of Justification: A New Reading of Edwards's Treatises, Sermons, and Miscellanies," 2014.3

"Jonathan Edwards's Doctrine of the Covenant of Redemption Within the Framework of the History of Redemption," 2019.59

"Jonathan Edwards's End of Creation: An Exposition and Defense," 2006.64

"Jonathan Edwards's Exegetical Practice," 2022.50

"Jonathan Edwards's Exegetical Reflections of Genesis: A Puritan Literal Hermeneutic?" 2014.50

"Jonathan Edwards's Five Stages of Homiletical Development: A Model for Contemporary Preaching," 2012.22

"Jonathan Edwards's Freedom of the Will and His Defense of the Impeccability of Jesus Christ," 2007.21

"Jonathan Edwards's Harmonic Interpretation of Hebrews 12:22–24," 2020.12

"Jonathan Edwards's 'Hermeneutics': A Case Study of the Sermon 'Christian Knowledge,'" 2006.61

"Jonathan Edwards's Interpretation of the Major Prophets: The Book of Isaiah, Jeremiah, and Ezekiel," 2011.62

"Jonathan Edwards's Judeo-Centric and Cosmic Vision of the Millennial Kingdom," 2019.74

"Jonathan Edwards's Metaphors of Sin in Indian Country," 2010.38

"Jonathan Edwards's Ontology: A Critique of Sang Hyun Lee's Dispositional Account of Edwardsian Metaphysics," 2010.19

Jonathan Edwards's Philosophy of History: The Reenchantment of the World in the Age of Enlightenment, 2009.91

Jonathan Edwards's Philosophy of Nature: The Re-Enchantment of the World in the Age of Scientific Reasoning, 2010.85

"Jonathan Edwards's Preaching of Romans 8: Presenting and Evaluating Two Previously Unpublished Sermons," 2017.61

"Jonathan Edwards's Reformed Doctrine of Theosis," 2016.65

"Jonathan Edwards's Reshaping of Lockean Terminology into a Calvinistic Aesthetic Epistemology in His Religious Affections," 2014.43

Jonathan Edwards's Sinners in the Hands of an Angry God: A Casebook, 2010.41

"Jonathan Edwards's Synthesis of Definitions of Beauty," 2020.14

Jonathan Edwards's Theology: A Reinterpretation, 2012.64, 2013.53

Review of *Jonathan Edwards's Theology: A Reinterpretation,*, 2014.49

"Jonathan Edwards's Thoughts on Prayer," 2016.30

Jonathan Edwards's Turn from the Classic-Reformed Tradition of Freedom of the Will, 2016.24

Review of *Jonathan Edwards's Turn from the Classic-Reformed Tradition of Freedom of the Will*, 2018.34, 2018.49, 2018.53, 2018.54

"Jonathan Edwards's Unique Role in an Imagined Church History," 2022.25

"Jonathan Edwards's View of Sympathy as It Relates to His Socio-Ethical Perspective," 2021.44

"Jonathan Edwards's View of That Great Act of Obedience: Jesus' Laying Down His Life," 2016.35

Jonathan Edwards's Vision of Reality: The Relationship of God to the World, Redemption History, and the Reprobate, 2011.6, 2012.10

Jones, Barry, 2022.20

Jones, Clay, 2023.21

Jones, Zachary, 2021.30

Jonik, Michael E., 2009.44

Joo, Yunsoo, 2023.20

"The Journal of Esther Edwards Burr," 2019.20

A Journey Toward Heaven: Daily Devotions from the Sermons of Jonathan Edwards, 2012.7

Juchno, Andrew, 2021.31, 2022.21

Jull, David, 2006.32, 2006.33

Jung, Peter B., 2015.31, 2017.39

The Justice of God in the Damnation of Sinners, Explained, Illustrated, and Proved, in a Sermon Upon Romans III:19, 2010.24

"Justified: The Pragmaticization of American Evangelicalism from Jonathan Edwards to the Social Gospel," 2020.57

Karcher, Justin G., SP.16
Kassen, Ernest Eugene, 2022.15
Kaufman, Matt, SP.6
Kay, William K., 2020.31
Kearney, John, 2022.22
Keller, Michael S., SP.41
Kellicut, Jordan, 2016.41, 2017.40
Kemeny, Paul C., 2017.41
Kemp, Raymond A., 2020.32
Kennedy, Rick, 2022.23
Kerley, Tyler, 2017.42
Kerr, Houston, 2023.22
Kidd, Thomas S., 2006.42, 2007.29, 2009.29, 2009.45, 2012.31
Kim, Eun Ju, 2023.23
Kim, Hong Youn, 2023.24
Kim, Hyunkwan, 2014.43
Kim, Isaac, 2019.28
Kim, Ji-Jyuk, 2018.35
Kim, Nam Joon, 2012.32
Kim, Song, 2021.32
Kim, Sun Wook, 2017.43
Kim, Youngrae, 2023.25
Kimble, Jeremy M., 2014.44, 2014.45, 2017.19, 2018.9, SP.34
Kimnach, Wilson H., 2006.22, 2007.58, 2009.46, 2010.41, 2010.65
King, Mason, 2023.26
The Kingdom of the Son of His Love: Jonathan Edwards Sermons on the Christ, 2014.25

Kinghorn, Kevin, 2007.30
Kirkland, E. Trevor, 2016.42
Kitanov, Severin V., 2021.33
Kiteley, Brian, 2009.47
Klaassen, Maarten, 2015.32
Kling, David W., 2006.70, 2014.46, 2019.29, 2020.33, 2021.64, 2022.24
Klosko, George, 2007.31
Knepper, Grant, 2008.41
Knight, Henry H., 2014.47
Knowing, Seeing, Being: Jonathan Edwards, Emily Dickinson, Marianne Moore and American Typological Interpretation, 2016.46
Review of *Knowing, Seeing, Being: Jonathan Edwards, Emily Dickinson, Marianne Moore and the American Typological Tradition*, 2016.52, 2017.44, 2017.71
"Knowledge and Reason Versus Experience and Practice: Jonathan Edwards and the Patristic Doctrine of Deification," 2021.49
Knutson, Andrea, 2006.34, 2010.42, 2011.29, 2012.12, 2017.44
Komline, David, 2018.36
Kornu, Kimbell, 2014.48
Korving, Willem J. (Jacob), 2011.30, SP.39
Kosits, Russell D., 2006.35, 2011.31
Kraus, Spencer, 2022.25
Kreider, Glenn R., 2006.36, 2006.37, 2007.57, 2008.42, 2008.43, 2008.44, 2010.40, 2011.32, 2013.27, 2013.28, 2014.49, 2015.33, 2016.43, 2016.44, 2017.45, 2018.37, 2019.30, 2019.31, 2019.32
Kuklick, Bruce, SP.1

La Pensée de Jonathan Edwards: Avec une concordance des différentes éditions de ses oeuvres, 2007.66
"La stupidité des damnés: Jonathan Edwards et sa doctrine de l'enfer," 2010.10
Labosier, Jeremy W., 2017.46
Landrum, Douglas Blake, 2014.50, 2015.34
Lane, Belden C., 2011.33, 2011.34
Lane, Mary M., 2014.51
Lange, Frederick de, 2007.32
Larsen, Christian N., SP.37
Larsen, Timothy, 2021.72
"The Last Edwardsean: Edwards Amasa Park and the Rhetoric of Improved Calvinism," 2006.58
"Latin America,," 2021.64
Launonen, Lari, 2023.27
Lawrence, Anna M., 2007.33
Lawson, Steven J., 2008.45, 2009.13, 2010.34, 2015.35, 2016.45
Leader, Jennifer L., 2006.38, 2016.46, 2016.52, 2017.44, 2017.71
"Learning to Love Wisdom from Masters: The Value of Jonathan Edwards' Philosophical Theology," 2022.33
Lee, Dongjun, 2022.26
Lee, Jeong, 2017.47
Lee, Joseph W., 2011.35, 2018.38
Lee, Robert Gordon, 2023.28
Lee, Sang Hyun, 2006.16, 2006.28, 2006.52, 2007.33, 2008.76, 2009.48, 2010.65, 2011.38, 2018.53
Review of *The Legacy of Jonathan Edwards: American Religion and the Evangelical Tradition*, 2006.43
"The Legacy of Jonathan Edwards in the Founder of American Deaf Education: An Historical Theology of Thomas Hopkins Gallaudet," 2017.7
The Legacy of Jonathan Edwards in the Theology of Andrew Fuller, 2012.15
Review of *The Legacy of Jonathan Edwards in the Theology of Andrew Fuller*, 2012.25, 2013.39, 2014.34

Leiburg, Fred van, 2008.46
Leidenhag, Joanna, 2017.48
Leithart, Peter J., 2008.47
Leitz, Robert C., III, 2006.24
Lengyel, Thomas Grant, 2018.39
Lesser, M. X., 2006.9, 2006.50, 2006.66, 2007.2, 2007.34, 2007.58, 2007.66, 2008.1, 2008.18, 2008.28, 2008.48, 2009.4, 2009.38, 2009.49, 2009.64, 2009.65, 2010.1, 2010.21, 2010.28, 2010.43, 2010.56, 2011.9, 2011.10, 2011.43, 2012.12, 2022.30
Liberty or Justice for All? A Conversation Across the American Centuries., 2023.17
A Library of the World's Best Literature: Ancient and Modern, 2008.77
Liem Yoe Gie, Jonathan, 2021.34
"The Life and Legacy of Jonathan Edwards, pt.1," 2015.35
"The Life and Legacy of Jonathan Edwards, pt.2," 2016.45
Review and Response to *Life in Christ: Union with Christ and the Twofold Grace in Calvin's Theology*, 2009.86
The Life of Andrew Fuller: A Critical Edition of John Ryland's Biography, 2021.25
"The Life of Brainerd and the State of the Church," 2007.5
Life of Jonathan Edwards, 2006.50
"The Literary Life of Jonathan Edwards," 2009.46
Littauer, Allison K., 2009.50
"The 'Little Church': Raising a Spiritual Family with Jonathan Edwards," 2010.5
"A Little Exercise for Those New to Interfaith Dialogue: Lessons on Spiritual Formation from Jonathan Edwards and Helmut Thielicke," 2018.67
The Lives of David Brainerd: The Making of an American Evangelical Icon., 2009.31

Living Justification: A Historical-Theological Study of the Reformed Doctrine in the Writings of John Calvin, Jonathan Edwards, and N. T. Wright, 2013.25
Review of *Living Justification: A Historical-Theological Study of the Reformed Doctrine of Justification in the Writings of John Calvin, Jonathan Edwards, and N. T. Wright*, 2015.32, 2015.61
Logan, Samuel T, 2007.35
"Logics of Similitude and Logics of Difference in American and Contemporary Continental Philosophy," 2006.67
Longaker, Mark G., 2006.39
"The Lord's Supper in the Hands of a Sensitive Preacher: The Bible in Edwards' Sermons on 1 Corinthians 10," 2019.53
"Losing Interest: Roger Sherman, Samuel Hopkins, and the Contest Between Disinterested Benevolence and SelfLove," 2022.53
Louie, K. Y, 2007.36
Lovi, David S., 2013.30, 2014.66, 2015.51, 2016.64
Lowe, John T. (Thomas), 2015.36, 2016.47, 2018.40, 2019.33, 2020.34, 2021.35, 2021.71, 2022.27, 2022.28
"Loyalty, Conscience and Tense Communion: Jonathan Edwards Meets Martha Nussbaum," 2014.38
Lucas, Sean Michael, 2006.43, 2008.49, 2011.36, 2012.6, 2013.28
Luke, D. N., SP.17
Luke, David, 2019.21, 2023.30
Luke, Sean, 2023.29
Lumpkin, Aaron L., 2020.35, 2023.31
Lundin, Roger, 2008.31

Madaras, Larry, 2017.49

"'Made for Other Worlds': The Preacher and the Imagination," 2020.41
Madueme, Hans, 2010.43
Madueme, Hans., 2008.50
Madureira, Jonas, 2019.34
Maffly-Kipp, Laurie F., 2006.40, 2006.69
"A Mainspring of Missionary Thought: Andrew Fuller on 'Natural and Moral Inability,'" 2006.13
"Making Friends with Locusts: Early ABCFM Missionary Perceptions of Muslims and Islam, 1818–50," 2009.41
"Making Sense of Hell," 2021.23
Making the American Self: Jonathan Edwards to Abraham Lincoln, 2009.38
"Making Their Hopes Prevail: The Stockbridge Indians and Jonathan Edwards," 2023.8
Mallèvre, Michel, SP.35, SP.40
Mancke, Elizabeth, 2006.2
Manger, Edward, 2023.32
Marini, Amelia, 2021.36
Marini, Stephen A., SP.18
Marko, Jonathan S., 2019.21
Marquette, Richard C. H., 2023.33
Marsden, George M., 2006.3, 2006.35, 2006.46, 2007.33, 2007.39, 2007.58, 2008.50, 2008.51, 2008.59, 2009.6, 2009.12, 2009.34, 2009.51, 2009.52, 2009.61, 2009.62, 2009.63, 2009.66, 2010.9, 2010.22, 2010.32, 2011.4, 2011.18, 2011.38, 2011.42, 2012.12, 2016.48, 2020.36, 2021.64, 2023.34, SP.23
Martin, James Alfred, 2014.52
Martin, Ryan J., 2010.44, 2013.31, 2018.41, 2019.60, 2019.69, 2020.9, 2021.27, 2021.56
Marty, Martin E., 2007.37
Maskell, Caleb, 2009.67
Masui, Shitsuyo, 2016.49
Matalu, Muriwali Yanto, 2021.37
Mather, Nicholas S., 2019.35
Mattei, Tobias A., 2013.32

Matthew Everhard, 2019.21
McCarthy, Keely, 2010.45
McCartney, D. G., 2009.52
McCleery, Jennifer Reagan, 2017.50
McClenahan, Michael J., 2006.41, 2006.42, 2006.45, 2007.38, 2012.33, 2012.34, 2013.38, 2014.8, 2014.29, 2014.54, 2014.75, 2015.44, SP.29
McClymond, Michael J., 2007.39, 2008.52, 2010.65, 2011.37, 2012.31, 2013.3, 2013.10, 2013.14, 2013.15, 2013.21, 2013.22, 2013.33, 2013.34, 2013.36, 2013.41, 2013.56, 2014.46, 2014.56, 2015.10, 2015.15, 2016.9, 2016.50, 2021.38, 2021.64, SP.27
McCollum, D., 2009.53
McDermott, Gerald R., 2006.44, 2008.53, 2009.42, 2009.54, 2009.80, 2009.82, 2010.46, 2010.47, 2010.50, 2010.59, 2010.65, 2011.37, 2011.38, 2011.45, 2012.11, 2012.24, 2012.31, 2012.34, 2013.3, 2013.10, 2013.14, 2013.15, 2013.21, 2013.22, 2013.33, 2013.34, 2013.36, 2013.41, 2013.56, 2014.46, 2014.53, 2014.54, 2014.55, 2014.56
McDermott, Gerald R. (cont.), 2015.10, 2015.15, 2015.36, 2015.38, 2015.69, 2016.9, 2016.48, 2016.51, 2017.13, 2018.42, 2018.43, 2018.44, 2019.36, 2019.70, 2020.37, SP.12, SP.27
McDowell, David Paul, 2010.48, 2012.35
McFadden, Ian D., 2008.54
McGee, Iain, 2021.39
McGlothlin, James C., 2021.40, 2023.35
McGraw, Ryan M., 2011.39, 2013.35, 2019.37, 2019.52, 2023.36
McKinley, David W, 2006.46
McMullen, Michael D., 2006.36, 2012.36, 2012.37
McNeill, John, 2013.36
McPherson, Jeffrey A., 2006.47

McRae, Richard J., 2010.49
"The Medieval and Scholastic Dimensions of Edwards' Philosophy of Nature," 2010.65
"The Medieval Puritan: Three Case Studies of Scholastic Themes in Jonathan Edwards," SP.33
Meeting Christ at His Table: Jonathan Edwards and the Lord's Supper, 2023.30
Meilaender, Gilbert, 2021.41
Melton, Frankie, Jr., 2013.37
Mensch, Elizabeth, 2006.48
"Mental vs. Top-Down Causation: Sic et Non: Why Top-Down Causation Does Not Support Mental," 2013.40
Menzies, William W, 2007.40, 2007.67
"The Merit of Christ's Obedience to God's Rule of Righteousness in the Theology of Jonathan Edwards," 2008.3
"The Metaphysics of Jonathan Edwards's End of Creation," 2016.61
"The Metaphysics of Jonathan Edwards's 'Personal Narrative': Continuous Creation, Personal Identity, and Spiritual Development," 2019.72
"The Methodist Edwards: John Wesley's Abridgement of the Selected Works of Jonathan Edwards.," 2012.3
"The Methodology of Persuasion in the Preaching of Jonathan Edwards," 2009.33
Mickle, Allen R., Jr., 2007.41, 2009.55
Milder, Robert, 2007.42
Millar, Robert, 2015.48
Miller, Mark J., 2006.49, 2012.38
Miller, Nicholas P., 2007.43
Miller, Paul, 2018.45
Miller, Perry, 2007.42
Miller, Rebecca, 2012.39
Miller, Samuel, 2006.50
Mills, D. E., 2006.51
"The Ministerial Ideal in the Ordination Sermons of Jonathan Edwards: Four Theological Portraits," 2013.8
"Ministry to the Bound and Enslaved,," 2021.64
Minkema, Kenneth P., 2007.58, 2009.56, 2009.67, 2010.50, 2010.65, 2011.40, 2011.41, 2012.40, 2012.41, 2012.42, 2012.60, 2013.13, 2013.48, 2013.49, 2014.33, 2015.39, 2015.40, 2016.52, 2017.51, 2017.56, 2019.38, 2019.39, 2019.40, 2019.41, 2019.42, 2019.43, 2020.28, 2021.42, 2021.43, 2021.55, 2021.64
Minor, Mitzi, 2009.57
Misak, Cheryl, 2008.55
The Miscellanies Companion, 2019.8
"Mission,," 2021.64
"A Missional Eschatology: Jonathan Edwards, Future Prophecy, and the Spread of the Gospel," 2009.68
"Missionary Benefactor and Strange Bedfellow: Isaac Hollis, Jonathan Edwards' English Correspondent," 2006.17
Mitchell, Louis J., 2006.52, 2007.44
Mitchell, Louis. J., 2010.51
Miyagi, Ken, 2021.44
Mizell, Stephen, 2017.52
"Models of Conversion in American Evangelicalism: Jonathan Edwards, Charles Hodge and Old Princeton, and Charles Finney," 2015.9
Modern Christianity to 1900, 2007.7
Moga, Dinu, 2019.44, 2019.45, 2019.46
Monescalchi, Michael John, Jr, 2019.47
"Monstrous Confessions: Early American Women and the Dangers of Divine Revelation," 2017.23
Moody, Josh, 2006.41, 2006.53, 2007.3, 2007.18, 2007.45, 2012.8, 2012.43, 2013.26, 2013.27, 2013.38, 2014.70, 2016.43
Moore, Darnell L., 2009.58

Moorhead, James H., 2008.56
Moorhead, Jonathan, 2009.59, 2014.56
Moots, Glenn, 2019.48
"Moral Character, Reformed Theology, and Jonathan Edwards," 2017.12
"The Moral Significance of Religious Affections: A Reformed Perspective on Emotions and Moral Formation," 2015.11
Morden, Peter J., 2013.39
"More Than Metaphors: Jonathan Edwards and the Beauty of Nature," 2010.52
Moreland, James P., 2013.40, 2013.41
Morgan, Christopher W., 2008.57
Morimoto, Anri, 2010.65, 2010.83, 2014.57, 2020.38
Moses, John A., 2011.42
Moye, Jerry, SP.31
Muller, Richard A., 2014.58, 2018.29, 2020.4, 2022.29
Review of *Multiple Reformation? The Many Faces and Legacies of the Reformation*, 2022.50
Music, David W., 2006.54
"Must We Believe? Jonathan Edwards and Conscious Faith in Christ," 2010.83
"My Top 5 Books: On Jonathan Edwards," 2011.38
"Mysticism in Jonathan Edwards's Theology of Spirituality: A Comparison Between Edwards's and Bernard of Clairvaux's Understanding of Union and Communion with Christ," 2021.32

Najapfour, Brian G., 2011.3, 2013.42, 2014.6, 2019.49
"Narcissism: The Root of All Hypocrisy in the Theological Psychology of Jonathan Edwards," 2014.24
Review of *A Natural History of Pragmatism: The Fact of Feeling from Jonathan Edwards to Gertrude Stein*, 2008.33, 2009.27

"A Natural History of the Mind: Edwards, Emerson, Thoreau, Melville," 2009.44
"Natural Morality or Splendid Vice? The Case of Paul Ramsey," 2021.41
"The Natural Sciences and Philosophy of Nature,," 2021.64
"Nature and Grace: Two Participations in the Thought of Jonathan Edwards," 2016.60
"The Nature of God and the Trinity,," 2021.64
"Natures Converts: Reading the Land and Nature in Early American Conversion, 1727–1831," 2021.7
Neele, Adriaan C., 2012.41, 2012.42, 2012.44, 2012.45, 2013.43, 2013.44, 2013.49, 2017.53, 2017.54, 2017.55, 2018.46, 2019.12, 2019.37, 2019.41, 2019.50, 2019.51, 2019.52, 2019.63, 2020.22, 2020.28, 2020.30, 2020.34, 2020.39, 2021.64, 2022.24, 2023.37
"'Neither Seen nor Heard': The Absent Child in the Study of Religion," 2010.17
Nelson, David R., 2007.46
"Neo-Aristotelean Rhetorical Criticism of Sermons from the Great Awakening," 2011.47
Nettles, Thomas J., 2008.58
"Neuroscience and Cognitive Psychology Insights into the Classical Theological Debate About Free Will and Responsibility," 2013.32
Neville, Jonathan E., 2021.45, 2022.25
New, Elza, 2006.55
"A New Edwards Document: Receipt for a Slave," 2019.39
"New England Baptist Alvah Hovey: A Later Chapter in Baptist Edwardsianism," 2020.48
"The New England Theology and the Atonement: Jonathan Edwards to Edwards Amasa Park," 2014.20

The New England Theology: From Jonathan Edwards to Edwards Amasa Park, 2006.68
Review of *The New England Theology: From Jonathan Edwards to Edwards Amasa Park*, 2007.25, 2007.56, 2007.60, 2008.11, 2008.16, 2008.43, 2008.56
"New Perspectives on the Northampton Communion Controversy II: Relations, Professions, and Experiences, 1748–1760," 2014.82
"New Perspectives on the Northampton Communion Controversy III," 2014.83
"New Perspectives on the Northampton Communion Controversy IV: Experience Mayhew's Dissertation on Edwards's Humble Inquiry," 2016.74
Nichols, Stephen J., 2006.43, 2006.56, 2008.44, 2009.56, 2010.52, 2015.41, 2018.47, 2021.46, 2022.30
Nichols, Stephen R. C., 2010.53, 2013.45, 2015.19, 2021.64
Niebuhr, Richard R., 2011.43
Nixon, C. Robert., 2008.59
Njoto, Ricky F., 2019.53, 2021.47, 2023.38
"'Nobles and Barons in the Court of Heaven': A Survey of Angelology from the Patristic Era to the Eighteenth Century with Particular Emphasis Given to Jonathan Edwards," 2018.5
Noll, Mark A., 2006.14, 2007.43, 2009.32, 2010.54, 2012.46, 2020.40
"Non-Penal Substitution," 2007.13
"North America,," 2021.64
Nossaman, Lucas, 2019.54
"Not From Ourselves: Holy Love in the Theology of Jonathan Edwards," 2016.16
The Notorious Elizabeth Tuttle: Marriage, Murder, and Madness in the Family of Jonathan Edwards, 2012.13
Review of *The Notorious Elizabeth Tuttle: Marriage, Murder, and Madness in the Family of Jonathan Edwards*, 2013.59, 2016.69
Novak, Barbara, 2008.60
Review of *A Novel of the Great Awakening*, 2014.4
Nuenke, Jonathan, 2023.39

O'Brien, Brandon J., 2013.46
O'Brien, Jill, SP.26
Oesterling, Jason, 2021.48
Ohst, Martin, 2009.60
Okubo, Masatake, 2016.53
"Old, Rested, and Reformed: Reflections on the Recovery of Edwards," 2020.36
Oliphint, K. Scott, 2011.22
Olson, Ray, 2008.61, 2008.62
"On the Orthodoxy of Jonathan Edwards," 2014.22
"One Alone Cannot Be Excellent: The Theology and Spirituality of Beauty in the Thought," 2010.36
One in a Thousand: The Calling and Work of a Pastor, 2014.42
"One-Mile-Wide, One-Inch-Deep: A Case Study of the Indigenization of Global Pentecostal Worship in Yoruba Context," 2023.23
"The Only Rule of Our Faith and Practice: Jonathan Edwards' Interpretation of the Book of Isaiah as a Case Study of His Exegetical Boundaries," 2009.3
"Ontology,," 2021.64
"Open Theism, Omniscience, and the Nature of the Future," 2006.60
Oppy, Dane, 2014.59
"Orderly but Not Ordinary: Jonathan Edwards's Evangelical Ecclesiology," 2011.5
Original Sin: A Cultural History, 2009.43
Ormond, Alexander T., 2010.28

Ortlund, Dane, 2010.55, 2014.41, 2014.60, SP.12, SP.34
The Other Jonathan Edwards: Selected Writings on Society, Love, and Justice, 2015.38
Review of *The Other Jonathan Edwards: Selected Writings on Society, Love, and Justice*, 2015.69, 2016.48, 2017.13, 2019.70
"Otterskins, Eagle Feathers, and Native American Alumni at Princeton," 2006.8
The Oxford Handbook of American Philosophy, 2008.55
The Oxford Handbook of Calvin and Calvinism, 2021.24, 2021.42
The Oxford Handbook of Jonathan Edwards, 2021.64
Review of *The Oxford Handbook of Jonathan Edwards*, 2021.15, 2022.21, 2022.32, 2022.34, 2023.35, 2023.36
Oxford Handbook of Religion and Emotion, 2008.52
The Oxford Handbook of Systematic Theology, 2007.19

Paeth, Scott R., 2011.44
Painter, Jeremy, 2020.41
Paisley, Katherine T., 2006.57
"Panentheism and Jonathan Edwards," 2016.34
"Paparazzi in the Hands of an Angry God: Jonathan Edwards, George Whitfield, and the Birth of American Celebrity Culture," 2011.55
Papers Presented at the Eighteenth International Conference on Patristic Studies Held in Oxford 2019, 2021.49
"Parish Ministry,", 2021.64
Park, Hyun Shin, 2012.47
Parker, David, 2009.61
Parmenter, Margaret Rose, 2012.48
"Part I: Puritan and Evangelical Practice in New England, 1630–1800,," 2006.40

"Participation in the Divine: The Method and Content of the Religious Epistemology of Jonathan Edwards," 2019.61
Particulars: The Telepathy of Archives, 2014.39
Parton, James, 2010.56
Pass, Bruce, 2016.54
"The Passions and the Interests: An Edwardsean Understanding of Populism," 2020.38
"Pastoral Necessity of Homiletical Application," 2023.21
"The Pastoral Theology of Jonathan Edwards: Reflections from Nine Ordination Sermons," 2015.55
Paul, Roy M., 2020.42
Pauley, Garth E., 2014.61
Pauw, Amy Plantinga, 2007.33, 2008.72, 2010.57, 2010.58, 2010.65, 2015.42, 2016.55, 2016.56
Payne, Jon D., 2016.57
Pederson, Randall J., 2009.63, 2009.64, 2009.65, 2010.59, 2011.45
"Penal Non-Substitution," 2008.14
Pendergrass, Aaron, 2020.43
Penner, Bradley M., 2022.32
Pennings, Ray, 2012.49
Pentecostal Theology and Jonathan Edwards, 2019.66
Review of *Pentecostal Theology and Jonathan Edwards*, 2020.31, 2021.2, 2021.37, 2023.54, SP.45
"'The Perfection of Beauty': Cotton Mather's Christological Interpretation of the Shechinah Glory in the 'Biblia Americana' and Its Theological Contexts," 2010.60
Perkins, Harrison, 2022.31
"Perry Miller and Yale's Proudest Moment," 2019.17
"The Person of Christ," 2021.64
Personal Narrative? 2007.22
The Personal Narrative of Jonathan Edwards and His Seventy Resolutions (Audiobook)? 2011.23

Peters, Nathaniel, 2009.62
Peterson, Cheryl M., 2014.62
Peterson, Paul Silas, 2010.60
Petrou, Irene, 2021.49
"Phenomenal Theology," 2007.16
Phillips, Charles W., 2006.58, 2018.48, 2018.59
Phillips, Christopher N, 2012.50
Pierpont, James, Jr., 2017.56
Piggin, Stuart, 2021.64
"Pilgrim's Progress," 2010.86
"The Pilgrim's Progress and Jonathan Edwards," 2019.40
Pino, Ryan, 2019.55
Piper, John, 2011.38, 2017.19, 2023.13
"The Place of Edwards in History," 2010.28
"Pneumatology,," 2021.64
"'A Point of Infinite Consequence': Jonathan Edwards' Experimental Calvinism on Trial," 2016.62
"Polemical Solidarity: John Wesley and Jonathan Edwards Confront John Taylor on Original Sin," 2012.54
"Politics and Economics,," 2021.64
Pollock, Darren M., 2015.43
"Population Genomics, Confessionalism, and the Metaphysics of Original Sin," 2023.53
Porterfield, Amanda, 2007.7
"Positive Mimesis in Jonathan Edwards's Charity and Its Fruits," 2020.54
"Positive Psychology: Friend or Foes of Religious Virtue Ethics?" 2008.29
"Postmillennialism: A Biblical Critique," 2023.44
Potgieter, Esmari, 2016.58, 2021.64
The Power of God: A Jonathan Edwards Commentary of the Book of Romans, 2013.30
Review of *The Power of God: A Jonathan Edwards Commentary on the Book of Romans*, 2014.66, 2015.51, 2016.64

"Practical Ecclesiology in John Calvin and Jonathan Edwards," 2010.57
"'The Practice That Prevails': Jonathan Edwards, Slavery, and Race," 2022.28
Practicing Protestants: Histories of Christian Life in America, 1630–965, 2006.40
Practicing Protestants: Histories of Christian Life in America, 1630–965, 2006.69
The Preaching of Jonathan Edwards, 2008.7
Review of *The Preaching of Jonathan Edwards*, 2010.2, 2010.33, 2011.39
"Preaching That Awakens the Heart: As Seen Through the Preaching of Jonathan Edwards and George Whitefield," 2010.49
Predicting the Past: The Paradoxes of American Literary History, 2021.9
"The Presence and Priority of the Spiritual Disciples in the Sermons of Jonathan Edwards," 2017.10
"A Previously Uncatalogued Letter," 2016.32
"A Previously Unpublished Sermon by Jonathan Edwards (1703–1758) on John 3:36," 2012.36, 2012.37
Price, Christopher, 2011.46
"Pride, Property, and Providence: Jonathan Edwards on Property Rights," 2011.26
Review of *The Princeton Companion to Jonathan Edwards*, 2006.16, 2006.28, 2006.52, 2008.76
The Princeton Companion to Jonathan Edwards, 2007.33, 2008.15, 2011.38
"Print, Predestination, and the Public Sphere," 2010.69
"Printing, Publics, and Pudding: Charles Chauncy's Universal Salvation and the Material Transformation

of New England Orthodoxy," 2023.3
"Proceed with Caution: Lessons from Saint Augustine, Jonathan Edwards, and Miroslav Volf," 2022.17
"A Profile of the Northampton Minority," 2017.50
"A Profoundly Theological Ethical Philosophy," 2021.40
"Progressive Millennialism," 2011.1
"Promoting Pure and Undefiled Religion: John Ryland, Jr. (1753–1825) and Edwardsean Evangelical Biography," 2017.24
"Proper Fourteen, Ordinary 19, Pentecost 10: August 9, 2009," 2009.57
Review of *The Protestant Interest: New England After Puritanism*, 2006.42
Providence, Freedom, and the Will in Early Modern Reformed Theology, 2022.29
"A Providential Plumbline for Pastoral Practice: Edwards's Exposition of the Kingdom of God," 2020.5
Prud'homme, Joseph Gilbert, 2012.51
Pryor, John M., 2006.59
Psychology and Christianity: Five Views, 2011.31
Puente, Eric, 2007.47
"Purchasing the Spirit: A Trinitarian Hermeneutic for Jonathan Edwards's Doctrine of the Atonement," 2018.60
"Puritan Involvement with Slavery," 2023.39
The Puritan Origins of the American Self, 2012.12
"Puritan Sermon Method and Church Government: Solomon Stoddard's Rhetorical Legacy," 2006.39
"Puritan Studies in the Twenty-First Century: Preamble and Projections," 2010.59
"Puritans, Presbyterians, and Jonathan Edwards," 2007.35

"The Queer Jeremiad: Jonathan Edwards, City upon a Hill, and City of Night," SP.16
Quinn, Philip L., 2023.40

"Radical Orthodoxy: William Goodell and the Abolition of American Slavery," 2018.26
Rager, Christopher, 2009.66
Rainey, David, 2015.44
Raley, Matthew, 2019.56
Ramini, Ashwin, 2023.41
Rast, Lawrence R., Jr., 2008.63
Rathel, David, 2023.42
"A Rational and Spiritual Worship: Comparing J. S. Bach and Jonathan Edwards," 2019.56
Ravished by Beauty: The Surprising Legacy of Reformed Spirituality, 2011.33
A Reader's Guide to the Major Writings of Jonathan Edwards, 2017.19
Review of *A Reader's Guide to the Major Writings of Jonathan Edwards*, 2018.9
Review of *Reading Jonathan Edwards: An Annotated Bibliography in Three Parts, 1729–2005*, 2009.4, 2009.64, 2009.65, 2010.43
Reading Jonathan Edwards: An Annotated Bibliography in Three Parts, 1729–2005, 2006.9, 2006.50, 2006.66, 2007.2, 2007.34, 2007.66, 2008.18, 2008.28, 2008.48, 2009.38, 2010.1, 2010.21, 2010.28, 2010.56, 2011.10, 2011.43, 2012.12, 2022.30
Reading "Religious Affections": A Study Guide to Jonathan Edwards' Classic on the Nature of True Christianity, 2012.9
"Reading the Gospels with Jonathan Edwards: Interpretive Practices of America's Greatest Theologian," 2020.35

Reason and Faith in Early Princeton: Piety and the Knowledge of God, 2014.2

Receptive Human Virtues: A New Reading of Jonathan Edwards's Ethics, 2011.16

"Recognizing Revelation: Illuminating the Epistemology Context of Biblical Worship," 2021.30

"Reconciling the Doctrine of Original Sin with Principles of Moral Responsibility," 2010.29

"Recovering the Disciplines: A Comparative Study on the Spiritual Disciplines as Expressed in the Lives, Teaching and Ministry of Jonathan Edwards, Charles Finney and Richard Foster," 2018.39

Reddinger, William, 2015.45

"The Redemption Discourse and Edwards the Missionary," 2021.47

"Redemptive History as a Paradigm for Jonathan Edwards' Exposition of Miracles," 2014.10

Reformed Dogmatics in Dialogue: The Theology of Karl Barth and Jonathan Edwards, 2022.47

"The Reformed Roots of Pentecostalism," 2007.40

Review of *Reformed Scholasticism: Recovering the Tools of Reformed Theology*, 2019.52

"A Reformed Vision of the World: Trinitarian Beauty and Environmental Ethics," 2011.34

"Regeneration, Revival, and Creation," 2020.10

Regeneration, Revival, and Creation: Religious Experience and the Purposes of God in the Thought of Jonathan Edwards, 2020.51

Review of *Regeneration, Revival, and Creation: Religious Experience and the Purposes of God in the Thought of Jonathan Edwards*, 2021.54

Rehnman, Sebastian, 2010.61, 2015.46, 2021.50, 2021.64, 2022.33

Reklis, Kathryn, 2014.63, 2016.12, 2016.39, 2016.56, 2016.72, 2017.57, 2017.62, 2017.73, 2021.64

"Relational Consent: Reflections on Disability and Jonathan Edwards's Aesthetics," 2018.12

"The Relationship Between God's Nature, God's Image in Man, and Freedom in the Philosophy of Jonathan Edwards," 2018.3

"The Relationship of the Old and New Testaments in the Theology of Jonathan Edwards (1703–58)," 2010.53

The Religious Affections, 2009.21

"The Religious Affections in Presbyterian Church (USA) Liturgy," 2017.14

"Religious Thought After the Period of Revivalism in Eighteenth-Century New England, c. 1739–1800," SP.3

"Remind, Rebuke, Refocus: Three Correctives After Investigating Edwards's Use of 'Known by God'," 2016.4

Rempel, Brent Anders, 2016.59

Renewing Spiritual Perception with Jonathan Edwards: Contemporary Philosophy and the Theological Psychology of Transforming Grace, 2016.76

"The Resolutions of Jonathan Edwards as a Contemporary Model for Emerging Leaders in the Twenty-First Century," 2009.73

"Re-Thinking Atonement in Jonathan Edwards and New England Theology," 2017.28

"A Retrieval of Jonathan Edwards's Concept of Free Will: The Relevance for Neuroscience," 2014.79

"Revelation,," 2021.64

"Revelation and Religions: Towards a More 'Harmonious' Jonathan Edwards," 2021.39
"Revelation as Divine Communication Through Reason, Scripture and Tradition," 2010.65
"The Reverend Jonathan Edwards: An American Radical," 2023.33
Review of *Revival Preaching: Twelve Lessons from Jonathan Edwards*, 2022.15
"Revival Types: A Look at the Leaders of the Great Awakening Through the Lens of Psychological Type and Temperament," 2007.24
"Revivals, Revivalism and the Baptist," 2009.5
"Revive Us Again: Evaluating a Sermon Series on Revival," 2023.41
"Rhetoric of Revival: An Analysis of Exemplary Sermons from America's Great Awakenings," SP.14
Review of *The Rhetoric of Revival: The Language of the Great Awakening*, 2018.55
Review of *The Rhetoric of Revival: The Language of the Great Awakening Preachers*, 2017.41
"Rhetoric of the Revival: A Pragma-Rhetorical Analysis of the Language of the Great Awakening Preachers," 2011.12
The Rhetoric of the Revival: The Language of the Great Awakening Preachers, 2016.15
"Rhetorical Influences Upon the Preaching of Jonathan Edwards," 2011.25
"Rhetorical Influences upon the Preaching of Jonathan Edwards," 2012.29
Rhoda, Alan R., 2006.60
Richardson, Herbert, 2017.58
Richardson, John, 2008.33, 2009.27
Rigney, Joe, 2015.47

The Rise of Evangelicalism: The Age of Edwards, Whitefield and the Wesleys, 2010.54
Ristau, Scott, 2011.47
Ritter, Luke, 2022.34
The River Gods, 2009.47
Rivera, Anthony, 2019.57
Rivera, Ted, 2006.61, 2007.48, 2010.62, 2012.27
Rivett, Sarah, 2009.67, 2011.48
"Robert Lewis Dabney and the Problem of Original Sin," 2022.51
Robinson, C. Jeffrey, Sr., 2012.52, 2014.35
Robinson, Marilynne, 2014.64
Rogers, Mark C., 2009.68, 2012.53
Rogers, Tony A., 2022.35
Roland, James W, 2006.62
"The Role of Beauty in Moral Discernment: An Appraisal from Rahnerian and Edwardsean Perspectives," 2006.12
"The Role of Perception in Jonathan Edwards's Moral Thought: The Nature of True Virtue Reconsidered," 2010.14
"The Role of Sanctification in the Ethics of Jonathan Edwards," 2019.27
Rolski, L. Benjamin, SP.22
Rosario, Jeffrey, 2017.59
Rosenbeck, Craig, 2018.49
Ross, Henry T., 2010.28
Ross, John S., 2007.49
Ross, Melanie, 2006.63, 2009.69
Ruetenik, Tadd, 2014.65, 2019.58
Russell, Andrew C., 2012.54
Ryu, Gilsun, 2018.50, 2018.51, 2019.59, 2021.51, 2021.61, 2022.23, 2023.15, 2023.43

"Sacramental Recital: Christological Use of Scripture in *A History of the Work of Redemption*," 2014.26
Saillant, John, 2021.64
"The Saints in Heaven as Spectators of Providence: Edwards and the Tradition," 2020.37

Salladin, James R., 2016.60, 2017.60, 2022.1, 2022.35, 2022.36, 2022.48, 2023.6
"Salvation History, Chronology, and Crisis: A Problem with Inclusivist Theology of Religions, Part 1 of 2," 2008.69
The Salvation of All Men Strictly Examined and the Endless Punishment of Those Who Die Impenitent, 2009.26
Review of *The Salvation of Souls, by Jonathan Edwards by Jonathan Edwards*, 2006.5
"'Salvation Shall Spread Through All the Tribes and Ranks of Mankind': Jonathan Edwards and World Mission," 2019.11
"Salvation Shall Spread to All the Tribes and Ranks of Mankind": Edwards and World Mission, 2021.12
Samuel, Josh P. S., 2008.64
"Samuel Kneeland and Daniel Henchman: Jonathan Edwards' Chief Printer and Publisher in Boston," 2015.68
"Samuel Miller (1769–1850): Reformed Orthodoxy, Jonathan Edwards, and Old Princeton," 2021.60
Samuel Miller (1769–1850): Reformed Orthodoxy, Jonathan Edwards, and Old Princeton, 2022.43
"Sanctification by Justification: The Forgotten Insight of Bavinck and Berkouwer on Progressive Sanctification," 2010.55
Sanders, E. Randall, 2007.50
Sanlon, Peter, 2009.70
Sasser, Daryl, 2010.63
Saunders, Dan, 2012.55
"'The Saving Change': New Birth and Conversion in Eighteenth-Century African-American Literature," 2009.11
"The SBJT Forum," 2013.24
Scalise, Brian T., 2010.64
Schafer, Thomas A., 2011.49

Schelberg, James Hoitsma, 2012.51
The Schlager Anthology of Early America: A Student's Guide to Essential Primary Sources, 2022.8
Schmidt, Darren, 2015.48
Schmidt, Leigh E., 2006.69
Schuit, John, 2014.66
Schultz, Walter J., 2006.64, 2013.47, 2014.67, 2014.68, 2016.61, 2018.52, 2020.44, 2021.57, 2022.37
Schuman, Andrew, SP.38
Schutter, David H., 2017.61
Schwanda, Tom, 2015.49, 2019.49, 2020.45, 2020.46
Schweitzer, Cameron, 2018.53, 2021.52, 2021.53, 2021.54, 2022.38, 2023.43
Schweitzer, Don, 2007.51, 2007.52, 2010.65, 2011.56, 2013.9, 2013.48, 2013.49, 2018.54, 2021.55, 2021.56
Schweitzer, William M., 2007.53, 2008.65, 2010.66, 2012.56, 2013.6, 2013.11, 2013.16, 2013.35, 2014.12, 2015.50, 2015.51, 2016.62, 2016.63, 2017.62, SP.27
The Science of the Soul in Colonial New England, 2011.48
Scorgie, Glen G., 2020.46
Scott, David, SP.9
Scott-Coe, Justin M., 2012.57
Seay, Scott D., 2006.65
Sederholm, Carl, 2012.58
Review of *Seeing God: The Beatific Vision in the Christian Tradition*, 2021.33
"The 'Sense of the Heart': Edwards's Public Expression of His Pietistic Understanding of Religious Experience," 2010.71
"'Sense of the Heart': Jonathan Edwards' Legacy in the Writings of Andrew Fuller," 2008.10
"Sereno Edwards Dwight, Biographer of Jonathan Edwards," 2020.58

Sermons and Discourses, 1743–1758. Vol. 25 of The Works of Jonathan Edwards, 2006.22
Sermons by Jonathan Edwards on the Church. Vol. 1: How Christians Are Come to Mt. Sion, 2019.43
Sermons by Jonathan Edwards on the Epistle to the Galatians, 2019.42
Review of *Sermons by Jonathan Edwards on the Matthean Parables*, 2013.49
Review of *Sermons by Jonathan Edwards on the Matthean Parables, vol. 1: True and False Christians (On the Parable of the Wise and Foolish Virgins)*, 2013.48
Review of *Sermons by Jonathan Edwards on the Matthean Parables, Vols. 1–3*, 2013.13
Sexton, Jeremy, 2023.44
"'A Shadow of Death': Jonathan Edwards and the Book of Job," 2018.56
Shammas, Carole, 2006.2
Sharansky, Rachel D., SP.32
Shaw, Ian J., 2008.66
Shea, William M., SP.23
Sherron, Tyler, 2022.39
Sherron, Tyler P, 2017.63
Sherry, Patrick, 2007.54
Shin, Joyce Sue-Mee, 2020.47
Shin, Moon-Ju, 2007.55
Shoemaker, Stephen P, 2007.56
Sholl, Brian K. (Keith), 2008.67, 2010.67
Review of *A Short Life of Jonathan Edwards*, 2008.50, 2008.59, 2009.12, 2009.34, 2009.61, 2009.62, 2009.63, 2010.9, 2010.22, 2010.32, 2010.50, 2011.4, 2011.18, 2011.42, SP.23
Review of *A Short Life of Jonathan Edwards* [Audiobook], 2009.52, 2009.66
A Short Life of Jonathan Edwards (Unabridged), 2009.51
A Short Life of Jonathan Edwards*, 2008.51, 2009.6, 2012.12
Shrader, Matthew C., 2020.48
Shukla, Abhishek, 2021.58

"The Significance of Edwards To-Day," 2010.28
Review of *Signs of the Spirit: An Interpretation of Jonathan Edwards' "Religious Affections*," 2012.1
Signs of the Spirit: An Interpretation of Jonathan Edwards' "Religious Affections," 2007.59
Simonson, Harold, 2009.71
Sims, David, 2009.72
Simut, Cornelius, C., 2022.40
"Sin and Evil,," 2021.64
"'Singly, Particularly, Closely': Edwards as Mentor," 2014.9
"Sinners in the Hands of a Gracious God," 2006.37
"Sinners in the Hands of an Angry God," 2022.8
Sinners in the Hands of an Angry God. A Sermon, Preached at Enfield, July 8, 1741, at a Time of Great Awakenings; And Attended with Remarkable Impressions on Many of the Hearers, 2010.25
Smart, Robert Davis, 2008.68, 2010.68, 2011.50
Smith, Craig, 2009.73
Smith, Egbert C., 2010.28
Smith, John E., 2011.38
Smith, John H., 2018.55
Smith, Marcus, 2007.57
Smith, Philip P., 2022.41
Smith, Phillip, 2018.56
Smith, Yvonne S., 2012.59
Smith. Ted A., 2015.52
Smolinski, Reiner, 2021.59
Snead, Jennifer, 2010.69
Snoddy, Richard M., 2015.53, 2015.54
Snoeberger, Mark A., 2019.60
"'So Much of the Gospel . . . Shining in It': Jonathan Edwards' Redemptive-Historical Vision of the Psalms," 2012.4
"'Some Agreeable Conversation': Jonathan Edwards Among Early American Baptists," 2023.31

"'Something That Is Seen, That Is Wonderful': Jonathan Edwards and the Feeling of Conviction," 2010.42

"The Son in the Hands of a Violent God? Assessing Violence in Jonathan Edwards's Covenant of Redemption," 2015.66

Song, J. Gaius, 2016.64

"'A Soul Inflamed with High Exercises of Divine Love': Affections and Passions in the Theology of Jonathan Edwards," 2013.31

"Soundly Gathered Out of the Text? Biblical Interpretation in 'Sinners in the Hands of an Angry God,'" 2014.61

"Sources of Edwards's Thought," 2021.64

Review of *Southern Edwards: The Southern Baptist Legacy of Jonathan Edwards*, 2023.32

Southern Edwardseans: The Southern Baptist Legacy of Jonathan Edwards, 2022.46

Spar, Natalie D., 2011.51

Sparkes, Adam, 2008.69

"Speaking Up and Out: The Subversion of Puritan Rhetorical Forms in the Writing of Lemuel Haynes," 2021.22

"The Speckled Bird: Nathanael Emmons, Consistent Calvinism, and the Legacy of Jonathan Edwards," 2016.7

"'Spectator' of Shadows: The Human Being in Jonathan Edwards's 'Images of Divine Things,'" 2018.7

"Spider and Fly: Novel Excerpt, August 1735, Northampton, Massachusetts," 2011.54

"Spider and Webs in American Literature," 2011.21

Spider in a Tree: A Novel of the First Great Awakening, 2013.51

Spiegel, James S., 2022.42

"The Spirit in Creation: A Unified Theology of Grace and Creation Care," 2008.73

Review of *The Spirit of Early Evangelicalism: True Religion in a Modern World*, 2018.31, 2020.6

The Spirit of Early Evangelicalism: True Religion in a Modern World, 2018.32

"The Spirit of Reform: St. Augustine and Jonathan Edwards on the Glory of God," 2009.50

The Spirit of Truth: The Holy Spirit and the Apologetics of Jonathan Edwards, 2021.46, 2022.30

"Spiritual and Devotion,," 2021.64

"The Spiritual and the Moral Sense: The Role of Theology and British Moral Sense Philosophy in Jonathan Edwards's 'True Virtue,'" 2018.33

"Spiritual Blindness, Self-Deception and Morally Culpable Nonbelief," 2007.30

Spiritual Disciplines: How to Become a Healthy Christian, 2023.26

"The 'Spiritual Music' of a Beautiful Word," 2014.55

"The Spirituality of David Brainerd: A Summary and Critique," 2018.63

"Spite or Spirit? Jonathan Edwards on the Imprecatory Language in the Psalms," 2015.3

Spurlock, R. Scott, 2012.60

St. John, Thomas, SP.19

Stahle, Rachel S., 2014.69

Stanton, Allen M., 2017.64, 2021.60, 2022.43

Steele, Richard B., 2008.70

Steffaniak, Jordan L., 2019.61

Stegeman, Daniel, 2015.55

Stein, Stephen J., 2006.20, 2007.17, 2007.20, 2007.58, 2008.12, 2008.15, 2008.34, 2008.41, 2008.75, 2009.35, 2009.60, 2009.74, 2010.70, 2011.38, 2013.50, 2015.56

Stenschke, Christoph W., 2006.66, 2009.74, 2015.24
Stetina, Karin Spiecker, 2009.75, 2010.71, 2011.52, 2012.5, 2014.70, 2015.57, 2022.44
Steven, Brian, 2020.49
Stevens, Chris S., 2021.61
Stewart, Carole Lynn, 2010.72, 2012.12, 2013.2, 2013.29
Stewart, Kenneth J., 2011.53
Stievermann, Jan, 2014.71, 2014.72, 2021.15, 2021.59, 2021.64, 2022.21, 2022.32, 2022.34, 2022.50, 2023.35, 2023.36
Stikkers, Kenneth W, 2006.67
Stinson, Susan, 2011.54, 2013.51, 2014.4
Stoever, William K. B., 2014.73, 2014.74, 2014.75
Storms, C. Samuel, 2010.73
Storms, Sam, 2007.59, 2012.1
Story, F. Allan, 2021.62
Story, Ronald, 2012.61, 2014.13, 2015.14, 2015.38, 2015.69, 2016.48
Stout, Harry S., 2007.58, 2008.71, 2009.67, 2010.65, 2017.65, 2018.1, 2018.10, 2018.66, 2019.10, 2019.32, 2019.57, 2021.64
Strachan, Owen, 2009.76, 2009.77, 2009.78, 2010.74, 2010.75, 2010.76, 2010.77, 2010.78, 2018.57, 2018.58, 2019.31, 2019.62
Strange, Alan D., 2007.60, 2010.79
Strange, Daniel, 2008.26
*Strange Jeremiahs: Civil Religion and the Literary Imaginations of Jonathan Edwards, Herman Melville, and W. E. B. Du Bois, 2010.72, 2012.12, 2013.2, 2013.29
Stratton, Gary David, 2009.79, 2011.55
Streams of Grace: Studies of Jonathan Edwards, Samuel Taylor Coleridge, and William James, 2011.43
Strobel, Kyle C., 2009.18, 2009.80, 2009.81, 2010.20, 2010.80, 2011.56, 2012.62, 2012.63, 2012.64, 2013.52, 2013.53, 2013.54, 2014.49, 2015.58, 2015.59, 2015.60, 2016.17, 2016.23, 2016.65, 2016.66, 2016.77, 2017.29, 2017.46, 2017.57, 2018.17, 2019.13, 2019.28, 2019.29, 2019.36, 2019.63, 2019.64, 2019.65, 2020.13, 2020.18, 2020.28, 2020.45, 2020.50, 2020.51, 2021.54, 2021.63, 2021.64, 2022.47, 2023.45, 2023.46, SP.28
Strom, Jonathan, 2023.47
"Struggling with God's Will: Jesus' Piety in Mark's Account of the Gethsemane in Light of Virgil's Aeneas," 2023.51
Strunk, Stephen R., 2014.76
Studebaker, Steven M., 2008.72, 2008.73, 2009.82, 2011.28, 2011.57, 2012.65, 2012.66, 2013.4, 2014.19, 2014.30, 2014.47, 2015.42, 2015.57, 2016.63, 2019.66, 2020.31, 2021.2, 2021.37, 2023.54, SP.28, SP.45
A Study Guide to Jonathan Edwards' Classic The Religious Affections, 2010.8
"A Study of Evangelicals and Revival Exercises from 1730–1805: Tracing the Development of Exercise Traditions Through the First Great Awakening Period to the Southern Great Revival," 2009.53
"A Study of Jonathan Edwards' Application of Preaching to Aid in Conversion," SP.25
"A Study on Jonathan Edwards' Sermon Influencing the Disciple-Making Ministry of the Modern Church," 2023.24
"Studying the History of American Protestantism Through Jonathan Edwards: Versions of 'America's Theologian' at Mid-Century," 2014.72

Sumner, George, 2015.61
Sundberg, Walter, 2011.58
Supreme Harmony, 2007.33
Sutanto, Nathaniel Gray, 2016.67
Světlíková, Anna, 2022.45, SP.24
Swan, Nick, 2020.52
Sweeney, Douglas A., 2006.68, 2006.70, 2007.25, 2007.56, 2007.58, 2007.60, 2007.61, 2008.11, 2008.16, 2008.43, 2008.56, 2009.59, 2009.76, 2009.77, 2009.78, 2009.83, 2010.3, 2010.40, 2010.65, 2010.67, 2010.74, 2010.75, 2010.76, 2010.77, 2010.78, 2010.79, 2011.14, 2011.19, 2011.32, 2011.46, 2012.19, 2013.12, 2013.50, 2013.55, 2014.17, 2014.28, 2014.85, 2015.4, 2015.23, 2015.53, 2016.19, 2016.68, 2017.5, 2018.1, 2018.4, 2018.13, 2018.58, 2018.59, 2019.31, 2019.48, 2019.64, 2019.71, 2020.11, 2021.15, 2021.35, 2021.64, 2022.21, 2022.32, 2022.34, 2022.50, 2023.35, 2023.36
"'A Sweet Union of Souls': The Dangers of Representing the Conversion in Jonathan Edwards' Biography of Missionary David Brainerd," 2010.45
"A Synthesis of Jonathan Edwards's Thoughts on Theodicy and Its Pastoral Implications., 2006.7
"The System of Being: A Study of the Metaphysics of Jonathan Edwards," 2021.58
Szczerba, Wojciech, 2020.8

Taking Hold of God: Reformed and Puritan Perspectives on Prayer, 2011.3, 2014.6
Tam, See-Kong, 2010.65
Tan, Seng-Kong, 2014.74, 2014.77, 2015.20, 2017.48, 2021.64
Tanner, Kathryn, 2007.19
Tarnsky, Will, 2021.65

"Taste and See That the Lord Is Good: The Aesthetic-Affectional Preaching of Jonathan Edwards," 2008.25
Tay, Edwin E. M., SP.29
Taylor, Justin, 2010.73
"Teresa of Avila and Jonathan Edwards on Prayer and Spirituality," 2021.34
"That Their Souls May Be Saved: The Theology and Practice of Jonathan Edwards on Church Discipline," 2014.45
"The Theological Aesthetics of Jonathan Edwards," 2007.36, 2007.44
"Theological Education of Nineteenth-Century French Missionaries: An Appropriation of the Catholicity of Classical Christian Theology," 2013.43
"The Theological Origins of Jonathan Edwards's Philosophy of Nature," 2009.92
Théologie et Lumières: Jonathan Edwards Entre Raison et Réveil, 2015.7, 2016.14
Theologies of the American Revivalists: From Whitefield to Finney, 2017.6
"Theology," 2012.46
Theology and the Kinesthetic Imagination: Jonathan Edwards and the Making of Modernity, 2014.63
Review of *Theology and the Kinesthetic Imagination: Jonathan Edwards and the Making of Modernity*, 2016.12, 2016.39, 2016.56, 2016.72, 2017.62, 2017.73
"Theology and Transformation in Society: The Scottish Evangelical Theological Society Finlayson lecture, 2008," 2008.66
Theology in America, 2009.32
"Theology of Jonathan Edwards," 2008.36
Review of *The Theology of Jonathan Edwards*, 2012.31, 2013.3, 2013.10, 2013.14, 2013.15,

2013.21, 2013.22, 2013.36, 2013.41, 2013.56, 2014.46, 2014.56, 2015.10, 2015.15, 2016.9, SP.27

The Theology of Jonathan Edwards, 2006.23, 2008.36, 2011.37, 2012.34, 2013.34

"A Theology of Joy: Jonathan Edwards and Eternal Happiness in the Holy Trinity," 2016.18

A Theology of Joy: Jonathan Edwards and Eternal Happiness in the Holy Trinity, 2018.22

Review of *A Theology of Joy: Jonathan Edwards and Eternal Happiness in the Holy Trinity*, 2020.3

"Theorizing the 'Black Body' as a Site of Trauma: Implications for Theologies of Embodiment," 2009.58

"'They Are Precious Gifts of Heaven': Jonathan Edwards's Works in Brazil," 2020.17

"'They Cannot Forbear Crying Out'—A Critical Study of Travailing Prayer as a Pattern of Preparedness for Revival, Examining It Historically in the Theology and Practice of Jonathan Edwards and Charles Finney," 2015.62

"'They Will Reign in Love': Spiritual Formation as Sanctified Affection in Jonathan Edwards," 2022.40

"The Third Use of the Law: John Calvin and Jonathan Edwards," 2021.28

"'This Awful Affair': Cousins, Communion, and the Collapse of Covenant Society in Jonathan Edwards's Northampton," SP.20

"This Loquacious Soil: Language and Religious Experience in Early America," 2011.51

Thomas, David R., 2015.62

Thomforde, James Henry, SP.42

The Thought of Jonathan Edwards, 2021.70

Thuesen, Peter J., 2008.19, 2010.81, 2011.9, 2013.56, 2016.69, 2021.64

Thunder God, Wonder God: Exploring the Emblematic Vision of Jonathan Edwards, 2023.5

"Thy Kingdom Come: The Missionary Theology and Practice of Jonathan Edwards," 2006.4

Timpe, Kevin, 2023.48

To Live Upon Hope: Mohicans and Missionaries in the Eighteenth-Century Northeast, 2008.78

To the Ends of the Earth: Calvin's Missional Vision and Legacy, 2014.35

"'To Understand Things as Well as Word': An Examination of Jonathan Edwards as an Educator and His Pedagogical Methodology," 2016.70

Todd, Obbie Tyler, 2017.66, 2018.60, 2018.61, 2019.21, 2019.67, 2019.68, 2021.66, 2022.46, 2023.32, 2023.49

"Tokutaro Takakura's Work Towards the Development of Evangelical Christianity in Japan: With Some References to Jonathan Edwards," 2016.53

Tooman, William A., 2009.84

Torrance, Iain, 2007.19

Torseth, Robb L., 2018.62, 2021.67

"Toward a Life-Changing Application Paradigm in Expository Preaching," 2012.47

"Towards a Clearer Understanding of Jonathan Edwards's Biblical Typology: A Case Study in the *Blank Bible*," 2022.38

"Towards a Solution to the 'Perennially Intriguing Problem' of the Sources of Jonathan Edwards' Idealism," 2015.46

"Towards an Understanding of the Effect of Revival Evidenced in the Writings of George Whitefield and Jonathan Edwards," 2006.33

Tracy, Joseph, 2020.32
"Training Up Children in the Way That They Should Go: Jonathan Edwards's Advice to Young Converts," 2016.3
Trakakis, N. N., 2014.59
"A Transcendentalist Conversion Narrative," 2009.49
"Transfiguring Light: The Moral Beauty of the Christian Life According to Gregory Palamas and Jonathan Edwards," 2008.70
Travel with Jonathan Edwards: A God-Centered Life, an Enduring Legacy, 2013.23
A Treatise Concerning Religious Affections, 2009.22
"A Treatise Concerning Religious Affections by Jonathan Edwards (1746)," 2017.54
A Treatise Concerning Religious Affections—In Three Parts, 2010.26
A Treatise on Jonathan Edwards, Continuous Creation and Christology, 2017.30
Review of *A Treatise on Jonathan Edwards, Continuous Creation and Christology*, 2021.10
Trementozzi, David, SP.45
Review of *The Trinitarian Ethics of Jonathan Edwards*, 2006.45, 2006.65, 2007.8, 2007.57, 2009.69
"The Trinitarian Missiology of Jonathan Edwards," 2006.59
"The Trinitarian Philosophy of Jonathan Edwards an Ontological and Typological Exposition," 2008.38
The Trinitarian Theology of Jonathan Edwards: Text, Context, and Application, 2012.65
Review of *The Trinitarian Theology of Jonathan Edwards: Text, Context, and Application*, 2013.4, 2014.19, 2014.30, 2014.47, 2015.42, 2015.57, 2016.63

Review of *The Trinitarian Vision of Jonathan Edwards*, 2012.66
The Trinitarian Vision of Jonathan Edwards: Text, Context, and Application, 2011.57
"Trinity and Beauty: The Theological Contribution of Jonathan Edwards," 2010.82
Trocchio, Rachel Donegan, 2017.67
"The Trouble with Grace: Reading Jonathan Edwards's Faithful Narrative," 2012.58
True and False Christians (On the Parable of the Wise and Foolish Virgins)., 2012.40
"True Excellency: The Missional Preaching of Jonathan Edwards," 2022.13
Trueman, Carl R., 2021.24, 2021.42
"Tuning the Heart: A Historical Survey of the Affections in Corporate Worship, with Special Reference to Jonathan Edwards," 2019.6
Turley, Stephen R., 2008.74
"Turretin and Edwards Once More," 2014.37
Twomey, Jay, 2009.85, SP.13
"Types in Nature: Jonathan Edwards on Typology," 2018.44
"Typology as Rhetoric: Reading Jonathan Edwards," SP.24
Tyrpak, Joseph Kirk, 2018.63
Tyson, Samuel Daley, 2011.59

Uche, Anizor, 2022.47
"An Uncommon Union: Understanding Jonathan Edwards's Experimental Calvinism," 2010.66
Underhill, Thomas, 2018.64, 2020.53
Review of *Understanding Affections in the Theology of Jonathan Edwards*, 2019.60
Review of *Understanding Affections in the Theology of Jonathan Edwards: "The High Exercises of Divine Love,"* 2019.69, 2020.9, 2021.27, 2021.56

Understanding Affections in the Theology of Jonathan Edwards: "The High Exercises of Divine Love," 2018.41

Understanding Jonathan Edwards: An Introduction to America's Theologian., 2009.54

Review of *Understanding Jonathan Edwards: An Introduction to America's Theologian*, 2009.42, 2009.80, 2009.82, 2010.58, 2011.45, 2012.11, 2012.24

"Unholy Hate: The Essence of Human Evil in the Theology of Jonathan Edwards," 2021.18

"The Unified Operations of the Human Soul Jonathan Edwards's Theological Anthropology and Apologetic," 2013.57

"The Union of Theology and Doxology: A Comparative Study of Jonathan Edwards and Anne Dutton," 2020.16

Review and Response to *Union with Christ: A Doctrine in Contention*, 2009.86

An Unpublished Essay of Edwards on the Trinity: With Remarks on Edwards and His Theology, 2009.23

The Unwavering Resolve of Jonathan Edwards, 2008.45

Review of *The Unwavering Resolve of Jonathan Edwards*, 2009.13, 2010.34

"Using Jonathan Edwards's Treatise Concerning Religious Affections to Equip Selected Members of Riverside Baptist Church, Denham," 2009.40

"Utilizing Biblical Persuasion Techniques in Preaching Without Being Manipulative," 2006.19

Utmost Endeavor: An Introduction to Jonathan Edwards on Revival, 2021.62

Valeri, Mark R., 2006.69, 2008.75, 2008.76, 2017.68, 2018.65, 2019.69, 2021.64

Van Andel, Kelly, 2011.60

Van Der Knijf, Cornelis, 2015.63

Van Engen, Abram, 2021.69

Van Wyk, John, 2016.70

VanBrugge, David, 2014.78

Vargas, Kristin, 2020.54

"Variety as Religious Experience: The Poetics of the Plain Style," 2006.55

Vaughan, David, 2007.62

Venter, Rian, 2010.82

"Very Two, Very One: Reading as Friendship," 2021.36

"Vestiges of Trinity," 2011.27

Vető, Miklós, 2007.66, 2021.70

Vincent, Markus, 2021.49

"'Violent Motions of Carnal Affections': Jonathan Edwards, John Owen, and Distinguishing the Work of the Spirit from Enthusiasm," 2010.44

"Virtue and the Hermeneutics of Culture," 2010.87

"'Virtue and 'True Virtue': Competing Ethical Philosophies in the American Founding Era," 2015.45

Virtue as Consent to Being: A Pastoral-Theological Perspective on Jonathan Edwards's Construct of Virtue, 2011.64

Review of *Virtue Reformed: Rereading Jonathan Edwards's Ethics*, 2008.35, SP.1

"The Vision of the Fullness of the Church: Jonathan Edwards' Interpretation of Zechariah 8 and 12–14," 2017.47

Vlastuin, Willem van, 2007.67, 2009.56, 2014.79, 2015.63, 2016.71, 2020.55, 2020.56, 2021.64, 2021.71, 2022.48, 2023.54

The Voice of Faith: Jonathan Edwards's Theology of Prayer, 2010.6

"Voicing Abjection: Evangelic Discourse, Suffering and Speech in Early American Literature," 2006.49
Vondey, Wolfgang, 2012.66

Waddington, Jeffrey C., 2009.86, 2010.83, 2013.57, 2015.64, 2017.69, 2018.66, 2019.70
Wainwright, William J., 2009.87, 2010.84, 2021.64
Walker, E. W., 2023.50
Walls, Taylor, 2021.68
Walton, Brad, 2013.17
Warner, Charles Dudley, 2008.77
"Was Jonathan Edwards a Christian Hedonist?" 2013.7
"We Are Them: The Golden Rule as a Theological Impetus in the Anti-Slavery and Abolitionist Movement," 2019.15
"Wealth and Poverty in the Life and Thought of Jonathan Edwards," 2022.5
"The Weather and Theology: The Influence of the Natural World on Religious Thought in Puritan New England," 2010.63
Webster, John, 2007.19
"Weighing the Evidence: Examining the Fruit of Charles Finney and Jonathan Edwards." DVD? 2012.2
Weimer, Adrian Chastain, 2009.88
Welch, Shawn, 2020.57
Wells, Christi, 2021.64
Welty, Kyle, 2022.49
Westerhoff. Benjamin, 2013.30, 2014.66, 2015.51, 2016.64
"What Ever Happened to Martha Root?" 2014.51
"What Is a Person? Three Essential Criteria for Jonathan Edwards' Doctrine of Personhood," 2018.61
Review of *What Is Saving Faith? Reflections on Receiving Christ as a Treasure*, 2023.13

"Whee! The People," SP.6
Wheeler, Rachel M., 2007.58, 2008.78
"When God Ceased Winking: Jonathan Edwards the Younger's Evolution on the Problem of Slavery," 2018.20
"When Whitefield Met Edwards," 2014.80
"Which Comes First, the Intellect or the Will? Alvin Plantinga and Jonathan Edwards on a Perennial Question," 2015.64
Whitefield, George, 2014.80
Whitlark, Jason A., 2023.51
Whitney, Donald S., 2014.81, 2015.36, 2015.49, 2015.59, 2016.20, 2017.72
"Who Lurks Behind Geerhardus Vos? Sources and Predecessors," 2021.21
"A Whole New World of Philosophy: Jonathan Edwards on Science, Nature and Miracles," 2014.11
"Whose Psychology? Which Christianity?" 2011.31
"Why Are We Here? A Biblical and Trinitarian Perspective on Man's End," 2021.68
"Why Edwards Did Not Understand Thomas Boston: A Comparison of Their Views on the Covenants," 2015.63
Wiersbe, Warren W., 2009.89
Wiess, James M., 2022.50
Wigginton, Caroline, 2021.69
Wigginton, Jesse C., 2017.70
"Wilderness Beauty: A Means to Resolve Volitional Doubt," 2010.64
Wilkening, Ann-Catherine, 2019.71
"The Will in Contemporary Evangelicalism: Or, How (Not) to Domesticate Jonathan Edwards," 2006.25
Willborn, C. N., 2022.51
Willemsen, Gerald F., 2016.72
Willi, Nora Lee, SP.43
William, Charles Scott, 2022.52
Wills, Garry, 2007.63, 2008.71

Wills, Gregory A., 2006.5
Willson, Cory B., 2018.67
Wilmoth, Daniel Ray, 2013.58
Wilson, Stephen A., 2008.35, SP.1
"Windows into Heaven: The Homiletic Scenes of Jonathan Edwards and the Preaching of Redemption," 2006.57
Winiarski, Douglas L., 2014.82, 2014.83, 2016.73, 2016.74, 2022.49
Winslow, Lisanne, 2022.44
Withrow, Brandon G., 2007.64, 2011.61
Wolosky, Shira, 2017.71
Woo, B. Hoon, 2014.84
Wood, Dustin A., SP.14
Wood, Timothy L., 2022.53
Woodbridge, John D., 2023.52
Wooddell, Joseph D., 2007.65
Woodyard, Jonathan D., 2022.54
Review of *The Works of Jonathan Edwards: The Catalogue of Books*, 2011.9
The Works of Jonathan Edwards: With a Memoir of His Life and Character, 2009.24
The Works of President Edwards, 2009.25
The Workshop of Being: Religious Affections and Their Pragmatic Value in the Thought of Jonathan Edwards and William James, 2011.10
Review of *The Workshop of Being: Religious Affections and their Pragmatic Value in the Thought of Jonathan Edwards and William James*, 2014.57

"Worship God with Our Minds: Theology as Doxology Among the Puritans," 2013.5
Woznicki, Christopher, 2015.65, 2015.66, 2019.21, 2019.72, 2023.53
Wright, Frank, SP.2
"Writing and Preaching Sermons," 2021.64

Yazawa, Reita, 2019.73, 2020.52
Yeager, Jonathan M., 2009.90, 2013.59, 2015.67, 2015.68, 2016.75, 2017.1, 2017.25, 2017.72, 2018.11, 2018.15, 2018.36, 2018.65, 2021.64, 2021.72
Yeo, Ray S., 2016.76
Yong, Amos, 2015.69, 2019.66, 2020.31, 2021.2, 2021.37, 2023.54
Yoo, Jeongmo, 2011.62
York, Alwyn, 2020.58
"'You Make All Things New': Jonathan Edwards and a Christian Environmental Ethic," 2011.44
Youngs, F., 2011.63

Zachman, Randall C., 2022.50
Zakai, Avihu, 2006.70, 2007.58, 2009.91, 2009.92, 2010.65, 2010.85, 2014.85, 2021.64
Zaleski, Carol, 2010.86
Zerra, Luke, 2017.73
Zhu, Victor, 2016.77, 2022.55
Zhu, Xinping, 2019.74
Zhu, Xinying, 2018.68
Zylla, Phil C., 2010.87, 2011.64

www.ingramcontent.com/pod-product-compliance
Lightning Source LLC
Chambersburg PA
CBHW061431300426
44114CB00014B/1641